THE NBA SUMMER ALMANAC

2019 Edition

by

Richard Lu

Credits:

Additional Scouting and Editing:
Alan Lu

Stats and Information:
Basketball-Reference.com
Sports-Reference.com/CBB
Kenpom.com
Spotrac
RealGM
Synergy Sports
probasketballtransactions.com/basketball
NBA.com/stats
NBAWowy.com
82games.com
Patricia Bender's website – https://www.eskimo.com/~pbender/

Cover:
Hayley Faye, fayefayedesigns on fiverr.com
Cover 1 photo based on a photo by Grant Halverson, Getty Images
Cover 2 photo based on a screengrab of the YouTube video, "Crazy Block! Zion at UVA" from Duke Basketball's channel

Back cover photo by:
Josh Springer
Josh Springer Photography, joshspringerphotography.com

For all comments, questions and requests, the author can be reached at lurv82@gmail.com or found on Twitter as @rvlhoops.

For all of the author's other work, please go to:
www.amazon.com/author/rvlhoops

As an additional show of support, you can leave a tip by finding the author on Venmo as @rvl82.

TABLE OF CONTENTS

What to Expect in the 2019 Edition	6
2019 NBA Offseason Primer	11
How Should Teams Handle the Supermax Contract?	12
Atlanta Hawks	18
Boston Celtics	23
Brooklyn Nets	28
Charlotte Hornets	33
Chicago Bulls	38
Cleveland Cavaliers	43
Dallas Mavericks	47
Denver Nuggets	52
Detroit Pistons	57
Golden State Warriors	62
Houston Rockets	67
Indiana Pacers	72
Los Angeles Clippers	77
Los Angeles Lakers	82
Memphis Grizzlies	87
Miami Heat	92
Milwaukee Bucks	97
Minnesota Timberwolves	102
New Orleans Pelicans	107
New York Knicks	112
Oklahoma City Thunder	117
Orlando Magic	122
Philadelphia 76ers	127
Phoenix Suns	132
Portland Trail Blazers	137
Sacramento Kings	142
San Antonio Spurs	147
Toronto Raptors	152
Utah Jazz	157
Washington Wizards	162
2019 Free Agency Projections	167
The Impact of Modern NBA Strategy on the Draft Evaluation Process	175

Analyzing the 2019 NBA Draft 184
   Glossary of Terms and Metrics 185

   Green Prospects 186
      Zion Williamson 187
      Ja Morant 190
      Jarrett Culver 193
      R.J. Barrett 196
      Cam Reddish 199
      De'Andre Hunter 202
      Bol Bol 205
      Coby White 208
      Romeo Langford 211
      Darius Garland 214
      Keldon Johnson 217

   Yellow Prospects

      <u>NCAA Guards</u> 220
      Carsen Edwards 221
      Ty Jerome 224
      Shamorie Ponds 227
      Tremont Waters 230
      Luguentz Dort 233
      Kyle Guy 236
      Jordan Poole 239
      Quinndary Weatherspoon 242
      Jaylen Nowell 245
      Ky Bowman 248
      Jaylen Hands 251
      Terence Davis 254
      Kerwin Roach 257
      Chris Clemons 260
      John Konchar 263
      Amir Hinton 266

      <u>NCAA 2 - 3 Wings</u> 269
      Nickeil Alexander-Walker 270
      Tyler Herro 273
      Chuma Okeke 276
      Nassir Little 279
      Cameron Johnson 282
      Dylan Windler 285
      Louis King 288
      Talen Horton-Tucker 291
      Ignas Brazdeikis 294
      Matisse Thybulle 297
      Admiral Schofield 300
      Kevin Porter, Jr. 303
      Kezie Okpala 306

NCAA 2-3 Wings (continued)

Miye Oni	309
Aubrey Dawkins	312
DaQuan Jeffries	315
Terance Mann	318
Kris Wilkes	321
Charles Matthews	324
Markis McDuffie	327
Caleb Martin	330
Cody Martin	333
Jaylen Hoard	336
Tyus Battle	339

NCAA Combo Forwards

	342
P.J. Washington	343
Brandon Clarke	346
Rui Hachimura	349
Dedric Lawson	352
Grant Williams	355
Isaiah Roby	358
Eric Paschall	361
Jalen McDaniels	364
Robert Franks	367

NCAA Big Men

	370
Charles Bassey	371
Bruno Fernando	374
Jaxson Hayes	377
Daniel Gafford	380
Mfiondu Kabengele	383
Naz Reid	386
Jontay Porter	389
Tacko Fall	392
Nicolas Claxton	395
Mike Daum	398
Dewan Hernandez	401
Aric Holman	404
Bennie Boatwright	407
Simi Shittu	410
Ethan Happ	413

Non-College Players

	416
Goga Bitadze	417
Sekou Doumbouya	420
Luka Samanic	423
Laurynas Birutis	426
Darius Bazley	429
Joshua Obiesie	431
Alen Smailagic	434
Jalen Lecque	437

Non-College Players (continued)
Marcos Louzada Silva   440
Santiago Yusta   443
Borisa Simanic   445
Vanja Marinkovic   448
Deividas Sirvydis   451
Abdoulaye N'Doye   454
Yovel Zoosman   457

Thank You to All My Readers   460

What to Expect in the 2019 Edition

If you have read any of my previous books, welcome back and thanks for picking up a copy of this new edition of The NBA Summer Almanac. Similar to the previous edition, you will get updated insights into the state of all 30 teams entering this next offseason as well as detailed, in-depth analysis of this year's set of draft prospects. In this edition, you will have access to original, deep-dive research that you will not be able to find anywhere else, either from other sources or even from some of my own articles on Medium. If you already know how my general process works, you can skip ahead and enjoy the rest of the book. If you need a quick refresher on my basic methods or are new to my work, then here are some answers to some of your most common questions.

1. *Who are you and what is your background?*

Based on over a decade of comprehensive research on the NBA, I have provided analytic consulting services to help the Phoenix Suns and Chicago Bulls and my primary area of expertise is the NBA Draft. With the Similarity Based Projection Model that I still use to evaluate and analyze draft prospects, I made a recommendation for the Bulls to use one of their first-round picks in 2011 to select Jimmy Butler from Marquette University. Since that time, Butler has gone to make several All-NBA teams and become one of the league's best two-way wing players. Before that, I performed advanced statistical analysis to help the Suns in their Western Conference Finals run in 2010. Specifically, I identified a critical defensive switch in the team's first-round series against Portland that allowed the Suns to win the series. Using various lineup analytics, I suggested for the defense to switch Grant Hill onto Andre Miller instead of having Jason Richardson guard Miller. As a result of the switch, Miller's effectiveness in the series was neutralized and Richardson broke out offensively, averaging over 25 points-per-game in the series' final five games. In all of my writing, I draw from past experiences to deliver the same premium analysis that I used to assist NBA front office personnel to give my readers a more enriched knowledge of everything that is going in the NBA to this point.

2. *What is the Similarity Based Projection Model that you use to evaluate draft prospects?*

This projection model is my own personal system that I have developed to analyze draft prospects through over ten years of meticulous refinement. As the name suggests, the system uses statistical similarity to compare the stats of any given current draft prospect to a pool of historical college players from the 1990 Draft to the present. From there, the model projects a prospect's possible career path based on the NBA performance of a set of comparable players. For the sake of this book, I have attached the most relevant comparable list to every listed player evaluation. These lists are not meant to overtly say if a prospect is good or bad, but if a player rates with a high degree of similarity to Kevin Durant, it implies a higher level of potential than if he were to be compared to someone like Anthony Bennett.

Because international players cover a smaller portion of the draft pool and they play in a lot of different leagues of varying strength, I don't have a separate methodology to perfectly analyze them. To get a best estimate for international players, I run their numbers as if they were college players. It's something of an apples-to-oranges comparison, so this process isn't absolute by any means. On the other hand, this type of analysis provides key insight into an international player's type and a possible degree to which that player's skills could translate.

3. *Why is there no Top 100 list of prospects?*

In my years of research, I have found that this sort of list is rather gratuitous after going in-depth to investigate an interesting comment made by current New York Knicks executive, Mark Warkentein in a conversation that I had with him at what was then called the D-League Showcase. To be specific, I found that on average, around ten players in any given draft are likely to become significantly productive, career starters and the rest will wind up being role players with varying degrees of interchangeability. Rather than split hairs over which player gets to be ranked 71st, I separate draft prospects into three color coded groups, and they are as follows:

Green: This subset of 10 to 15 players are the prospects with the highest probability of becoming highly impactful, career starters in the NBA.

Yellow: This groups contains the set of prospects that are likely to be drafted. However, players in this subset have some kind of red flag attached to them that prevents them from being in the Green Group.

Red: This group consists of lower probability prospects that are not likely to be selected in the draft and will most likely be players that will be used to fill out Summer League rosters or spend a few years in a league outside of the NBA. For the purposes of keeping the length of this book manageable, I did not include these prospects. If you want additional notes on anyone from this group, you can contact me through the information listed in the Credits section of this book.

4. *What does the three-numbered slash line at the top of a prospect's evaluation page mean?*

The three-numbered slash line at the top of any prospect's evaluation is my standardized numerical rating of that player. The values are based on a scale between 20 and 80, and each value is represented as follows:

- 80: Once-in-a-lifetime prospect
- 75: Elite generational talent
- 70: MVP caliber talent
- 65: Legitimate All-Star
- 60: Solid starter
- 55: Sixth man type or borderline starter
- 50: Rotation player
- 45: Fringe rotation player
- 40: End of the roster player
- 35: G-Leaguer
- 30 and below: Fringe G-League to non-professional level player

The three values in the slash line are in the format: Present/Likely Future/Ceiling and each value is explained in the following:

- Present: This value is based on the role or production level that a prospect is likely to have when he immediately enters the league as a rookie with minimal development time.

- Likely Future: This number corresponds to the prospect's most likely career role or production level according to my analytics and scouting information.

- Ceiling: Using all relevant data, this value is the prospect's best-case scenario or most attainable level of upside.

To provide an example, I rated last year's third overall pick, Luka Doncic as the best prospect in the 2018 NBA Draft and gave him a rating of 55/60/65. The first number indicates that immediately, he would be expected to produce at a level similar to a starter on a bad team or a typical sixth man. Typically, on average, a player with his overall profile tends to become a productive career NBA starter and in highly favorable scenarios, a player with Doncic's profile could potentially become a perennial All-Star.

5. What are the Cap Value and RCV numbers in the tables in the Offseason Primer section?

In last year's edition, I introduced a methodology to evaluate contracts based on team payrolls, current player salaries, as well as a player's overall production using readily available PER and Win Share metrics. Based on the formula outlined in the 2018 edition, I calculate any given player's Cap Value based on his performance relative to his current salary to get a sense of not just a player's raw dollar value, but also the amount of return a team is getting on that player's salary as well as any potential surplus value. The actual calculation for a player's Cap Value is fairly simple, and it goes as follows.

Step 1: Calculate the Win Share Part
- Cost per Win * Win Shares * (1230 / Total League Win Shares)

Step 2: Calculate the PER Part
- Cost per Minute Played * Minutes Played * (PER / 15)

Step 3: Calculated Dollars Earned
- Average Step 1 and Step 2

Step 4: Calculate the Surplus Value
- Dollars Earned – Actual Salary

Step 5: Calculate Overall Cap Value
- Dollars Earned + Surplus Value

Based on league payroll data, the cost of one win was approximately $2.813M and the cost of one minute of play was about $5,860. Anyway, I adapted Basketball-Reference's Simple Projection System methods to project Cap Values for all future seasons left in any given player's contract to get a projection of the **Remaining Cap Value (RCV)**, which is essentially the total estimated value of the remainder of that player's contract at this point in time.

In essence, the answers to these basic questions should be enough to get you up to speed if you are new to my brand of analysis or if you just needed to remember how everything in this book works. Every piece of information in this book was thoroughly researched with absolute care to ensure that you can gain a deeper knowledge and appreciation of the NBA, the Draft and basketball as a whole. If you want well-informed insights into the NBA heading into this offseason as well as a fun read in general, please turn the page and enjoy the 2019 edition of The NBA Summer Almanac.

2019 NBA OFFSEASON PRIMER

NBA Rosters are accurate as of May 30, 2019

How Should Teams Handle the Supermax Contract?

In response to the formation of the Miami Heat's super-team in the summer of 2010, the owners and the Players Association collectively agreed in 2011 to institute the Designated Player Rule as a way to give teams a greater advantage in retaining their homegrown players. Initially, this rule applied to younger players that were eligible for an extension to their rookie contract. However, after Kevin Durant's defection from Oklahoma City to Golden State, the rule was expanded to include veterans as well, resulting in what is commonly referred to as the Supermax. Like the original rule, the Supermax was intended to help teams keep their stars by allowing them to sign those players to a more lucrative contract than they could sign if they went elsewhere in free agency, but unintended consequences emerged. In 2017, the Supermax was in play for Paul George, Jimmy Butler and DeMarcus Cousins because they either met the criteria or were very close to meeting the required marks. But instead of being re-signed to a Supermax extension, all three of those players were eventually traded to other teams. Since that time, Kawhi Leonard was eligible for a Supermax extension with the San Antonio Spurs, but rather than re-sign, he forced a trade to end up in Toronto. Then, this season at the trade deadline, Anthony Davis unsuccessfully attempted to force a trade away from New Orleans by essentially announcing his intentions of declining his potential Supermax extension. In this sense, the Supermax has not had its intended effect because a lot of the eligible players have either changed teams or are in the process of trying to do so. A few Supermax contracts or extensions have been signed, but the results appear to be mixed at the moment. James Harden, Stephen Curry and Russell Westbrook to some extent are performing at a high enough level to warrant the higher maximum. On the flip side, a combination of performance regression and a catastrophic series of complications arising from an Achilles injury have potentially made John Wall's Supermax extension the most onerous contract in the NBA. With all of this mind, the two questions that arise are, "why has the Supermax contract caused more problems than benefits and how should teams approach it to efficiently build their teams?"

The best way to address this overall question is to start with the original rule. The original rule that was put in place in 2011 is now the rookie contract portion of the overall Designated Player Rule. Initially, teams were allowed to designate one player coming off a rookie contract to receive a longer extension, but the rules were later amended to allow teams to have two designated players as long as at most one was acquired by trade. Then, if a designated player meets the criteria specified by the CBA or in their contract, they can receive a higher maximum, and this is commonly referred to as the Derrick Rose Rule. Specifically, this rule states that a designated player can qualify for a higher maximum salary starting at 30% of the cap instead of 25% if they meet any of the following criteria.

- The player was named to an All-NBA team in the most recent season or both of the seasons before it.
- The player was named as Defensive Player of the Year in the most recent season or both of the seasons before it
- The player was named as the NBA's MVP in any of the three most recent seasons

If a designated player doesn't meet any of the criteria above in any of his first three seasons, a team can put language into the contract to allow a player to qualify for a higher maximum if he meets certain approved benchmarks in his fourth year. For example, the Phoenix Suns put in conditions for Devin Booker's starting salary when his contract begins in the 2019-20 season. Specifically, the Suns tied his starting salary to making one of the All-NBA teams. He didn't actually qualify for the higher maximums, but these were the conditions for his starting salary for his extension.

- Booker's salary would be 25% of the cap if he didn't make an All-NBA team.
- He would start at 27.5% of the cap if he was named to the All-NBA Third Team.
- His salary would start at 28.5% of the cap if he was named to the All-NBA Second Team.
- He would receive a starting salary of 30% of the cap if he was named to the All-NBA First Team.

The idea behind this rule was that young players already producing at elite levels would have more incentives to stay with the teams that drafted them by providing an avenue to earn more money up front and have more long-term security. Then, the team would have similar advantages for the next contract because they could provide continually compounding raises through an extension. However, this was based on the assumption that the cap would remain relatively static. After all, the cap stayed at a figure between around $53.1 million in the 2006-07 season to just over $58.6 million in the 2013-14 season. But then, revenues exploded in the league, resulting in multiple cap spikes from the summer of 2015 to the present. Because of this, some of the older Designated Player contracts became outdated. For example, Kevin Durant agreed to a five-year maximum extension with no opt-outs in the summer of 2010, right before the last year of his rookie contract was set to expire and before the 2011 lockout. If the cap stayed at a level close to what it was in 2011, Oklahoma City would have had some advantages to extend his contract, but the cap was set for a significant spike in the summer of 2016. As a result, an extension of Durant's outdated contract was simply not going to happen because the salary numbers were based on the lower caps from earlier in the decade, which meant that he would have to leave a lot of money on the table to stay with Oklahoma City. Also, because there were no opt-outs in his second contract, the Thunder had no means to renegotiate an extension based on an anticipated future cap spike. If the last year of Durant's contract was an option year, the team and Durant could have mutually agreed to tear up the option and replace it with a brand new contract that was guaranteed for the maximum percentage of the future cap, but they didn't have an option in place to do this. Therefore, Durant had no choice but to hit the open market to get a contract that reflected his true value, which more or less, leveled the playing field for any potential suitor and now the rest is history.

As it was alluded to earlier, the Designated Player Rule was amended in 2017 to include qualifying veteran players in response to the outcome of the Durant situation. This amendment to the rule was a rather short-sighted move because the owners were unable to anticipate some of the negative consequences that followed. This is mainly because the idea of paying a player heading into their ninth or tenth season a starting salary of 35% of the cap is usually unreasonable, as only about a handful of players per season actually come close to producing at that high of a level. In addition to this, a Supermax contract tends to be a multi-year deal with compounded raises of up to 8% per season. If this is factored in, then the back-end of the contract eventually eats up so much cap space that it potentially limits any flexibility that a team might have to make moves. Unless the contract is for one of the few exceptional players, the Supermax is more likely to be an albatross than a positive value for teams. To illustrate the riskiness of the Supermax contract, the following will estimate the production level that is necessary to make this type of deal worthwhile to a team. If a player were to sign a four-year Supermax contract this summer, the starting salary would be 35% of $109 million with an 8% raise in each season after that to bring the total to about $171.9 million. Using the Win Share portion of this book's contract evaluation formula where one win in 2019 is worth about $2.813 million, this $171.9 million total would be equal to approximately 63 Win Shares in a four-year period. To get a sense of how high this number is, here are the players that accumulated 60 or more Win Shares in a four-year period from either their ninth to twelfth seasons or their tenth to thirteenth seasons in the modern three-point era of the NBA.

- Karl Malone, 62, 1994-95 to 1997-98
- LeBron James, 60, 2011-12 to 2014-15
- Kevin Garnett, 60, 2003-04 to 2006-07

As a side note, Michael Jordan's tenth season was his shortened return from baseball in 1995. If that particular season was discarded and only the four full seasons that he played between his ninth and thirteenth seasons are accounted for, he would have been on top of the list because he accumulated 71.7 Win Shares in those four years, which would have made him the only qualifying veteran player that produced at a level above a Supermax in modern NBA history, at least according to a portion of the formula. From a PER perspective, the Supermax bar is simply too high for any qualifying veteran to match the necessary production level. Using the PER portion of the contract evaluation formula in this book where one minute of play is worth $5,860 in 2019, a player would have to have a four-year PER of just over 33.5 if they consistently played 40 minutes per game in all 328 games to reach a level equal to the Supermax. This is unreachable because no player in NBA history has ever had a PER of 33.5 in one season, let alone a four-year period. If we adjust for a somewhat reasonable PER for the highest possible performing player, the Supermax would still be tough to reach. Under this part of the calculation, a player with a four-year PER of 30 would have to average just over 44.7 minutes per game and play in all 328 games to play at a Supermax level. This is theoretically possible but unlikely because the back-end of the Supermax usually coincides with a player's early-to-mid-30's, a time where NBA players are typically declining and have to take on reduced workloads. With all of this in mind, the Supermax or even the standard ten-year-plus max contract should only be reserved for the very best of the best and no one else because those type of players would be the only ones capable of coming close to the extremely high production bar to make sure that this kind of contract doesn't become a long-term cap killer. Among the players in the league right now that could qualify for a Supermax in the future, Giannis Antetokounmpo is probably the only one that could justify this kind of contract, if he continues on his current career trajectory. With any of the other possible qualifiers, there may be enough question marks in their overall profile to be concerned about the potential negatives of a contract of that size.

    In a hypothetical world where NBA executives operate with an unwavering dedication to efficiency and value optimization, the Supermax or ten-year-plus max contract would only be given to players like James Harden, Giannis Antetokounmpo or somebody else that performs at an extraordinarily elite level and has an established track record of durability. Then, with every other potential max contract player, they would hold firm and stick to the 25% or 30% max contract to serve as their value. However, this isn't the world that the NBA operates in. In the real world of the NBA, executives don't really haggle much with mid-level role players, let alone max-level stars. Therefore, it would suddenly be a shock to the current system if a team were to shift to a ruthlessly efficient negotiating style and try to pinch a few pennies with a star player. If it is not a viable option to negotiate for a more cost-efficient price, then trading a questionable Supermax qualifier before they reach that status is likely to produce the best long-term outcome. Consider the Sacramento Kings' situation in 2017 regarding DeMarcus Cousins. Because he had made the All-NBA Second Team in both 2014-15 and 2015-16, he was set to qualify for a Supermax extension in the summer of 2017 if he remained a member of the Kings. Sacramento on the other hand recognized that they were a losing team that couldn't handle a cap situation with Cousins occupying a large portion of the payroll, so they promptly traded him to New Orleans. In the years since the trade, the Kings have been operating with mostly clean books, which enabled them to stockpile young talent and foster a significant overall improvement to the point where they were closer to the playoffs than they have ever been in the last decade, an outcome that is more favorable than if they had signed Cousins to an inflated contract. Chicago employed a similar strategy with Jimmy Butler, but the execution has been clunky to say the least. Even so, they still have young players with asset value and cap flexibility on their side to potentially improve their situation, which probably wouldn't have been the case if they had committed to Butler on a Supermax contract. On the flip side, the Washington Wizards are going to serve as the cautionary tale for the Supermax. John Wall became eligible for the Supermax when he made the All-NBA Third Team in the 2016-17 season. Though Wall had made the Eastern Conference All-Star team in the previous three seasons, he had never made an All-NBA team until that season, which planted a little seed of doubt of whether he was actually worthy of this kind of contract. Rather than wait another season to allow Wall to establish his true value, the Wizards immediately signed him to the Supermax extension. Since then, Wall's play has regressed to a level below his career averages and he will miss at least a full season with a ruptured left Achilles' tendon. For a player that's highly dependent on his athleticism, these circumstances will likely result in a decline that's going to be very expensive for the Wizards, as he'll also occupy a massive chunk of their payroll for the next four years to severely limit the team's overall flexibility. In hindsight, the most sensible move would have been to trade him once he became eligible to avoid what is now a cap crippling contract.

On average, the best strategy to handle a potential Supermax contract is to just avoid the commitment altogether and just trade the player either right before he qualifies or once he becomes eligible. This is usually because two factors have to come together to make the Supermax viable. First off, the player has to have an impeccable track record of elite production and have a fairly reliable aging profile to offset the increasing back-end of the contract. Also, the team has to have a championship-level core already in place to compensate for the future limitations in cap flexibility. Because there are only a handful of truly special players in the league that could justify this type of contract and the fact that the majority of teams are closer to average than they are to contention, the Supermax is more likely to be an impractical expenditure in most situations, so teams would be best served to steer clear of it whenever possible. As a result, the Supermax has not achieved its intended effect, and unintentionally, Supermax eligibility has essentially become a new inflection point where teams have to assess the state of their own franchise and true value of the player in question. In the rare cases where a no doubt, MVP-level, future Hall of Famer is involved and the team is trying to keep a championship-level team together, then the Supermax may be worthwhile. In almost every circumstance, a team would need honestly evaluate the situation and show a willingness to make a difficult decision. If they do that, then the team in question could make a move that could allow them to be better in the long-term even though they may take a hit in the short-term. However, if they act with irrational confidence and elect to make a short-sighted move, they could do serious damage to the long-term health of their franchise by committing a sizeable chunk of the cap to one person that would also reduce the number of ways to maneuver and improve their roster. To put it simply, the Supermax really isn't a mechanism to provide an advantage for teams to retain their star players. It actually is a high-stakes point in the building process where teams have to choose a clear direction for their franchise. A rash decision could result in a potentially bleak future where a team is stuck in mediocrity for a long time with no real way to escape their situation. On the other hand, a measured action may not pay off in the short-term, but simply being free of a massive burden could give a team a much better chance at a brighter future.

ATLANTA HAWKS

Season in Review

Last summer, the Atlanta Hawks took the first steps to create an identity for themselves while they continue to execute their multi-year rebuilding project. Specifically, General Manager, Travis Schlenk made moves to build the Hawks in the image of his former employer, the Golden State Warriors, mainly by trading the rights to Luka Doncic to Dallas for the rights to Trae Young and an additional first round pick. Atlanta also drafted Kevin Huerter and Omari Spellman to give them two additional prospects with outside shooting potential and they hired former Philadelphia 76ers assistant, Lloyd Pierce as their new head coach to implement a fast paced system with similar principles. Because the team was in the early stages of its developmental process, they took some lumps and finished near the bottom of the Eastern Conference. However, their record was a bit better than expected and they showed some signs of promise in the future.

Individually speaking, Trae Young had a very strong rookie season. To be specific, he displayed good playmaking skills and he was a very good shot creator, particularly in isolation situations. He seemed to be a little overextended at first, but later his efficiency improved considerably towards the end of the season. In addition to Young, John Collins continued to improve in his second season and first full year as a starter. His effectiveness increased in virtually offensive metric and situationally, he excelled as a roll man in the pick-and-roll game. From there, Huerter and Spellman showed promise as floor spacers and Taurean Prince flashed some potential as a three-and-D wing player. The only real negative from an individual standpoint was that they stayed relatively quiet at the trade deadline and only chose to make a minor move by swapping Tyler Dorsey for Shelvin Mack without picking up any additional draft assets. Otherwise, the team's primary young core displayed enough future upside to give them something to build upon for the next few seasons.

From a team standpoint, they were among the league's worst teams on both sides of the ball, as they ranked in the bottom third of the league in both Offensive and Defensive Efficiency. Offensively, the Hawks were simply too inexperienced to properly execute the team's fast paced system. On the positive side, they ranked in the top half of the league in almost every passing metric and they ranked in the top ten in both Three-Pointers Made and Attempted while playing at the league's fastest pace. In addition to this, they were one of the league's best offensive rebounding teams, finishing in the top ten in Offensive Rebound Percentage. However, the team's offensive efficiency suffered because, like many young teams before them, they turned the ball over at a high rate and struggled to generate open shots, resulting in lower shooting percentages. Also, the team was taking more of a process-oriented approach than a results-based one, so they didn't play to their immediate strengths on offense. To be specific, the Hawks were better in isolation and post-up situations due to the individual abilities of Young and Collins, respectively. However, they didn't use these plays very often, as they were focusing on developing their younger players for a movement-based offense that they will continue to implement as these players become more polished. As a result, the Hawks made a lot of mistakes on the offensive end because their primary young players were still trying to find their place in the league.

The team's ineffectiveness on offense hurt them on the defensive end because their frequent missed shots and tendency to turn the ball over made them one of the league's worst teams at playing transition defense. Specifically, they rated among the league's five worst teams for most of the season in per-possession defense in transition situations. In addition to this, they were a young team that struggled with its defensive rotations, so they gave up a lot of wide open looks and opposing teams were able to shoot very efficiently against them, as the Hawks ranked near the bottom of the league in Opponents' Effective Field Goal Percentage. Additionally, the team struggled a bit on the defensive glass, and they fouled at a very high rate, allowing opponents to frequently get to the free throw line. In fact, their Opponents' Free Throws per Field Goal Attempt Rate was the league's worst. On the positive side, they forced turnovers at a high rate, ranking in the upper half of the league in Opponents' Turnover Percentage, and they excelled at defending isolations. They were able to rank in the top five in per-possession isolation defense by keeping opposing offenses away from going one-on-one against their weaker defenders and forcing the action over towards players that were better at guarding their specific match-up. Even despite these positives, the Hawks still have their work cut out for them to improve their defense in the future.

Based on the team's performance this past season, Atlanta has a couple of pieces to build around in Young and Collins, but they will definitely need some more help, particularly on the wings to become a consistent winner in the Eastern Conference. Fortunately for the Hawks, the Eastern Conference is rather top heavy with only six teams that could consistently finish with records above the 0.500 mark. This may give the team an easier pathway to a future playoff spot, but the team has to resist any temptation to win in the short-term because the core is still a few years away from being polished enough to be a legitimate contender. Therefore, the Hawks should remain patient and focus on improving their youngest players to the fullest of their abilities while accumulating assets to make bigger moves in the future. If they can do that and get some good luck in either this lottery or a future one, they could eventually contend in the future.

2019-20 Outlook

Players Under Contract for 2019-20

* Age and Salary numbers are for 2019-20. See page 9 for explanation for Cap Value and RCV. A number in parentheses indicates that the value is negative.

	Age	Salary	Years Left	2018-19 Cap Value	RCV
Kent Bazemore	30	$19.27M	0	($8.54M)	($7.30M)
Miles Plumlee	31	$12.50M	0	($9.86M)	($8.27M)
Trae Young	21	$6.27M	2 Team Options	$20.27M	$61.86M
Alex Len	26	$4.16M	0	$14.76M	$16.29M
Taurean Prince	25	$3.48M	0	$8.78M	$9.51M
John Collins	22	$2.69M	Team Option	$29.65M	$56.88M
Kevin Huerter	21	$2.64M	2 Team Options	$9.92M	$29.82M
DeAndre' Bembry	25	$2.60M	0	$8.97M	$3.82M
Omari Spellman	22	$1.90M	2 Team Options	$5.55M	$15.43M
Deyonta Davis*	23	$1.65M	0	$0.15M	$3.81M
Jaylen Adams*	23	$1.42M	0	$1.31M	$0.20M
Isaac Humphries*	22	$1.42M	0	($0.25M)	($1.62M)

* Adams' contract for 2019-20 is not guaranteed. Humphries' contract for 2019-20 is not guaranteed. Davis' contract for 2019-20 is not guaranteed.

Two-Way Contracts

* In this section, listings are read: Player, Current Age, Height, Weight, College or Country

- Alex Poythress, 25, 6'9", 235, Kentucky

2019 Free Agents

* Age and Salary numbers are for 2019-20. See page 9 for explanation for Cap Value and RCV. A number in parentheses indicates that the value is negative.

	Age	Status	Salary	2018-19 Cap Value	RCV
Justin Anderson	26	Restricted	N/A	$0.60M	N/A
Dewayne Dedmon	30	Unrestricted	N/A	$13.77M	N/A
Vince Carter	43	Unrestricted	N/A	$9.80M	N/A

Estimated Cap Space for 2019 Free Agency

Note: Salary cap estimated to be at $109 million for 2019-20, as of September 17, 2018.

- **$53.5 million** if Adams, Humphries and Davis are waived
- **$49.0 million** if Adams, Humphries and Davis remain on the roster

2019 Draft Picks and Future Assets until 2022
- 2019 own first round – **8th overall**
- 2019 first round from Dallas (Luka Doncic/Trae Young trade) – **10th overall**
- 2019 own second round – **35th overall**
- 2019 second round from L.A. Lakers (Richard Jefferson trade) – **41st overall**
- 2019 second round from Charlotte (Devonte' Graham trade) – **44th overall**
- 2020 own first round
- 2020 first round from Cleveland, top 10 protected (Kyle Korver trade)
- 2020 own second round, top 55 protected, otherwise goes to Boston (Jabari Bird trade)
- 2021 own first round
- 2021 own second round
- 2022 own first round
- 2022 first round from Oklahoma City, lottery protected (Dennis Schroder trade)
- 2022 own second round

Draft Rights Held

	Year	Round	Pick
Alpha Kaba	2017	2	60
Marcus Eriksson	2015	2	50

Offseason Recommendations

The Atlanta Hawks are still a long way from becoming playoff team in the Eastern Conference. With this in mind, the team's offseason goals should be the same as they were last season. Specifically, **they should look to land a potential core player with one of their two lottery picks and use their ample cap space to accumulate additional assets.** Ideally, the Hawks would look to target a wing prospect because they currently have a sizeable hole in that portion of the roster and most of the better prospects in this draft are projected to play on the wing. From there, the Hawks are in a prime position to pick up some extra draft picks or young players because they are projected to have over $50 million in cap space in addition to potentially having the reasonably large expiring contracts of Kent Bazemore and Miles Plumlee to use in a salary dump trade. Therefore, Atlanta can get creative to find teams that are willing to part with valuable assets for the sake of cap relief. They could even absorb some of the worst contracts in the league because most of the team's core is still on rookie contracts and the Hawks are in a rebuilding mode anyways. Therefore, if Minnesota or Washington is willing to pair a sizeable pick package that includes multiple unprotected first round picks to the contracts of either Andrew Wiggins or John Wall, the Hawks should consider making a deal, as it could give their franchise much more optionality as they continue to rebuild their roster. If they absorb an onerous contract to add extra assets, they could then take a more prudent approach to building the rest of the team. They could do this by focusing on loading up their roster with developing young players on rookie contracts and possible low-cost trade deadline bait to offset the sunk costs of taking on a major contract. If the team plays its cards right, some extra tradeable assets could set the Hawks up to make bigger moves in the future and put the team closer to contention. Otherwise, their rebuild could take longer than expected with a more passive approach or even worse, they could be stuck in mediocrity if they make a rash move to use their cap space to sign middling veterans for the short-term.

BOSTON CELTICS

Season in Review

Last season, the Boston Celtics came within one game of reaching the NBA Finals with an undermanned roster. Expectations for this season were very high, as they were set to have both Kyrie Irving and Gordon Hayward return from their respective injuries. Because of this, they were viewed by many as the favorite to come out of the East and reach this season's NBA Finals. However, things didn't go as smoothly for the Celtics at the start of the season. They stumbled to a 10-10 start because they basically had difficulties incorporating everyone into new roles. This resulted in a few chemistry clashes and an unsettled rotation. Then, head coach, Brad Stevens made a tweak to the rotation by starting Marcus Smart and Marcus Morris and moving Hayward and Jaylen Brown to the bench. From there, Boston began to play more like than they did in the last couple of seasons for a while. The team's performance didn't stay that high for a consistent amount of time because the team's chemistry problems lingered throughout the season and they ended up finishing with a middle playoff seed in the Eastern Conference.

This season, Boston didn't really defend at the same level that it did last year, but they still were one of the league's best defensive teams, ranking in the top ten in Defensive Efficiency. The Celtics mainly relied on using their versatility to aggressively switch screens and make clean rotations. This allowed them to be one of the better teams in the league at forcing misses, as evidenced by the fact that they ranked in the upper half of the league in Opponents' Effective Field Goal Percentage. Furthermore, their defensive flexibility made them one of the best teams at defending the three-point line, as they ranked in the top ten in Opponents' Three-Point Percentage. Their aggressive switching also helped them force a lot of turnovers, as they could consistently apply pressure to opposing ball handlers and play passing lanes. They ranked in the top ten in Opponents' Turnover Percentage and Steals per Game as a result. For most of the season, Boston struggled on the defensive glass mainly because they were playing smaller lineups on a regular basis, as they had to incorporate all of their talented perimeter players. However, their rebounding improved a little bit at the end of the season, but they were still a below average defensive rebounding team. The only real negative for the Celtics' defense was that their effort wasn't always consistent on a night-to-night basis. Most likely, the reason for their inconsistency was related to the Celtics' disconnected chemistry, so they weren't a cohesive enough unit to play elite team defense in every game. As a result, they would sometimes get sloppy and commit some unnecessary fouls, which allowed their opponents to get to the free throw line a little more than they did last season. Specifically, they were below the league average in Opponent Free Throws per Field Goal Attempt this past season.

Offensively, the Celtics improved greatly over the performance from last season, as they became one of the league's better offensive teams, ranking in the top ten in Offensive Efficiency this past season. Not only did they benefit from a talent boost by having Irving and Hayward healthy for the whole season, the stylistic change to a slightly faster pace and an increased level of ball movement helped them get better shots on a consistent basis. The result of this was that they were one of the league's best shooting teams, ranking in the top ten in Effective Field Goal Percentage. They also were effective at spreading out opposing defenses, as they often put four or five credible three-point threats on the floor to enhance the offensive skills of Irving and Jayson Tatum. They shot very well on their threes because of this and they even got a career shooting season from Smart, which allowed them to rank in the top ten in Three-Point Percentage. In addition to shooting well, the Celtics limited turnovers to the point where they finished in the top ten in Turnover Percentage. Because the team was more perimeter-oriented, they didn't really draw fouls or do much damage on the offensive boards. Specifically, they finished with one of the league's lowest Free Throw Attempt Rates and they ranked in the bottom half of the league in Offensive Rebound Percentage.

The Celtics failed to meet the high expectations of this season, as they were bounced out quickly in the second round by Milwaukee. Their future is also murky because of Kyrie Irving's impending free agency. If they can re-sign him and overcome their chemistry issues, they would remain contenders in the Eastern Conference with the chance to rise even higher if they make some other moves. If he elects to go elsewhere, the team is still in a solid position to compete because they could easily pivot to building around Tatum and using their collection of assets to find the appropriate complementary pieces. Because the future of the Eastern Conference is in flux due to the possible departures of several big name free agents from contending teams, Boston shouldn't try to make any kind of sudden move. Their best bet is to let the events of the summer play out and then make prudent decisions on the fly. If they don't lock themselves into a long-term deal with a middling veteran or irrationally give up their assets, they still could be a solid playoff team in the East with the flexibility to improve in future years in a worst-case scenario.

2019-20 Outlook

Players Under Contract for 2019-20

* Age and Salary numbers are for 2019-20. See page 9 for explanation for Cap Value and RCV. A number in parentheses indicates that the value is negative.

	Age	Salary	Years Left	2018-19 Cap Value	RCV
Gordon Hayward	29	$32.70M	Player Option	($6.49M)	($30.80M)
Marcus Smart	25	$12.55M	2	$14.06M	$25.72M
Jayson Tatum	21	$7.83M	Team Option	$21.42M	$46.45M
Jaylen Brown	23	$6.53M	0	$13.10M	$13.11M
Guerschon Yabusele	24	$3.12M	Team Option	($0.09M)	($2.42M)
Robert Williams	22	$1.94M	2 Team Options	$3.70M	$9.35M
Semi Ojeleye*	25	$1.62M	Team Option	$2.50M	$6.13M

* Ojeleye's contract for 2019-20 is not guaranteed. His contract for 2020-21 is a team option and is not guaranteed until July 1, 2020. The Celtics also used the stretch provision to waive Demetrius Jackson on July 15, 2017. They will be assessed a cap hit of **$92,857** until the end of the 2022-23 season.

Two-Way Contracts

* In this section, listings are read: Player, Current Age, Height, Weight, College or Country
- P.J. Dozier, 22, 6'6", 205, South Carolina
- R.J. Hunter, 25, 6'5", 185, Georgia State

2019 Free Agents

* Age and Salary numbers are for 2019-20. See page 9 for explanation for Cap Value and RCV. A number in parentheses indicates that the value is negative.

	Age	Status	Salary	2018-19 Cap Value	RCV
Al Horford	33	Player Option	$30.12M	$7.10M	$5.47M
Kyrie Irving	27	Player Option	$21.33M	$25.74M	$24.38M
Aron Baynes	33	Player Option	$5.45M	$5.84M	$7.09M
Terry Rozier	25	Restricted	N/A	$14.71M	N/A
Daniel Theis	27	Restricted	N/A	$14.20M	N/A
Brad Wanamaker	30	Restricted	N/A	$3.81M	N/A
Jonathan Gibson	32	Restricted	N/A	($0.02M)	N/A
Marcus Morris	30	Unrestricted	N/A	$18.50M	N/A

Estimated Cap Space for 2019 Free Agency

Note: Salary cap estimated to be at $109 million for 2019-20, as of September 17, 2018.

- **$44.2 million**, maximum cap space if Horford, Irving and Baynes opt out and Ojeleye is waived

- **Basically over the cap**, most likely scenario, Horford and Baynes opt in and Irving opts out. Their spending power would be lower with cap space than it would be if they stayed over the cap and used their cap exceptions.
    - **Non-taxpayer Mid-Level Exception**

2019 Draft Picks and Future Assets until 2022

- 2019 first round from Sacramento via Philadelphia (Jayson Tatum trade) – **14th overall**
- 2019 first round from L.A. Clippers via Memphis (Deyonta Davis trade, Jeff Green trade) – **20th overall**
- 2019 own first round – **22nd overall**
- 2019 own second round – **51st overall**
- 2020 own first round
- 2020 first round from Memphis, top 6 protected (Jeff Green three-team trade)
- 2020 own second round
- 2020 second round from Atlanta, top 55 protected (Jabari Bird trade)
- 2021 own first round
- 2021 own second round
- 2022 own first round
- 2022 own second round

Draft Rights Held

None

Offseason Recommendations

This summer could be an eventful one for the Celtics because Kyrie Irving is hitting the open market in free agency and he's given mixed indications about if he'll re-sign. Even though Irving is extremely talented, **it might be best for the franchise if he moves on**. There have been rumblings that the Celtics will make an aggressive move to trade for Anthony Davis. If they could somehow pry him away from New Orleans without giving up Jayson Tatum, it might be worth the trade price. However, given the events of the most recent trade deadline, Boston should seriously reconsider any trade for Davis if Tatum is involved. For starters, Davis' camp has reportedly stated that he's not willing to re-sign with Boston after his current contract expires. This likely means that Boston would only be getting Davis for one season because he would probably opt out of his final year. This combined with possibly giving up Tatum, an extremely valuable player on a rookie contract as well as other assets could make this potential deal very risky on Boston's end because two years from now, Davis could walk and leave them with nothing. Additionally, it's unclear if they even have valuable enough assets outside of Tatum to make a palatable deal. The pick that they have from Memphis may be valuable in the future, but their other assets have decreased in value because their three first round picks are all in the middle portion of that round. In addition to this, the future of the contenders in the Eastern Conference is mostly unsettled because every single team could suffer a critical personnel loss. As of now, many of Milwaukee's primary rotation players are set to hit free agency, Toronto could lose Kawhi Leonard and Philadelphia dealt away most of its assets to acquire Jimmy Butler and Tobias Harris, but both could potentially go elsewhere this summer. This might take away some of the incentive to take an all-in approach because Boston may not have to do much to wind up with the most talented team in the conference, even if they lose Irving. With all of this in mind, **Boston would be better served to pivot in its strategy and hold onto their assets to maintain their optionality**. The team's success in the playoffs last season without Irving and Hayward suggest that they might be able withstand a heavy personnel loss if Irving leaves in free agency. Therefore, the Celtics could look to re-sign Terry Rozier at an appropriate price and then use the picks or cap exceptions to fill the holes on the roster to build around Tatum, Brown and their other young players. If Boston maintains its discipline in what looks to be a wild summer, they still could remain contenders in the East no matter what happens with Kyrie Irving because the quality of young talent on the roster gives them the ability to exercise some patience and they don't need to rush to make hasty decisions to stay competitive. If they continue to make sound, rational decisions and they catch a lucky break or two, they still could be one of the best teams in the Eastern Conference next season.

BROOKLYN NETS

Season in Review

After spending the last couple of seasons in an adverse rebuilding period where they had no access to elite talent of any kind, the Brooklyn Nets made a significant improvement this past season. This was mainly because they were one of the few teams that maintained a semblance of continuity and their primary core players like Spencer Dinwiddie, Joe Harris and Caris LeVert developed a high level of on-court chemistry after spending more than a season together. Also, D'Angelo Russell took a major leap forward in his development to the point where he made his first All-Star team. Additionally, the Eastern Conference was a bit weaker as a whole, so they picked up a few more wins than they were expected to get, so all of this enabled the Nets to reach the playoffs for the first time since the 2014-15 season.

At the offensive end, head coach, Kenny Atkinson has adapted his style as his team's talent level has improved. Specifically, he's moved from using a frenetic, pace and space attack to a slightly slower paced offense that incorporated more isolations and a heavy use of the pick-and-roll because of Russell's growth to becoming an All-Star level player. Because of Russell's effectiveness as an on-ball playmaker, he can draw defenders to him to create open looks for his teammates. As a result, the Nets ranked in the top five in Open Three-Point Field Goal Frequency according to the NBA's tracking metrics. They were one of the league's better teams at making threes in volume, as they ranked in the top ten in Three-Pointers Made. They also were somewhat efficient as well because they shot threes at around the league average. In addition to being a good outside shooting team, the Nets got to the free throw line very frequently, as they ranked in the top ten in Free Throw Attempt Rate. This was mainly because LeVert and Dinwiddie continued to improve and became even more effective at getting penetration to force defenders to commit fouls. On another positive note, the addition of Ed Davis to go along with second-year big man, Jarrett Allen gave them a boost on the offensive boards, which allowed Brooklyn to finish in the top ten in Offensive Rebound Percentage. On the flip side, the Nets were still a young team, so they were a bit turnover prone as a result and they wound up ranking in the bottom third of the league in Turnover Percentage. They also weren't as efficient a shooting team as their three-point shooting ability suggests because they had a lot of trouble finishing shots inside. In fact, they were among the NBA's worst teams at finishing shots inside of five feet according to the league's tracking metrics. Their roll men with exception to Allen really struggled in pick-and-roll situations and as a whole, the team finished in the bottom third in the league in per-possession efficiency in plays that ended with the roll man in the pick-and-roll game.

At the other end of the floor, the Nets were able to improve to being around an average defensive unit because of the team's chemistry. Individually, they don't really have any significant standouts, but they did a couple of things well as a team. Specifically, they were fairly good at forcing misses and keeping teams off the free throw line, as they rated in the upper half of the league in Opponents' Effective Field Goal Percentage and Opponent Free Throws per Field Goal Attempt. Moreover, they were a team that consistently made clean rotations on the defensive end, which allowed them to have some success in a few subtle areas. They almost always got back on defense, which enabled them to be one of the league's best teams at preventing transition offense. In fact, according to Synergy, they ranked in the top ten at defending in transition situations. They also excelled at defending cuts to the basket and closing out on spot-up shooters. As further evidence of the latter, they were particularly good at limiting their opponents' three-point attempts, as they ranked in the top ten in Three-Pointers Allowed. On the negative side, the Nets are still rather inexperienced, so they had some struggles against opponents in pick-and-roll situations and they wound up being one of the league's worst teams at defending these kinds of plays. Also, because they played smaller lineups as a whole, they had trouble defending post-ups. In fact, they were among the league's worst teams at defending in post-up situations on a per-possession basis according to Synergy. On top of this, they were still below average at forcing turnovers and grabbing defensive rebounds, as they finished in the bottom third of the league in Opponent Turnover Percentage and Defensive Rebound Percentage.

Brooklyn took a sizeable step forward this season by taking advantage of a weakened Eastern Conference to make the playoffs. The team has a lot working in its favor because they have a solid system in place, some chemistry to help them grow even further and the cap space to add another major piece to give them a talent boost. However, they will have to be careful in making a big acquisition because they don't want to negate some of this positive momentum by adding a player that might disrupt their chemistry or force them to make major changes to the team's system. If they can do their due diligence to find the right fit and re-sign D'Angelo Russell at a reasonable price, the Nets could take another step to becoming legitimate contenders in the East. Otherwise, the conference might just be weak enough where they still may be a solid playoff team next season.

2019-20 Outlook

Players Under Contract for 2019-20

* Age and Salary numbers are for 2019-20. See page 9 for explanation for Cap Value and RCV. A number in parentheses indicates that the value is negative.

	Age	Salary	Years Left	2018-19 Cap Value	RCV
Allen Crabbe	27	$18.50M	0	($12.91M)	($7.51M)
Spencer Dinwiddie	26	$10.61M	1 + Player Option	$23.63M	$44.42M
Joe Harris	28	$7.67M	0	$18.77M	$15.53M
Caris LeVert	25	$2.63M	0	$9.12M	$10.30M
Jarrett Allen	21	$2.38M	Team Option	$34.12M	$58.44M
Dzanan Musa	20	$1.91M	2 Team Options	($1.82M)	($8.10M)
Rodions Kurucs	21	$1.70M	1 + Team Option	$8.31M	$26.69M
Treveon Graham*	26	$1.65M	0	$1.56M	$3.05M

* Graham's contract for 2019-20 is not guaranteed. The stretch provision was used to waive Deron Williams in July 2015, so the Nets are still assessed a cap hit of **$5.47M** until the end of the 2019-20 season.

Two-Way Contracts

* In this section, listings are read: Player, Current Age, Height, Weight, College or Country

- Alan Williams, 26, 6'8", 265, UC – Santa Barbara

2019 Free Agents

* Age and Salary numbers are for 2019-20. See page 9 for explanation for Cap Value and RCV. A number in parentheses indicates that the value is negative.

	Age	Status	Salary	2018-19 Cap Value	RCV
Shabazz Napier	28	Team Option	$1.85M	$9.39M	$10.66M
D'Angelo Russell	23	Restricted	N/A	$25.17M	N/A
Rondae Hollis-Jefferson	25	Restricted	N/A	$6.83M	N/A
Theo Pinson	24	Restricted	N/A	$0.66M	N/A
DeMarre Carroll	33	Unrestricted	N/A	$1.11M	N/A
Jared Dudley	34	Unrestricted	N/A	($0.90M)	N/A
Ed Davis	30	Unrestricted	N/A	$20.87M	N/A

Estimated Cap Space for 2019 Free Agency

Note: Salary cap estimated to be at $109 million for 2019-20, as of September 17, 2018.

- **$56.3 million**, most likely scenario, Napier's option is picked up and Graham is waived

2019 Draft Picks and Future Assets until 2022
- 2019 own first round – **17th overall**
- 2019 first round from Denver (Kenneth Faried trade) – **27th overall**
- 2019 second round from New York via Philadelphia (Jahlil Okafor trade, Arnett Moultrie trade) – **31st overall**
- 2020 own first round
- 2020 second round from Denver (Kenneth Faried trade)
- 2020 second round from Portland via Orlando, Cleveland, and Atlanta, top 55 protected (Jeremy Lin trade, Richard Jefferson trade to Atlanta, Joe Harris trade to Orlando, Maurice Harkless trade to Portland)
- 2020 second round from Indiana, protected from picks 45 – 60 (Caris LeVert trade)
- 2021 own first round
- 2021 second round from Toronto (Greg Monroe trade)
- 2021 second round from Phoenix, protected from picks 31 – 35 (Jared Dudley trade)
- 2022 own first round
- 2022 own second round

Draft Rights Held

	Year	Round	Pick
Aleksandar Vezenkov	2017	2	57
Isaia Cordinier	2016	2	44
Juan Pablo Vaulet	2015	2	39

Offseason Recommendations

Brooklyn is a prime position to improve this summer because they have loads of cap space and they're a playoff team in the NBA's largest market. Therefore, they could be attractive to big name free agents. In fact, when Jimmy Butler was making his trade demands at the beginning of the season, the Nets were one of his preferred destinations. However, the Nets **could look to aim higher and take their best shot to land Kevin Durant**. Durant and the Nets could be a pretty good match for one another. After all, Brooklyn could give Durant a new challenge, if that's what he desires, while also providing him with a solid base of complementary talent, a dynamic pace and space system to match his abilities and a relatively stable organization to make the appropriate moves to compete for a championship. Otherwise, if Durant decides to go elsewhere, then Brooklyn could move on to some of the other options. Among the available free agents, the best fit for the Nets would be the combination that's commonly known across social media circles as "Bobi and Tobi", or **Boban Marjanovic and Tobias Harris. The best use of the team's cap space would be to aggressively pursue that duo** as a way to significantly improve Brooklyn's roster.

In order of importance, Harris would warrant a max contract because he probably would have been an All-Star if he had been in the Eastern Conference all season. His skill set would be a great fit for the Nets because he could give them an excellent two-way, floor spacing combo forward that would also provide efficient volume scoring without demanding the ball. This would allow the Nets to improve its offense without stifling the development of the team's key perimeter players like Dinwiddie or LeVert. Harris' on-ball defense could also help Brooklyn contain opposing wing players as well. Next, Marjanovic could give the Nets some additional scoring efficiency inside and rim protection on the defensive end. Because of his plodding foot speed, Marjanovic has always been a limited use player that has never averaged more than 15 minutes per game. However, his limited usage could benefit the Nets because Marjanovic's presence would still give ample playing time to Jarrett Allen, which would allow him to continue his growth as a player. The combination of Harris and Marjanovic not only allows the team to fill its two biggest needs, a floor spacing four-man and a reliable rim running, rim protecting big man, but this duo could also enhance the team's chemistry, which appears to be a strong intangible strength. From there, the team could **target another veteran three-and-D wing player** along the lines of Danny Green with their remaining cap space to add more floor spacing and better on-ball perimeter defense. Then, they could finish off their offseason by matching any kind of reasonable offer for D'Angelo Russell to keep an All-Star level talent on the roster and maintain continuity. Brooklyn is favorably positioned this summer because they have the means to make a significant addition, but they don't rush to make a move because the Eastern Conference is weaker from an overall standpoint and there's considerable uncertainty with most of the top teams in the conference. With this in mind, they can afford to be more selective and only target impact free agents that could enhance their existing culture. If they can find the players that best fit their program, they could take a big step towards being contenders in the Eastern Conference in the next few years.

CHARLOTTE HORNETS

Season in Review

The Charlotte Hornets came into this season with its roster from last year mostly intact. They only made minor changes by dumping Dwight Howard's contract, shuffling backup big men to acquire Bismack Biyombo along with a couple of future second round picks and picking up veteran point guard, Tony Parker to serve as their new backup. In addition, they hired former Spurs assistant, James Borrego as their new head coach last summer and he made a few tweaks to their rotation. Namely, he moved Michael Kidd-Gilchrist to the bench and inserted Jeremy Lamb into the starting lineup. The Hornets also got another All-Star season out of Kemba Walker, but the team's overall performance was pretty similar to last year. However, they were able to pick up a few extra wins because the lower part of the Eastern Conference was weakened due to various injury issues or roster defections. Even so, the Hornets barely missed the playoffs and were a lottery team for the third consecutive year.

Like the season before, the Hornets success was largely by having an above average offense, as they finished in the top half of the league in Offensive Efficiency. Stylistically, they switched to a more simplified, slower paced, pick-and-roll heavy attack that mainly relied on Walker's individual brilliance. As a result, Walker posted career highs almost across the board. Because opponents had to pay extra attention to Walker, three-point opportunities opened up for the others, as the Hornets ranked in the upper half of the league in Three-Pointers Made. Also, putting the ball in Walker's hands on a more frequent basis in a slowed down attack allowed the team to drastically cut its turnover rate to the point where they were the league's best team at limiting turnovers. The change to a slower offense did have some negative effects, as the Hornets had some trouble getting quality looks because there was simply less ball movement. Overall, the team ranked in the bottom third of the league in Effective Field Goal Percentage and this mainly because they were one of the league's worst teams at finishing shots inside of five feet, according to the NBA's tracking metrics. Additionally, the team was only about average at generating transition offense and they weren't especially effective at using screens or cuts to get open looks. Also, they tended to play smaller, perimeter-oriented lineups, so they didn't do a whole lot of damage on the offensive glass because they ranked in the bottom third of the league in Offensive Rebounding Percentage.

Defensively, the Hornets dropped off a little bit because they finished in the bottom third of the league in Defensive Efficiency. The main reason for this was that they struggled to defend around the basket. As a result, they were very vulnerable against post-ups, cuts to the basket and penetrating ball handlers in pick and roll situations. To compensate for their rim protection deficiencies, the Hornets often had to bring extra help, which left a lot of shooters open on the perimeter. All of this meant that Charlotte was one of the league's worst teams at forcing misses, as they finished in the bottom third of the league in Opponents' Effective Field Goal Percentage. Also, a lot of the scrambling that they had to do to give help left them out of position and unable to consistently keep pressure on opposing ball handlers or play passing lanes. Therefore, they also didn't force turnovers at a high rate. Additionally, the Hornets were also a below average defensive rebounding team, posting a Defensive Rebound Percentage just below the league average. On the positive side, they really excelled at keeping opponents off the free throw line, ranking in the top five in Opponent Free Throw Attempts per Field Goal Attempt. In addition to this, when the team had its defense set, it did very well in isolation situations because they ranked in the top ten on a per-possession basis according to Synergy. It was only a small sample size, but Miles Bridges' performance as a one-on-one defender really stood out, as he ranked in the 100th percentile at per-possession defense in isolation situations this past season. If the Hornets incorporated him into the rotation more in the future, their defense could incrementally improve.

      Generally speaking, Charlotte is in a precarious position. They really aren't good enough to really be a legitimate contender in the East, but they aren't bad enough to really consider a full-scale rebuild, especially after several other franchises have beaten them in the race to the bottom. Also, they don't have many additional assets to swing a major trade to move upwards and Kemba Walker will be a free agent this summer. So far, the team has made every indication that they will try to re-sign him and bring him back. If that happens, they still have a lot of work to do to put quality pieces around him to compete. Therefore, it's unlikely that they could do enough to make them better than they currently are now, so they'll probably still be a team that consistently competes for a lower playoff seed if Walker comes back. If Walker chooses to sign elsewhere, the Hornets will have no choice but to overhaul their roster and commit to a complete rebuilding project, as they don't have the assets to do anything else.

2019-20 Outlook

Players Under Contract for 2019-20

* Age and Salary numbers are for 2019-20. See page 9 for explanation for Cap Value and RCV. A number in parentheses indicates that the value is negative.

	Age	Salary	Years Left	2018-19 Cap Value	RCV
Nicolas Batum	31	$25.57M	Player Option	($2.96M)	($9.93M)
Bismack Biyombo	27	$17.00M	0	($7.14M)	($4.37M)
Cody Zeller	27	$14.47M	1	$5.46M	$3.84M
Tony Parker	37	$5.25M	0	$3.45M	$3.98M
Malik Monk	21	$4.03M	Team Option	$3.17M	$2.23M
Miles Bridges	21	$3.76M	2 Team Options	$13.38M	$40.34M
Willy Hernangomez*	25	$1.68M	0	$12.02M	$11.41M
Dwayne Bacon*	24	$1.62M	0	$5.37M	$3.09M
Devonte' Graham*	24	$1.42M	1	$3.10M	$5.42M

* Hernangomez's contract for 2019-20 is not guaranteed. Bacon's contract for 2019-20 is not guaranteed until August 1, 2019, then it is fully guaranteed. Graham's contract for 2020-21 is not guaranteed.

Two-Way Contracts

* In this section, listings are read: Player, Current Age, Height, Weight, College or Country

- Joe Chealey, 23, 6'3", 190, College of Charleston
- J.P. Macura, 23, 6'5", 205, Xavier

2019 Free Agents

* Age and Salary numbers are for 2019-20. See page 9 for explanation for Cap Value and RCV. A number in parentheses indicates that the value is negative.

	Age	Status	Salary	2018-19 Cap Value	RCV
Marvin Williams	33	Player Option	$15.01M	$6.78M	$7.21M
Michael Kidd-Gilchrist	26	Player Option	$13.00M	($0.05M)	$3.36M
Frank Kaminsky	26	Restricted	N/A	$6.24M	N/A
Kemba Walker	29	Unrestricted	N/A	$32.46M	N/A
Jeremy Lamb	27	Unrestricted	N/A	$22.18M	N/A
Shelvin Mack	29	Unrestricted	N/A	$5.01M	N/A

Estimated Cap Space for 2019 Free Agency

Note: Salary cap estimated to be at $109 million for 2019-20, as of September 17, 2018.

- **$37.5 million**, maximum cap space, Williams and Kidd-Gilchrist opt out, Hernangomez and Bacon are waived

- **Basically over the cap**, most likely scenario, Williams and Kidd-Gilchrist opt in. Their spending power would be lower with cap space than it would be if they stayed over the cap and used their cap exceptions

    - **Non-taxpayer Mid-Level Exception**
    - **Bi-Annual Exception**

2019 Draft Picks and Future Assets until 2022

- 2019 own first round – **12th overall**
- 2019 second round from Washington (Bismack Biyombo three-team trade, Jarred Vanderbilt trade to Denver) – **36th overall**
- 2019 second round from Oklahoma City (Hamidou Diallo trade) – **52nd overall**
- 2020 own first round
- 2020 second round from Cleveland via Portland, Cleveland, Orlando and L.A. Clippers (Miles Bridges trade, C.J. Wilcox trade to Orlando, Channing Frye trade to Cleveland, Anderson Varejao trade to Portland, Mike Miller trade to Portland)
- 2020 second round from either Brooklyn or New York via Orlando and Philadelphia (Bismack Biyombo three-team trade, Anzejs Pasecniks draft day trade to Philadelphia, Andrei Kirilenko trade to Philadelphia, Willy Hernangomez trade to New York)
- 2021 own first round
- 2021 second round from Brooklyn (Dwight Howard/Timofey Mozgov trade)
- 2021 second round from L.A. Clippers (Miles Bridges trade)
- 2022 own first round
- 2022 own second round

Draft Rights Held

	Year	Round	Pick
Arnoldas Kulboka	2018	2	55

Offseason Recommendations

The Charlotte Hornets backed themselves into a corner because their offseason plans are going to revolve around Kemba Walker's free agent decision. Because they don't have a lot of high-end assets, the team's best bet is to **try to re-sign Walker**. It's a bit of a risky bet because the Hornets would have to commit to a fifth year that would pay him a maximum salary into his mid-30's. However, there's not really another pathway for them to stay competitive with their current roster. If Charlotte is successful in keeping him, then they could look to **acquire a rim protecting big man that could also be a pick-and-roll partner for Walker**. Ideally, they would try to target a player that fits this profile in the draft because productive big men are now skewing younger and an established big man would also be out of Charlotte's price range anyways. From there, they could make a rotational tweak to set themselves up the future by **increasing Miles Bridges' minutes** and gradually phasing Michael Kidd-Gilchrist and Marvin Williams out, as they are set to become free agents in the summer of 2020 if they pick up their player options for next season. Next, they have some flexibility with Jeremy Lamb because they have his Bird Rights. They could re-sign him if the price is reasonable, but if the bidding gets out of hand, they could pivot and use their cap exceptions to bargain hunt for pieces to fill out the roster. If Walker decides to play elsewhere, the Hornets should commit to an aggressive plan to flip any of their veteran players for additional draft assets and pursue buy-low opportunities to potentially land a future rotational player at a discounted rate. This would allow them to take a proactive approach in rebuilding their roster with the goal of building a coherent system around a group of young players while maintaining their cap flexibility to eventually compete in the future even if the worst-case scenario happens where Walker decides to leave Charlotte in the summer.

CHICAGO BULLS

Season in Review

It was already expected to be a long season for the Chicago Bulls because they were heading into the second year of their rebuilding project. They made some curious moves in the offseason by a making long-term commitment to Zach LaVine and signing Jabari Parker to a lucrative short-term deal. Even with these moves, the team stumbled out of the gates and they fired head coach, Fred Hoiberg in early December. The Bulls replaced Hoiberg with assistant coach, Jim Boylen and immediately promoted to the full-time head coaching position within a few months. Boylen used drastically different managing style where he tended to be a bit more confrontational and used a more abrasive tone to his players. The attempts to shake up Chicago's culture didn't really work, and the Bulls continued to be one of the league's worst teams, finishing near the bottom of the Eastern Conference this past season.

Chicago's performance on the offensive end was rather emblematic of the considerable dysfunction that surrounds this team. From an individual standpoint, the team's most important players were quite productive. LaVine had his best season as a pro, posting career highs in PER as well as many other per-game categories like Points, Rebounds and Assists. Lauri Markkanen missed some games early on, but he improved his efficiency in his second season. Then, Wendell Carter, Jr. was productive in his rookie season before he injured his thumb in January and Otto Porter played well after coming to the Bulls in a trade at the deadline. However, this group couldn't really function as a unit and they wound up being one of the league's least efficient offensive units, finishing near the bottom of the league in Offensive Efficiency. They also finished in the bottom third of the league in every driving component metric for offensive effectiveness, as they struggled to make shots efficiently, maintain control of the ball, get to the free throw line or grab offensive rebounds. Stylistically, they elected to play an archaic, slow-down style that de-emphasized many of the team's potential strengths. For instance, the Bulls are young team that has a few players that excel at running the floor, but their slow pace limited their transition opportunities, so they weren't especially good at creating early offense. Also, the team wasn't bad from the three-point line, as they were just below the league average from a percentage standpoint, but they finished near the bottom of the NBA in Three-Point Attempts. The team made free throws at a high percentage, but they don't really use kind of motion to create mismatches and force opponents into fouling them, so they rarely get to the foul line. All of this suggests that the team really needs to overhaul its offensive system to maximize the individual talents of their key players in a way that is more conducive to effective performance in the modern NBA.

On defense, the Bulls were a little bit better, but they still ranked in the bottom third of the league in Defensive Efficiency. They didn't really excel in any one particular area, but if the coaching change had any effect, it may be that the team appeared to tighten some of its rotations. They did a solid job of keeping opponents off the free throw line, as they finished in the top half of the league in Opponents' Free Throws per Field Goal Attempt. According to Synergy, they were good at preventing cuts and rolls to the rim. However, Boylen's old-school approach may have detrimental effects on the team's defensive performance because the Bulls often over-protected the paint, which left them vulnerable on the outside. Specifically, they ranked in the upper half of the league at preventing Two-Point Attempts, but they finished in the bottom third of the league in giving up Three-Point Attempts. As a result, opposing teams shot much more efficiently against them and they ranked in the bottom third of the league in Opponents' Effective Field Goal Percentage. In addition to not playing effective shot defense, the Bulls also struggled to force turnovers. If there was another potential positive factor for their defense, it was that they were just above the league average in Defensive Rebound Percentage.

Though the Bulls may have some solid pieces in place to build a team around, the team's problems may be much greater than just finding the right personnel on the roster. To be specific, Chicago's organization needs to address the overall sense of dysfunction in their management operations and coaching staff because it's apparent that their culture is a bit toxic. If this issue isn't addressed, then the team is not likely to progress in a constructive fashion, and they could stay at the bottom of the Eastern Conference for the foreseeable future. As a result, they may need to make a drastic move to replace their current staff and break this current cycle by bringing in outside help that's more in tune to the ways of the modern NBA and can install a positive culture. That type of major change may be the only way that the Bulls could improve their fortunes in the future. Otherwise, the outlook for the next few years doesn't really look especially bright at the moment.

2019-20 Outlook

Players Under Contract for 2019-20

* Age and Salary numbers are for 2019-20. See page 9 for explanation for Cap Value and RCV. A number in parentheses indicates that the value is negative.

	Age	Salary	Years Left	2018-19 Cap Value	RCV
Otto Porter	26	$27.25M	Player Option	($6.83M)	($0.96M)
Zach LaVine	24	$19.50M	2	$4.00M	($4.06M)
Cristiano Felicio	27	$8.16M	1	($0.75M)	$2.21M
Lauri Markkanen	22	$5.30M	Team Option	$14.07M	$29.47M
Wendell Carter, Jr.	20	$5.20M	2 Team Options	$7.33M	$20.81M
Kris Dunn	25	$5.35M	0	$4.14M	$3.66M
Denzel Valentine	26	$3.38M	0	($2.28M)	$0.13M
Chandler Hutchison	23	$2.33M	2 Team Options	$2.72M	$6.16M
Antonio Blakeney	23	$1.59M	0	$0.72M	$0.23M
Shaquille Harrison*	26	$1.59M	0	$9.40M	$7.15M

* Harrison's contract for 2019-20 is not guaranteed. The Bulls waived Omer Asik on October 21, 2018. They are still assessed a cap hit of **$3.00M** until the end of the 2019-20 season.

Two-Way Contracts

* In this section, listings are read: Player, Current Age, Height, Weight, College or Country

- Rawle Alkins, 21, 6'5", 225, Arizona
- Brandon Sampson, 21, 6'5", 184, LSU

2019 Free Agents

* Age and Salary numbers are for 2019-20. See page 9 for explanation for Cap Value and RCV. A number in parentheses indicates that the value is negative.

	Age	Status	Salary	2018-19 Cap Value	RCV
Ryan Arcidiacono	25	Restricted	N/A	$17.63M	N/A
Wayne Selden	25	Restricted	N/A	$2.30M	N/A
Walter Lemon, Jr.	25	Restricted	N/A	$1.24M	N/A
Robin Lopez	31	Unrestricted	N/A	$2.98M	N/A
Timothe Luwawu-Cabarrot	24	Unrestricted	N/A	$1.09M	N/A

Estimated Cap Space for 2019 Free Agency

Note: Salary cap estimated to be at $109 million for 2019-20, as of September 17, 2018.
- **$27.9 million**, maximum cap space if Harrison is waived
- **$26.4 million**, if Harrison remains under contract

2019 Draft Picks and Future Assets until 2022
- 2019 own first round – **7th overall**
- 2019 second round from Memphis (Justin Holiday trade) – **38th overall**
- 2020 own first round
- 2020 own second round, top 55 protected, otherwise goes to Oklahoma City (Timothe Luwawu-Cabarrot trade)
- 2020 second round from Memphis, top 55 protected, otherwise goes to Houston (Justin Holiday trade, Michael Carter-Williams trade)
- 2021 own first round
- 2021 own second round, option to swap with New Orleans (Nikola Mirotic trade)
- 2022 own first round
- 2022 own second round, option to swap with Detroit (Willie Reed/Jameer Nelson trade)

Draft Rights Held

	Year	Round	Pick
Tadija Dragicevic	2008	2	53

Offseason Recommendations

Before the Bulls do anything to try to improve the team this summer, their organization needs to get its house in order. Though they actually signed Jim Boylen to a long-term extension, they **should rethink that decision and reverse course with a long-term head coach that is better versed in the ways of today's NBA.** As it stands now, the Bulls are stuck in the Stone Age with their approach and their key young players are suffering because of it, as they are not playing in a system that enhances their talent for the benefit of the team. Therefore, Chicago should look to poach an assistant from a forward-thinking, smaller market team like Milwaukee or Denver to implement a more effective system that plays to the strengths of players like Lauri Markkanen, Wendell Carter, Jr., Zach LaVine and Otto Porter.

With the long-term in mind, Chicago is still a long way from being contenders in the East, so they should **use their cap space and any other means to aggressively accumulate more assets to give them greater optionality in the future.** Right now, the Bulls don't have a whole lot of extra draft picks aside from a couple of extra second round picks. Because of this, there's not a lot of room for error and there's more pressure on them to nail their draft picks because they don't have the assets to make a worthwhile trade. If they can figure out a way to rent out some of their cap space to land an extra first round pick or two, it could give them a better chance to land some higher-end talent down the line. From an on-court perspective, **the Bulls would be best served to target a primary ball handler, preferably in the draft**. The modern NBA game has become much more perimeter-oriented, as teams continue to emphasize the importance of spacing and ball movement. For the Bulls to catch up, they will need to develop a dynamic primary ball handler to catch up with their competition. If a viable target doesn't present itself in the draft, the team shouldn't force their hand to reach for a lesser option. If they strike out in the draft, they could try to target a restricted free agent, but D'Angelo Russell might be the only player that would be worth an offer sheet. If they could sign him at a reasonable price, he could be worth it. **Otherwise, the team should look to experiment by making Zach LaVine their full-time point guard**. He played at the point for most of his rookie season before former Timberwolves coach, Sam Mitchell moved him to the two-guard spot, where he's been ever since. Since that time, his playmaking skills have improved over the last three seasons and his Assist Percentage has risen significantly in each of those years. Therefore, he may be able to handle the responsibilities of being a full-time point guard. Also, his scoring abilities could allow him to draw extra attention, which could give his teammates easier shots to improve the team's offensive efficiency. From there, the team could use any remaining space to target some inexpensive three-and-D wing players or rim protecting big men to round out the roster and help them incrementally on both sides of the ball.

CLEVELAND CAVALIERS

Season in Review

For the second time in franchise history, LeBron James parted ways with the Cleveland Cavaliers and the team had no choice but to move in a different direction. The Cavs were a bit better prepared this time around because they locked up Kevin Love to a four-year extension this past summer and they used the lottery pick that they picked up in the Kyrie Irving trade to select Collin Sexton. However, things didn't get off to a good start, as they lost their first six games and head coach, Tyronn Lue lost his job as a result. The team then hired Larry Drew as the team's interim head coach, but their performance still didn't improve very much. After trading veterans like Kyle Korver, George Hill and Rodney Hood away for an assortment of draft assets, Cleveland wound up finishing the season as one of the league's worst teams.

For the previous couple of seasons, the Cavs were among the league's worst defensive teams even with LeBron James on the roster, so it's not surprising that they were the worst defensive team in the NBA this past season. A lot of the team's ineffectiveness at this end was a result of the coaching change and all of the personnel shuffling, so the Cavs couldn't defend as a cohesive unit. Because of this, they really struggled to make sound rotations and opposing offenses got a lot of open shots, making it difficult for the Cavs to force misses on a consistent basis. In fact, Cleveland finished last in the league in Opponents' Effective Field Goal Percentage. Additionally, the team didn't really force turnovers and was below average at grabbing defensive rebounds because Love missed around 50 games with a foot injury. The team's situational metrics didn't look much better, as they ranked in the bottom half of the league in virtually every category except for defense in post-up situations. The Cavs' slightly above average post-up defense was largely attributed to strong situational play from Cedi Osman, Tristan Thompson and Ante Zizic. The team's only real positive was that it didn't foul very frequently, which kept opponents off the free throw line. As a result, they ranked in the top ten in the league in fewest Personal Fouls and Opponent Free Throws per Field Goal Attempt.

At the offensive end, the team really felt the loss of James and Love for the first half of the season because they couldn't generate quality shots on a consistent basis, and they ended up ranking in the bottom third of the league in Offensive Efficiency. Because the Cavs were an undermanned unit as a whole, the team had to over-extend Sexton to give him more responsibility than he was capable of handling. As a result, the team had trouble getting into its sets and the ball movement was stilted a bit, which hurt their shooting efficiency to the point where they were ranked near the bottom of the league in

Effective Field Goal Percentage. The team was good at knocking down spot-up threes, as they shot threes at an above average rate. However, they didn't have enough offensive flow to generate open looks consistently. Additionally, the team's lack of motion or flow didn't help them create mismatches to force defenders to commit fouls, so the Cavs rarely got to the free throw line. In fact, the team was in the bottom third of the league in Free Throw Attempt Rate. On the positive side, Cleveland was above average at limiting turnovers and grabbing offensive rebounds, as they ranked in the top half of the league in both Turnover Rate and Offensive Rebound Percentage.

Cleveland is at the start of a long rebuilding process. They currently don't have any major core pieces on the roster but selling off some veterans for draft picks was a step in the right direction. Implementing a consistent structure to maximize talent has been a problem in the past, as Cleveland has had a lot of turnover with its coaching staffs in the last decade. However, they may have taken a step to rectify that by hiring former Michigan coach, John Beilein to oversee the on-court portion of their rebuilding process. If they can fully commit to him to give the team a sense of stability, they could focus on rebuilding the roster to put them in contention once again. Otherwise, if the situation remains chaotic, they could remain at the bottom of the Eastern Conference for the foreseeable future.

2019-20 Outlook

Players Under Contract for 2019-20

* Age and Salary numbers are for 2019-20. See page 9 for explanation for Cap Value and RCV. A number in parentheses indicates that the value is negative.

	Age	Salary	Years Left	2018-19 Cap Value	RCV
Kevin Love	31	$28.94M	3	($16.02M)	($56.48M)
Tristan Thompson	28	$18.54M	0	($1.77M)	($1.86M)
J.R. Smith*	34	$15.68M	0	($14.59M)	($11.82M)
Brandon Knight	28	$15.64M	0	($12.07M)	($14.12M)
Jordan Clarkson	27	$13.44M	0	$6.94M	$6.16M
Larry Nance, Jr.	27	$12.73M	3	$24.14M	$60.45M
John Henson	29	$10.48M	0	($8.44M)	$1.26M
Matthew Dellavedova	29	$9.61M	0	($4.72M)	($4.48M)
Collin Sexton	21	$4.76M	2 Team Options	$6.51M	$18.96M
Cedi Osman	24	$2.91M	0	$12.30M	$8.57M
Ante Zizic	23	$2.28M	Team Option	$10.35M	$15.06M

* J.R. Smith's contract for 2019-20 is partially guaranteed for $3.87M until June 30, 2019.

Two-Way Contracts

* In this section, listings are read: Player, Current Age, Height, Weight, College or Country

- Jaron Blossomgame, 25, 6'7", 220, Clemson
- Deng Adel, 21, 6'7", 200, Louisville

2019 Free Agents

* Age and Salary numbers are for 2019-20. See page 9 for explanation for Cap Value and RCV. A number in parentheses indicates that the value is negative.

	Age	Status	Salary	2018-19 Cap Value	RCV
David Nwaba	27	Restricted	N/A	$7.11M	N/A
Marquese Chriss	22	Unrestricted	N/A	($1.96M)	N/A
Channing Frye	36	Unrestricted	N/A	($0.05M)	N/A
Nik Stauskas	26	Unrestricted	N/A	$5.70M	N/A

Estimated Cap Space for 2019 Free Agency

Note: Salary cap estimated to be at $109 million for 2019-20, as of September 17, 2018.

- **Over the cap**, but not over luxury tax, can only use exceptions
  - **Non-taxpayer Mid-Level Exception**

2019 Draft Picks and Future Assets until 2022

- 2019 own first round – **5th overall**
- 2019 first round from Houston (Alec Burks/Brandon Knight three-team trade) – **26th overall**
- 2020 own first round, protected top 10, otherwise goes to Atlanta (Kyle Korver trade)
- 2020 second round from Utah (Alec Burks/Kyle Korver trade)
- 2021 own first round
- 2021 own second round
- 2021 second round from Portland (Rodney Hood trade)
- 2022 own first round
- 2022 first round from Milwaukee, top 10 protected (George Hill/Matthew Dellavedova trade)
- 2022 own second round
- 2022 second round from Houston (Alec Burks/Brandon Knight three-team trade)
- 2022 second round from Washington (George Hill/Matthew Dellavedova trade)

Draft Rights Held

	Year	Round	Pick
Arturas Gudaitis	2015	2	47
Sir'Dominic Pointer	2015	2	53
Ilkan Karaman	2012	2	57
Milan Macvan	2011	2	54
Chukwudiebere Maduabum	2011	2	56
Sergiy Gladyr	2009	2	49
Renaldas Seibutis	2007	2	50
Edin Bavcic	2006	2	56

Offseason Recommendations

Interestingly, the Cavaliers hired John Beilein to oversee their rebuild. The history of college coaches transitioning to the NBA is checkered, so Cleveland will have to do everything they can to make his adjustment as smooth as possible. **Ideally, they would look to fill out his staff with experienced assistants that are also well-versed in modern tactics and strategies.** They have been a fairly chaotic operation in recent years, so they will have to commit to building a coherent structure from the top down. If they can overcome their past history, they could install a sound system to lead their core into a new era.

Finding that core is going to be tough at the moment because the team has a lot of high-salaried veterans on the roster. In particular, the Cavs will have to find a way to salvage any kind of value from Kevin Love because his four-year extension will kick in next summer and that contract could be an albatross due to his age and injury history. If Love's contract becomes a sunk cost, then Cleveland **will have to figure out a way to sell off the remaining expiring contracts to take back more draft assets as a way to increase the team's future maneuverability**. Most likely, they will have to wait until next season's trade deadline to make these kinds of moves. After all, the cap is about to increase next summer, a lot of teams will have space to spend and several of those teams could experience some buyer's remorse, giving the Cavs an opportunity to make a deal. As far as the summer goes, Cleveland will probably have to take a quieter approach because they will still be capped out. Therefore, they **would be best served to target a major core piece in the draft and use their cap exceptions to bargain hunt for some buy-low opportunities**. This would increase the team's base of young talent and give them a much clearer direction to move into. Cleveland is in for a long rebuild, so putting as many young pieces into a distinct system would be helpful to accelerate their timetable. If they can stay relatively patient and get their organization in order, they could get closer to winning in the near future. However, if Cleveland operates as they have for the last decade, they could be at the bottom of the standings for a while.

DALLAS MAVERICKS

Season in Review

Though the Dallas Mavericks missed the playoffs for the third straight season, there's considerable hope for the franchise's future. This is mainly because the team's bold move to trade up in the draft for the rights to Luka Doncic paid off in a major way, as he showed considerable potential as a future franchise cornerstone by having one of the most productive seasons by a teenager in modern NBA history. In addition to this, the Mavericks opportunistically pounced on the New York Knicks' eagerness to clear cap space for the summer and wound up with Kristaps Porzingis, another superstar level talent that's still recovering from an ACL injury. The team took a short-term hit with that trade and the subsequent one that sent Harrison Barnes to Sacramento, but the team's long-term outlook appears promising for the first time in several years.

The Mavericks were competitive all season long because they were pretty solid on the defensive end for most of the season. However, their defense tapered off towards the end of the season and they finished as a below average defensive unit. They had a little bit of success on defense mainly because the acquisition of Doncic allowed them to play bigger lineups than they were using in the past, which gave them the versatility to switch screens and not give opponents an obviously exploitable mismatch. Because of this, the Mavericks were very good at defending isolations, according to Synergy. Also, they were fairly good at defending the three-point line, as they finished in the top ten in Three-Point Percentage Allowed. On the other hand, the personnel shuffling at the trade deadline hurt their ability to force misses overall and they wound with a slightly below average shot defense. Specifically, they ranked just below the league average in Opponents' Effective Field Goal Percentage. On the positive side, the greater level of defensive versatility also kept the Mavericks away from situations where they had to foul, so they were one of the league's better teams at keeping opponents off the free throw line. Interestingly enough, Dallas' defensive rebounding improved a bit after they dealt DeAndre Jordan away to the Knicks in the Porzingis deal and they ranked in the upper half of the league in Defensive Rebound Percentage. Conversely, they played a conservative style where they didn't really look pressure their opponents. Because of this, they didn't force turnovers very often and ranked in the bottom half of the league in Opponents' Turnover Percentage.

Despite Doncic's individual brilliance, Dallas was actually a below average offensive unit, ranking in the bottom half of the league in Offensive Efficiency. They really only did a couple things well. The team's biggest positive was that they drew fouls and made free throws with great frequency. A good chunk of this can be attributed to Doncic, as he was very good at turning the corner on pick-and-rolls to put pressure on defenders to draw fouls. As an interesting side note, the team benefitted in the first half of the season from the presence of Jordan for their success at the free throw line. Initially, opposing teams looked to intentionally foul him because of his history as a poor free throw shooter, but Jordan's Free Throw Percentage spiked by over 10% and made more free throws as a result. The Mavericks were also around average at grabbing offensive rebounds, although they had some difficulty finishing on put-back attempts, as the team was only average in those situations. On the downside, Dallas struggled to knock down shots, as they were a bottom third team from behind the three-point line and they didn't really get many attempts around the rim. Because of this, they ranked in the bottom half of the league in Effective Field Goal Percentage. Also, due to the team's relative youth, they turned the ball quite frequently and they ranked in the bottom half of the league in Turnover Percentage as a result.

In the short-term, Dallas was competitive but not quite at same level as the playoff teams in the Western Conference. However, their future could be very bright if they get a commitment from Kristaps Porzingis to re-sign with them on a long-term contract as a restricted free agent. If he can recover from his ACL injury and stay healthy, the Mavericks could possess one of the league's most dynamic ball handler-big man combinations, which could give them a very clear direction for them to build their franchise. The biggest key to Dallas' future success is to keep Porzingis on the court as much as possible, so he and Doncic can develop the necessary chemistry to maximize both of their enormous talents. From there, the Mavericks may not really need to make any drastic moves to round out their roster to find other complementary pieces. If they stay relatively patient and keep their focus on Porzingis' health, they could become contenders in the Western Conference in the near future.

2019-20 Outlook

Players Under Contract for 2019-20

* Age and Salary numbers are for 2019-20. See page 9 for explanation for Cap Value and RCV. A number in parentheses indicates that the value is negative.

	Age	Salary	Years Left	2018-19 Cap Value	RCV
Tim Hardaway, Jr.	27	$20.03M	Player Option	($3.36M)	($4.15M)
Courtney Lee	34	$12.76M	0	($9.44M)	($2.64M)
Luka Doncic	20	$7.68M	2 Team Options	$24.56M	$75.57M
Justin Jackson	24	$3.28M	Team Option	$12.23M	$17.54M
Jalen Brunson*	23	$1.42M	2	$13.82M	$42.67M
Ryan Broekhoff*	29	$1.42M	0	$3.24M	$2.66M

* Broekhoff's contract for 2019-20 is not guaranteed. Brunson's contract for 2021-22 is not guaranteed.

Two-Way Contracts

* In this section, listings are read: Player, Current Age, Height, Weight, College or Country

- Kostas Antetokounmpo, 21, 6'10", 200, Dayton
- Daryl Macon, 23, 6'3", 185, Arkansas

2019 Free Agents

* Age and Salary numbers are for 2019-20. See page 9 for explanation for Cap Value and RCV. A number in parentheses indicates that the value is negative.

	Age	Status	Salary	2018-19 Cap Value	RCV
Kristaps Porzingis	24	Restricted	N/A	($5.70M)	N/A
Dorian Finney-Smith	26	Restricted	N/A	$15.99M	N/A
Maxi Kleber	28	Restricted	N/A	$15.86M	N/A
Dwight Powell	28	Unrestricted	N/A	$24.08M	N/A
Dirk Nowitzki	41	Unrestricted	N/A	($1.20M)	N/A
J.J. Barea	35	Unrestricted	N/A	$3.81M	N/A
Trey Burke	27	Unrestricted	N/A	$10.64M	N/A
Devin Harris	36	Unrestricted	N/A	$7.06M	N/A
Salah Mejri	33	Unrestricted	N/A	$3.43M	N/A

Estimated Cap Space for 2019 Free Agency

Note: Salary cap estimated to be at $109 million for 2019-20, as of September 17, 2018.

- **$63.8 million**, maximum cap space, if Broekhoff is waived
- **$62.4 million**, if Broekhoff remains on the roster

2019 Draft Picks and Future Assets until 2022

- 2019 own second round – **37th overall**
- 2020 own first round
- 2020 own second round, protected from picks 56 to 60, otherwise goes to Philadelphia (Nerlens Noel trade)
- 2020 second round from Golden State, option to swap with Houston (Andrew Bogut trade, Chinanu Onuaku trade)
- 2021 own second round
- 2022 own first round
- 2022 own second round

Draft Rights Held

	Year	Round	Pick
Satnam Singh	2015	2	52
Petteri Koponen	2007	1	30

Offseason Recommendations

The Mavericks have a lot of options available to them because they are expected to have over $50 million in cap space to spend on free agents. Because of this, they could be in play for some of the bigger names that will be available. However, they have been unsuccessful at landing free agents of significance in recent years, so it might not necessarily be worthwhile go down this road this summer. Also, their timeline doesn't match up with the marquee free agents because their cornerstone piece, Doncic is still very young and in a developmental stage. Therefore, **Dallas' best option is to roll over their cap space to next summer and see how Doncic and Porzingis mesh next season before they push any chips into the middle.** This way, they can get a better sense of Porzingis' health, how their two dynamic talents fit together and what they need moving forward. Also, they wouldn't be introducing other variables like a ball-demanding high salary player into the equation, which could throw off the chemistry of Doncic and Porzingis, which is much more important for Dallas' future. With the long-term future as the primary focus, **Dallas can fill holes in the roster in the short-term by targeting multi-positional three-and-D players to provide additional spacing on offense and build up the team's defensive versatility**. Among their upcoming free agents, they could look to bring back Dorian Finney-Smith and Maxi Kleber if their respective price tags are reasonable and would allow the Mavericks to maintain cap space for a maximum salary player in the future. Otherwise, the team should look to keep its discipline and only sign veterans to one-year contracts to preserve their flexibility in the coming years. Right now, the Mavericks are in a favorable position because they don't have to rush to make a major move. It also doesn't really make sense to do so because even though the combination of Doncic and Porzingis looks incredible on paper, they still don't know what they have yet. Therefore, the team should do its best to stay patient and see how everything plays out next season when Porzingis returns. If he stays healthy, develops chemistry with Doncic and the team retains its cap flexibility, Dallas could be on the path to contention in the Western Conference very soon. However, if they try to take a shortcut by pushing their chips in right now, it could backfire, and the team could waste Doncic's prime years by clogging up their cap sheet with aging veterans that would stagnate the team's overall growth by keeping them stuck in mediocrity.

DENVER NUGGETS

Season in Review

Rather than overreact to the disappointment of missing the playoffs in each of the last two seasons, the Denver Nuggets decided to remain committed to their core by re-signing Nikola Jokic and Will Barton to long-term contracts. The team's faith was rewarded because the Nuggets took a giant leap forward this past season. They improved significantly despite the fact that they were dealing with various injuries to key players like Barton and Gary Harris because they got a lot of internal growth from younger contributors like Monte Morris, Malik Beasley and Juan Hernangomez. Also, Jokic had his best season as a pro and wound up making his first All-Star team. As a result, Denver spent the bulk of the season as one of the best teams in the Western Conference.

In the previous two seasons, defense was the team's Achilles heel. Even though they had a dynamic offense, they were held back by a defense that was often ranked near the bottom of the league in Defensive Efficiency. Without making any major personnel moves, the team's performance at the defensive end improved to the point where they were in the top ten in Defensive Efficiency because they took a more aggressive approach. In fact, the Nuggets were average or better in most of the defensive situations this past season, according to Synergy, and this wasn't the case in either of the past two years. In the past, head coach, Mike Malone used a lot of drop coverages in screen situations to try to cover up Jokic's lack of foot speed and keep him in the paint. However, this left the team vulnerable on the perimeter and they gave up a lot of open outside shots in the past. This season, Malone and the coaching staff changed their defensive coverages to have Jokic aggressively hedge screens instead of dropping back on them, and in other situations, they switched more frequently. This kept the team more engaged and they did a much better job of defending the three-point line to the point where they were consistently in the upper half of the league in Three-Point Percentage and Three-Point Attempts Allowed. The increased activity also allowed them to force more turnovers, as they improved to being in the upper half of the league in Turnover Percentage. In addition to this, they rarely fouled, which kept opponents off the free throw line and because of interior players like Jokic, Mason Plumlee and Paul Millsap, they maintained their defensive rebounding prowess from a year ago. Though the team's new approach allowed them to do a lot of good things defensively, they still were rather vulnerable inside because opposing teams shot a better than average percentage from inside 14 feet and in. They also didn't have a whole lot of rim protection because they finished in the bottom third of the league in Blocked Shots.

Offensively, they continued to be one of the league's best offenses, as they ranked in the top five in Offensive Efficiency. Because of the team's abundance of playmakers like Jokic, Jamal Murray, Barton and others, the Nuggets were one of the most effective teams at using ball movement to create efficient shooting opportunities. Specifically, they were among the league leaders in every relevant passing category such as Passes Made per Game and Assists per Game. This high-quality ball movement allowed them to be one of the league's better shooting teams because they were consistently getting open looks to the point where their Effective Field Goal Percentage was in the upper half of the league. This season, the Nuggets slowed down their pace as a part of their strategy to improve their team's defense. However, they were still very effective at generating transition offense by finding opportunities to selectively run. In fact, they were one of the league's most efficient teams in transition situations, ranking in the upper half of the NBA, according to Synergy. Furthermore, Denver continued to be one of the league's best offensive rebounding teams and they shored up a weak area from a season ago by drastically cutting the team's turnover rate to the point where they finished in the top ten in Turnover Percentage. The main weakness that Denver showed was that they didn't really have anyone that could break a defense down one-on-one in a late clock, isolation situation. To be specific, they were one of the league's worst per-possession isolation teams this past season. This didn't really hurt them in the regular season, but this weakness could hurt them in a future playoff series when opponents start to figure out how to defend their ball movement and force them into these situations.

This past season was a major step forward for the Nuggets and they appear to be on track to being a contender in the Western Conference for the next few years. The landscape of the league could change considerably this summer, so Denver is in good position in the moment. After all, their primary core is fairly young and locked up for the next couple of seasons, so they don't have to make any drastic moves to stay in contention. If they can make some minor tweaks to shore up their defense a little bit and Jamal Murray improves as a one-on-one player to address the offense's only weakness, the Nuggets could make another leap to being title contenders. Otherwise, Denver will still be one of the Western Conference's top teams even if they stay at their current level.

2019-20 Outlook

Players Under Contract for 2019-20

* Age and Salary numbers are for 2019-20. See page 9 for explanation for Cap Value and RCV. A number in parentheses indicates that the value is negative.

	Age	Salary	Years Left	2018-19 Cap Value	RCV
Nikola Jokic	24	$26.57M	3	$33.31M	$114.44M
Gary Harris	25	$17.84M	2	($1.61M)	$3.09M
Mason Plumlee	29	$14.04M	0	$14.94M	$11.60M
Will Barton	29	$12.78M	1 + Player Option	($3.45M)	$5.88M
Jamal Murray	22	$4.44M	0	$25.71M	$24.70M
Michael Porter, Jr.	21	$3.39M	2 Team Options	($2.89M)	($12.20M)
Juan Hernangomez	24	$3.32M	0	$11.85M	$6.85M
Malik Beasley	23	$2.73M	0	$20.93M	$11.92M
Torrey Craig	29	$2.00M	0	$12.29M	$8.47M
Monte Morris*	24	$1.59M	1	$28.03M	$39.63M
Jarred Vanderbilt*	20	$1.42M	1	($0.23M)	($1.78M)

* Monte Morris' contract for 2020-21 is not guaranteed until June 30, 2020. Vanderbilt's contract for 2020-21 is not guaranteed until July 15, 2020.

Two-Way Contracts

* In this section, listings are read: Player, Current Age, Height, Weight, College or Country
- Thomas Welsh, 22, 7'0", 255, UCLA
- Brandon Goodwin, 23, 6'2", 180, Florida Gulf Coast

2019 Free Agents

* Age and Salary numbers are for 2019-20. See page 9 for explanation for Cap Value and RCV. A number in parentheses indicates that the value is negative.

	Age	Status	Salary	2018-19 Cap Value	RCV
Paul Millsap	34	Team Option	$30.15M	$0.66M	($4.95M)
Trey Lyles	24	Restricted	N/A	$5.47M	N/A
Tyler Lydon	23	Unrestricted	N/A	($0.99M)	N/A
Isaiah Thomas	30	Unrestricted	N/A	($1.84M)	N/A

Estimated Cap Space for 2019 Free Agency

Note: Salary cap estimated to be at $109 million for 2019-20, as of September 17, 2018.

- **$18.4 million**, maximum cap space, if Millsap's option is not picked up
- **Over the cap**, but not over luxury tax if Millsap's option is picked up, can only use exceptions
    - **Non-taxpayer Mid-Level Exception**

2019 Draft Picks and Future Assets until 2022

- 2020 own first round
- 2021 own first round
- 2022 own first round
- 2022 own second round, Philadelphia has the option to swap picks (Wilson Chandler trade)

Draft Rights Held

	Year	Round	Pick
Vlatko Cancar	2017	2	49
Petr Cornelie	2016	2	53
Nikola Radicevic	2015	2	57
Izzet Turkyilmaz	2012	2	50

Offseason Recommendations

Heading into the summer, the Denver Nuggets are in a good position because most of the team's core is still under contract. Even if they don't do very much, they still could be one of the best teams in the Western Conference next season. The team does have to decide if they want to pick up Paul Millsap's sizeable option for next season. On the one hand, he's heading into his mid-30's, showing some signs of decline and his performance hasn't quite matched his price tag, which is expected to be above $30 million. On the other hand, he's still a relatively productive player even at an advanced age and he's had a very positive effect on Denver's success when he's been healthy. Specifically, the Nuggets are an average of plus-6.7 points per 100 possessions with him on the floor during his two seasons with the team. Because Denver's a middle market team that doesn't really attract free agents, they would be best served **to pick up Millsap's option and use their cap exceptions to fill the other holes on the roster.** Millsap only has a year left on his contract, so picking up his option is a relatively low risk move. If his play drops off significantly, the Nuggets could always use his expiring contract to find some kind of replacement. From there, the Nuggets should **split up their Mid-Level Exception or find veteran's minimum options to target another three-and-D wing player and a rim**

protector to shore up their defense. Ideally, they would look to find a wing player that could play both forward spots and guard elite scoring wings to add to the team's defensive versatility and improve their overall on-ball defense. Rim protection was also a problem this season, so bringing in an effective shot blocking presence to occasionally spell Jokic could help to prevent a few extra shots around the basket. Depending on who they sign, a quality rim protecting big man on a reasonably priced contract could make Mason Plumlee expendable. Plumlee's contract is set to expire after next season, so the Nuggets could dangle his contract out on the trade market to see if they could get something in return to improve the roster. Overall, Denver doesn't really have to make any major changes to its roster to be a top team in the Western Conference next season. If they really wanted to go all in for a title, they could try to trade for an All-Star level wing player to help them create shots in late clock situations, but it's uncertain if a player of that caliber is available or if the Nuggets have enough assets to make a deal without giving up a major piece of its core. Therefore, their best plan would be to keep their roster intact and make some smaller additions to shore up the defense. If they can do that, they could be an even better team next season.

DETROIT PISTONS

Season in Review

The Detroit Pistons couldn't really make any big changes to their team for this past season because the transactions from the Stan Van Gundy regime left them capped out with very little flexibility to maneuver. To account for this limitation, their new front office headed by Ed Stefanski hired last season's Coach of the Year, Dwane Casey as the new head coach and they looked to build a more functional unit around Blake Griffin and Andre Drummond. From a personnel standpoint, they brought a few role players like Zaza Pachulia and Glenn Robinson III in free agency and shuffled some pieces around at the trade deadline. However, the team's performance wasn't dramatically different from what it was a season ago. Fortunately, because the Eastern Conference was weaker this season, the Pistons were able to squeak into the playoffs on the final day of the regular season.

Detroit was able to be competitive this past season because it was one of the league's better defensive teams, ranking in the upper half of the league in Defensive Efficiency. Drummond has been the NBA's best overall rebounder for the last six seasons, so it's not a surprise that he was the anchor of a defensive unit that ranked in the top ten in Defensive Rebound Percentage. In addition to this, the Pistons were a team that made clean rotations and made it tough for opponents to get easy looks off motion plays. According to Synergy, they were average or better in almost every movement-oriented situation, which included pick-and-rolls, screens, cuts and so forth. They were also very good at defending the three-point line, as they were among the league leaders in fewest Three-Point Attempts Allowed and they finished in the top ten in Three-Point Percentage Allowed. On the negative side, they didn't force misses as regularly as expected because opposing teams were able to get some open looks inside. This was mainly because they were one of the league's worst teams at defending in one-on-one situations, as they ranked near the bottom of the league at guarding isolations. As a result, opponents were regularly getting to the rim and the Pistons ended up being one of the league's worst teams at defending shots inside of five feet. This also put them in positions where they had no choice but to foul, so they sent opponents to the free throw line quite frequently. In fact, they ranked in the bottom of third of the league in Opponents' Free Throws per Field Goal Attempt.

Despite a stellar individual season from Griffin, the Pistons were a below average offensive team, finishing in the bottom third of the league in Offensive Efficiency. Because Detroit's talent is concentrated inside with very few quality playmakers on the perimeter, the team has to play at a slower pace. As a result, the team doesn't really move the ball very much and the ball tended to stay in the hands of either Griffin or Reggie Jackson.

Detroit had some success with pick-and-rolls and dribble hand-offs, but they really struggled to consistently generate open looks. Their lack of reliable outside shooters also didn't help either, so they ended up being one of the league's least efficient shooting teams, ranking in the bottom third of the league in Effective Field Goal Percentage. In addition to this, the Pistons struggled to make free throws because they ranked in the bottom third of the league in Free Throw Percentage. This negated their above average ability to get to the free throw line. One of their main positives on offense was that they were one of the league's best offensive rebounding teams because they usually had either Drummond or Zaza Pachulia on the floor to actively crash the glass. Also, they were fairly careful with the ball because they posted a Turnover Percentage just over the league average.

Detroit is in a tough situation at the moment because they appear to be stuck in mediocrity for the next few seasons. Because Blake Griffin and Andre Drummond are still producing at All-Star levels, they will be just good enough to compete for one of the lower seeds in the Eastern Conference. However, their cap sheet is clogged with middling veterans on inflated contracts and they don't have a lot of additional draft assets, so they don't have the ability to swing any kind of major move to improve their situation. Also, they probably aren't in a position to launch a full-scale rebuild because several other teams in the East were much quicker to bottom out for higher lottery odds. With all this in mind, the Pistons may just have to tread water and stay as competitive as possible while they get out from some of their bad contracts. Then, if they don't do any more damage to their cap sheet, they could formulate a clearer plan for the future of their franchise in one way or the other. On the flip side, if things continue as they are, Detroit will be stuck on the treadmill of mediocrity for the foreseeable future.

2019-20 Outlook

Players Under Contract for 2019-20

* Age and Salary numbers are for 2019-20. See page 9 for explanation for Cap Value and RCV. A number in parentheses indicates that the value is negative.

	Age	Salary	Years Left	2018-19 Cap Value	RCV
Blake Griffin	30	$34.45M	1 + Player Option	$11.25M	$5.28M
Andre Drummond	26	$27.09M	Player Option	$26.04M	$47.00M
Reggie Jackson	29	$18.09M	0	$10.19M	$3.53M
Jon Leuer	30	$9.51M	0	($5.47M)	($4.51M)
Langston Galloway	28	$7.33M	0	$9.57M	$6.13M
Luke Kennard	23	$3.83M	Team Option	$10.23M	$19.49M
Thon Maker	22	$3.57M	0	$6.95M	$6.11M
Svi Mykhailiuk*	22	$1.42M	Team Option	($0.73M)	($1.44M)
Bruce Brown*	23	$1.42M	1	$7.16M	$13.62M
Khyri Thomas*	23	$1.42M	1	($0.37M)	($2.08M)

* Mykhailiuk's contract for 2019-20 is not guaranteed. Bruce Brown's contract for 2021-22 is not guaranteed. Khyri Thomas' contract for 2020-21 is not guaranteed. Detroit used the stretch provision to waive Josh Smith on December 22, 2014 and they are assessed a cap hit of **$5.33M** until the end of the 2019-20 season.

Two-Way Contracts

* In this section, listings are read: Player, Current Age, Height, Weight, College or Country

- Isaiah Whitehead, 23, 6'4", 213, Seton Hall
- Kalin Lucas, 29, 6'1", 195, Michigan State

2019 Free Agents

* Age and Salary numbers are for 2019-20. See page 9 for explanation for Cap Value and RCV. A number in parentheses indicates that the value is negative.

	Age	Status	Salary	2018-19 Cap Value	RCV
Glenn Robinson III	26	Team Option	$4.28M	($0.09M)	$0.41M
Ish Smith	31	Unrestricted	N/A	$4.41M	N/A
Wayne Ellington	32	Unrestricted	N/A	$6.29M	N/A
Jose Calderon	38	Unrestricted	N/A	$1.88M	N/A
Zaza Pachulia	35	Unrestricted	N/A	$9.46M	N/A

Estimated Cap Space for 2019 Free Agency

Note: Salary cap estimated to be at $109 million for 2019-20, as of September 17, 2018.

- **Over the cap**, but not over luxury tax, only have cap exceptions to use
  - **Non-taxpayer Mid-Level Exception**
  - **Bi-Annual Exception**

2019 Draft Picks and Future Assets until 2022

- 2019 own first round – **15th overall**
- 2019 own second round – **45th overall**
- 2020 own first round
- 2021 own first round
- 2021 second round from L.A. Lakers (Reggie Bullock/Svi Mykhailiuk trade)
- 2022 own first round

Draft Rights Held

None

Offseason Recommendations

The Pistons dug themselves pretty deep into a hole because of the mistakes of the previous regime and as a result, they will be over the cap going into the summer. On the positive side, many of the team's larger mid-level contracts, like the ones to Reggie Jackson, Jon Leuer and Langston Galloway, are set to expire at the end of next season. They could dangle those contracts to try to take back some value, but it's not certain that they could get anything of substance back for those players without taking on more money. Additionally, Andre Drummond could opt out at the end of next season and he may be the only player on the roster with meaningful trade value. Therefore, Detroit **should look to shop Drummond around before the draft and into the early parts of free agency to see if they could take back valuable assets in return**. If they can get at least one high-end first round pick and a promising young player on a rookie contract in a trade for Drummond, it might be worthwhile to make a deal. Otherwise, if the return stays consistent with the current trade market for centers, then the Pistons should hold onto him and adjust their plans accordingly. No matter what happens with Drummond, the team should then use its cap exceptions to **add playmakers and shooters to put around Griffin**. The Pistons really struggled to score efficiently because they couldn't really space the floor and they didn't move the ball very much. If they can target some cost effective shooters, preferably on the wings, they can give Griffin more room to operate. Also, a few more playmakers could allow them to generate open shots on a more consistent basis to improve the team's offensive efficiency. Detroit doesn't have many options to maneuver this offseason, so their best bet is to tweak the roster with short-term contracts to fill holes and buy time until some of their more onerous contracts come off the books. Then, once they get a better sense of where they stand in the Eastern Conference, they probably have to operate on Blake Griffin's timeline because he has up to three years left on his max contract and it's not likely that Detroit will be able to move him, as he progresses into his 30's. Because of this, they should maximize the next three years but still maintain its cap flexibility. This way, the Pistons can easily pivot when Griffin's contract expires and move towards building a more sustainable model for the franchise's future success.

GOLDEN STATE WARRIORS

Season in Review

The Golden State Warriors made one of the biggest moves of the summer by adding All-Star, DeMarcus Cousins to an already loaded roster. The Warriors stumbled a bit in the early part of the season because Stephen Curry missed a few weeks with a groin injury and the team was dealing with some minor chemistry issues, as a result of a sideline verbal spat between Kevin Durant and Draymond Green. However, Golden State found its footing when Curry returned. Then, they got a boost when Cousins was inserted into the starting lineup in mid-January after spending the last calendar year recovering from his Achilles injury. Overall, the Warriors made it clear that they were still the team to beat and finished as the heavy favorite to potentially win their third title in four years.

During this entire run under head coach, Steve Kerr, the Warriors have established themselves as one of the league's most dangerous offensive teams and this season was no different, as they led the NBA in Offensive Efficiency. The team was able to score at such a staggering level of efficiency because not only do they have an incredible amount of talent, they use excellent ball and player movement to constantly generate quality looks. They led the league in Assists per Game for the fifth consecutive year. Also, according to Synergy, they were the league's best team at scoring off screens on a per-possession basis by a considerable margin. All of this effective movement allowed them to be the NBA's most efficient shooting team, as they led the league in Effective Field Goal Percentage. They also managed to improve upon a few weaknesses from the previous season. Most notably, the Warriors cut their turnover rate a bit, but they still posted a Turnover Percentage that was just below the league average. In addition to this, they were a little more effective on the offensive glass because they were no longer in the bottom third of the league in Offensive Rebound Percentage, as they improved to being around average. This was mainly because they leaned on younger, more active big men like Kevon Looney to crash the boards early in the season rather than some of the older veterans that they had in their previous title runs. As a result, the Warriors got a few more second chance opportunities than they did in previous years. If the team had any weakness on offense, it was probably that they were a bit too jump shot dependent and didn't look to go inside to draw fouls, as they were in the bottom third of the league in Free Throw Attempt Rate.

Defensively, the Warriors' effort level fluctuated a bit, but they still were a solid defensive team that ranked in the upper half of the league in Defensive Efficiency. First off, they were one of the league's better teams at forcing misses, as they ranked in the top five in Opponents' Effective Field Goal Percentage. On average, they made clean rotations and forced tough shots because according to Synergy, they were among the league's best teams at defending in transition and closing out in spot-up situations. They were also very effective at containing pick-and-roll ball handlers. On the downside, the Warriors were a little bit vulnerable on the interior because they tended to allow scores to the roll man in pick-and-roll situations. They also were a little exposed in isolation situations, as opposing offenses frequently looked to target Cousins and Andre Iguodala showed some signs of age-related regression. On the plus side, the Warriors were a better defensive rebounding team than were last season, as they moved into the upper half of the league in Defensive Rebounding Percentage. This was mainly due to Looney's emergence and the addition of Cousins. Because the team played younger, more inexperienced big men early on and players like Iguodala and Shaun Livingston aged a bit, the Warriors were a little more foul prone than they were in the past and opposing teams were able to get to the free throw line with more frequency. Specifically, the team finished in the bottom half of the league in Opponent Free Throws per Field Goal Attempt this past season. They also couldn't really be as aggressive at pressuring their opponents, so they didn't force a lot of turnovers and they wound up ranking in the bottom third of the league in Opponents' Turnover Percentage.

    The final verdict on Golden State's season is still undetermined because the playoffs are still going on as this book is being written. They had some struggles early on and their focus has been inconsistent in the regular season, but the addition of Cousins gives them a different dimension to their game. If they play up to their abilities, they should be able to win their third straight championship. However, their title chances may have taken a hit after Kevin Durant suffered a calf strain in their second round series against Houston. Even if they do win another title, the team's future is still unclear because Durant and Klay Thompson are expected to hit the open market as free agents this summer. If they can find a way to bring both players back, they can continue this impressive run. However, if one of those two players decide to play elsewhere, the Warriors will have no choice but to retool their roster around Curry to give themselves the best chance to remain contenders in the Western Conference in the next few seasons.

2019-20 Outlook

Players Under Contract for 2019-20

* Age and Salary numbers are for 2019-20. See page 9 for explanation for Cap Value and RCV. A number in parentheses indicates that the value is negative.

	Age	Salary	Years Left	2018-19 Cap Value	RCV
Stephen Curry	31	$40.23M	2	$11.23M	$13.40M
Draymond Green	29	$18.54M	0	$4.67M	$7.80M
Andre Iguodala	36	$17.19M	0	$3.53M	$1.88M
Shaun Livingston*	34	$7.69M	0	$1.57M	$2.35M
Damian Jones	24	$2.31M	0	$5.00M	$1.63M
Jacob Evans	22	$1.93M	2 Team Options	($1.64M)	($7.53M)
Alfonzo McKinnie*	27	$1.42M	0	$8.77M	$4.82M

* Livingston's contract for 2019-20 is partially guaranteed for **$2.00M**. McKinnie's contract for 2019-20 is not guaranteed.

Two-Way Contracts

* In this section, listings are read: Player, Current Age, Height, Weight, College or Country

- Damion Lee, 26, 6'6", 210, Louisville
- Marcus Derrickson, 22, 6'7", 249, Georgetown

2019 Free Agents

* Age and Salary numbers are for 2019-20. See page 9 for explanation for Cap Value and RCV. A number in parentheses indicates that the value is negative.

	Age	Status	Salary	2018-19 Cap Value	RCV
Kevin Durant	31	Player Option	$31.50M	$26.92M	$23.54M
Quinn Cook	26	Restricted	N/A	$8.79M	N/A
Jordan Bell	25	Restricted	N/A	$6.96M	N/A
Klay Thompson	29	Unrestricted	N/A	$12.67M	N/A
DeMarcus Cousins	29	Unrestricted	N/A	$7.66M	N/A
Jonas Jerebko	32	Unrestricted	N/A	$13.91M	N/A
Kevon Looney	23	Unrestricted	N/A	$24.87M	N/A
Andrew Bogut	35	Unrestricted	N/A	$1.21M	N/A

Estimated Cap Space for 2019 Free Agency

Note: Salary cap estimated to be at $109 million for 2019-20, as of September 17, 2018.
- **$26.8 million**, maximum cap space, if Livingston and McKinnie are waived
- **$25.4 million**, if Livingston is waived and McKinnie remains on the roster
- **$19.7 million**, if Livingston and McKinnie remain on the roster

2019 Draft Picks and Future Assets until 2022
- 2019 own first round – **28th overall**
- 2019 own second round – **58th overall**
- 2020 own first round
- 2021 own first round
- 2021 own second round
- 2022 own first round
- 2022 own second round

Draft Rights Held

None

Offseason Recommendations

Even if the Warriors win another championship in June, the team could look different next season. After all, Kevin Durant and Klay Thompson are set to explore their options in free agency and it's unlikely that they'll be able to retain DeMarcus Cousins, as he should receive an offer closer to his true market value, now that he's healthy. Before they can address the other parts of the roster, the Warriors **will have to make every effort to re-sign Durant and Thompson in free agency.** This will allow the team to maintain the most dynamic elements of its prolific offense and keep them in title contention for the next few years. No matter what happens in free agency, the Warriors **may have to explore the idea of trading Draymond Green** because his contract is set to expire after next season, and he could be due for a significant max-level raise. This type of contract for a player like Green is risky because he will be approaching his 30's and historically, slightly undersized defensive players like him have not aged well. Therefore, the team could shop him around to see if they can either get equally productive younger players or possibly package him with Andre Iguodala to land a bigger piece. Otherwise, if they can't find a worthwhile trade, they could just hold onto him and see how things play out next season. Once the Warriors have a solid idea of what their core is going to look like, the team **should try to re-sign Kevon Looney if they can retain him at a reasonable price**. Looney was probably Golden State's most valuable big man this past season, as he provided them with a quality rim runner, rebounder, and switchable defender. He's coming off his age-22 season, so he still has considerable room to grow and he could become a valuable part of the team's future. If they have additional space, the Warriors should **look to get younger on the wings** because Iguodala and Shaun Livingston are now showing signs of age-related decline, as a result of being in their mid-30's. The pickup of Alfonzo McKinnie in training camp was a step in the right direction, but they need to find more young wing players like him to help them maintain their defensive versatility. Golden State is probably going to transition to a different-looking roster in one way or the other this summer. If they can at least retain one of their two free agent All-Stars, they still could be a very good team in the Western Conference next season. Even in a worst-case scenario, the Warriors probably aren't going to drop off completely because they still have one of the league's best players, Stephen Curry, under contract for the next three seasons. If some of kind of adverse scenario happens, the Warriors will have to get creative to retool their roster and remain among the league's best teams.

HOUSTON ROCKETS

Season in Review

The Houston Rockets came into this season with a retooled roster after they lost Trevor Ariza and Luc Mbah a Moute in free agency and traded away Ryan Anderson. They initially brought in Carmelo Anthony among others to replace those players, but that experiment ended after the team posted a sub-0.500 record after the first 25 games, so Anthony was dealt away to Chicago. However, the Rockets got back on track by leaning on reigning MVP, James Harden even more and he proceeded to go on a prolific scoring streak. They also reworked their rotation with the waiver wire pickups of Austin Rivers and Kenneth Faried, and they made a modest addition at the trade deadline by acquiring Iman Shumpert in a three-team deal. As a result, Houston overcame their bad start and wound up being a top-four seed in the Western Conference this past season.

This season, Houston was still one of the best offensive teams in the league, as they ranked in the top five in Offensive Efficiency, even though head coach, Mike D'Antoni employed a very simplified offensive style. Specifically, they were the league's most isolation heavy offense, so they didn't use a lot of motion or dynamic ball movement. The Rockets were able to succeed this way because of the extraordinary individual skills of Harden, who used his one-on-one talents to either score, draw fouls or force defenders to help, which opened up spot-up opportunities for his teammates. They also continued their extreme method of shot selection by avoiding taking mid-range shots almost entirely and continuing to focus on taking threes at the league's most frequent rate while also making a concerted effort to draw fouls. As a result, they ranked in the top ten in Free Throw Attempt Rate and they were one of the league's most efficient shooting teams despite shooting a below average percentage from behind the three-point line. Because the ball was in Harden's hands so frequently and they didn't pass much, the Rockets were among the league's better teams at limiting turnovers, which was evidenced by the fact that they finished in the upper half of the NBA in Turnover Percentage. The pickup of Faried also allowed them to maintain their above average ability to grab offensive rebounds even though Clint Capela missed more than a month with a thumb injury.

On the other side ball, the changes to the roster hurt their defense, as they went from having a top ten defense to one that was just below average. They didn't really replace the defensive versatility that they lost when Ariza and Mbah a Moute left in free agency, so their rotations were thrown off as a result. After they shuffled their lineup in the middle of the season, they wound up leaning on a three-guard lineup with Harden, Chris Paul and Eric Gordon. Though this helped them offensively, this combination's lack of size gave opponents a mismatch that they could exploit on a consistent basis.

Specifically, opposing teams often had success targeting Eric Gordon by finding ways to get him matched up against their top scoring wing player in isolation situations. In addition to this, the team really struggled to protect the rim because they were among the league's worst teams at defending shots inside of five feet, according to the league's tracking metrics. Their vulnerability around the basket also put them in a lot of situations where they had to foul, so they frequently allowed opponents to get to the free throw line. As a result, the team finished in the bottom half of the league in Opponents' Effective Field Goal Percentage and Opponent Free Throws per Field Goal Attempt. Furthermore, their rebounding performance dropped off significantly due to Capela's injury and the fact that they were frequently playing smaller lineups. On the positive side, the smaller lineups allowed them to be a little more active, which made them pretty good at defending the three-point line. In fact, they were among the league's best teams at limiting their opponents' Three-Point Attempts and three-point shooting efficiency. They also forced turnovers at a high rate, ranking in the top ten in Opponents' Turnover Percentage.

Houston took a little step back this past season after nearly making the Finals a season ago. The landscape of the league has changed very quickly in the last year and the best teams in the league are moving towards building well-rounded rosters that incorporate multiple star players. Therefore, it's unclear if the Rockets can continue to rely on James Harden as much they do and match up with opponents that have more talent from top to bottom. Therefore, they may have to rethink their approach and make some adjustments. If they can strike a balance between maximizing Harden and building a more balanced roster, they could bounce back and become an elite contender in the Western Conference once again. Otherwise, they will probably stay where they are as a very good playoff team for the next few years.

2019-20 Outlook

Players Under Contract for 2019-20

* Age and Salary numbers are for 2019-20. See page 9 for explanation for Cap Value and RCV. A number in parentheses indicates that the value is negative.

	Age	Salary	Years Left	2018-19 Cap Value	RCV
Chris Paul	34	$38.51M	1 + Player Option	($3.36M)	($15.43M)
James Harden	30	$37.80M	2 + Player Option	$45.32M	$124.71M
Clint Capela	25	$16.40M	3	$35.08M	$125.73M
Eric Gordon	31	$14.06M	0	$3.88M	$6.16M
P.J. Tucker	34	$8.35M	1	$15.74M	$26.16M
Nene	37	$3.83M	0	$2.71M	$5.19M
Isaiah Hartenstein*	21	$1.42M	1	$1.39M	$1.62M
Gary Clark*	25	$1.42M	1	$4.44M	$7.26M

* Hartenstein's contracts for 2019-20 and 2020-21 are not guaranteed. Gary Clark's contract for 2019-20 is partially guaranteed. Clark's contract for 2020-21 is guaranteed after August 1, 2020. Houston used the stretch provision to waive Troy Williams on February 14, 2018 and they will be assessed a cap hit of **$122,741** until the end of the 2022-23 season.

Two-Way Contracts

* In this section, listings are read: Player, Current Age, Height, Weight, College or Country

- Vincent Edwards, 22, 6'8", 225, Purdue
- Trevon Duval, 20, 6'2", 189, Duke

2019 Free Agents

* Age and Salary numbers are for 2019-20. See page 9 for explanation for Cap Value and RCV. A number in parentheses indicates that the value is negative.

	Age	Status	Salary	2018-19 Cap Value	RCV
Danuel House	26	Restricted	N/A	$10.69M	N/A
Chris Chiozza	24	Restricted	N/A	$0.00M	N/A
Iman Shumpert	29	Unrestricted	N/A	($1.93M)	N/A
Gerald Green	34	Unrestricted	N/A	$10.23M	N/A
Austin Rivers	27	Unrestricted	N/A	($4.20M)	N/A
Kenneth Faried	30	Unrestricted	N/A	($0.39M)	N/A

Estimated Cap Space for 2019 Free Agency

Note: Salary cap estimated to be at $109 million for 2019-20, as of September 17, 2018.

- **Over the cap**, but not over luxury tax, can only use cap exceptions
    - **Non-taxpayer Mid-Level Exception**
    - **Bi-Annual Exception**

2019 Draft Picks and Future Assets until 2022

- 2020 own first round
- 2020 own second round or 2020 second round from Golden State, depends on pick swap with Dallas, higher second round pick between their own and Golden State goes to Sacramento (Chinanu Onuaku trade, Iman Shumpert three-team trade)
- 2021 own first round
- 2021 own second round, have option to swap with Philadelphia (James Ennis trade)
- 2022 own first round

Draft Rights Held

	Year	Round	Pick
Marko Todorovic	2013	2	45
Jon Diebler	2011	2	51
Sergio Llull	2009	2	34
Maarty Leunen	2008	2	54
Axel Hervelle	2005	2	52

Offseason Recommendations

For better or for worse, the Rockets are locked into its core of James Harden, Clint Capela and Chris Paul for the next three seasons. Even if Paul's play declines due to his age, the team should still be in playoff contention because the tandem of Harden and Capela. However, the Rockets will need to make some changes to the roster if they want to do more than just make the playoffs. Doing so is going to require some creativity because they don't have any draft picks this year and they're going to be over the cap. Despite these limitations, Houston **should look to add as many three-and-D wing players as possible to help them regain some defensive versatility**. The team didn't really have a lot of quality wing players, so they were forced to almost exclusively use smaller lineups, which made it easier for their opponents to find exploitable matchups. Therefore, a deeper group of wings could allow them to aggressively switch and defend different types of lineups. More capable wing players could limit some wear and tear on the bodies of Paul and P.J. Tucker because they are now older players in their mid-30's and could use some additional rest in the coming years. As for specific players to target, it would be worthwhile for the Rockets to start by **re-signing Gerald Green and Danuel House**. Green was arguably the team's most productive wing player this past season. Even though he'll be going into his age-34 season, his solid on-ball defense and above average three-point shooting makes him a great fit for Houston's system. House was an efficient shooter in his limited minutes with the Rockets, but due to a contractual quirk regarding Two-Way Contracts, he was unable to stay on the active roster for the full season. He did get picked up for a full-time contract at the end of the season, so if they bring him back at a reasonable price, he could be a productive part of their rotation next season. From there, Houston will have to bargain hunt for other wing players on veteran's minimum contracts or they could expand their search to players that are currently overseas. If the Rockets can rebuild its depth, they have a chance to improve and become prime contenders in the Western Conference once again. Otherwise, they will remain as they are and be a solid playoff team next season.

INDIANA PACERS

Season in Review

This season, the Indiana Pacers were out to prove that last season's playoff berth wasn't a fluke. Last summer, they kept their core intact and added Tyreke Evans, Doug McDermott and Kyle O'Quinn to their rotation. With these additions, the Pacers were able to be one of the Eastern Conference's better teams. However, the team was dealt a significant blow when All-Star, Victor Oladipo ruptured his right quadricep tendon, which forced him to miss the second half of the season. Despite his absence, Indiana managed to regroup a bit and they still made the playoffs as a top-five seed in the East.

The Pacers were able to build on their success from a season ago because they improved by becoming one of the league's best defensive teams, ranking in the top five in Defensive Efficiency. Statistically, they were very good across the board and didn't show many weaknesses. Individually, almost every key player in the team's rotation was an average defender or better. Also, the team consistently made clean rotations and their lineup was versatile enough to give head coach, Nate McMillan a variety of options to match up with his opponents, making it harder for opposing teams to score efficiently against them. In fact, according to Synergy, they were ranked in the top ten in almost every situation except scores off cuts, dribble hand-offs and spot-up jumpers. This allowed them to be one of the better teams in the league at forcing misses, as they ranked in the upper half of the league in Opponents' Effective Field Goal Percentage. Because of their depth, they were able to aggressively pressure opponents to frequently force turnovers and wound up finishing in the top five in Opponents' Turnover Percentage as a result. They also managed to put pressure on their opponents without fouling because they were one of the league's best teams at keeping opposing offenses off the free throw line, ranking in the top five in Opponent Free Throws per Field Goal Percentage. The only weakness that they showed was that they weren't an elite defensive rebounding team. To be specific, they ranked in the bottom half of the league in Defensive Rebound Percentage, mainly because they were playing a lot of smaller lineups over the course of the season.

At the offensive end, the Pacers really felt the loss of Oladipo because they struggled to consistently generate quality offense. Specifically, their Offensive Efficiency slipped to the bottom half of the league this season. The main reason for the team's offensive struggles was that Oladipo was really the team's only consistent shot creator. Therefore, the team had to compensate by relying on effective ball movement to get good looks at the basket. A lot of times, they were a pretty good passing team because they ranked near the top of the league in every relevant passing category including Assists per

Game, where they finished in the top ten. They also were successful at finding open shooters either in spot-up situations or coming off screens, hitting cutters and selectively running to get shots in transition. Because of this, they were one of the league's better shooting teams, ranking in the upper half of the league in Effective Field Goal Percentage and ranking in the top ten in Three-Point Percentage. However, as a product of having a limited amount of individual talent, they had to play at a much slower pace, so they couldn't stay with some of the more higher-powered offenses in the league. They also couldn't consistently get to the free throw line, which was evidenced by the fact that they finished near the bottom of the league in Free Throw Attempt Rate. In addition to this, they weren't particularly effective on the offensive glass and because of their reliance on passing to generate shots, they were a little more turnover prone than they were last year.

Overall, the Pacers were a solid regular season team, but they had trouble competing in the playoffs, as they were swept in the first round by Boston. Their future is a little bit clouded by Oladipo's injury. If he can make a full recovery, they can continue to build on the success over the last couple of seasons by trying to find some way to add more offensive help to complement their excellent defense. Indiana's position as a smaller market team makes this tough, but if they can creatively figure out a way to boost their firepower, they could take another step closer to becoming contenders in the Eastern Conference. Otherwise, they will likely remain a very competitive team that consistently makes the playoffs but doesn't do very much beyond that.

2019-20 Outlook

Players Under Contract for 2019-20

* Age and Salary numbers are for 2019-20. See page 9 for explanation for Cap Value and RCV. A number in parentheses indicates that the value is negative.

	Age	Salary	Years Left	2018-19 Cap Value	RCV
Victor Oladipo	27	$21.00M	1	($6.84M)	$5.42M
Myles Turner	23	$18.00M	3	$28.68M	$57.47M
Doug McDermott	28	$7.33M	1	$6.65M	$13.11M
Domantas Sabonis	23	$3.53M	0	$33.80M	$27.51M
T.J. Leaf	22	$2.81M	Team Option	$5.40M	$6.31M
Aaron Holiday	23	$2.24M	2 Team Options	$3.57M	$8.78M
Edmond Sumner*	24	$1.59M	0	$0.45M	($0.37M)
Alize Johnson*	23	$1.42M	0	($0.68M)	($1.25M)

* Alize Johnson's contract for 2019-20 is not guaranteed. Sumner's contract for 2019-20 is not guaranteed. Indiana used the stretch provision to waive Monta Ellis on July 5, 2017. They will be assessed a cap hit of **$2.245M** until the end of the 2021-22 season.

Two-Way Contracts

* In this section, listings are read: Player, Current Age, Height, Weight, College or Country

- Davon Reed, 23, 6'5", 208, Miami (FL)

2019 Free Agents

* Age and Salary numbers are for 2019-20. See page 9 for explanation for Cap Value and RCV. A number in parentheses indicates that the value is negative.

	Age	Status	Salary	2018-19 Cap Value	RCV
Thaddeus Young	31	Unrestricted	NA	$20.81M	NA
***Tyreke Evans**	30	Unrestricted	NA	($5.28M)	NA
Bojan Bogdanovic	30	Unrestricted	NA	$24.24M	NA
Darren Collison	32	Unrestricted	NA	$22.53M	NA
Cory Joseph	28	Unrestricted	NA	$10.47M	NA
Kyle O'Quinn	29	Unrestricted	NA	$0.71M	NA
Wesley Matthews	33	Unrestricted	NA	($3.36M)	NA

* Evans has been dismissed from NBA for violating its Anti-Drug Program. He can apply for reinstatement after two seasons.

Estimated Cap Space for 2019 Free Agency

Note: Salary cap estimated to be at $109 million for 2019-20, as of September 17, 2018.

- **$51.8 million**, maximum cap space, if Johnson and Sumner option are waived
- **$50.4 million**, if Johnson remains on the roster and Sumner is waived
- **$50.3 million**, if Sumner remains on the roster and Johnson is waived
- **$48.8 million**, if Johnson and Sumner are both on the roster

2019 Draft Picks and Future Assets until 2022

- 2019 own first round – **18th overall**
- 2019 own second round – **50th overall**
- 2020 own first round
- 2020 own second round, protected from picks 45 to 60, otherwise goes to Brooklyn (Thaddeus Young trade)
- 2021 own first round
- 2021 own second round
- 2021 second round from Milwaukee (Nik Stauskas trade, Brandon Knight three-team trade to Cleveland, George Hill trade to Milwaukee)
- 2022 own first round
- 2022 own second round

Draft Rights Held

None

Offseason Recommendations

The Pacers are going to be in a good position this summer because they will have a considerable amount of cap space and flexibility to improve their roster. However, they will have to resolve the general conundrum regarding their two talented big men, Myles Turner and Domantas Sabonis. The main issue with these two players is that though both are productive as individuals, they have had some difficulty playing at the same time. Over the last two seasons, according to NBAWowy.com, Indiana was a plus-1.6 points per 100 possessions with both players at the same time. When only one of the two big men was on the floor, the team's performance improved significantly. Specifically, the Pacers were a plus-3.9 points per 100 possessions with Turner on the floor without Sabonis and they were a plus-4.2 points per 100 possessions with Sabonis on the floor without Turner. This arrangement has worked for the last two seasons because both players were still on their rookie contracts. However, Turner signed a four-year, $72 million extension last October. Next season, Sabonis will be in the last year of his rookie contract and he's likely to be due a significant eight-figure per-year salary on his next deal. Sabonis has been one of the team's most productive players and would be worth re-signing, but not being able to play two high salaried players at the same time is not really an efficient use of the team's cap dollars. Therefore, the Pacers **should explore trading one of them to add more offensive firepower to the roster**. Of the two of them, it might make more sense to shop Turner in July because his new salary point is high enough to create a workable framework for a trade that could allow Indiana to bring back a polished veteran player that fits into Victor Oladipo's timeline. An ideal scenario for this would be if Washington's Bradley Beal grows dissatisfied with his situation, Indiana could offer Turner as a centerpiece of a package that could allow the Pacers to acquire Beal and pair him with Oladipo as part of a dynamic new backcourt. Otherwise, if they could try to explore trade options with Sabonis during the draft, but teams in recent years have not been able to fetch a great deal of value for big men in the trade market, so the team would probably be better off holding onto Sabonis for now. If they hold onto to both big men, they could look to free agency to add some more offense. It's not worthwhile for them to go after any of the big name veterans because Indiana is a smaller market that doesn't typically attract free agents on a regular basis. Therefore, they **probably will have to explore younger options and even try to target a restricted free agent**. Of the available names, the most worthwhile target may be Brooklyn's D'Angelo Russell. The Nets are in similar situation to the Pacers, but because they are in a larger market, they could be tempted to aim higher and set their sights on the marquee unrestricted free agents like Kevin Durant or Kyrie Irving. If the Nets try to sign a bigger name, then their cap dollars will be occupied to the point where Indiana could swoop in and get Russell at a reasonable price. If that scenario comes into fruition, it could be a significant way to improve the team. From there, the Pacers will **have to either re-sign Thaddeus Young and Bojan Bogdanovic or retool their group of wings with cheaper options to maintain the team's defensive versatility**. The Pacers' defense was the main reason for its success this past season, so ideally, they would want to re-sign their two most important wing players at reasonable salaries to stabilize their lineups. Otherwise, they will have to do their due diligence to find cost effective substitutes that could provide similar value, particularly on defense. If Indiana effectively uses its cap space or trade assets to maintain the team's defensive identity while adding some more offensive talent, they could take another step forward in their development and possibly become legitimate contenders in the Eastern Conference next season. Otherwise, their situation is stable enough that they could remain a solid playoff team, assuming Oladipo recovers from his quad injury.

LOS ANGELES CLIPPERS

Season in Review

The Los Angeles Clippers came into this season with one eye on the present and the other eye on the summer. Therefore, they didn't make any significant commitments beyond this season during free agency. As a result, they kept much of their roster intact, even though they let DeAndre Jordan leave for Dallas. Even without making any major moves, the Clippers stayed in playoff contention for the entire season. Then, close to the trade deadline, they dealt Tobias Harris, Boban Marjanovic and Mike Scott to Philadelphia for a package that included multiple first round picks, rookie Landry Shamet and Wilson Chandler. It was an interesting move considering that Harris was having arguably his best season in the NBA and nearly made the All-Star team. Also, the team was still in the hunt for one of the lower playoff seeds in the West. Even despite the trade, the Clippers had enough talent left over to consistently give themselves a chance to win games and they were rewarded with a playoff spot in the Western Conference.

The Clippers were able to compete for the playoffs because they were one of the league's better offensive teams, ranking in the top ten in Offensive Efficiency. In general, they were able to consistently score because they were one of the league's best pick-and-roll teams, as they ranked in the top ten in both plays finished by the ball handler and roll man due to the consistency of Lou Williams and the emergence of rookie, Shai Gilgeous-Alexander and fourth-year player Montrezl Harrell. Because the team's pick-and-roll attack put pressure on opponents going to the rim, they were able to generate a lot of free throw attempts. In fact, the Clippers led the league in Free Throw Attempt Rate and Free Throws Made per Field Goal Attempt. Their ability to draw extra help inside opened up quality spot-up opportunities on the outside. Though they didn't shoot threes very often, they made them at a very high percentage, and they ranked in the top five in Three-Point Percentage. In addition to this, they were one of the league's best teams at making shots in spot-up situations to the point where they ranked in the top five in points per possession on those plays. Because the team took a lot of mid-range shots, their shooting efficiency wasn't as high as it could have been. As a result, their Effective Field Goal Percentage was just above the league average. On the negative side, head coach, Doc Rivers shuffled his lineups around quite a bit, so the Clippers prone to some bouts of miscommunication, which led to them being in the bottom half of the league in Turnover Percentage. They also didn't really hit the offensive glass because they ranked in the bottom third of the league in Defensive Rebound Percentage. Some of this was by design, as they tended to intentionally punt the offensive glass to focus on preventing the opposing team from getting quality opportunities in transition. The other factor involved was that they tended to play smaller lineups, so they weren't quite equipped to grab a lot of offensive boards anyway.

Defensively, the Clippers were a bit of a mixed bag. On the positive side, they were excellent at playing shot defense, as they forced misses at a frequent rate, and they ranked in the top ten in Opponents' Effective Field Goal Percentage. They were able to accomplish this because they were good at defending opponents in one-on-one situations either on the perimeter or in the post. Also, they limited their opponents' opportunities in transition and did a good job of closing out on spot-up shooters. However, the Clippers were only a below average defensive team, as they actually ranked in the bottom half of the league in Defensive Efficiency. Because there was a lot of roster and lineup shuffling over the course of the season, the team wasn't as crisp when making defensive rotations. As a result, they were really exposed in pick-and-roll situations, as they ranked near the bottom of the league at containing the ball handler and they were only about average at guarding the roll man. The team's struggles with miscommunication also made them more prone to commit fouls and put opponents on the free throw line. In fact, the Clippers ranked near the bottom of the league in Opponent Free Throws per Field Goal Attempt this past season. In addition to this, their tendency to play small didn't allow them to finish off defensive possessions with a rebound and they gave up a lot of second chance opportunities. As evidence of this, they ranked in the bottom third of the league in points per possession allowed off put-backs and Defensive Rebound Percentage. To compound matters even more, they played with a more conservative approach. Because of this, they rarely looked to pressure opponents or play passing lanes, so they ranked near the bottom of the league in Opponents' Turnover Percentage.

The Clippers are in a fluid situation because one of their goals was to preserve cap space for the summer, so they could go after a couple of big name free agents. If they are successful in attracting an elite free agent or two, they could be on a quick path to contending in the Western Conference. Otherwise, the assets gained from the Tobias Harris trade along with the emergence of Shai Gilgeous-Alexander could allow the team to pivot and rebuild their roster in a more gradual fashion if they strike out with some of the bigger names. Either way, the Clippers have some flexibility and multiple options available to them to find the right model to build their franchise. Depending on what happens, they could set themselves for success in the coming years as long as they don't overreact and make a rash move in one way or another.

2019-20 Outlook

Players Under Contract for 2019-20

* Age and Salary numbers are for 2019-20. See page 9 for explanation for Cap Value and RCV. A number in parentheses indicates that the value is negative.

	Age	Salary	Years Left	2018-19 Cap Value	RCV
Danilo Gallinari	31	$22.62M	0	$17.68M	$5.40M
Lou Williams	33	$8.00M	1	$22.42M	$49.06M
Montrezl Harrell	26	$6.00M	0	$37.46M	$30.83M
Shai Gilgeous-Alexander	21	$3.95M	2 Team Options	$17.01M	$52.18M
Jerome Robinson	22	$3.57M	2 Team Options	($1.87M)	($8.87M)
Landry Shamet	22	$2.00M	2 Team Options	$15.86M	$48.00M
Sindarius Thornwell*	25	$1.62M	0	($0.74M)	$1.17M
Tyrone Wallace	25	$1.59M	0	($0.45M)	$1.07M

* Thornwell's contract for 2019-20 is not guaranteed until June 20, 2019.

Two-Way Contracts

* In this section, listings are read: Player, Current Age, Height, Weight, College or Country
- Johnathan Motley, 23, 6'10", 230, Baylor
- Angel Delgado, 24, 6'10", 245, Seton Hall

2019 Free Agents

* Age and Salary numbers are for 2019-20. See page 9 for explanation for Cap Value and RCV. A number in parentheses indicates that the value is negative.

	Age	Status	Salary	2018-19 Cap Value	RCV
Ivica Zubac	22	Restricted	N/A	$14.86M	N/A
Rodney McGruder	28	Restricted	N/A	$9.33M	N/A
Wilson Chandler	32	Unrestricted	N/A	($4.80M)	N/A
Garrett Temple	33	Unrestricted	N/A	$4.78M	N/A
JaMychal Green	29	Unrestricted	N/A	$8.12M	N/A
Patrick Beverley	31	Unrestricted	N/A	$12.08M	N/A

Estimated Cap Space for 2019 Free Agency

Note: Salary cap estimated to be at $109 million for 2019-20, as of September 17, 2018.

- **$61.3 million**, maximum cap space, if Thornwell is waived
- **$59.7 million**, if Thornwell remains on the roster

2019 Draft Picks and Future Assets until 2022

- 2019 own second round – **48th overall**
- 2019 second round from Portland via Orlando and Detroit (Blake Griffin trade, various other trades) – **56th overall**
- 2020 own first round
- 2020 first round from Philadelphia, lottery protected (Tobias Harris trade)
- 2020 own second round
- 2021 own first round
- 2021 first round from Miami via Phoenix and Philadelphia (Tobias Harris trade, Mikal Bridges trade to Phoenix, Goran Dragic trade to Miami)
- 2021 second round from Detroit via Philadelphia (Tobias Harris trade, Khyri Thomas trade to Detroit)
- 2022 own first round
- 2022 own second round

Draft Rights Held

	Year	Round	Pick
David Michineau	2016	2	39
Vladimir Veremeenko	2006	2	48

Offseason Recommendations

There are a lot of variables in play for the Clippers this summer, as they are positioned to clear the decks to make a run at two marquee free agents. They don't quite have the space at the moment, but if they attach the draft picks that they acquired in the Tobias Harris trade to Danilo Gallinari's contract, they could easily get more room. If they are successful and land any combination of two major free agents, then all they would have to do is use their remaining space or draft picks to cobble together a workable bench to build a contending team. If they only land one of the big names, they could use one-year deals to possibly roll over some cap space to try again next summer to land someone like Anthony Davis. Otherwise, **if they strike out, the Clippers would be best served to hold onto its assets and take a more gradual approach to building the roster**. The Clippers don't have many significant long-term contracts on their roster, so they could keep rolling over its cap space until they eventually land somebody big. However, if they don't land anybody, then constantly rolling over space and shuffling pieces around could have negative consequences. In particular, they could stunt the growth of their younger players by placing them in a destabilized environment where their roles are uncertain and they're unable to develop positive chemistry with their teammates. If no major free agent signs with the Clippers this summer, the team **should look to expand its core of young players.** They're off to a solid start by adding Landry Shamet in the Tobias Harris trade to add to Shai Gilgeous-Alexander. Also, if they re-signed Montrezl Harrell to a two or three-year market value deal after his current contract expires, he could give them a highly productive interior presence to go along with them. From there, the Clippers should probably shop Lou Williams around because even though he's one of the league's most effective bench players, he wouldn't quite fit the timeline of a team building around a younger core, as he will be approaching mid-30's. Also, Williams' cap number is low enough to potentially boost his trade value because he would be easier to fit into any contending team's cap sheet, allowing the Clippers possibly receive a first round pick or more in return. No matter what happens this summer, the Clippers have more enough flexibility to go in any direction, as long as they maintain their discipline and not overreact if their best laid plans go awry. If they irrationally spend for the sake of spending, they could get stuck in mediocrity. However, if stay patient and maintain some optionality, they could eventually put themselves on the path to contention, even if it takes a few years more than expected.

LOS ANGELES LAKERS

Season in Review

Expectations were raised considerably for the Los Angeles Lakers when they signed LeBron James to a four-year contract last summer. The Lakers took a different route from James' previous stops in Miami and Cleveland by holding onto its key young players and preserving cap space for this summer. They were playing like a solid playoff team until James suffered a groin injury that caused him to miss time from after Christmas to the end of January. While he was out, they had to lean on their key young players like Brandon Ingram, Kyle Kuzma and Lonzo Ball, but the team was unable to maintain its level of play without James, so they dropped in the standings as a result. Then, the bizarre public negotiations to unsuccessfully trade all of their main young players for Anthony Davis disrupted chemistry to the point where the Lakers had to scramble to stay competitive and they missed the playoffs for the sixth consecutive season.

In the last couple of seasons, the Lakers have been a solid defensive team under head coach, Luke Walton and this year, they ranked in the upper half of the league in Defensive Efficiency. This is mainly because they have been emphasizing defensive versatility by playing taller perimeter players and favoring mobile big men to allow them to constantly switch screens and stay attached to shooters to force misses. Because of this, the Lakers were pretty good at keeping opponents away from the basket, as opposing offensive players struggled to effectively finish shots against them inside. As a result, the Lakers ranked in the upper half of the league in Opponents' Effective Field Goal Percentage. Also, the constant switching also kept them out of positions where they had to foul, so they were above average at keeping opponents off the free throw line. The mid-to-late season chemistry issues did have a negative effect on the defense because the team's overall effort was not especially consistent and this showed in the team's transition defense, which was rated by Synergy as being in the bottom third of the league. They also weren't especially active to pressure their opponents because they didn't force turnovers at a high rate. In fact, the Lakers ranked in the bottom half of the league in Opponents' Turnover Percentage. In addition to this, opponents had success against their defense by targeting the Lakers' younger players on isolation plays, and they ended up ranking in the bottom third of the league in these situations. Finally, because the team tended to play smaller lineups, they had trouble finishing off possessions with defensive rebounds and wound up ranking in the bottom third of the league in Defensive Rebound Percentage.

Offensively, the Lakers struggled from an efficiency standpoint, as they ranked in the bottom third of the league in Offensive Efficiency. On the positive side, James' presence helped them generate a lot of quality shots around the rim and the Lakers ended up taking the most shots inside of five feet, according to the league's tracking metrics. The team was able to get a lot of these inside shots because of James' individual isolation skills as well as his ability to find cutters at the rim. In fact, the Lakers were one of the league's better cutting teams, ranking in the upper half of the league in those situations on a per-possession basis, according to Synergy. As a result, the team was a pretty efficient shooting team, finishing in the upper half of the league in Effective Field Goal Percentage, even though they weren't particularly effective from the outside. Their ability to attack the basket did allow the Lakers to draw fouls, but they really had problems making free throws, as they posted one of the league's worst Free Throw Percentages because most of the team's regular rotation players, except Kyle Kuzma, Kentavious Caldwell-Pope and Reggie Bullock shot below 70% from the free throw line. In addition to this, Lonzo Ball's free throw shooting is a cause for concern in the future because his Free Throw Percentage decreased to the point where he's making free throws at a rate that's just over 40%, so opponents could utilize the Hack-a-Shaq strategy on him to stagnate the Lakers' offense in the future if he doesn't improve. In addition to being a poor free throw shooting team, the team's hectic pace had some negative effects. Primarily, it made them prone to committing turnovers at a pretty high rate, as the Lakers ranked near the bottom of the league in Turnover Percentage and Turnovers per Game. Also, the team's tendency to play smaller lineups hurt them on the offensive boards and they wound up finishing in the bottom half of the league in Offensive Rebound Percentage.

  At this stage, the Lakers are betting so big on the idea that they will land another superstar to play with LeBron James to the point where it has become rather detrimental to the team as a whole. Specifically, many of the team's younger players have stalled in their development and it's uncertain if any of them will grow into becoming high-end players in the future. In addition to this, Magic Johnson abruptly resigned from his position as President of Basketball Operations and the team relieved Luke Walton of his coaching duties. With a lack of focus on player development and the continually increasing level of toxicity to the team's overall environment, the Lakers could run the risk of following in the path of the New York Knicks by covering up its obvious flaws in organizational structure and inability to develop their young players by bringing in quick fix, name brand replacements, only to produce mediocre to bad results. To avoid this potential path, the Lakers will need to place a greater emphasis on improving the team's system and culture to give their younger players a better chance to reach their full potential. This way, the team has better odds of becoming legitimate contenders in the Western Conference. Otherwise, they could be stuck in mediocrity for the next few years, even with James on the roster.

2019-20 Outlook

Players Under Contract for 2019-20

* Age and Salary numbers are for 2019-20. See page 9 for explanation for Cap Value and RCV. A number in parentheses indicates that the value is negative.

	Age	Salary	Years Left	2018-19 Cap Value	RCV
LeBron James	35	$37.44M	1 + Player Option	$3.36M	$27.29M
Lonzo Ball	22	$8.72M	Team Option	$3.41M	$5.75M
Brandon Ingram	22	$7.27M	0	$8.91M	$8.47M
Moritz Wagner	22	$2.06M	2 Team Options	$0.54M	($0.69M)
Kyle Kuzma	24	$1.97M	Team Option	$19.42M	$40.29M
Josh Hart	24	$1.93M	Team Option	$10.31M	$22.78M
Isaac Bonga*	20	$1.42M	1	($0.99M)	($3.04M)
Jermerrio Jones*	24	$1.42M	0	$1.17M	($0.07M)

* Bonga's contract for 2020-21 is not guaranteed. Jones' contract for 2019-20 is not guaranteed. The Lakers used the stretch provision to waive Luol Deng on September 1, 2018. They will be assessed a cap hit of **$5.00M** until the end of the 2021-22 season.

Two-Way Contracts

* In this section, listings are read: Player, Current Age, Height, Weight, College or Country

- Alex Caruso, 24, 6'5", 186, Texas A&M
- Johnathan Williams, 23, 6'9", 228, Gonzaga

2019 Free Agents

* Age and Salary numbers are for 2019-20. See page 9 for explanation for Cap Value and RCV. A number in parentheses indicates that the value is negative.

	Age	Status	Salary	2018-19 Cap Value	RCV
Kentavious Caldwell-Pope	26	Unrestricted	N/A	$9.17M	N/A
Rajon Rondo	33	Unrestricted	N/A	$1.02M	N/A
Mike Muscala	28	Unrestricted	N/A	$7.33M	N/A
Lance Stephenson	29	Unrestricted	N/A	$3.73M	N/A
Reggie Bullock	28	Unrestricted	N/A	$13.67M	N/A
JaVale McGee	32	Unrestricted	N/A	$28.81M	N/A
Tyson Chandler	37	Unrestricted	N/A	($5.36M)	N/A

Estimated Cap Space for 2019 Free Agency

Note: Salary cap estimated to be at $109 million for 2019-20, as of September 17, 2018.

- **$43.2 million**, maximum cap space

2019 Draft Picks and Future Assets until 2022

- 2019 own first round – **4th overall**
- 2020 own first round
- 2020 own second round
- 2021 own first round
- 2022 own first round
- 2022 own second round

Draft Rights Held

	Year	Round	Pick
Chinemelu Elonu	2009	2	59
Brad Newley	2007	2	54

Offseason Recommendations

Even if the Lakers add another All-Star caliber player in free agency this summer, they still have a lot of work to do build a championship level roster. Most importantly, they will have to make some key decisions on some of their younger players, as their rookie contracts are set to expire at the end of either next season or the one after it. In particular, Brandon Ingram will be in the last season of his rookie contract and his play over the last three years has been inconsistent enough where it's likely that he'll hit restricted free agency when his contract expires. Therefore, there is a non-zero chance that the Lakers could lose him for nothing at the end of the next season if they are in the process of star chasing. If they can't include him in a trade for Anthony Davis, they probably **should look to shop him to acquire a young player that has a skill set that is a better fit around LeBron James**. Because the Lakers are going to come into the summer with relatively clean books, they probably won't have enough salary to pair with Ingram to trade for an established veteran, so targeting another player on a rookie contract might provide them with a more worthwhile return. Ideally, the Lakers could look to deal Ingram in an apples-for-oranges to acquire someone that's talented, but not quite a perfect fit for their current team. An example of this kind of trade could something like Ingram and draft pick compensation to Indiana for Domantas Sabonis to give the Lakers a mobile rim runner and rebounding presence. From there, the Lakers should use whatever means are **leftover to add more outside shooting to improve the team's offensive efficiency**. This season, the Lakers took a different approach by surrounding James with additional playmakers instead of perimeter shooters. However, this didn't really translate into an efficient offense because teams could often pack in the paint and dare the Lakers to beat them from the perimeter due to the team's lack of three-point shooting. With this in mind, the Lakers would be best served to target above average shooting wing players to give them more spacing on offense and enough length to maintain the team's defensive versatility. Having better shooters would have another residual effect because typically, good three-point shooters tend to also be good at shooting free throws, so the team's poor free throw shooting could improve with better shooters on the roster. Then, the Lakers don't have a center under contract for next season, so they could figure out a way to bring JaVale McGee back or find others to help them rebound and protect the rim.

    Even if the Lakers land a key free agent to team up with LeBron James, they still have work to build a cohesive system to maximize the other parts of the roster and allow them to compete against the elite teams in the league. Their operation has become much more chaotic in recent years, which was evident in Magic Johnson's sudden resignation at the end of the season and their bungled coaching search that eventually landed them on their third or fourth choice, Frank Vogel. They will have to resolve those issues and get their house in order or the situation could become even more toxic in the future. If they can get everybody on the same page, improve the talent level and play according to a more defined structure, they could move closer to being contenders in the Western Conference. Otherwise, if the situation stays the same, the returns might not be high as expected and the Lakers could just be a team that consistently competes for a playoff spot in the next few seasons.

MEMPHIS GRIZZLIES

Season in Review

After having a lost season last year, the Memphis Grizzlies looked to bounce back this past season by returning to their "Grit and Grind" roots. In the offseason, they made additions to improve the defense by drafting Jaren Jackson, Jr. to serve as modern rim protector and signing Kyle Anderson and Garrett Temple to give them the ability to defend multiple positions. These changes appeared to pay off at the beginning of the season because they won 12 of their first 17 games. However, the schedule and the brutal competition in the Western Conference kicked in and their play dropped off to the point where they fell to almost the bottom of the conference standings. As a result, the team sold off a few pieces at the trade deadline to take back some value for players that were bound for free agency. Most notably, the Grizzlies sent Marc Gasol to Toronto for Jonas Valanciunas, Delon Wright, C.J. Miles and a future second round pick. Because they raised the white flag on the season, they were once again a lottery team and appear to be headed for a rebuild in the coming years.

The Grizzlies were able to get off to an early hot start because they were one of the league's better defensive teams, ranking in the top ten in Defensive Efficiency. The team's offseason moves did have their intended effect because the boost in versatility and athleticism helped them play a more aggressive style of defense against modern offenses. As a result, they could be active to switch screens and be more disruptive to opposing offensive players, which allowed them to be one of the league's best teams at forcing turnovers. Specifically, they ranked in the top five in Opponents' Turnover Percentage. The extra versatility helped them wall off the paint and not give opponents easy looks inside. In fact, they were among the league's best teams at preventing shots inside of five feet, according to the NBA tracking metrics. This enabled them to force misses at an above average rate, even though they were prone to giving their fair share of open threes. To be specific, they finished in the upper half of the league in Opponents' Effective Field Goal Percentage. Additionally, they were a good defensive rebounding team this season even though they traded away their two best rebounders, Gasol and JaMychal Green, at the trade deadline. Besides being vulnerable to giving up shots on the outside, the Grizzlies were among the league's most foul prone teams, so they allowed opponents to get to the free throw line quite frequently to the point where they ranked near the bottom of the league in Opponent Free Throw Attempts per Field Goal Attempt.

Though the team's defense improved to where it had been in the past, the Grizzlies were held back by a stagnant offense that was among the league's worst units, as they were almost at the bottom of the league in Offensive Efficiency. Despite the fact that Gasol and Mike Conley were healthy and fairly productive for the entire first half of the season, the team's offense as a whole really struggled to generate efficient offense. This was mainly because they were playing a slow-down, inside-out style that couldn't keep up with opponents with a much more modern approach. Specifically, they played at the league's slowest pace and wasted a lot of seconds on the shot clock by trying to dump the ball into the post. Because of this, they weren't in a position to attack the defense and force bad rotations to get open looks. They also were caught against the shot clock quite a bit and had to force up tougher shots with the clock winding down. All of this meant that Memphis was one of the league's worst shooting teams, ranking near the bottom of the league in Effective Field Goal Percentage. The team's tendency to force the ball into the post negatively affected their ability to effectively pass because the Grizzlies were among the league's most turnover prone teams, finishing in the bottom third of the league in Turnover Percentage. Additionally, the Grizzlies made a concerted effort to punt the offensive glass to improve their transition defense, so they rarely pulled down offensive boards to the point where they posted one of the league's lowest Offensive Rebounding Percentages. If there was any kind of positive regarding the Grizzlies' offense, it was that the focus on going inside allowed them to draw fouls at an above average rate and they wound up ranking in the upper half of the league in Free Throw Attempt Rate. According to Synergy, they were actually pretty good at selectively running in transition and they ranked in the top ten in per-possession offense in transition situations. If the team wanted to move to a modernized attack in the future, this could be a base to work from.

      The Marc Gasol trade was an indication that Memphis is going to go through with a full-scale rebuild that probably should have happened at least a year ago. They still will have to find a trade partner for Conley to take back some more assets and possibly add more young pieces to complement Jaren Jackson, Jr. Once the season ended, the team crystallized their intentions of changing directions by firing head coach, J.B. Bickerstaff and reshuffling their front office to put a different set of people in charge. Now that it's clear that the team will follow a different plan, the Grizzlies should do whatever is possible to move the team towards playing a style that fits today's NBA. If they can find a solid core of young players and modernize the team's structure, they could become competitive in a few years if they maintain their cap flexibility and work to accumulate some more assets. Otherwise, their rebuild could take longer and keep them near the bottom of the Western Conference standings.

2019-20 Outlook

Players Under Contract for 2019-20

* Age and Salary numbers are for 2019-20. See page 9 for explanation for Cap Value and RCV. A number in parentheses indicates that the value is negative.

	Age	Salary	Years Left	2018-19 Cap Value	RCV
Mike Conley	32	$32.51M	Player Option	$10.88M	($7.63M)
Chandler Parsons	31	$25.10M	0	($22.46M)	($21.94M)
Avery Bradley*	29	$12.96M	0	($5.53M)	($5.69M)
Kyle Anderson	26	$9.07M	2	$5.13M	$26.00M
C.J. Miles	32	$8.73M	0	($3.41M)	$0.36M
Jaren Jackson, Jr.	20	$6.93M	2 Team Options	$12.79M	$37.48M
Bruno Caboclo*	24	$1.85M	0	$7.45M	$3.02M
Dillon Brooks*	24	$1.62M	0	($0.40M)	$3.64M
Jevon Carter	24	$1.42M	0	$0.92M	$0.41M

* Avery Bradley's contract for 2019-20 is partially guaranteed for **$2.00M** if he's not waived before July 3, 2019. Dillon Brooks' contract for 2019-20 is not guaranteed. Bruno Caboclo's contract for 2019-20 is partially guaranteed. Memphis used the stretch provision to waive Dakari Johnson on August 31, 2018. They will be assessed a cap hit of **$459,414** until the end of the 2020-21 season.

Two-Way Contracts

* In this section, listings are read: Player, Current Age, Height, Weight, College or Country

- Yuta Watanabe, 24, 6'9", 205, George Washington
- Julian Washburn, 27, 6'8", 210, UTEP

2019 Free Agents

* Age and Salary numbers are for 2019-20. See page 9 for explanation for Cap Value and RCV. A number in parentheses indicates that the value is negative.

	Age	Status	Salary	2018-19 Cap Value	RCV
Jonas Valanciunas	27	Player Option	$17.62M	$5.32M	$10.57M
Ivan Rabb	22	Team Option	$1.62M	$8.89M	$7.56M
Delon Wright	27	Restricted	N/A	$19.48M	N/A
Tyler Dorsey	23	Restricted	N/A	$3.31M	N/A
Justin Holiday	30	Unrestricted	N/A	$11.53M	N/A
Joakim Noah	34	Unrestricted	N/A	$9.94M	N/A
Tyler Zeller	30	Unrestricted	N/A	$1.31M	N/A

Estimated Cap Space for 2019 Free Agency

Note: Salary cap estimated to be at $109 million for 2019-20, as of September 17, 2018.

- **$22.8 million**, maximum cap space, if Valanciunas opts out, Rabb's option is not picked up, Bradley, Brooks and Caboclo are waived
- **Basically over the cap**, most likely scenario, Valanciunas opts in and Brooks remains on the roster. Their spending power would be lower with cap space than it would be if they stayed over the cap and used their cap exceptions
    - **Non-taxpayer Mid-Level Exception**
    - **Bi-Annual Exception**

2019 Draft Picks and Future Assets until 2022

- 2019 own first round – **2nd overall**
- 2020 own first round, top 6 protected, otherwise goes to Boston (Jeff Green three-team trade)
- 2021 own first round
- 2022 own first round
- 2022 own second round
- 2022 second round from either Detroit or Chicago, whichever is less favorable (James Ennis trade)

Draft Rights Held

	Year	Round	Pick
Wang Zhelin	2016	2	57
Tyler Harvey	2015	2	51

Offseason Recommendations

The Grizzlies have already started the rebuilding process when they traded Marc Gasol to Toronto, so they need to **continue to sell off veterans for assets**. Most importantly, they should look to deal Mike Conley, but his injury history and max contract might make it tough to get a big return. If they could identify a trade partner like possibly Utah or Detroit that might be in the market for a point guard upgrade, they should try to make a deal. Otherwise, their best bet is wait until next January when this summer's free agents are eligible to be traded. After all, the cap is set to rise, many teams will have space, and there may be some teams that could have some buyer's remorse after signing free agents to unfavorable deals. If this situation were to occur, the Grizzlies could be in a position to make a trade that nets them a few additional assets.

From there, Memphis has to address its biggest concern, which is its outdated offensive system. Unlike the defense, the offense has not adjusted to modern strategy trends, so they still favor a slowed down pace, an attack with limited spacing and very little player movement. This archaic offensive style puts them at an extreme disadvantage because they either have to play perfect defense or they are left to be outgunned by their opponents. Therefore, **the Grizzlies will really have to nail their next coaching hire and they could do so by identifying an assistant with ties to an elite offensive team like the Warriors or a coach like Mike Budenholzer.** Overall, the Grizzlies are in a state of transition and the next few years are set to be rather lean. Because the team is in the middle of a long rebuild in a tough Western Conference, wins and losses aren't going to be as important as building up a young core around Jaren Jackson, Jr. and implementing a modernized system to maximize everyone's talents. If they continue to add additional draft assets and install a cohesive structure, they could return to being a competitive playoff level team in the next few years. Otherwise, the team's rebuild could take longer than expected and the Grizzlies could remain near the bottom of the standings for the foreseeable future.

MIAMI HEAT

Season in Review

The Miami Heat have been a competitive playoff team in the Eastern Conference over the last couple of seasons and the team was expected remain that way once again this past season. This was mainly because they kept their roster intact and made no major moves. However, they were dealt a significant blow when Goran Dragic had to miss a significant portion of the season due to arthroscopic knee surgery and the team's performance suffered a bit as a result. Fortunately for the Heat, the Eastern Conference was weak enough as a whole that they still remained in the hunt for the eighth seed. They spent the bulk of Dwyane Wade's farewell season battling for that final playoff spot but fell a little short and they missed the playoffs this past season.

   The Heat stayed competitive because they were one of the league's best defensive teams, as they finished in the top ten in the NBA in Defensive Efficiency. For the last few seasons, defensive versatility has been a hallmark of the head coach, Erik Spoelstra's defense. Because their personnel didn't change very much, they were a versatile unit that could aggressively switch screens and limit their opponent's opportunities to find exploitable matchups. As a result, the Heat were average or better in most situations, according to Synergy. This allowed them to be one of the best teams in the league at forcing misses, as they ranked in the top five in Opponents' Effective Field Goal Percentage. The team's aggressive style also allowed them to force turnovers at an above average rate, as they finished in the upper half of the league in Opponents' Turnover Percentage. In addition to this, the presence of Hassan Whiteside and Bam Adebayo allowed them to be one of the league's better defensive rebounding teams, as they wound up ranking in the upper half of the NBA in the Defensive Rebounding Percentage. Miami's defense wasn't without its flaws, even though they were rather minor. In particular, they would occasionally fall asleep at times, so they sometimes didn't close out on spot-up shooters. According to Synergy, they were just below average at defending plays that ended with a spot-up jumper. They also tended to foul a bit more and they were also below average at keeping opponents off the foul line. The Heat also had some difficulties in isolation situations because opponents would often target Whiteside or Adebayo on switches to gain good looks at the basket.

   At the offensive end, the Heat really felt the loss of Dragic because he was the team's primary shot creator and without him, they really struggled to generate quality shots. Because of this, they were among the league's worst offensive teams, finishing in the bottom third of the league in Offensive Efficiency. According to Synergy, Miami was only effective at scoring off rolls to the rim and making spot-up jumpers. In every other situation, they were below average or worse. This was mainly because they didn't have a lot of movement in their offense, so they didn't force defenses into making difficult rotations to potentially open up opportunities to get easy shots. If there wasn't an obvious breakdown that allowed a shooter to get a wide open look or big man to get free on a roll to the basket, the team had to take a difficult contested shot. As a result, the Heat were among the league's worst shooting teams, ranking in the bottom third in the league in Effective Field Goal Percentage. They also couldn't get to the free throw line at a high rate because they weren't especially effective at putting defenders in vulnerable positions. Additionally, because they were without their best playmaker, they struggled to keep control of the ball and were one of the league's most turnover prone teams, as they finished near the bottom of the league in Turnover Percentage. Their offense's only real positive was that it was one of the league's best offensive rebounding teams because of the athleticism of their two primary big men and the energy of Derrick Jones, Jr. In fact, the Heat ranked in the top five in Offensive Rebounding Percentage this past season.

Miami's growth as a team has stagnated to the point where it is now stuck in mediocrity. Because of this, they will have to carefully examine their situation to figure out the best direction for their franchise. With limited assets and cap space, they don't have any real ability to swing a major move to put them in the class of the contenders in the Eastern Conference. Therefore, they may have to seriously consider a rebuild of some kind to give themselves a better chance to succeed in the long-term. If they can find a reliable core to build around, they could move themselves closer to a sustainable model of success. Otherwise, they could be stuck in the middle of the Eastern Conference or slowly fade into the lottery for the next few years.

2019-20 Outlook

Players Under Contract for 2019-20

* Age and Salary numbers are for 2019-20. See page 9 for explanation for Cap Value and RCV. A number in parentheses indicates that the value is negative.

	Age	Salary	Years Left	2018-19 Cap Value	RCV
Ryan Anderson*	31	$21.26M	0	($20.39M)	($13.45M)
James Johnson	32	$15.35M	Player Option	($5.60M)	($1.84M)
Kelly Olynyk	28	$13.07M	Player Option	$10.48M	$21.71M
Justise Winslow	23	$13.00M	1 + Team Option	$13.71M	$8.83M
Dion Waiters	28	$12.10M	1	($3.21M)	($9.96M)
Josh Richardson	26	$10.12M	1 + Player Option	$19.80M	$52.64M
Bam Adebayo	22	$3.45M	Team Option	$28.97M	$48.84M
Derrick Jones, Jr.*	22	$1.65M	0	$12.71M	$8.15M
Duncan Robinson*	25	$1.42M	1	$1.01M	($0.98M)
Yante Maten*	23	$1.42M	1	$0.02M	($3.02M)
Kendrick Nunn*	24	$1.42M	1	($0.01M)	($3.08M)

* Anderson's contract for 2019-20 is partially guaranteed for **$15.60M** if he's not waived on or before July 10, 2019. Jones' contract for 2019-20 is not guaranteed. Robinson's contracts for 2019-20 and 2020-21 are not guaranteed. Maten's contracts for 2019-20 and 2020-21 are not guaranteed. Nunn's contracts for 2019-20 and 2020-21 are not guaranteed. Miami used the stretch provision to waive A.J. Hammons on February 8, 2018. They will be assessed a cap hit of **$350,087** until the end of the 2020-21 season.

Two-Way Contracts
None

2019 Free Agents

* Age and Salary numbers are for 2019-20. See page 9 for explanation for Cap Value and RCV. A number in parentheses indicates that the value is negative.

	Age	Status	Salary	2018-19 Cap Value	RCV
Hassan Whiteside	30	Player Option	$27.09M	$7.12M	$5.40M
Goran Dragic	33	Player Option	$19.22M	($8.36M)	($1.15M)
Udonis Haslem	39	Unrestricted	N/A	($1.68M)	N/A
Dwyane Wade	38	Unrestricted	N/A	$16.67M	N/A

Estimated Cap Space for 2019 Free Agency

Note: Salary cap estimated to be at $109 million for 2019-20, as of September 17, 2018.

- **$26.3 million**, maximum cap space, if Whiteside and Dragic opt out, Anderson, Jones, Maten, Nunn and Robinson are waived

- **Over the cap**, just under luxury tax, most likely scenario, Whiteside and Dragic opt in, Jones, Maten, Nunn and Robinson remain on the roster, can only use cap exceptions
    - **Non-taxpayer Mid-Level Exception**

2019 Draft Picks and Future Assets until 2022

- 2019 own first round – **13th overall**
- 2020 own first round
- 2022 own first round
- 2022 own second round

Draft Rights Held

None

Offseason Recommendations

Miami is in a precarious position because they will probably be pressed against the luxury tax, assuming Hassan Whiteside and Goran Dragic opt in for next season. Though they have a Mid-Level Exception available to them, it wouldn't be wise to use any portion of it because it could result in them being hard capped next season, which would really restrict their maneuverability. Instead they should **explore the trade market to any find any possible way to flip the expiring contracts of Whiteside and Dragic for future assets**. The Heat are stuck with some onerous contracts that will be difficult to trade, so they might not have much of a choice but to shop their two most valuable veteran players. They may not be able to get a big return for either of them because the market for big men is depressed and Dragic is a declining player coming off a major injury. However, they have a depleted number of assets and any additional draft picks would give them a better chance to build for the future than they could in their current situation. Because of the team's limited flexibility, they can only fill holes on their roster with minimum salary players. Therefore, the Heat **should scour the G-League or the end of other team's benches for potential diamonds in the rough similar to how they found Derrick Jones, Jr.** Instead of adding veterans that may only be an incremental short-term help, they should target younger players that could fit into their system and possibly grow into rotation players. Ideally, they should target multi-positional defenders that could allow the team to maintain its defensive versatility to keep them competitive. From there, Miami will have to make some tactical changes to find an offensive system that is a better fit for their younger players like Josh Richardson, Justise Winslow and Bam Adebayo. If they can find a way to maximize those players, Miami could accelerate their timetable and reaffirm their position as a solid playoff team. However, their roster and cap sheet may be too flawed for any kind of minor tweak to work in a significant fashion, so it may take several years for Miami to get out from its current situation. As a result, they will have to exercise some patience and use their limited means to find pieces to help them in the long-term. If they stay disciplined and make sensible moves to pick up assets or add young players to their core group, they could be a factor in the Eastern Conference in the future. Otherwise, if they rush things and take short-sighted actions, they could find themselves at the bottom of the standings for the foreseeable future.

MILWAUKEE BUCKS

Season in Review

Last summer, the Milwaukee Bucks arguably made the best move of the offseason by hiring former Coach of the Year, Mike Budenholzer to be their new head coach. With a few minor roster tweaks like the additions of Brook Lopez and Ersan Ilyasova, Budenholzer reworked the team's entire on-court strategy to make the Bucks a dramatically better team than they were a year ago. From an individual perspective, Giannis Antetokounmpo took another leap forward in his development and became a leading contender for the MVP award. Then, the team finished with the NBA's best regular season record and they emerged as one of the contenders to possibly represent the Eastern Conference in the NBA Finals.

The Bucks had a pretty effective offense last season, but they became a much more dangerous and dynamic unit this season, as they ranked in the top five in Offensive Efficiency. The main reason for the team's improvement on offense was that they switched from a slower, isolation based attack that almost relied solely on Antetokounmpo to using a more modernized attack that incorporated more ball movement and floor spacing to enhance the abilities of their elite superstar. In fact, according to Synergy, the Bucks were good or better in almost every situation. Because Milwaukee played at a significantly faster pace and made more threes in volume, Antetokounmpo had more open driving lanes to attack the rim to the point where he scored more points inside of five feet than anybody in the league by a wide margin. Antetokounmpo's brilliance at the rim combined with the team's league average Three-Point Percentage made the Bucks one of the league's most efficient shooting teams, as they ranked in the top five in Effective Field Goal Percentage. The Bucks also improved their ability to limit turnovers as the season progressed to the point where they ranked in the top ten in Turnover Percentage. The team's highly efficient shooting and ability to avoid turnovers masked a couple of flaws. For starters, they weren't being fouled as frequently because the floor was spread out and they were taking more jump shots, so they posted a slightly below average Free Throw Attempt Rate. From a tactical standpoint, they essentially turned Brook Lopez into a spot-up shooter. Though this really helped them space the floor, this didn't make them very effective on the offensive boards because they simply didn't have anyone positioned inside on offense. As a result, they finished near the bottom of the league in Offensive Rebound Percentage.

Over the past few seasons, Milwaukee had always had tremendous length up and down its roster, but they always had trouble converting it into effective defense. This season, the Bucks finally harnessed all of their length under Budenholzer to become the league's best defensive team. They mainly accomplished this feat by moving away from the unnecessary gambling that was put in by the previous head coach, Jason Kidd and by playing simpler coverages. As a result, the team's length and defensive versatility allowed them to switch screens and not allow opponents to find exploitable matchups. In fact, they were pretty effective on defense across the board, as they were rated as average or better in almost every defensive situation, according to Synergy. The simpler defensive coverages also made it easier for Antetokounmpo to pick and choose his spots to rotate to block shots on the weak side, which made the Bucks one of the league's best at protecting the rim. This shot blocking prowess combined with the team's ability to disrupt shots with its overall length made Milwaukee the league's toughest team to shoot against, as they led the NBA in Opponents' Effective Field Goal Percentage. Additionally, they were able to be this disruptive without fouling, so they ended up becoming the league's best team at keeping opponents off the free throw line. Because they generally played lineups with more length and usually had Antetokounmpo on the floor, the Bucks were very effective on the defensive glass to the point where they led the league in Defensive Rebound Percentage. If the team had any weakness on the defensive end, it was that their more simplified style didn't allow them to force turnovers with any sort of frequency, as they were in the bottom half of the league in Opponents' Turnover Percentage. However, this possible negative was greatly outweighed by the positives.

    Milwaukee's fortunes changed in the best possible way this season to the point where they went all-in by dealing away some picks for George Hill and Nikola Mirotic. It's uncertain if these moves paid off because the playoffs are still going on as this book is being written. If the Bucks manage to come out of the Eastern Conference and go to the Finals, they could look to re-sign many of their key free agents to maintain their position as title contenders. Otherwise, if they fall short of their goals, they may be forced to retool their roster. However, the combination of Antetokounmpo's leap to being an MVP-caliber player and Budenholzer's ability to maximize talent should allow the Bucks to keep their place as one of the Eastern Conference's top teams.

2019-20 Outlook

Players Under Contract for 2019-20

* Age and Salary numbers are for 2019-20. See page 9 for explanation for Cap Value and RCV. A number in parentheses indicates that the value is negative.

	Age	Salary	Years Left	2018-19 Cap Value	RCV
Giannis Antetokounmpo	25	$25.84M	1	$43.59M	$81.81M
George Hill*	33	$18.00M	0	($5.21M)	($1.76M)
Eric Bledsoe	30	$15.63M	3	$24.50M	$76.98M
Tony Snell	28	$11.39M	Player Option	$3.57M	$5.35M
Ersan Ilyasova*	32	$7.00M	1	$6.76M	$18.50M
D.J. Wilson	23	$2.96M	Team Option	$5.65M	$3.67M
Donte DiVincenzo	23	$2.91M	2 Team Options	$0.62M	($0.86M)
Pat Connaughton*	27	$1.72M	0	$15.70M	$12.88M
Sterling Brown*	24	$1.62M	0	$8.75M	$6.52M

* Hill's contract for 2019-20 is guaranteed for **$1.00M** until July 1, 2019. Ilyasova's contract for 2020-21 is not guaranteed. The 2019-20 contracts for Connaughton and Brown are not guaranteed. Milwaukee used the stretch provision to waive Larry Sanders on February 21, 2015 and they will be assessed a cap hit of **$1.87M** until the end of the 2021-22 season. Milwaukee also used the stretch provision to waive Spencer Hawes on September 1, 2017 and they will be assessed a cap hit of **$2.01M** until the end of the 2019-20 season.

Two-Way Contracts

* In this section, listings are read: Player, Current Age, Height, Weight, College or Country

- Bonzie Colson, 23, 6'6", 224, Notre Dame

2019 Free Agents

* Age and Salary numbers are for 2019-20. See page 9 for explanation for Cap Value and RCV. A number in parentheses indicates that the value is negative.

	Age	Status	Salary	2018-19 Cap Value	RCV
Khris Middleton	28	Player Option	$13.00M	$19.07M	$18.97M
Malcolm Brogdon	27	Restricted	N/A	$28.93M	N/A
Nikola Mirotic	28	Unrestricted	N/A	$5.41M	N/A
Brook Lopez	31	Unrestricted	N/A	$28.14M	N/A
Pau Gasol	39	Unrestricted	N/A	($10.08M)	N/A
Tim Frazier	29	Unrestricted	N/A	$8.76M	N/A

Estimated Cap Space for 2019 Free Agency

Note: Salary cap estimated to be at $109 million for 2019-20, as of September 17, 2018.

- **$38.4 million**, maximum cap space, if Middleton opts out, Hill, Connaughton, and Brown are waived

- **$36.7 million**, if Middleton opts out, Connaughton remains on the roster, Hill and Brown are waived

- **$21.4 million**, if Middleton opts out, Hill remains on the roster, Connaughton and Brown are waived

- **$19.7 million**, if Middleton opts out, Hill and Connaughton remain on the roster, Brown is waived

- **$18.1 million**, if Middleton opts out, Hill, Connaughton, and Brown remain on the roster

2019 Draft Picks and Future Assets until 2022

- 2019 own first round – **30th overall**
- 2020 own first round, top 7 protected, otherwise goes to Phoenix (Eric Bledsoe trade)
- 2021 own first round
- 2022 own first round, top 10 protected, otherwise goes to Cleveland (George Hill trade)
- 2022 own second round

Draft Rights Held

None

Offseason Recommendations

The Milwaukee Bucks could look very different next season because Giannis Antetokounmpo and Eric Bledsoe are the only players in the team's starting five that are not free agents. Therefore, the Bucks will have to figure out which players are the most sensible to keep. Most likely, Brook Lopez and Khris Middleton have priced themselves out of Milwaukee's range. Lopez has played well enough this season that he won't be available at the same discounted rate. By virtue of his career year, Middleton might be due for an expensive, long-term max contract that may not be worthwhile for Milwaukee in the next few years. Also, the team can make back some of Middleton's three-and-D abilities by giving a few more minutes to Tony Snell, even though he's not quite the same as a volume scorer. On the other hand, if Middleton were to agree to a team-friendly deal that's just under the max, it would be worthwhile for the Bucks to bring him back. Of their key free agents, it might **make the most sense to re-sign Malcolm Brogdon**. In his three years in the NBA, he's been a massive bargain because of his shooting, playmaking and multi-positional versatility. Players of his skill set and production level are rarely available on the open market, so he would be pretty difficult to replace. Also, Brogdon's a restricted free agent, so Milwaukee has the option to match any offer as long as it's reasonable. As long as another team doesn't come in with an irrationally large offer sheet, the team should work to keep him around. **To fill the remaining holes, Milwaukee will have to do their due diligence to bargain hunt for role players to surround their core**, much like how they found Lopez last summer. If they can find a few hidden gems and get some internal growth from their younger players like D.J. Wilson and Donte DiVincenzo, they could remain an elite team in the Eastern Conference. Even if a worst-case scenario happens and they have to overhaul the roster, the bottom will not completely fall out because they still have a strong system overseen by Mike Budenholzer and they will have Antetokounmpo under contract for the next couple of seasons. Because of this, Milwaukee should be able to utilize their means to put together a solid roster that will allow them to be a factor in the Eastern Conference for the next few seasons.

MINNESOTA TIMBERWOLVES

Season in Review

The news cycle in the NBA moves at such a high velocity that it's tough to remember that the Minnesota Timberwolves' season began with Jimmy Butler's public pre-season trade demand. The situation was awkwardly handled to the point where the team's environment became intensely toxic, so much so that it spilled over into their on-court performance and the Timberwolves got off to a poor start. Minnesota got a brief boost after they dealt Butler to Philadelphia in November for Robert Covington, Dario Saric, Jerryd Bayless and a future second round pick. However, their play stalled to the point where they remained under 0.500 and they eventually relieved Tom Thibodeau of his coaching and executive duties while appointing Ryan Saunders to serve as interim head coach. The environment surrounding the team stabilized a bit in the second half, but it was not enough to put them in a playoff spot and Minnesota finished as a lottery team this past season.

The Timberwolves were somewhat competitive all season long because they were one of the league's better offensive teams, as they ranked in the upper half of the league in Offensive Efficiency. This was interesting because Minnesota was actually not a very good shooting team. In fact, the team finished in the bottom third of the league in Effective Field Goal Percentage, even though they got an All-Star season from Karl-Anthony Towns. This was mainly because they didn't surround Towns with enough perimeter shooting on a consistent basis, so opposing defenses often helped off a lower-percentage shooter like Andrew Wiggins or Josh Okogie and dared them to beat them from outside. They also didn't really move the ball very much and their primary playmakers really struggled to draw defenders to create openings for others. The team's ball handlers were among the worst in the league at finishing plays efficiently in pick-and-roll situations. Despite Minnesota's shooting inefficiencies, they were effective in other areas. Strangely, because space was congested and they spent most of their time trying to attack the basket, they were able to draw fouls at a high rate and they ranked in the top ten in almost every free throw shooting metric. Also, they tended to play bigger players in the frontcourt, so they wound up being one of the league's best offensive rebounding teams. Specifically, they finished in the top ten in Offensive Rebounding Percentage. Furthermore, they were one of the league's best ball control units because they rarely looked to make risky passes and as a result, they ranked in the top five in Turnover Percentage.

On defense, Minnesota continued to have some difficulties getting stops and they were among the league's worst defensive teams, finishing in the bottom third of the league in Defensive Efficiency. Their defense mainly struggled because their lineups were not very versatile, and they didn't feature many players that were capable of guarding multiple positions. Therefore, opponents could easily pinpoint exploitable matchups to get quality looks at the basket. To compensate for this issue, the Timberwolves often had to bring extra help, but that usually made them prone to giving up a lot of open threes to the point where they among the league's worst teams at defending the three-point line. As a result, opposing teams were able to shoot very efficiently against them and they ranked in the bottom third of the league in Opponents' Effective Field Goal Percentage. Additionally, their lineups were put at a disadvantage because their perimeter players were ineffective rebounders. Most of Minnesota's opponents embraced modern offensive principles and took threes with greater frequency. This produced a lot of long rebounds, but Minnesota's perimeter players consistently couldn't pull down these boards, so opponents were able to get a lot of second chance opportunities. As evidence of this, the Timberwolves finished near the bottom of the league in Defensive Rebound Percentage. On the positive side, Minnesota played with more activity, especially towards the end of the season. This allowed them to force turnovers at a fairly high rate and they wound up ranking in the top ten in Opponents' Turnover Percentage. They also played fairly under control by rarely fouling, so they were pretty good at keeping opposing teams off the free throw line.

Minnesota took a step back this season and the team is in very tough position because Tom Thibodeau's moves left them hard capped with very little flexibility to get out from their current situation. As a result, there's a chance that Timberwolves could be stuck in mediocrity for the foreseeable future if nothing changes in a major way. At the moment, Minnesota appears to be headed in a different direction because they hired former Houston Rockets' assistant GM, Gersson Rosas to be their new President of Basketball Operations and they also made Ryan Saunders the permanent head coach. If the new front office can implement a more coherent structure from top to bottom, they could move their franchise in the right direction. Otherwise, they will remain a middling team that will struggle to consistently compete in a difficult Western Conference.

2019-20 Outlook

Players Under Contract for 2019-20

* Age and Salary numbers are for 2019-20. See page 9 for explanation for Cap Value and RCV. A number in parentheses indicates that the value is negative.

	Age	Salary	Years Left	2018-19 Cap Value	RCV
Andrew Wiggins	24	$27.50M	3	($11.51M)	($50.13M)
Karl-Anthony Towns	24	$27.25M	4	$46.68M	$149.50M
Jeff Teague	31	$19.00M	0	($5.39M)	$1.48M
Gorgui Dieng	30	$16.23M	1	($0.24M)	($0.61M)
Robert Covington	29	$11.30M	2	$2.61M	$17.84M
Dario Saric	25	$3.48M	0	$17.38M	$19.97M
Josh Okogie	21	$2.53M	2 Team Options	$7.57M	$21.96M
Keita Bates-Diop*	24	$1.42M	Team Option	$1.87M	$2.55M
Cameron Reynolds*	24	$1.42M	0	$2.04M	$0.79M

* Bates-Diop's contract for 2020-21 is not guaranteed. Reynolds' contract for 2019-20 is not guaranteed. Minnesota used the stretch provision to waive Cole Aldrich on June 30, 2018 and they will be assessed a cap hit of **$685,340** until the end of the 2020-21 season.

Two-Way Contracts

* In this section, listings are read: Player, Current Age, Height, Weight, College or Country

- C.J. Williams, 28, 6'5", 226, NC State
- Jared Terrell, 23, 6'3", 227, Rhode Island

2019 Free Agents

* Age and Salary numbers are for 2019-20. See page 9 for explanation for Cap Value and RCV. A number in parentheses indicates that the value is negative.

	Age	Status	Salary	2018-19 Cap Value	RCV
Tyus Jones	23	Restricted	NA	$14.09M	NA
Mitch Creek	27	Restricted	NA	$0.87M	NA
Taj Gibson	34	Unrestricted	NA	$11.64M	NA
Jerryd Bayless	31	Unrestricted	NA	($6.39M)	NA
Anthony Tolliver	34	Unrestricted	NA	$1.15M	NA
Luol Deng	34	Unrestricted	NA	$2.91M	NA
Derrick Rose	31	Unrestricted	NA	$17.28M	NA

Estimated Cap Space for 2019 Free Agency

Note: Salary cap estimated to be at $109 million for 2019-20, as of September 17, 2018.

- **Over the cap**, but not over luxury tax, only have cap exceptions
    - **Non-taxpayer Mid-Level Exception**

2019 Draft Picks and Future Assets until 2022

- 2019 own first round – **11th overall**
- 2019 second round from Miami via Charlotte (Gary Neal/Troy Daniels trade, Shabazz Napier draft day trade) – **43rd overall**
- 2020 own first round
- 2020 own second round
- 2021 own first round
- 2021 own second round
- 2022 own first round
- 2022 own second round
- 2022 second round from either Philadelphia or Denver, whichever is more favorable (Jimmy Butler trade, Wilson Chandler trade to Philadelphia)

Draft Rights Held

	Year	Round	Pick
Bojan Dubljevic	2013	2	59
Henk Norel	2009	2	47
Lior Eliyahu	2006	2	44

Offseason Recommendations

The Timberwolves are in a bind because if they continue on their current path, they could wind up in the same position as the New Orleans Pelicans are now. Specifically, they could be a capped out, mediocre team that squanders the prime years of their elite, All-Star big man. To avoid this fate, Minnesota has to reassess its situation and figure out some way to escape mediocrity. It isn't going to be easy because their resources are going to be very limited. After all, they don't have a lot of additional draft picks to use as trade bait. Even though Jeff Teague's contract will probably come off the books after next season, the team will probably still be capped out because Dario Saric's rookie contract will expire and he's due for a raise. In addition to this, the team still has four years left on Andrew Wiggins' max contract and because of his declining production, this contract has become rather immovable. Without attaching draft picks, the only way that Minnesota could unload this and gain positive long-term value would be to trade Wiggins and Karl-Anthony Towns together, but that would mean that the Timberwolves would have to commit to a full-scale rebuild. This is not ideal because Towns' extension has not kicked in yet, so the team should try to do their best to salvage the current situation before taking the drastic measure of blowing everything up. To improve their long-term prospects without making a major change, the Timberwolves will have to find some way to boost Wiggins' production to make his contract less of an albatross. **Most likely, Minnesota has to simplify his role because at this stage, Wiggins is probably miscast and overextended as a shot creating wing player**. This is mainly because he's struggled to shoot efficiently from perimeter and his playmaking skills aren't developed enough for him to be a primary ball handler. To get the most out of him, they should limit his offensive responsibilities to the few things that he does well. Particularly, he should be used as a post-up wing similar to someone like Shaun Livingston. According to Synergy, posting up smaller players is Wiggins' best skill and he's been rated average or better in post-up situations every year that he's been the league. Therefore, the Timberwolves should tweak their lineups and schemes to put him in the post on a more frequent basis. A way to do this may be **to replace Teague with either a taller ball handler or another mid-size wing player**. This way, the team could increase their odds of getting a smaller guard switched onto Wiggins to increase his post-up opportunities. Essentially, the team should employ a four-around-one attack but treat Wiggins as if he were a non-shooting big man instead of a wing player. If this type of tactical switch doesn't work and the team is still stuck in the middle of the Western Conference, then they may no choice but to start over and rebuild from scratch. However, if the new front office stabilizes their overall operation and makes a few creative moves to give them a little more flexibility, they might be able to figure a way out of their current mess. Otherwise, tearing everything down is probably the best option to give them a better chance at a more sustainable long-term future.

NEW ORLEANS PELICANS

Season in Review

The New Orleans Pelicans were expected to be a playoff team coming into this season because they still had most of the core of last season's playoff roster intact. They made some minor tweaks to the rotation last summer by bringing in Julius Randle and Elfrid Payton to replace an injured DeMarcus Cousins and Rajon Rondo. However, the results didn't go as planned for the Pelicans. They were a bit unlucky in close games and the Western Conference was more competitive, so their record fell to below 0.500. Then, around the trade deadline, Anthony Davis dropped a bombshell by publicly demanding a trade, but nothing came of it and the team had to awkwardly manage the second half of the season. The team fired General Manager, Dell Demps and Davis' availability from game-to-game was a constant question mark towards the end of the season. Because of all this, the Pelicans ended up as a lottery team this past season.

Despite all of the chaos that came from Davis' trade demand, head coach, Alvin Gentry managed to help the Pelicans become one of the league's better offensive teams, as they ranked in the upper half of the league in Offensive Efficiency this past season. They mainly relied a fast paced attack that used great ball movement to generate easy shots around the basket. In fact, they were one of the league's best teams at making shots at the rim and they ranked in the top five in both Field Goals Made and Field Goal Percentage on shots inside of five feet. They also were one of the NBA's best teams at scoring on cuts and they excelled at scoring on put-backs and finishing plays with the roll man in pick-and-roll situations, according to Synergy. This effectiveness from inside negated their reluctance to shoot threes and they were one of the league's better overall shooting teams, as they finished in the upper half of the league in Effective Field Goal Percentage. Because of the aggressiveness of both Davis and Randle, the Pelicans were able to consistently grab offensive rebounds, as evidenced by the fact that they wound up in the top ten in Offensive Rebound Percentage. As a slight negative, the Pelicans' Turnover Percentage was just below the league average, so were a little susceptible to turning the ball over. Also, as it was mentioned earlier, they weren't a great outside shooting team, as they ranked in the bottom half of the league in Three-Point Percentage. Therefore, opposing defenses had success by packing in the paint and daring them to beat them from outside. Additionally, the Pelicans only drew fouls at a below average rate because Davis missed a lot of games towards the end of the season, which hurt the team's ability to put pressure on opposing defenses on a consistent basis.

This season, New Orleans' defensive performance dropped to the point where they were one of the league's worst defenses, as they finished in the bottom third of the league in Defensive Efficiency. On the positive side, Davis' interior presence allowed them to be very effective at defending around the basket. His shot blocking abilities allowed the Pelicans to limit their opponent's effectiveness on cuts and rolls to the rim. The team's ability to defend the basket also helped them be an above average team at keeping opponents off the free throw line. However, the Pelicans really didn't defend well enough on the perimeter to complement their interior defense. They struggled to defend shooters off screens, and they gave up a lot of wide open threes in general. As a result, they among the league's worst teams at defending the three-point line, which allowed opponents to score very efficiently against them. As evidence of this, New Orleans ranked in the bottom third of the league in Opponents' Effective Field Goal Percentage. They also weren't a very active defensive team because they didn't really put pressure on opposing offensive players, so they rarely forced turnovers. Because opponents were shooting so many threes against them, their lack of size on the perimeter was exposed because the Pelicans' perimeter players struggled on the defensive boards and opponents were able to get some more second chance opportunities. In fact, the Pelicans ranked in the bottom half of the league in Defensive Rebound Percentage.

The Pelicans are headed for a rebuild because of Davis' publicly stated intentions to leave the team after his contract expires. As a result, the team probably has to trade him to take back some valuable assets to help them rebuild for the future. Ideally, they would be best served to hold out for a significant package that lands them either a high-end lottery pick, or a talented young player on a rookie contract. However, the situation may be so toxic that dealing him immediately could make it easier for the team to move forward. Either way, this situation has to be resolved and then, once the rebuild commences, they should take a more prudent approach than they did under the Dell Demps regime. If they focus on accumulating draft assets and avoiding long-term deals to mid-level players, they could be a competitive team in the Western Conference in a few years. Otherwise, the franchise could languish near the bottom of the standings for a long time.

2019-20 Outlook

Players Under Contract for 2019-20

* Age and Salary numbers are for 2019-20. See page 9 for explanation for Cap Value and RCV. A number in parentheses indicates that the value is negative.

	Age	Salary	Years Left	2018-19 Cap Value	RCV
Anthony Davis	26	$27.09M	Player Option	$22.38M	$55.86M
Jrue Holiday	29	$26.71M	1 + Player Option	$6.96M	$22.91M
Solomon Hill	28	$12.76M	0	($8.56M)	($9.24M)
E'Twaun Moore	30	$8.66M	0	$2.40M	$6.83M
Christian Wood*	24	$1.65M	0	$2.82M	$0.73M
Frank Jackson*	21	$1.62M	0	$4.01M	$4.08M
Kenrich Williams*	25	$1.44M	0	$6.52M	$6.10M
Dairis Bertans*	30	$1.42M	0	($0.61M)	($1.84M)

* Jackson's contract for 2019-20 is only guaranteed for **$506,000**. Williams' contract for 2019-20 is guaranteed for **$50,000** if he's not waived on or before July 22, 2019, then it is guaranteed for **$200,000** if he's not waived on or before the first regular season game. Bertans' contract for 2019-20 is guaranteed for **$150,000** if he's not waived on or before August 1, 2019, then it is guaranteed for **$300,000** if he's not waived on or before November 4, 2019. Wood's contract for 2019-20 is not guaranteed.

Two-Way Contracts

* In this section, listings are read: Player, Current Age, Height, Weight, College or Country

- Trevon Bluiett, 24, 6'6", 198, Xavier

2019 Free Agents

* Age and Salary numbers are for 2019-20. See page 9 for explanation for Cap Value and RCV. A number in parentheses indicates that the value is negative.

	Age	Status	Salary	2018-19 Cap Value	RCV
Julius Randle	25	Player Option	$9.07M	$26.31M	$25.53M
Jahlil Okafor	24	Team Option	$1.70M	$10.97M	$8.14M
Stanley Johnson	23	Restricted	N/A	$1.95M	N/A
Cheick Diallo	23	Restricted	N/A	$11.67M	N/A
Elfrid Payton	25	Unrestricted	N/A	$7.93M	N/A
Darius Miller	29	Unrestricted	N/A	$7.93M	N/A
Ian Clark	28	Unrestricted	N/A	$1.37M	N/A

Estimated Cap Space for 2019 Free Agency

Note: Salary cap estimated to be at $109 million for 2019-20, as of September 17, 2018.

- **$33.8 million**, maximum cap space, if Randle opts out, Okafor's option is not picked up, Wood, Jackson, Williams and Bertans are waived

- **$25.9 million**, most likely scenario, Randle opts out, Okafor's option is picked up, Wood, Jackson, Williams and Bertans remain on the roster

- **$16.9 million**, Randle opts in, Okafor's option is picked up, Wood, Jackson, Williams and Bertans remain on the roster

2019 Draft Picks and Future Assets until 2022

- 2019 own first round – **1st overall**
- 2019 own second round – **39th overall**
- 2019 second round from Denver via Milwaukee (Nikola Mirotic trade to Milwaukee, Roy Hibbert trade to Denver) – **57th overall**
- 2020 own first round
- 2020 own second round
- 2020 second round from Milwaukee (Nikola Mirotic trade to Milwaukee)
- 2020 second round from Washington via Milwaukee (Nikola Mirotic trade to Milwaukee)
- 2021 own first round
- 2021 own second round, Chicago has the option to swap picks (Nikola Mirotic trade from Chicago)
- 2021 second round from Washington via Utah, Cleveland and Milwaukee (Nikola Mirotic trade to Milwaukee, George Hill three-team trade to Milwaukee, Kyle Korver trade to Utah, Trey Burke trade to Washington)
- 2022 own first round
- 2022 own second round

Draft Rights Held

	Year	Round	Pick
Tony Carr	2018	2	51
Latavious Williams	2010	2	48

Offseason Recommendations

The Pelicans were stuck as a decent playoff level team for the last few seasons, but strangely enough, the trade demand of Anthony Davis now gives the franchise a clear direction for the first time in years, as the team is likely headed for a full-scale rebuild. New Orleans got off to a pretty good start by getting a sizeable haul of four second round picks from Milwaukee in the trade involving Nikola Mirotic at the trade deadline. This summer, the Pelicans would be best served to keep going and **sell any veterans with value for assets**. Obviously, the starting point of this rebuild is to deal Davis. Because the negotiations between New Orleans and the Lakers went public during the trade deadline, a minimum bar was set, as the Lakers reportedly offered all three of their main young players and multiple first round picks. Therefore, if other teams can beat that offer, the Pelicans could land a pretty big return to give them some optionality for the next few years. From there, the team should **look to shop Jrue Holiday around the league** as well. After all, if the team is losing Davis and the Pelicans go in a rebuilding mode, it makes little sense to keep a veteran like Holiday. Also, if Memphis is serious about a possible trade involving Mike Conley, the teams in pursuit of Conley would probably be interested in Holiday as well, if he were to be available. Of the two, Holiday is a more attractive option than Conley for a team looking for a point guard upgrade because Holiday is three years younger and he's on a cheaper contract. Therefore, the Pelicans could come away with a lot of draft picks or young players if they sell off their two best players. On top of this, they will have some cap space to work with, so they could go even further by renting out their cap space to other teams that are looking to dump salary and take back a few extra draft picks. On the surface, it seems like the Pelicans are in a rough spot, but they are positioned well to turn lemons into lemonade if they assess their situation realistically and fully commit to rebuilding from scratch. If they have any delusions of competing in the short-term, they could do considerable damage to themselves in the long-term by making the same kind of short-sighted moves that got them into their current mess. If they can maximize the return on an Anthony Davis trade and they stay patient during their rebuilding process, they could ultimately build a more sustainable model for their success and return to being competitive in the Western Conference.

NEW YORK KNICKS

Season in Review

The New York Knicks weren't expected to be competitive this year, especially considering the fact that All-Star, Kristaps Porzingis was going to miss most of the season to recover from his ACL injury. Initially, the Knicks took a patient rebuilding approach by focusing their effort on developing younger players like Kevin Knox, Allonzo Trier, Frank Ntilikina and others. Then, around the trade deadline, they pivoted and made their offseason intentions clear by trading Porzingis, Tim Hardaway, Jr. and Courtney Lee to Dallas for Dennis Smith, Jr., the expiring contracts of DeAndre Jordan and Wesley Matthews, and multiple future first round picks. Basically, the Knicks attached Porzingis to the contracts of Hardaway and Lee to clear enough space to pursue two max salary free agents in an attempt to quickly turnaround the franchise through free agency this summer. As for the season, the team was one of the worst teams in the league before the trade and their play fell off even further afterwards to the point where they finished with the league's worst record.

From an individual perspective, a few of the team's young players showed some positive signs of growth. Specifically, Allonzo Trier went from playing on a two-way contract to become one of the team's most reliable outside shooters and earning a full-time contract in the process. Damyean Dotson also showed improvement in his second year and he also has turned into an above average three-point shooter. In addition to these two players, Mitchell Robinson and Luke Kornet were effective in limited minutes. Robinson flashed potential as a rim running and rim protection big man while Kornet showed that he could eventually develop into a decent floor spacing big man. From there, Emmanuel Mudiay had his best season as a pro and Dennis Smith, Jr. saw his production increase while he was in a Knicks uniform. On the negative side, Frank Ntilikina's growth stagnated a bit because he struggled to figure out his role under head coach, David Fizdale. Also, Kevin Knox was a bit overextended because though he put up solid counting numbers, his production was very inefficient.

As a team, the Knicks were among the league's worst teams on both sides of the ball, as they ranked near the bottom of the league in both Offensive and Defensive Efficiency. Offensively, they actually did do a couple of things rather well. In particular, because of the youth and athleticism, they were pretty aggressive and attacked the basket quite frequently. As a result, they were one of the league's better teams at getting to the foul line and they finished in the top ten in Free Throw Attempt Rate. For a team that was as young as the Knicks were, they were not bad at avoiding turnovers and they hovered around the league average in Turnover Percentage. On the downside, their ability to avoid turnovers was mainly due to the fact that their offense didn't feature a whole lot of ball movement and they tended to take a lot of forced, inefficient shots. Because of this, the Knicks were last in the league in both Effective Field Goal Percentage and Assists per Game. The Knicks were around average on the offensive glass for the bulk of the season, and then the team's offensive rebounding rate dropped a little bit after they waived Enes Kanter after the trade deadline. As a result, the Knicks finished the season with a below average Defensive Rebound Percentage. On the defensive side, the Knicks were fairly bad across the board and they were below average or bad in every component metric. This was mainly because the team struggled to make clean rotations and they couldn't build a cohesive unit due to all of the various personnel shuffling. If there was anything resembling a positive about their defense, it was that they were actually effective at defending the ball handler in pick-and-roll situations, according to Synergy. However, this positive was negated significantly by the fact that they were the league's worst team at defending the roll man.

The Knicks have a lot riding on this summer because they gave up a superstar talent to clear the necessary cap space. It's a major gamble because they pretty much have to land multiple elite players to justify the deal. Otherwise, they could be in a much worse situation in the future because the Knicks have tried to take shortcuts like this in the past and they generally have not panned out. If they get lucky either in the lottery or in free agency, they could be competitive in the Eastern Conference once again. However, things don't go as planned, they will need to reconsider their approach and possibly overhaul their operation to implement a system that is more conducive to sustainable success. Because if they operate as they are, they could be stuck in their permanent rut and continue to produce diminishing returns on their teams.

2019-20 Outlook

Players Under Contract for 2019-20

* Age and Salary numbers are for 2019-20. See page 9 for explanation for Cap Value and RCV. A number in parentheses indicates that the value is negative.

	Age	Salary	Years Left	2018-19 Cap Value	RCV
Lance Thomas*	31	$7.58M	0	($4.89M)	($3.97M)
Frank Ntilikina	21	$4.86M	Team Option	($4.22M)	($9.32M)
Dennis Smith, Jr.	22	$4.46M	Team Option	$3.43M	$6.22M
Kevin Knox	20	$4.38M	2 Team Option	$0.05M	($1.57M)
Henry Ellenson*	23	$1.65M	0	$0.22M	$0.35M
Damyean Dotson*	25	$1.62M	0	$11.17M	$7.78M
Mitchell Robinson*	21	$1.56M	1 + Team Option	$26.85M	$85.77M

* Thomas' contract for 2019-20 is partially guaranteed for **$1.00M**. Dotson's contract for 2019-20 is not guaranteed until July 15, 2019. Robinson's contract for 2020-21 is not guaranteed. Ellenson's contract for 2019-20 is not guaranteed. New York used the stretch provision to waive Joakim Noah on October 13, 2018 and they will be assessed a cap hit of **$6.43M** until the end of the 2021-22 season.

Two-Way Contracts

* In this section, listings are read: Player, Current Age, Height, Weight, College or Country
- Isaiah Hicks, 24, 6'9", 230, North Carolina
- Kadeem Allen, 26, 6'3", 192, Arizona

2019 Free Agents

* Age and Salary numbers are for 2019-20. See page 9 for explanation for Cap Value and RCV. A number in parentheses indicates that the value is negative.

	Age	Status	Salary	2018-19 Cap Value	RCV
Allonzo Trier	24	Team Option	$3.55M	$6.03M	$6.19M
Emmanuel Mudiay	23	Restricted	N/A	$7.05M	N/A
Luke Kornet	24	Restricted	N/A	$6.73M	N/A
Billy Garrett	25	Restricted	N/A	$0.20M	N/A
DeAndre Jordan	31	Unrestricted	N/A	$11.67M	N/A
Mario Hezonja	24	Unrestricted	N/A	($1.69M)	N/A
Noah Vonleh	24	Unrestricted	N/A	$16.57M	N/A

Estimated Cap Space for 2019 Free Agency

Note: Salary cap estimated to be at $109 million for 2019-20, as of September 17, 2018.

- **$86.3 million**, maximum cap space, if Thomas, Dotson and Ellenson are waived, Trier's option is not picked up

- **$82.8 million**, if Thomas, Dotson and Ellenson are waived, Trier's option is picked up

- **$81.1 million**, if Thomas is waived, Dotson remains on the roster, Trier's option is picked up

Note: If Ellenson remains on the roster, subtract **$1.65M** from the numbers above.

2019 Draft Picks and Future Assets until 2022

- 2019 own first round – **3rd overall**
- 2019 second round from Houston (Pablo Prigioni trade) – **55th overall**
- 2020 own first round
- 2020 second round from Charlotte (Willy Hernangomez trade)
- 2021 own first round
- 2021 first round from Dallas (Kristaps Porzingis trade)
- 2021 second round from Charlotte (Willy Hernangomez trade)
- 2022 own first round
- 2022 own second round

Draft Rights Held

	Year	Round	Pick
Ognjen Jaramaz	2017	2	58
Louis Labeyrie	2014	2	57

Offseason Recommendations

Once the Knicks made the move to trade Kristaps Porzingis, their plans for this summer have become crystal clear, as they intend to use their considerable cap space to sign two elite free agents. If they happen to be successful in landing some combination of Kevin Durant, Kyrie Irving and Kawhi Leonard, then their plans to fill out the rest of roster are fairly straightforward, as they would likely target useful veteran role players that are willing to take minimum salary deals. If they don't come away with at least one elite free agent, they should not panic and spend their cap dollars on mid-level players. Instead, they **should continue the rebuilding process and use their space to accumulate assets and potentially expand their core.** Right now, the Knicks don't have any solid cornerstones to build around because their last two first round picks, Frank Ntilikina and Kevin Knox, have gotten their careers off to a slow start. Also, Dennis Smith, Jr. has been a little inconsistent in his two seasons in the league. Of their young players, Mitchell

Robinson is probably the closest thing that they have to a building block, but he only started to get regular playing time in the second half of the season. If he can maintain his high efficiency in a larger role, he could become a very valuable part of the Knicks' future, especially considering the fact that he'll be playing on a very team-friendly contract for at least two more seasons. From there, the Knicks will have to hit on their lottery pick to give themselves a better opportunity to move forward and clarify the team's overall direction. Then, the Knicks would be better served to use their cap space to take on some money to acquire additional draft picks if they don't land any of the elite free agents. This way, they can give themselves some more options to maneuver and build a stronger base of young talent. Even if the Knicks' plan to land multiple elite free agents is successful, they still have some work to do to build a completely balanced roster that can compete for a championship. If they can find the right mix of elite talent, role playing veterans and internal growth from their young players, they could once again be a factor in the Eastern Conference. Otherwise, if things don't go as planned, they will have to work smartly to salvage their situation by avoiding the short-sighted moves that have plagued them in the past. If they can make prudent moves that give them more assets and quality young talent, they can build a team that has a better chance of sustaining its success over a longer period of time.

OKLAHOMA CITY THUNDER

Season in Review

The Oklahoma City Thunder came into this season with its core intact after Paul George decided to re-sign with the team last summer. The team made a few tweaks to the roster to forge an identity as an athletic, high energy, versatile defensive-oriented unit by trading Carmelo Anthony to Atlanta for Dennis Schroder and picking up Nerlens Noel in free agency. They also promoted Jerami Grant and Terrance Ferguson to more significant roles. In addition to these changes, George took his play up a notch and became an MVP candidate for most of the season due to his excellent two-way abilities. Also, Russell Westbrook averaged a triple-double for the third straight season. Even with a more stable core and improved chemistry, the Thunder sputtered towards the end of the season and finished with a back-end playoff seed in the Western Conference.

Opposing teams had difficulties against the Thunder because they were one of the league's best defensive teams, ranking in the top five in Defensive Efficiency. Their versatility and athleticism allowed them to be very aggressive in pressuring opponents. It also allowed them to switch screens and not give opponents easy matchups to exploit. Therefore, Oklahoma City was rated as average or better in every defensive situation, according to Synergy. Their high pressure style helped them force turnovers at a very high rate, as they led the league in Opponents' Turnover Percentage and Steals per Game. Individually, Paul George and Russell Westbrook were ranked first and fourth, respectively in Steals per Game this past season. They also were one of the league's better defensive rebounding teams, as they ranked in the upper half of the league in Defensive Rebound Percentage. The team's emphasis on playing a high pressure style did have some drawbacks. Specifically, the Thunder tended to get caught gambling quite a bit and allowed a lot of shots inside of five feet. Their defenders often over-played their man, so they were vulnerable against cuts and rolls to the rim. In fact, according to Synergy, the Thunder finished in the bottom half of the league at defending in situations that ended in a cut or with a roll to the rim. Even though, the team was pretty good at defending perimeter shots, they were only about average at limiting their opponents' shooting efficiency, as their Opponents' Effective Field Goal Percentage hovered around the league average. Also, they could be over-aggressive, which led to some fouls that allowed opponents to get to the free throw line at an above average rate.

Offensively, the Thunder dropped off a bit and they finished just below the league average in Offensive Efficiency. A major factor in the team's overall drop-off was that Westbrook had his worst shooting season since his second year and his percentages dipped across the board. Opposing defenses were able to take advantage of this and had some success in baiting him into taking inefficient shots. This negated some of the positive developments from their other perimeter players because he was basically taking shots away from more efficient shooters. Because Westbrook was still assuming a lot of volume, the team posted an Effective Field Goal Percentage well below the league average. Also, even though the Thunder got to the free throw line on a frequent basis, it didn't really help their offense because they posted one of the league's worst Free Throw Percentages. On the positive side, Oklahoma City's offense hovered around average because they played at a very high pace that allowed them to score a lot of points in volume in transition situations. They also got a lot of second shot opportunities because they were one of the league's best offensive rebounding teams, largely due to the presence of Steven Adams and Nerlens Noel off the bench. Finally, because the ball wasn't changing hands very frequently, they generally didn't commit turnovers and they ranked in the top ten in Turnover Percentage this past season.

This season, Oklahoma City established a strong identity as an aggressive, high-energy defensive team under head coach, Billy Donovan. However, they haven't had much success in the playoffs because they were knocked out in the first round this season. Therefore, they may need to rethink their approach to improve their future playoff performance. Westbrook's shooting struggles are something to watch out for because the team is fairly dependent on him and Paul George to generate offense. If either of them drops off considerably, then the team could be in a serious bind because most of the team's cap space is tied up between those two and they wouldn't have a lot of ways to maneuver if a worst-case scenario were to happen. Given that Westbrook doesn't appear to be diminished physically, these struggles could just be seen as an aberration and he could easily bounce back next season. If that is the case and he can return to shooting somewhere around his career averages, then Oklahoma City should be one of the better teams in the Western Conference for the next few years. Otherwise, the Thunder will have to consider making either a tactical or personnel change to address the possible decline of one of its superstars.

2019-20 Outlook

Players Under Contract for 2019-20

* Age and Salary numbers are for 2019-20. See page 9 for explanation for Cap Value and RCV. A number in parentheses indicates that the value is negative.

	Age	Salary	Years Left	2018-19 Cap Value	RCV
Russell Westbrook	31	$38.51M	2 + Player Option	$4.58M	$11.64M
Paul George	29	$33.01M	1 + Player Option	$27.76M	$53.25M
Steven Adams	26	$25.84M	1	$19.96M	$36.22M
Dennis Schroder	26	$15.50M	1	$3.89M	$10.86M
Andre Roberson	28	$10.74M	0	($10.00M)	($6.87M)
Jerami Grant	25	$9.35M	Player Option	$25.34M	$42.73M
Terrance Ferguson	21	$2.48M	Team Option	$10.35M	$14.68M
Abdel Nader*	26	$1.62M	Team Option	$3.46M	$3.32M
Hamidou Diallo	21	$1.42M	Team Option	$3.42M	$5.95M
Deonte Burton	26	$1.42M	0	$0.78M	($0.47M)

* Nader's contract for 2019-20 is not guaranteed until July 5, 2019. Burton's contract for 2019-20 is not guaranteed. Oklahoma City used to the stretch provision to waive Kyle Singler on August 31, 2018 and they will be assessed a cap hit of **$999,200** until the end of the 2022-23 season.

Two-Way Contracts

* In this section, listings are read: Player, Current Age, Height, Weight, College or Country

- Donte Grantham, 23, 6'8", 215, Clemson
- Jawun Evans, 22, 6'0", 185, Oklahoma State

2019 Free Agents

* Age and Salary numbers are for 2019-20. See page 9 for explanation for Cap Value and RCV. A number in parentheses indicates that the value is negative.

	Age	Status	Salary	2018-19 Cap Value	RCV
Patrick Patterson	30	Player Option	$5.71M	$0.27M	$2.79M
Nerlens Noel	25	Player Option	$1.99M	$17.93M	$13.91M
Raymond Felton	35	Unrestricted	N/A	$2.06M	N/A
Markieff Morris	30	Unrestricted	N/A	$1.14M	N/A

Estimated Cap Space for 2019 Free Agency

Note: Salary cap estimated to be at $109 million for 2019-20, as of September 17, 2018.

- **Over the cap**, over the luxury tax, can only use exceptions
  - **Taxpayer Mid-Level Exception**

2019 Draft Picks and Future Assets until 2022

- 2019 own first round – **21st overall**
- 2020 own first round, top 20 protected, otherwise goes to Philadelphia via Orlando and Philadelphia (Jerami Grant trade, Anzejs Pasecniks trade, Markelle Fultz trade)
- 2020 own second round
- 2020 second round from Chicago, top 55 protected (Timothe Luwawu-Cabarrot trade)
- 2021 own first round
- 2021 own second round
- 2022 own first round, lottery protected, otherwise goes to Atlanta (Dennis Schroder trade)
- 2022 own second round

Draft Rights Held

	Year	Round	Pick
Devon Hall	2018	2	53
Kevin Hervey	2018	2	57
Sofoklis Schortsanitis	2003	2	34
Szymon Szewczyk	2003	2	35

Offseason Recommendations

Oklahoma City is in a decent position heading into this summer. After all, they have the talent to be a legitimate contender in the Western Conference and a good chunk of their primary rotation is under contract for next season. They are also going to be above the luxury tax and pressed up against the apron, so they probably shouldn't dip into their cap exception to sign free agents or else they could be hard capped, which would limit their flexibility significantly. Therefore, the Thunder is likely to find a potential contributor with their first round pick and fill the remaining holes on the roster with veterans on minimum salary contracts. Ideally, they **should look to find some way to acquire a stretch big to offset Russell Westbrook's shooting decline**. The large drop-off in Westbrook's shooting percentage is a cause for concern because his Supermax extension is going to kick in next season. That high cap figure could be an even heavier burden on a smaller market team like Oklahoma City if Westbrook is diminished in some way, so the team must figure out some way to get him closer to his previous efficiency level. With this in mind, pairing Westbrook with a stretch big for a few minutes would theoretically give him more space to operate by opening up driving lanes and giving him easier shots around the basket to increase his shooting efficiency. The main issue is that there is a scarce amount of readily available, quality shooting big men in the league and they can really only offer the league minimum, so the team's options are fairly limited. The only established stretch big in the Thunder's price range may be Jeff Green. This front office did originally draft him, so a reunion between Green and the Thunder could make some sense if Green is willing to play on the veteran's minimum once again. Most likely, they will have to home grow a stretch big by either taking a projectable shooting big man prospect in the first round or by taking on a reclamation project of sorts in free agency. An intriguing option for a reclamation project could be former Suns lottery pick, Dragan Bender. Bender hasn't been effective as an overall player in his three seasons, but he wasn't really put in a position to succeed. In particular, the situation in Phoenix has been chaotic to say the least and he's played for three different coaches in three years. A move to a more stable environment and a simplified role could allow him to gradually develop into a useful role player. He hasn't established any real strengths, but he's flashed an ability to knock down threes. With steady playing time in the season before, he was effective on pick-and-pop plays and pretty good at making no dribble spot-up jumpers to the point where his Three-Point Percentage was just above the league average. With some time with Oklahoma City's development staff, he could be a decent buy-low option. The Thunder could also take a flyer on Luke Kornet from the Knicks because he's flashed some stretch potential this past season. In general, the Thunder has to make some tweaks to their roster to get into contention in the Western Conference and Westbrook holds the key to their future. If his play continues to decline, then the team has to find some way to make up for any possible loss of production. On the other hand, if this season was just a fluke, then the Thunder could become a prime contender in the Western Conference for the next few seasons.

ORLANDO MAGIC

Season in Review

The Orlando Magic came into this season with very few expectations because they were still a team in transition. The front office moved on from the previous regime by replacing the last season's head coach, Frank Vogel with former Charlotte Hornets coach, Steve Clifford. The team didn't really make any major changes to the roster, but the Magic were able to take advantage of being in a weakened Eastern Conference. It also helped that Nikola Vucevic had a career best season that enabled him to make his first All-Star team. Therefore, they picked up a few extra wins and were able to hang around the fringes of the Eastern Conference playoff race for most of the season. Their play really picked up in the last month of the season and they ended up making the playoffs for the first time in seven years.

Clifford is known around coaching circles as being one of the league's better defensive coaches due to his previous work with the Van Gundy brothers. This season, his team's performance on defense lived up to his reputation and the Magic were able to compete in the Eastern Conference by being one of the NBA's best defensive teams. In fact, Orlando ranked in the top ten in Defensive Efficiency. Despite not having any standout individual defenders, the Magic defended well as a team because they were very good at steering opponents away from the high yield areas of the floor, as they were effective at protecting the rim and limiting their opponents' Three-Point Attempts. On the other hand, the team's youth and inexperience made them susceptible to giving up a few open mid-range shots. However, their ability to limit high yield shots outweighed this negative and Orlando was generally good at forcing misses, as they ranked in the top ten in Opponents' Effective Field Goal Percentage. In addition to being able to force more misses, the team's improved structure and rotation schemes allowed them to stay out of foul trouble, so Orlando became one of the league's best teams at keeping opponents off the free throw line to the point where they finished in the top ten in Opponent Free Throws per Field Goal Attempt. From a physical standpoint, the Magic was one of the league's bigger teams because they only had one player on the roster that was shorter than 6'3". As a result of having a lot of length and size, the team was one of the league's most effective defensive rebounding teams and they wound up in the top five in Defensive Rebound Percentage. The only real negative that Orlando showed was that they weren't really able to force turnovers at a high rate, as they ranked in the bottom third in Opponents' Turnover Percentage. Their relative inability to create turnovers may have been a byproduct of their conservative rotation scheme, as they had to compensate for the team's lack of quality on-ball defenders. If they can bring in better individual defenders, the team's defense could improve and be even better in the future.

Even though the Magic greatly improved on the defensive end, they still struggled to score efficiently, and they were among the league's worst offensive teams, ranking in the bottom third of the league in Offensive Efficiency. Even though Vucevic produced at an All-Star level, the team had difficulty generating quality shots on a regular basis. Some of this was tied to their style, as they played at a very slow pace and they didn't really move the ball very much. As a result, Orlando had to take a lot of difficult shots because they couldn't get easy looks around the rim. Because of this, they were very jump shot dependent and ended up having to take a lot of long twos. This hurt the team's overall efficiency and they ranked in the bottom half of the league in Effective Field Goal Percentage. Additionally, because of the lack of movement in their offense, they didn't put enough pressure on opposing defensive players to draw fouls, so they posted one of the league's worst Free Throw Attempt Rates. They also didn't grab offensive rebounds with great frequency, but this was probably a part of the team's defensive strategy, as the Magic often punted the offensive boards to be more effective at playing transition defense. As a positive, because the team was taking a more conservative, defense-oriented approach, Orlando reduced their turnover rate to the point where they ranked in the top ten in Turnover Percentage.

The Magic took a step forward by making the playoffs this season. The team's future is uncertain at this point because Vucevic is set to hit free agency this summer and the Magic have invested their last two first round picks in young big men like Mohamed Bamba and Jonathan Isaac. Therefore, they may be a little more willing to take a slight step back to develop those players rather than retain Vucevic. If they decide to continue to rebuild around their younger players, it may still take them another year or two for them to return to the playoffs because their roster isn't especially balanced. If they find some high-end perimeter prospects to pair with their interior players, then the Magic could have a fairly promising future and build on their improvement from this past season. Otherwise, they may still be competitive, but they might be too flawed to be a high-end playoff team in the Eastern Conference next season.

2019-20 Outlook

Players Under Contract for 2019-20

* Age and Salary numbers are for 2019-20. See page 9 for explanation for Cap Value and RCV. A number in parentheses indicates that the value is negative.

	Age	Salary	Years Left	2018-19 Cap Value	RCV
Aaron Gordon	24	$19.83M	2	$7.85M	$28.43M
Evan Fournier	27	$17.00M	Player Option	$4.00M	$8.21M
Timofey Mozgov	33	$16.72M	0	($16.00M)	($15.69M)
Markelle Fultz	21	$9.75M	Team Option	($5.77M)	($17.11M)
D.J. Augustin	32	$7.25M	0	$25.49M	$19.58M
Jonathan Isaac	22	$5.81M	Team Option	$16.08M	$15.86M
Mohamed Bamba	21	$5.70M	2 Team Options	$4.23M	$10.02M
Melvin Frazier	23	$1.42M	Team Option	($1.30M)	($3.60M)

Orlando used the stretch provision to waive C.J. Watson on July 10, 2017 and they will be assessed a cap hit of **$333,333** until the end of the 2019-20 season.

Two-Way Contracts

* In this section, listings are read: Player, Current Age, Height, Weight, College or Country

- Troy Caupain, 23, 6'4", 210, Cincinnati
- Amile Jefferson, 25, 6'9", 222, Duke

2019 Free Agents

* Age and Salary numbers are for 2019-20. See page 9 for explanation for Cap Value and RCV. A number in parentheses indicates that the value is negative.

	Age	Status	Salary	2018-19 Cap Value	RCV
Wesley Iwundu	25	Team Option	$1.62M	$8.00M	$6.18M
Jerian Grant	27	Restricted	N/A	$5.96M	N/A
Jarell Martin	25	Restricted	N/A	$0.15M	N/A
Khem Birch	27	Restricted	N/A	$11.08M	N/A
Nikola Vucevic	29	Unrestricted	N/A	$39.31M	N/A
Terrence Ross	28	Unrestricted	N/A	$14.17M	N/A
Michael Carter-Williams	28	Unrestricted	N/A	$2.97M	N/A

Estimated Cap Space for 2019 Free Agency

Note: Salary cap estimated to be at $109 million for 2019-20, as of September 17, 2018.

- **$25.2 million**, maximum cap space, if Iwundu's option is not picked up
- **$23.5 million**, if Iwundu's option is picked up

2019 Draft Picks and Future Assets until 2022

- 2019 own first round – **16th overall**
- 2019 second round from Brooklyn via Charlotte and Memphis (Ivan Rabb trade, Courtney Lee three-team trade, Juan Pablo Vaulet trade) – **46th overall**
- 2020 own first round
- 2020 own second round
- 2021 own first round
- 2021 own second round
- 2022 own first round
- 2022 own second round

Draft Rights Held

	Year	Round	Pick
Justin Jackson	2018	2	43
Janis Timma	2013	2	60
Fran Vazquez	2005	1	11

Offseason Recommendations

The Orlando Magic are in an interesting position because they surprisingly made the playoffs and they are expected to have some cap space available this summer. However, Orlando has not really been a free agent destination in recent years and there's a distinct possibility that their season was something of a fluke because the bottom of the conference was weaker than usual. Therefore, the team should take a more patient approach this summer and try to sort their situation out. Specifically, the Magic have important players on three different timelines and their roster is still rather imbalanced, so the team's direction is not exactly clear at the moment.

    First off, the team has to make decision on whether or not to re-sign Nikola Vucevic, as he'll be an unrestricted free agent this summer. Vucevic has been the team's most consistently productive player, but he might not match the team's timeline because he's in his late-20's and the rest of the roster is significantly younger. Also, it might be risky to sign him to a long-term contract because his position is somewhat devalued, and he's missed a lot of games in the past due to minor injuries. As a result, it might be **more worthwhile for the Magic to work out a sign-and-trade deal to take back some value for Vucevic, preferably a perimeter player or two, to recoup some value for losing**

him. From there, Orlando has to figure out what to do with Aaron Gordon because his skill set overlaps with Jonathan Isaac and he's the only productive player on the roster entering his prime years, so he might not be the best fit with the team's base of young talent. However, Gordon may have some trade value because he signed a front-loaded contract last summer, which would make it easier for the Magic to find a suitable trade partner. If **they could swap Gordon for an equally talented perimeter player, they should really consider making a deal** because all of their most valuable players are at their best on the interior, so this could work to balance out their roster. Otherwise, if no deal comes to fruition, they should continue to expand Isaac's shooting range. In his two seasons in the league, he has demonstrated that he can repeat his shooting stroke because he has made almost 84% of his free throws, so there may be some potential for him to become a decent three-point shooter in the future. The team did acquire Markelle Fultz at the trade deadline, but he really can't be looked at as a real solution until he shows that he can play a full season and take perimeter shots without hesitation. At this stage, he's a wild card that may or may not pan out. The Orlando Magic have some key decisions to make this offseason, but they shouldn't buy into the relative success of this season too much because they were only two games above 0.500 this past season. If they can find some quality young perimeter players to go along with their solid base of interior players, they could solidify their place as a playoff team in the Eastern Conference either next season or in a couple seasons after that. Otherwise, if they try to cash in their chips now, they could get stuck in mediocrity for the foreseeable future.

PHILADELPHIA 76ERS

Season in Review

After years of asset accumulation and patient rebuilding through "the Process", new General Manager, Elton Brand quickly made his mark by dramatically shifting the direction of the Philadelphia 76ers. Specifically, he pushed all of the team's chips into the middle and decided to go all-in. He started by trading Robert Covington and Dario Saric to Minnesota for Jimmy Butler. Then, around the trade deadline, the Sixers flipped a series of assets including multiple first round picks and Markelle Fultz to acquire Tobias Harris, Boban Marjanovic, Mike Scott, Jonathon Simmons and James Ennis to provide more reinforcements to their rotation. These moves allowed the Sixers to become one of the best teams in the Eastern Conference, as they were able to land a top-four playoff seed.

Despite all of the various roster changes, the Sixers succeeded in the regular season because they were one of the league's best offensive teams, ranking in the top ten in Offensive Efficiency. From a style perspective, head coach, Brett Brown maintained a lot of core principles because the Sixers relied on a lot of quick ball movement and they played at a fairly fast pace. However, they incorporated some new elements to adjust to their new personnel. In particular, they put Jimmy Butler on the ball more in isolation situations and as the ball handler in pick-and-rolls to give them another way to create offense. From there, the Sixers got All-Star seasons from both Joel Embiid and Ben Simmons. In addition to this, J.J. Redick continued to be a reliable outside shooter and the addition of Harris gave them another high-end player to space the floor even more. With this level of high-end production, the offense was very effective across the board and they were average or better in almost every situation, according to Synergy. Because the Sixers were good at generating quality looks, they were one of the league's best shooting teams, as they finished in the top ten in Effective Field Goal Percentage. They also got to the free throw line at a very high rate because Embiid, Simmons and Butler consistently put pressure on defenders by aggressively attacking the basket. As a result, the team ranked in the top five in Free Throw Attempt Rate. The Sixers weren't quite as aggressive on the offensive glass as they were last year, mainly because they were focusing on getting back to play better transition defense. Even with this tactical change, they were in the upper half of the league in Offensive Rebound Percentage. As a negative, the Sixers were still one of the league's most turnover prone teams, although they were a little better than they were a season ago. Even still, they ranked in the bottom third of the league in Turnover Percentage this past season.

On the defensive end, the team's performance slipped a bit because they couldn't become a cohesive unit until the latter portion of the season. Even with a decrease in effectiveness, the Sixers were still one of the league's better defensive teams, as they ranked in the upper half of the league in Defensive Efficiency. Because the Sixers frequently had a size and length advantage over their opponents, they were pretty effective on the defensive boards, as they were in the top ten in Defensive Rebounding Percentage. Additionally, opposing teams struggled to shoot efficiently against them, mainly because they were one of the league's best teams at defending in the high yield areas. Specifically, the shot blocking abilities of Embiid allowed them to be effective at protecting the rim. Also, the team overall was one of the league's best at defending the three-point line, as they excelled at limiting their opponent's Three-Point Percentage and preventing Three-Point Attempts. This success at defending high yield shot attempts allowed the Sixers to rank in the top ten in Opponents' Effective Field Goal Percentage. However, the personnel shuffling over the course of the season had some negative effects. For starters, they had to be a bit more conservative with their rotations to allow the new players to adjust, so they couldn't be very aggressive to pressure opponents. As a result, they were one of the league's worst teams at forcing turnovers. Furthermore, the constant change in personnel made them prone to bouts of miscommunication. Therefore, the team was susceptible to allowing scores on cuts and they had some breakdowns in pick-and-rolls. They also were put in more situations where they had to foul, and they ended up allowing opponents to get to the free throw line fairly frequently. Specifically, they were in the bottom third of the league in Opponent Free Throws per Field Goal Attempt this past season.

  The Sixers took a sizeable risk by cashing in their chips to acquire Butler and Harris and they still fell short, as they lost in the second round on a buzzer beater from Kawhi Leonard in Game 7. They went all-in for this season, but now their roster situation is in flux because many players are set to hit free agency. Namely, Butler and Harris are going to hit the market this summer, so there's a chance that they could go elsewhere and leave the team with very little help and depleted assets to build around Embiid and Simmons. If they can re-sign one of those two key free agents, it could alleviate some concerns and the Sixers should be able to stay in contention in the Eastern Conference for the next few seasons. Otherwise, if the worst-case scenario happens, then they may have to take a slight step back to replenish their assets to build a more balanced roster and put the team on a more sustainable long-term path.

Players Under Contract for 2019-20

* Age and Salary numbers are for 2019-20. See page 9 for explanation for Cap Value and RCV. A number in parentheses indicates that the value is negative.

	Age	Salary	Years Left	2018-19 Cap Value	RCV
Joel Embiid	25	$27.50M	3	$20.23M	$42.97M
Ben Simmons	23	$8.11M	0	$37.03M	$38.14M
Jonathon Simmons*	30	$5.70M	0	($1.65M)	$2.23M
Zhaire Smith	20	$3.06M	2 Team Options	($1.93M)	($8.94M)
Jonah Bolden*	24	$1.70M	2	$5.30M	$16.51M

*Jonathon Simmons' contract for 2019-20 is guaranteed for **$1.00M** until July 1, 2019. The 2020-21 and 2021-22 contracts for Jonah Bolden are not guaranteed.

Two-Way Contracts

* In this section, listings are read: Player, Current Age, Height, Weight, College or Country
- Shake Milton, 22, 6'6", 207, SMU
- Haywood Highsmith, 22, 6'7", 220, Wheeling Jesuit

2019 Free Agents

* Age and Salary numbers are for 2019-20. See page 9 for explanation for Cap Value and RCV. A number in parentheses indicates that the value is negative.

	Age	Status	Salary	2018-19 Cap Value	RCV
Jimmy Butler	30	Player Option	$19.84M	$18.35M	$23.05M
Tobias Harris	27	Unrestricted	N/A	$23.70M	N/A
J.J. Redick	35	Unrestricted	N/A	$17.88M	N/A
Boban Marjanovic	31	Unrestricted	N/A	$7.62M	N/A
Mike Scott	31	Unrestricted	N/A	$4.73M	N/A
Justin Patton	22	Unrestricted	N/A	($2.58M)	N/A
James Ennis	29	Unrestricted	N/A	$10.76M	N/A
Furkan Korkmaz	22	Unrestricted	N/A	$4.31M	N/A
T.J. McConnell	27	Unrestricted	N/A	$14.01M	N/A
Amir Johnson	32	Unrestricted	N/A	$4.20M	N/A

Estimated Cap Space for 2019 Free Agency

Note: Salary cap estimated to be at $109 million for 2019-20, as of September 17, 2018.

- **$67.6 million**, maximum cap space, most likely scenario, if Butler opts out and Jonathon Simmons is waived
- **$62.9 million**, if Butler opts out and Jonathon Simmons remains on the roster

2019 Draft Picks and Future Assets until 2022

- 2019 own first round – **24th overall**
- 2019 second round from Cleveland via New York and Orlando (Markelle Fultz trade to Orlando, Kyle O'Quinn trade to New York, J.R. Smith three-team trade) – **33rd overall**
- 2019 second round from Chicago via L.A. Lakers (Isaac Bonga trade, Jose Calderon trade to L.A. Lakers) – **34th overall**
- 2019 second round from Sacramento (Casper Ware/Marquis Teague trade, Jason Kidd head coach compensation, Luc Mbah a Moute trade to Sacramento) – **42nd overall**
- 2019 own second round – **54th overall**
- 2020 own first round, lottery protected, otherwise goes to L.A. Clippers (Tobias Harris trade)
- 2020 first round from Oklahoma City via Orlando and Philadelphia, top 20 protected (Markelle Fultz trade to Orlando, Anzejs Pasecniks trade, Jerami Grant trade to Oklahoma City)
- 2020 own second round
- 2020 second round from either Brooklyn or New York, whichever is most favorable (Willy Hernangomez trade to New York, Brandon Davies/Andrei Kirilenko trade)
- 2020 second round from Dallas, protected from picks 56 to 60 (Nerlens Noel trade)
- 2021 own first round
- 2021 own second round, Houston has the option to swap picks (James Ennis trade)
- 2021 second round from New York (Willy Hernangomez trade)
- 2021 second round from Denver (Wilson Chandler trade)
- 2022 own first round
- 2022 own second round, if less favorable than Denver, otherwise goes to Minnesota (Wilson Chandler trade, Jimmy Butler trade)
- 2022 second round from Toronto (Malachi Richardson trade)

Draft Rights Held

	Year	Round	Pick
Anzejs Pasecniks	2017	1	25
Mathias Lessort	2017	2	50
Vasilije Micic	2014	2	52

Offseason Recommendations

The Sixers are going to come into this summer in a relatively fluid state because even though they will have a lot of cap space to work with, they will also have a lot of holes on the roster to fill, as Joel Embiid and Ben Simmons will be only two members of their primary rotation under contract for next season. As a result, the Sixers have some important decisions to make. Most notably, they have to figure out if they want to re-sign Jimmy Butler or Tobias Harris or bring them both back. Butler and Harris have established themselves as All-Star caliber players and both could be due for max level contracts. The team could decide to bring both players back, but Simmons is in the last season of his rookie contract and he's due for a big raise. Therefore, it may not make sense to have four players on max contracts because it could press the team against the luxury tax and limit their flexibility, so the Sixers probably have to choose between Butler and Harris. **Of the two, it may be more sensible to re-sign Harris because he's three years younger than Butler and his lower volume skill set may be a better long-term fit with Simmons and Embiid**. Also, signing Butler to a long-term, max contract could be pretty risky. After all, Butler's next contract will cover his early 30's and he's something of an injury risk due his very aggressive, high contact playing style. This suggests that there's a significant chance that the back-end of Butler's contract could hurt the Sixers in the future, whereas they might able to stomach the back-end of Harris' next deal because there's simply less wear and tear on Harris' body. From there, they could look to re-sign some of their role players as long as the price tag is reasonable. Ideally, **they should bring back J.J. Redick, Mike Scott, James Ennis and Boban Marjanovic to keep the rotation relatively intact**. Redick and Scott would provide reliable outside shooting to open up space for Embiid and Simmons. Ennis would give them a three-and-D wing player to boost the team's depth on the wings. Finally, Marjanovic allows the Sixers to have one of the league's most effective backup centers to help the team manage Embiid's minutes over the long season. Then with the remaining space, the team could target some additional three-and-D wings to help the team maintain its defensive versatility and find a cost effective pick-and-roll ball handler to offset the possible loss of Butler's shot creating abilities. To fill the latter role, the Sixers could try to sign someone like Jeremy Lin to a short-term deal because when healthy, he's been rated good or better as a pick-and-roll ball handler by Synergy in every season that he's been in the league. The Sixers have a lot of moving parts to put together their roster for next season, but they still should be in a good spot because they have two very solid building blocks in Embiid and Simmons. Even in a worst-case scenario, they should be able to cobble together a solid enough team to be one of the top teams in Eastern Conference next season.

PHOENIX SUNS

Season in Review

In the early part of last summer, it seemed like the Phoenix Suns were taking baby steps towards moving in the right direction. They hired former Utah Jazz assistant, Igor Kokoskov to be their new head coach and they came away with DeAndre Ayton, Mikal Bridges and Elie Okobo from last year's draft. Then, they made a couple of relatively head-scratching moves by adding veterans like Trevor Ariza and Ryan Anderson that didn't exactly fit the team's timeline. From there, the wheels came off before the season really started and the Suns fired their General Manager, Ryan McDonough in October and replaced him with James Jones. Over the course of the season, the team's usual dysfunction and chaos set in to the point where Ayton passive aggressively vented some frustrations about his role late in the season and the Suns once again finished with one of the NBA's worst records.

As a team, the Suns were pretty bad on both sides of the ball, as they ranked near the bottom of the league in both Offensive and Defensive Efficiency. The team didn't show many strengths overall, but it did a few things well on defense. Because the Suns were pretty young as a whole, they used their youth and energy to aggressively close out on perimeter shooters and jump passing lanes to force turnovers. They ended up finishing in the top ten in Opponents' Turnover Percentage and Opponents' Three-Point Attempts. However, the Suns didn't play under control and they were usually caught out of position taking bad gambles. This allowed their opponents to get a lot of easy looks around the basket. It also didn't help that they only played one big man in their regular rotation. As a result, the Suns were rated as average or worse in almost every situation, according to Synergy. Their struggles to make effective rotations didn't allow them to be in any kind of position to force misses, grab defensive rebounds and keep opponents off the line and they wound up ranking near the bottom of the league in Opponents' Effective Field Goal Percentage, Defensive Rebound Percentage and Opponent Free Throws per Field Goal Attempts. Offensively, the Suns didn't demonstrate any real strengths because they ranked in the bottom third of the league in almost every component metric. From a style standpoint, they tried to incorporate some more ball movement, but it wasn't especially effective because plays would often break down, leading players to take inefficient shots. Specifically, the Suns often settled for mid-range shots and weren't effective at generating high yield shot attempts. In fact, they were in the bottom half of the league in Three-Point Attempts and shots taken inside of five feet. As a result, they were among the league's worst shooting teams. The Suns were also one of the league's most turnover prone teams because of their youth and inexperience. On the positive side, they became more effective at drawing fouls as the season progressed and they wound up finishing in the upper half of the league in Free Throw Attempt Rate.

From an individual standpoint, the Suns may have some worthwhile pieces to build around. Devin Booker signed a five-year max extension in the offseason, and he continued his improvement to the point where he had his best season as a pro. Additionally, Ayton and Bridges had strong rookie seasons. Ayton was arguably the Suns most effective player, as he led the team in Win Shares this past season. Also, Bridges flashed some promise as a three-and-D wing player. Specifically, he posted a solid True Shooting Percentage and according to Synergy, he defended well in the majority of situations. From there, the team got solid seasons from T.J. Warren and Richaun Holmes, and Kelly Oubre's efficiency improved significantly after he arrived in a trade from Washington. On the negative side, Josh Jackson's development has stalled a bit because he's still a high volume, low efficiency shooter. This is mainly because he's miscast as an on-ball shot creator, as he hasn't been effective in any on-ball situation in each of his two seasons in the league. Because of this, opposing defenses have had success in baiting him to take outside shots to the point where his True Shooting Percentage has remained under 50%. To change Jackson's trajectory, the Suns will need to adjust his role to minimize these weaknesses and give him a better chance to play to his strengths.

Generally speaking, the Suns continue to be stuck at the bottom of the league because they haven't done much to stabilize their overall operation. In fact, the team fired Kokoskov at the end of the season and replaced him with former Pelicans coach, Monty Williams. As long as their situation remains chaotic and disorganized, the roster isn't really going to matter very much because there's always a strong possibility that everything is still going to be mismanaged. As a result, the future doesn't look very promising and it's likely that they will still be rebuilding for the next few years. If they miraculously change their direction by becoming a more disciplined, rational organization, then they could gradually take steps to eventually become competitive in the future. However, nothing about Robert Sarver's ownership history has indicated that this could happen anytime soon.

Players Under Contract for 2019-20

* Age and Salary numbers are for 2019-20. See page 9 for explanation for Cap Value and RCV. A number in parentheses indicates that the value is negative.

	Age	Salary	Years Left	2018-19 Cap Value	RCV
Devin Booker	23	$27.25M	4	$23.93M	($25.48M)
T.J. Warren	26	$10.81M	2	$2.64M	$19.14M
DeAndre Ayton	21	$9.56M	2 Team Options	$25.14M	$75.09M
Josh Jackson	22	$7.06M	Team Option	($2.45M)	($5.23M)
Mikal Bridges	23	$4.16M	2 Team Options	$14.56M	$43.21M
Elie Okobo*	22	$1.42M	1 + Team Option	$0.24M	$0.11M
De'Anthony Melton	21	$1.42M	0	$2.86M	$2.64M
Ray Spalding*	22	$1.42M	0	$0.37M	$0.04M
Jimmer Fredette*		$1.42M	0	($0.65M)	($1.71M)

* Okobo's contract for 2020-21 is not guaranteed. Spalding's contract for 2019-20 is not guaranteed. Fredette's contract for 2019-20 is not guaranteed.

Two-Way Contracts

* In this section, listings are read: Player, Current Age, Height, Weight, College or Country

- George King, 25, 6'6", 225, Colorado

2019 Free Agents

* Age and Salary numbers are for 2019-20. See page 9 for explanation for Cap Value and RCV. A number in parentheses indicates that the value is negative.

	Age	Status	Salary	2018-19 Cap Value	RCV
Tyler Johnson	27	Player Option	$19.25M	($5.56M)	($1.41M)
Kelly Oubre	24	Restricted	N/A	$14.28M	N/A
Dragan Bender	22	Unrestricted	N/A	($0.23M)	N/A
Troy Daniels	28	Unrestricted	N/A	$0.47M	N/A
Richaun Holmes	26	Unrestricted	N/A	$19.71M	N/A
Jamal Crawford	39	Unrestricted	N/A	$4.57M	N/A

Estimated Cap Space for 2019 Free Agency

Note: Salary cap estimated to be at $109 million for 2019-20, as of September 17, 2018.

- **$47.3 million**, maximum cap space, if Tyler Johnson opts out, Spalding and Fredette are waived
- **$25.2 million**, most likely scenario, Tyler Johnson opts in, Spalding and Fredette remain on the roster

2019 Draft Picks and Future Assets until 2022

- 2019 own first round – **6th overall**
- 2019 own second round – **32nd overall**
- 2020 own first round
- 2020 first round from Milwaukee, top 7 protected (Eric Bledsoe trade)
- 2020 own second round
- 2021 own first round
- 2021 own second round, protected from picks 31 to 35, otherwise goes to Brooklyn (Darrell Arthur/Jared Dudley trade)
- 2022 own first round
- 2022 own second round

Draft Rights Held

None

Offseason Recommendations

Phoenix is entering this offseason in the same situation that they were in last year. Specifically, they will be a team with plenty of cap space to work with, but the Suns are so far away that it wouldn't really make sense to spend big on free agents. Also, their situation has been so chaotic that they probably will not be able to bring in any free agent of substance without a significant overpay. Therefore, the Suns should **do the opposite of what they did last summer and instead, they should look to take a more sensible approach and rent out their cap space to accumulate future assets**. This way, the team would gain some more room to maneuver or more opportunities to expand their core through the draft.

Because their situation has been constantly changing in the last four seasons, the Suns have been operating without any kind of consistent structure. As a result, they haven't really defined anyone's role, so their roster has always been managed rather inefficiently. This is even true for one of their best players, Devin Booker because he's had to produce while playing different roles for four different head coaches throughout his career. It's important for the Suns to clarify Booker's role because his max extension is going to kick in next season, and he will need to raise his level of play, so his production matches his high salary figures. To do this, the team will **need to move Booker to the point and make him their primary ball handler**. Skill-wise, Booker has improved his playmaking skills every year that he's been in the league and this season, he set career highs in Assists per Game and Assist Percentage. Therefore, he should have the necessary skills to transition to being a full-time point guard. This move would accomplish a couple of things. First off, the Suns would be able to attack defenses sooner because the ball would already be in Booker's hands, so they won't waste additional seconds trying to get him the ball. More importantly, using Booker at the point would allow the Suns to put an extra wing player on the floor to increase their length and defensive versatility. From this point, **Phoenix would then need to target cost effective two-way wing players** to surround Booker and DeAndre Ayton to complement their skills and give those players the best chance to succeed. On another note, the Suns will probably have to change Josh Jackson's role because he doesn't quite fit in as a traditional wing player due to his lack of outside shooting. The team may just have to simplify things a bit and concentrate on the few things that he does well. In particular, he's much better around the basket than he is on the perimeter. According to Synergy, he's been a very effective cutter in his two seasons in the league and in a limited number of possessions, he's shown some effectiveness as a post-up player. To play to these strengths, the Suns should move Jackson to the bench and utilize him in a post-up perimeter player role similar to how the Warriors use Shaun Livingston. A switch to this type of role could unlock some additional efficiency and allow him to be a more significant contributor in the future. These tactical adjustments are dependent on whether or not the team follows a consistent and organized structure. The Suns haven't done so over the last decade, so they will need to get their house in order. If they can straighten out their overall organization, they could make their situation work and eventually become competitive in the Western Conference. Otherwise, if they continue to make short-sighted moves and constantly change the staff around them, the Suns will remain in a rebuilding phase for the foreseeable future.

PORTLAND TRAIL BLAZERS

Season in Review

The Portland Trail Blazers seemingly find new ways to sneak up on people. After all, they have been coming into the last few seasons with a roster that seems flawed on paper and they don't make any attention grabbing moves in the offseason to suggest that they could improve. This season, Portland followed along the same pattern, as they kept their rotation pretty much intact and only added Seth Curry in the offseason. By maintaining their continuity from last season, the Blazers were able to get productive seasons from their high-powered backcourt of Damian Lillard and C.J. McCollum as well as a career best season from Jusuf Nurkic. As a result, Portland was a solid playoff team in the Western Conference for pretty much the whole year and wound up with a top four seed this past season.

Over the last few seasons, head coach, Terry Stotts has been very good at adapting his system in a way that best suits his roster. This means that Portland will sometimes have more of an offensive lean and in other years, they may be more defensive-minded. This season, Stotts was able to help keep the Blazers near the top of the Western Conference by molding them into one of the best offensive teams in the league, as they ranked in the top five in Offensive Efficiency. Stylistically, the Blazers had a pretty simple approach, as they relied on a pick-and-roll heavy attack that featured their two playmaking guards, Lillard and McCollum. To make this attack more effective than it was last year, Stotts moved Evan Turner to the bench and replaced him in the starting lineup with either Jake Layman or Maurice Harkless to provide the Blazers with a more efficient shooting option. As a result, Portland was more effective at generating quality shots and they ranked in the upper half of the league in Effective Field Goal Percentage. Additionally, the Blazers were one of the best free throw shooting teams in the league, as they ranked in the top five in Free Throw Percentage. This allowed them to make the most of their free throw opportunities even though they got to the free throw line at an average rate. Because they kept the ball in the hands of their best players, they didn't commit turnovers very often, as they finished in the top ten in Turnover Percentage. Furthermore, the team got improved play from their primary interior players, Nurkic and Zach Collins and their aggressiveness and activity allowed the Blazers to be the league's most effective offensive rebounding team, which was evidenced the fact that they posted the league's best Offensive Rebound Percentage.

At the defensive end of the floor, the Blazers slipped a bit because opponents did a better job of finding ways to attack their defense, so they fell to being a slightly below average unit this past season. Last season, Portland was an effective defensive team because they consistently steered opponents into the inefficient parts of the floor. They tried to employ the same strategy this season, but they weren't nearly as successful in their execution. Positively speaking, they were very good at limiting their opponents' three-point shots and often forced them into taking long twos. Because of this, they were still one of the league's better teams at forcing misses, as they ranked in the upper half of the league in Opponents' Effective Field Goal Percentage. They were also generally good at avoiding fouls, but they were only around average at keeping teams off the free throw line. In addition to this, the play of Nurkic and Al-Farouq Aminu allowed the Blazers to be one of the best defensive rebounding teams in the NBA, as they finished in the top five in Defensive Rebound Percentage. On the negative side, opposing teams were much more effective at using the pick-and-roll game to generate quality looks against the defense. As a result, they were a little more vulnerable around the basket and allowed more shots at the rim. This forced their defense to bring additional help, so many of the threes that opponents did get were open looks. The additional scrambling put them out of position, which made them unable to pressure their opponents to force turnovers. Because of this, Portland was ranked last in the league in Opponents' Turnover Percentage this past season.

      The Blazers continued to be a very competitive team in the Western Conference. Even though Nurkic was forced to miss the end of the season due to a leg fracture, the Blazers overcame this loss to reach the Western Conference Finals, but they were later swept by Golden State. Over the course of the regular season, they have been able to maximize their roster without making major moves, but it might not be enough to become legitimate title contenders. If they can find some way to add a significant piece to this core group, they could step up to the next level and contend with the elite teams in the Western Conference. Otherwise, if they stay as they are, they will continue to be a solid playoff team as long as their core group is under contract.

Players Under Contract for 2019-20

* Age and Salary numbers are for 2019-20. See page 9 for explanation for Cap Value and RCV. A number in parentheses indicates that the value is negative.

	Age	Salary	Years Left	2018-19 Cap Value	RCV
Damian Lillard	29	$29.80M	1	$31.31M	$56.92M
C.J. McCollum	28	$27.56M	1	$5.29M	$11.00M
Evan Turner	31	$18.61M	0	($5.14M)	($5.44M)
Jusuf Nurkic*	25	$12.00M	2	$28.21M	$69.63M
Maurice Harkless	26	$11.51M	0	$5.74M	$5.48M
Meyers Leonard	27	$11.29M	0	$3.01M	($0.52M)
Zach Collins	22	$4.24M	Team Option	$11.43M	$13.62M
Skal Labissiere	23	$2.34M	0	$0.14M	$2.69M
Anfernee Simons	20	$2.15M	2 Team Options	($0.95M)	($5.44M)
Gary Trent, Jr.	21	$1.42M	1	($1.23M)	($3.88M)

* Nurkic's contract for 2021-22 is partially guaranteed for **$4.00M**. Portland used the stretch provision to waive Andrew Nicholson on August 30, 2017 and they will be assessed a cap hit of **$2.84M** until the end of the 2023-24 season. Portland also used the stretch provision to waive Anderson Varejao on February 18, 2016 and they will be assessed a cap hit of **$1.91M** until the end of the 2020-21 season. Finally, Portland used the stretch provision to waive Festus Ezeli on June 30, 2017 and they will be assessed a cap hit of **$333,333** until the end of the 2019-20 season.

Two-Way Contracts

None

2019 Free Agents

* Age and Salary numbers are for 2019-20. See page 9 for explanation for Cap Value and RCV. A number in parentheses indicates that the value is negative.

	Age	Status	Salary	2018-19 Cap Value	RCV
Jake Layman	25	Restricted	N/A	$13.91M	N/A
Al-Farouq Aminu	29	Unrestricted	N/A	$20.69M	N/A
Rodney Hood	27	Unrestricted	N/A	$12.72M	N/A
Seth Curry	29	Unrestricted	N/A	$9.98M	N/A
Enes Kanter	27	Unrestricted	N/A	$9.91M	N/A

Estimated Cap Space for 2019 Free Agency

Note: Salary cap estimated to be at $109 million for 2019-20, as of September 17, 2018.

- **Over the cap**, but not over luxury tax, can only use exceptions
  - **Non-taxpayer Mid-Level Exception**
  - **Bi-Annual Exception**

2019 Draft Picks and Future Assets until 2022

- 2019 own first round – **25th overall**
- 2020 own first round
- 2020 own second round, top 55 protected, otherwise goes to Brooklyn via Atlanta, Cleveland and Orlando (Maurice Harkless trade, Joe Harris trade to Orlando, Richard Jefferson trade to Atlanta, Jeremy Lin trade to Atlanta)
- 2021 own first round
- 2021 second round from Miami (Brian Roberts trade)
- 2022 own first round
- 2022 own second round

Draft Rights Held

	Year	Round	Pick
Dani Diez	2015	2	54
Milovan Rakovic	2007	2	60

Offseason Recommendations

The Portland Trail Blazers are in an interesting position because they are very close to getting out from under the luxury tax, as the contracts of Evan Turner, Maurice Harkless and Meyers Leonard will expire after next season. This means that the Blazers could have as much as $30 million of cap space in the summer of 2020 if they don't make any major commitments this summer. This will require Portland to pull off a tough balancing act because a few key rotational players are set to be free agents. Of the team's free agents, the most important ones are Al-Farouq Aminu, who has been a starter for the last couple of seasons and Jake Layman, who emerged as key rotational piece this season. Of the two, Layman might be the easiest to re-sign because he's a restricted free agent and the team has matching rights. As long as he doesn't sign a large offer sheet with another team, the Blazers could bring him back on a reasonable short-term deal. From there, the market will dictate their decisions on their other free agents. If they bring back any of them on one-year deals that won't put them over the apron, then it would be worthwhile to re-sign them.

Otherwise, **the Blazers should look to bargain hunt for shooters and two-way wing players that would be willing to accept a minimum salary to allow them to keep their cap space for the summer of 2020**. In the meantime, they could also shop around their expiring contracts to see if they could land a big piece this summer as a way to hedge their bets. After all, Portland hasn't really been a free agent destination, so the trade market could offer another option to add another big piece, preferably a wing player or combo forward to go along with the trio of Lillard, McCollum and Nurkic. Depending on their agenda, Orlando could be a match if they elect to lean more on their younger players and the Blazers could offer a package of Turner's contract, a young player like Anfernee Simons and a draft pick to land a player like Aaron Gordon to replace Aminu and potentially give them a more dynamic fourth option. However, if they don't find a workable trade, then the team shouldn't rush to make a move because they can just let those contracts expire and get the cap space. Even though the Blazers may have to retool their roster a little bit with little short-term flexibility, they still have a very productive base to work with that will allow them to stay competitive in the Western Conference. If they avoid making rash, short-sighted decisions this summer, then they could give themselves a chance to make one more big push with this core group to put them in a better position to become legitimate contenders. Otherwise, they will stay as they are and be a very good regular season team that consistently finds production from unheralded sources and can occasionally make a deep run in the playoffs if they get some favorable matchups.

SACRAMENTO KINGS

Season in Review

Not much was expected from the Sacramento Kings this past season, as they were set to develop around their base of young talent. However, even in a loaded Western Conference, the Kings exceeded all expectations and spent most of the season competing for a playoff spot. In his typical fashion, head coach, Dave Joerger maximized his team's performance and they were much better than their point differentials would indicate. This is mainly because the team saw a significant improvement from both De'Aaron Fox and Buddy Hield, and they wound up becoming one of the league's most dynamic young backcourts. They also had a very strong rookie season out of Marvin Bagley III to the point where he was arguably the team's most effective player even though he came off the bench. Overall, the Kings took a major step forward this past season and even though they missed the playoffs this season, they could eventually get there in the coming years.

The Kings were a slightly below average team on a per-possession on both sides of the ball, but they showed considerable improvement on offense. This is mainly because they changed their style for the better this season. Instead of walking the ball up and pounding the ball into the post like they did last season, the Kings moved to a much faster attack to better utilize Fox's raw speed and they incorporated more ball movement into the offense. Additionally, they spread the floor with more credible three-point threats. As a result, Sacramento was one of the league's best per-possession transition teams and ranked in the top five in Three-Point Percentage. More impressively, they were able to increase the tempo while cutting down on their turnovers to the point where they ranked in the top ten in Turnover Percentage. Even though the Kings took a more perimeter-oriented approach and their lineups skewed smaller, they were above average on the offensive boards and they posted an Offensive Rebound Percentage that was in the upper half of the league. As a byproduct of taking more perimeter shots, they didn't attack the basket as much, so they didn't really get to the free throw line very often. The Kings were also among the NBA's worst free throw shooting teams from a percentage standpoint because opposing teams could use the Hack-a-Shaq tactic on Willie Cauley-Stein to slow down the team's offense.

At the defensive end, the Kings were still a below average unit overall, but they improved significantly from the season before. The switch to a higher tempo approach made them much more aggressive when pressuring opponents and they had more freedom to jump passing lanes. As a result, the Kings were one of the league's best teams at forcing turnovers, as they ranked in the top ten in both Steals per Game and Opponents' Turnover Percentage. Though they still allowed opponents to take a lot of threes in volume, they were very active to close out on perimeter shooters to the point where they were among the league's more effective teams at limiting the opposing team's Three-Point Percentage. On the flip side, the Kings were still a young team that struggled to consistently grasp NBA defensive rotation schemes. Therefore, they were still prone to some breakdowns that allowed opponents to get open looks at the basket. They also didn't have a standout individual defender in their primary rotation, so opposing offenses could easily target their players in isolation situations. Because of all this, the Kings ranked in the bottom third of the league in Opponents' Effective Field Goal Percentage. They were also a bit foul prone, so opposing teams were able to get to the free throw line with a little more frequency. Finally, as a product of playing smaller, perimeter-oriented lineups, the Kings really struggled on the defensive glass, as they ranked among the league's worst teams in Defensive Rebound Percentage.

For the first time in years, the Sacramento Kings have shown some promise as a future contender in the Western Conference. After all, they have a solid young core in Fox, Hield and Bagley. Then, the trade deadline pickup of Harrison Barnes was another step in the right direction. Interestingly enough, the Kings elected to make a coaching change despite the team's vast improvement by letting Joerger go and immediately replacing him with Luke Walton. It's uncertain if this move will have any effect on the team's progress in any way, but Walton's philosophies do match up with the team's personnel. Therefore, the team could still continue on their upward trajectory even with a different head coach. From a personnel standpoint, if they can find some more complementary pieces to round out their roster, they could take the next step and be a solid playoff team next season. Otherwise, as long as their main core players don't regress, they should be a very competitive unit for years to come.

Players Under Contract for 2019-20

* Age and Salary numbers are for 2019-20. See page 9 for explanation for Cap Value and RCV. A number in parentheses indicates that the value is negative.

	Age	Salary	Years Left	2018-19 Cap Value	RCV
Marvin Bagley III	20	$8.56M	2 Team Options	$14.09M	$40.82M
Bogdan Bogdanovic	27	$8.53M	0	$9.09M	$10.33M
Nemanja Bjelica	31	$6.83M	1	$16.53M	$24.24M
De'Aaron Fox	22	$6.39M	Team Option	$27.81M	$34.76M
Buddy Hield	27	$4.86M	0	$30.14M	$23.04M
Yogi Ferrell*	26	$3.15M	0	$7.48M	$10.12M
Harry Giles	21	$2.58M	Team Option	$5.13M	$9.10M
Caleb Swanigan	22	$2.03M	Team Option	($1.96M)	($5.54M)
Frank Mason*	25	$1.62M	0	$1.55M	$2.77M

* Ferrell's contract for 2019-20 is not guaranteed. Mason's contract for 2019-20 is not guaranteed until October 15, 2019. Sacramento used the stretch provision to waive Matt Barnes on February 20, 2017 and they will be assessed a cap hit of **$2.13M** until the end of the 2019-20 season.

Two-Way Contracts

* In this section, listings are read: Player, Current Age, Height, Weight, College or Country

- Wenyen Gabriel, 21, 6'9", 205, Kentucky
- Troy Williams, 24, 6'7", 218, Indiana

2019 Free Agents

* Age and Salary numbers are for 2019-20. See page 9 for explanation for Cap Value and RCV. A number in parentheses indicates that the value is negative.

	Age	Status	Salary	2018-19 Cap Value	RCV
Harrison Barnes	27	Player Option	$25.10M	($2.31M)	($0.32M)
Willie Cauley-Stein	26	Restricted	N/A	$29.14M	N/A
B.J. Johnson	24	Restricted	N/A	$0.47M	N/A
Alec Burks	28	Unrestricted	N/A	($0.62M)	N/A
Kosta Koufos	30	Unrestricted	N/A	($4.42M)	N/A
Corey Brewer	33	Unrestricted	N/A	$2.96M	N/A

Estimated Cap Space for 2019 Free Agency

Note: Salary cap estimated to be at $109 million for 2019-20, as of September 17, 2018.

- **$67.1 million**, maximum cap space, if Barnes opts out, Ferrell and Mason are waived

- **$38.8 million**, most likely scenario, Barnes opts in, Ferrell remains on the roster, Mason is waived

* If Mason is on the roster subtract **$1.62M** from the numbers above.

2019 Draft Picks and Future Assets until 2022

- 2019 second round Minnesota via Cleveland and Portland (Gary Trent, Jr. trade, Mike Miller trade to Portland, Tyus Jones trade to Minnesota) – **40th overall**
- 2019 second round from Orlando via New York (compensation for hiring Scott Perry) – **47th overall**
- 2019 second round from Milwaukee (Luc Mbah a Moute trade) – **60th overall**
- 2020 own first round
- 2020 own second round
- 2020 second round from Miami via Boston and Cleveland (George Hill three-team trade to Cleveland, Kyrie Irving trade, Zoran Dragic trade)
- 2020 second round from Detroit via Phoenix (Bogdan Bogdanovic trade, Marcus Morris trade to Detroit)
- 2020 second round from either Houston or Golden State via Dallas, whichever is more favorable (Iman Shumpert/Alec Burks three-team trade)
- 2021 own first round
- 2021 own second round
- 2021 second round from Memphis (Garrett Temple/Ben McLemore trade)
- 2022 own first round
- 2022 own second round

Draft Rights Held

	Year	Round	Pick
Dimitrios Agravanis	2015	2	59
Luka Mitrovic	2015	2	60
Alex Oriakhi	2013	2	57

Offseason Recommendations

The Kings are in a unique position because most of the team's core is still on their rookie contracts and they will have plenty of cap space to try to lure free agents this summer. They could try to **take advantage of this situation by adding a few veterans on short-term deals** to help them take the next step to become a solid playoff team in the Western Conference. Ideally, the Kings could use this **summer to add a solid rim protector and a three-and-D wing player to address some of their main weaknesses**. Of the two roles, it might be easier to find a rim protecting big man because big men are a little bit devalued these days, so they might be able to find a player at a reasonable price tag. The most intriguing option could be Marc Gasol if he opts out of his last year in Toronto because his passing, floor spacing and rim protection would be a good fit with this current Kings squad. Interestingly enough, the coaching change cleared away a potential obstacle in acquiring Gasol because he had clashed with former coach, Dave Joerger in Memphis. Now that Joerger has been replaced, the Kings could look to bring in Gasol and he could be a very impactful interior presence that could elevate Sacramento's performance on both sides of the ball. From there, the Kings should then try to either add one high-end three-and-D wing player or try to acquire multiple lower-tier options to bolster their depth and give them more defensive versatility. The team's ample cap space gives them a bunch of different options. If they wanted to splurge, they could take a run at Khris Middleton or if they wanted to go to a veteran route, they could look at players like Danny Green or Trevor Ariza. Mainly, the team should try to come away with a solid three-and-D wing player because they sorely need someone to take on the tougher defensive assignments, so they can be a better defensive team as a whole. Sacramento is well-positioned this summer and if they play their cards right, they could step up a level in the Western Conference as soon as next season. If they can make sensible moves to improve in the short-term while keeping an eye on the future, they could set themselves for an interesting run in the future. Otherwise, if they focus too much on the short-term, they could be better next season, but they may not give themselves enough flexibility to reach the highest levels of contention.

SAN ANTONIO SPURS

Season in Review

For the last two decades, it seemed as if the San Antonio Spurs were immune from all of the noise that other teams had to deal with. However, that changed in the last offseason when Kawhi Leonard made it clear that that he was going to leave the team after this season, and he would prefer to be traded. The Spurs made the most of a potentially bad situation, and they sent him along with Danny Green to Toronto for All-Star, DeMar DeRozan, Jakob Poeltl and a 2019 first round draft pick. From there, San Antonio looked to do as they have always done under head coach, Gregg Popovich, which is adjust their system to their personnel to make the team as competitive as possible. This time around, the Western Conference was loaded to the point where the Spurs were in danger of missing the playoffs for the first time in 21 seasons, but the team stayed in the hunt until the very end and managed to land a playoff spot once again.

The Spurs were able to stay competitive despite the major personnel changes because they had one of the league's most effective offenses, ranking in the top ten in Offensive Efficiency. The team's style was interesting because it was a definitive antithesis to all of the recent trends. While most of the league was moving to a faster pace-and-space attack, the Spurs utilized a slower, half-court oriented attack that featured a lot of post-ups for LaMarcus Aldridge and isolations for DeRozan. As a team, they took more mid-range shots than any other team in the league and they got away with this because they were one of the league's most effective teams from that range. The Spurs didn't shoot threes as frequently as other teams in the league did. In fact, they were last in the NBA in Three-Point Attempts per Game, but they were far more selective with their three-point opportunities to the point where they were almost always open when they took a three. Specifically, almost 87% of their three-pointers were either categorized by the league's tracking metrics as open or wide open. Because of this high percentage of open threes, they shot the league's highest Three-Point Percentage and they were one of the NBA's best shooting teams, ranking in the top ten in Effective Field Goal Percentage. As another byproduct of playing more methodically and moving the ball more selectively, the Spurs were one of the league's best teams at avoiding turnovers and they finished in the top five in Turnover Percentage. Though the team's mid-range shooting tendency didn't allow them to draw fouls at a high rate, they were one of the more effective teams from the free throw line, as they led the league in Free Throw Percentage this past season. On the negative side, they weren't especially on the offensive glass, as they wound up in the bottom third of the league in Offensive Rebound Percentage. However, this may have been more of a conscious choice, as Popovich in his past has been known to punt the offensive boards to get back and play transition defense, so this very well could have been the case this season.

Defensively, the Spurs struggled because they weren't really equipped to keep up with modern offenses and they ranked in the bottom half of the league in Defensive Efficiency as a result. On the positive side, the Spurs made a conscious effort to defend their own basket even though they didn't really have a traditional rim protector. Even without an obvious deterrent around the rim, they were one of the league's best teams at preventing shots from inside five feet. Additionally, according to Synergy, they were one of the better teams in the league at defending roll men in pick-and-roll situations. They were also one of the league's best defensive rebounding teams and they ranked in the top five in Defensive Rebound Percentage. In addition to focusing on defending the basket, the Spurs played a more conservative rotation scheme and rarely looked to make big gambles. The main positive of this was that the team was very good at avoiding fouls to the point where they led the league in least Personal Fouls Committed per Game, so they were one of the best teams at keeping opponents off the free throw line as a result. The downside of their conservative rotation schemes was that they were the league's worst team at forcing turnovers, so they were rarely able to pressure opponents to get extra possessions for themselves. Because their opponents were employing a more modernized, three-point centric approach, the Spurs gave up a lot of three-point attempts, more than half of which were wide open looks. As a result, the Spurs were one of the worst teams at defending the three-point line, as they finished in the bottom half in Three-Points Attempts Allowed and Three-Point Percentage Allowed. Due to the team's struggles at preventing their opponents from shooting threes, the Spurs were among the league's worst teams when it came to shooting defense and they ranked in the bottom half of the league in Opponents' Effective Field Goal Percentage.

The San Antonio Spurs have continued to take everything one season at a time, and they continue to figure out ways to keep themselves competitive in the short-term. As the Western Conference continues to get stronger and new challengers consistently emerge, this may not be enough for them to continue their run and ultimately build towards winning another championship. If long-term contention is the team's goal, then they may have to take a step back or two to get the necessary cornerstone pieces to build a title contender. Otherwise, if they want to stay a solid playoff team for the next few years, they could go on as they are and rely on their staff's ability to adjust their strategies to maximize the performance of their roster.

Players Under Contract for 2019-20

* Age and Salary numbers are for 2019-20. See page 9 for explanation for Cap Value and RCV. A number in parentheses indicates that the value is negative.

	Age	Salary	Years Left	2018-19 Cap Value	RCV
DeMar DeRozan	30	$27.74M	Player Option	$10.03M	$27.62M
LaMarcus Aldridge*	34	$26.00M	1	$27.06M	$47.51M
Patty Mills	31	$13.29M	1	$6.96M	$13.57M
Davis Bertans	27	$7.00M	0	$12.20M	$10.12M
Marco Belinelli	33	$5.85M	0	$9.10M	$11.12M
Jakob Poeltl	24	$3.75M	0	$20.61M	$19.33M
Bryn Forbes	26	$2.88M	0	$17.99M	$13.01M
Lonnie Walker IV	21	$2.76M	2 Team Options	($1.86M)	($8.46M)
Dejounte Murray	23	$2.32M	0	($1.55M)	$1.61M
Derrick White	25	$1.95M	Team Option	$18.15M	$22.23M
Chimezie Metu	22	$1.42M	1	($1.29M)	($4.00M)

* Aldridge's contract for 2020-21 is guaranteed for **$7.00M** until June 29, 2020. San Antonio bought out and waived Pau Gasol on March 1, 2019 and they will be assessed a cap hit of **$5.10M** until the end of the 2019-20 season.

Two-Way Contracts

* In this section, listings are read: Player, Current Age, Height, Weight, College or Country

- Drew Eubanks, 21, 6'10", 245, Oregon State
- Ben Moore, 23, 6'8", 220, SMU

2019 Free Agents

* Age and Salary numbers are for 2019-20. See page 9 for explanation for Cap Value and RCV. A number in parentheses indicates that the value is negative.

	Age	Status	Salary	2018-19 Cap Value	RCV
Rudy Gay	33	Unrestricted	N/A	$14.51M	N/A
Dante Cunningham	32	Unrestricted	N/A	$6.39M	N/A
Quincy Pondexter	31	Unrestricted	N/A	$2.18M	N/A
Donatas Motiejunas	29	Unrestricted	N/A	($0.34M)	N/A

Estimated Cap Space for 2019 Free Agency

Note: Salary cap estimated to be at $109 million for 2019-20, as of September 17, 2018.

- **Basically over the cap**, most likely scenario, their spending power would be lower with cap space than it would be if they stayed over the cap and used their cap exceptions

    - **Non-taxpayer Mid-Level Exception**
    - **Bi-Annual Exception**

2019 Draft Picks and Future Assets until 2022

- 2019 own first round – **19th overall**
- 2019 first round from Toronto (Kawhi Leonard trade) – **29th overall**
- 2019 own second round – **49th overall**
- 2020 own first round
- 2020 own second round
- 2021 own first round
- 2021 own second round
- 2022 own first round

Draft Rights Held

	Year	Round	Pick
Nikola Milutinov	2015	1	26
Cady Lalanne	2015	2	55
Nemanja Dangubic	2014	2	54
Adam Hanga	2011	2	59
Giorgos Printezis	2007	2	58
Erazem Lorbek	2005	2	46
Sergei Karaulov	2004	2	57

Offseason Recommendations

The San Antonio Spurs have been able to keep themselves afloat for the last couple of seasons, but they may not be able to do this for a whole lot longer. Their team featured an older rotation, as a majority of their key players were 30 or older. In addition to this, DeMar DeRozan could hit free agency after next season and LaMarcus Aldridge could leave the season after. Therefore, the Spurs will have to find some way to build up their core in order to give them a chance of competing in the future. To do this, they will have to **find a way to incorporate younger players into key roles to give those players a chance to become higher-end contributors**. If Dejounte Murray fully recovers from his ACL injury, he could give them a dynamic point guard option if his shot improves. Otherwise, the Spurs may have look at their other internal options. Out of their young players, Derrick White may have the most potential to at the very least become an upper-tier role player. In his first full season with considerable playing time, White showed that he can contribute on offense with solid playmaking skills and a good enough outside shot. At the defensive end, he excelled as a versatile, multi-position defender that could effectively defend both guard spots. With an expanded role, White could build upon these skills to become a greater part of the team's future. Because the Spurs have been so successful over the last two decades, they have been unable to pick at the top of the draft to land high-end prospects. To find a younger potential core piece, they may have to explore their options on the trade market and **to land a substantial piece, they may have to shop their most valuable trade chip, DeMar DeRozan.** If the Spurs could land a similar but younger talent in a trade for DeRozan, it might be worthwhile to do so. After all, DeRozan is still an All-Star caliber entering his age-30 season, he's had no significant injury history and given that the cap will rise in each of the next two seasons, his relatively inexpensive contract could slightly increase his trade value. If there's an opportunity to deal somebody like DeRozan for a high-level return, this could be the year. Otherwise, if the Spurs don't receive trade offer of substance, they could just run back this team, compete for the playoffs and build their teams on the fly as they have been doing for the last few seasons. If the Spurs have greater designs and want to build a legitimate long-term title contender, they may have to make a couple of moves that are a bit out of character to adapt to these times. If they carefully take the right risks, they could reach an even higher level than they are at right now. However, if they simply want to stay true to who they have been for over twenty years, they will still be a solid team that has a good shot at making the playoffs in the Western Conference next year.

TORONTO RAPTORS

Season in Review

After experiencing several years of playoff disappointment, the Toronto Raptors recognized an opportunity to change their fortunes and they sought to make a major change. Even after former head coach, Dwane Casey had won Coach of the Year the season before, he was replaced on the bench by Nick Nurse. Then, the Raptors altered its core significantly by trading All-Star DeMar DeRozan, Jakob Poeltl and a first round draft pick for Kawhi Leonard and Danny Green. At the trade deadline, the team went even further and dealt Jonas Valanciunas, Delon Wright, C.J. Miles and a future second round pick to Memphis to acquire Marc Gasol. The Raptors have always been an excellent regular season team and the changes enabled them to maintain their status as one of the Eastern Conference's best teams. However, they fared much better against the other contenders in the East, so they may be better prepared for a long playoff run than they were in other years.

This season, the Raptors continued to be one of the league's best defensive teams, as they once again rated in the top five in Defensive Efficiency, but they accomplished this in a slightly different way than they did a season ago. Last year's defense was propped up significantly by their disproportionately strong bench unit. This unit had a tremendous effect in the regular season last year because teams use their bench a little more to manage the 82-game schedule. In the playoffs, that unit's effectiveness was limited because opposing teams play their starters more and simply don't use their bench as much. This season, the Raptors made their moves to improve the defense from their first unit and they became less reliant on their bench as they season went on. The insertion of Leonard, Green and an emerging Pascal Siakam into the starting lineup gave the Raptors much more length, activity and defensive versatility. Then, they slid Serge Ibaka down to the center spot to give them much more mobility than they had in previous years where they had to account for the slower-footed Valanciunas. As a result, the Raptors could aggressively switch screens and cover more ground on the court, so they were good at forcing misses to the point where they ranked in the top five in Opponents' Effective Field Goal Percentage. The extra length and activity allowed them to put more pressure on opponents, so they were able to force a lot of turnovers. In fact, they finished in the top ten in Opponents' Turnover Percentage. Additionally, the extra mobility helped them to stay out of situations where they had to foul, so they were one of the league's better teams at keeping their opponents off the free throw line. If there was anything resembling a negative about their defense, it was that they were only about average on the defensive glass, as their Defensive Rebound Percentage was right at the league average.

Offensively, the team only changed in a subtle way. In a general sense, the Raptors still had an offense ranked in the top five in Offensive Efficiency. Stylistically, their attack was still pick-and-roll heavy with a lot of isolations mixed in. However, the changes affected them in the following ways. First off, because the defense was forcing more turnovers, the Raptors were able to generate more early offense in transition to the point where they were one of the best teams in the league in transition situations, according to Synergy. Next, the team played lineups featuring players that were much more comfortable shooting threes, so they did a much better job at spacing the floor and the team's Three-Point Percentage increased a bit as a result. Therefore, the Raptors were one of the best shooting teams in the league, ranking in the top five in Effective Field Goal Percentage. Though they didn't get to free throw line at a high rate, they still were very effective from the free throw line, as they placed in the top five in Free Throw Percentage this past season. In fact, all five starters shot 75% or better from the free throw line this season. The moves at the trade deadline made them prone to bouts of miscommunication, which caused them to turn the ball a bit more and they ended up posting a Turnover Percentage just around the league average. Also, because the Raptors took a more perimeter-oriented approach, they weren't quite as effective on the offensive glass as they were last season and they were in the bottom third of the league in Offensive Rebound Percentage.

The Raptors took a bold approach by essentially going all-in for this season. The end result is unclear at this moment because the playoffs are still are going as this book is being written. If they reach the Finals, then their season could be considered a success and there may be some chance that they could bring back Kawhi Leonard to take another run at a title. Otherwise, if events go as they have gone in previous years, the Raptors may have to change to an entirely different course altogether because they could suffer some serious personnel losses in addition to Leonard. If this worst-case scenario happens, they may not need to completely blow everything up because they still have interesting players like Siakam and Fred VanVleet under contract but winning would be much harder than it has been over the last few years. In this situation, the Raptors would just retool without making any long-term commitments and then evaluate their roster to figure out the next steps to do what's best for the franchise moving forward.

Players Under Contract for 2019-20

* Age and Salary numbers are for 2019-20. See page 9 for explanation for Cap Value and RCV. A number in parentheses indicates that the value is negative.

	Age	Salary	Years Left	2018-19 Cap Value	RCV
Kyle Lowry	33	$33.50M	0	$1.07M	$4.22M
Serge Ibaka	30	$23.27M	0	$9.66M	$6.20M
Norman Powell	26	$10.12M	1 + Player Option	$3.03M	($0.27M)
Fred VanVleet	25	$9.46M	0	$12.50M	$10.39M
OG Anunoby	22	$2.28M	Team Option	$8.68M	$18.79M
Pascal Siakam	25	$2.35M	0	$42.44M	$31.75M
Chris Boucher*	27	$1.59M	0	$2.87M	($0.36M)
Malcolm Miller*	26	$1.59M	0	$0.45M	($0.61M)

* Boucher's contract for 2019-20 is partially guaranteed. Miller's contract for 2019-20 is not guaranteed. Toronto used the stretch provision to waive Justin Hamilton on July 14, 2017 and they will be assessed a cap hit of **$1.00M** until the end of the 2019-20 season.

Two-Way Contracts

* In this section, listings are read: Player, Current Age, Height, Weight, College or Country

- Jordan Loyd, 25, 6'4", 210, Indianapolis

2019 Free Agents

* Age and Salary numbers are for 2019-20. See page 9 for explanation for Cap Value and RCV. A number in parentheses indicates that the value is negative.

	Age	Status	Salary	2018-19 Cap Value	RCV
Marc Gasol	35	Player Option	$25.60M	$6.86M	$5.47M
Kawhi Leonard	28	Player Option	$21.33M	$23.37M	$14.48M
Patrick McCaw	24	Restricted	N/A	$1.42M	N/A
Danny Green	32	Unrestricted	N/A	$17.35M	N/A
Jeremy Lin	31	Unrestricted	N/A	($0.95M)	N/A
Jodie Meeks	32	Unrestricted	N/A	($2.18M)	N/A
Eric Moreland	28	Unrestricted	N/A	($0.14M)	N/A

Estimated Cap Space for 2019 Free Agency

Note: Salary cap estimated to be at $109 million for 2019-20, as of September 17, 2018.

- **$27.0 million**, maximum cap space, Leonard and Gasol opt out, Boucher and Miller are waived

- **$23.8 million**, Leonard and Gasol opt out, Boucher and Miller remain on the roster

2019 Draft Picks and Future Assets until 2022

- 2019 own second round – **59th overall**
- 2020 own first round
- 2020 own second round
- 2021 own first round
- 2022 own first round

Draft Rights Held

	Year	Round	Pick
Emir Preldzic	2009	2	57

Offseason Recommendations

Toronto's all-in approach has left them in a reactive position for this summer. If they can convince Kawhi Leonard to re-sign with them, much like how Oklahoma City did with Paul George last summer, their offseason plan would be pretty straightforward, and they would use their means to bring back some of their free agents to run everything back for another year. However, Leonard's future is rather uncertain, as he's not really made an indication about any of his future plans, so there's a significant chance that he could leave. If he does leave, the Raptors would be **best served to consider all of their options to help their team move forward.** They could make retool their roster in a subtle way by tweaking their roster to build around Kyle Lowry and Pascal Siakam. A few smaller moves to bring in some extra wing depth might keep them competitive next year. However, the upside of this sort of strategy isn't especially high because all of the remaining players under contract are probably best suited to being complementary players. Also, Lowry and Serge Ibaka would both be on the wrong side of age-30 and they would be entering the last year of their contracts, so they may not be around for very long either. Therefore, the Raptors may have to consider dealing for assets to get a head start on a potential rebuild. One of the issues with this strategy is that Toronto can't really put its best trade chip in play until after Leonard's decision. Specifically, the Raptors can't really dangle the last season of Siakam's rookie contract to acquire a prime asset during this year's NBA Draft because making that move would almost certainly hurt their chances of retaining Leonard, as it would make them less competitive in the short-term, and thus less attractive to him overall. If Leonard leaves, their best course may be just to retool around Lowry and Siakam with short-term contracts. That way, if things don't go as planned, they can be positioned well for next year's trade deadline because they would have at least three solid trade chips to sell off with the potential of adding somebody like Fred VanVleet as a deal sweetener to extract more value. In general, the Raptors have to work with what the market gives them this offseason. If they get lucky and successfully convince Leonard to come back, they should once again be contenders in the Eastern Conference next season. In all likelihood, they will probably have to retool in some way to account for Leonard's departure. Fortunately, their base of talent is solid enough that they still could cobble together a fairly competitive team next season. However, their future is not going to be as clear because a lot of their existing core is getting older and the Raptors will have to deal with their potential aging to find the best way to move forward. If they figure out a plan for their long-term future, then their strong system and culture could allow them to move faster in rebuilding their franchise and enabling them to regain their excellence much sooner than expected. Otherwise, if they take too much of a short-term focus, they could be stuck in mediocrity for a while.

UTAH JAZZ

Season in Review

The Utah Jazz snuck up on teams last season but this year, opponents had a better idea of what to expect, so the team stumbled a bit out of the gate. In late November, the Jazz gained some traction and their play started to pick up. In the middle of the season, they made a modest trade to re-acquire Kyle Korver by sending Alec Burks to Cleveland. From there, their key players, Donovan Mitchell, Rudy Gobert and Joe Ingles got going and put in performances similar to last year. In the end, despite some early struggles, Utah finished the season as a solid playoff team in the Western Conference.

Throughout head coach, Quin Snyder's tenure, the Jazz have been successful because they have been one of the league's best defensive teams. This season was no different, as they ranked in the top five in Defensive Efficiency. Their defensive success over the last few seasons including this one is mainly due to the presence of Gobert, who is arguably the NBA's best rim protector. His presence has helped the Jazz limit their opponent's shots from inside of five feet, forcing opposing teams outside to beat them over the top. By having Gobert inside to deter opponents from aggressively driving to the basket, Utah's perimeter players can be more aggressive to close out on three-point shooters to force them into the more inefficient mid-range area. As a result, Utah had one of the best shooting defenses in the league, ranking in the top five in Opponents' Effective Field Goal Percentage. In addition to having Gobert inside, most of the other players in Utah's rotation were solid rebounders, so it's not a surprise that they were one of the NBA's best defensive rebounding teams. Specifically, the finished in the top five in Defensive Rebound Percentage. In addition to having sound interior defense, the Jazz generally made sound rotations on the defensive end, so they didn't foul at an especially high rate. This allowed them to be one of the better teams in the league at keeping opponents off the free throw line to the point where they ranked in the upper half of the league in Opponent Free Throws per Field Goal Attempt. On the one hand, Utah's defensive scheme did consistently allow the team to force turnovers and they ended up in the upper half of the league in Opponents' Turnover Percentage. However, they weren't in position to force as many turnovers as they did last season because they had some trouble adjusting to playing a faster overall pace. Because they were scrambling a little more, opponents had an easier time making passes around the perimeter to relieve any potential pressure to avoid committing a turnover. Most notably, the team's transition defense suffered considerably, as the quicker misses on offense were often converted into easy looks the other way. In fact, according to Synergy, the Jazz dropped from being a good transition defense to being one of the league's worst per-possession transition defenses this past season.

At the offensive end, Utah really had to work hard to score. Their personnel from the year before one was basically intact, so they produced similar results and were about an average offensive team this past season. Stylistically, Utah's offense was very much like last year. Donovan Mitchell took up volume with above average efficiency, which allowed the others to fall into their roles. As it was alluded to earlier, the Jazz tried to speed up their pace, but the effects of this change were very minimal at best. If anything, the faster tempo made them a little bit worse because they just played wilder. In fact, Utah's Turnover Percentage increased to the point where they were one of the league's most turnover prone teams. On top of this, they continued to maintain a conservative approach on the boards, so they were just around the league average in Offensive Rebound Percentage. Positively speaking, Utah was one of the better shooting teams in the league because they made a concerted effort to take high-yield shots. In particular, they rarely took mid-range shots and looked to either attack the basket aggressively or shoot threes. Even though they shot below the league average on threes, they still were in the upper half of the league in Effective Field Goal Percentage, simply by being more effective around the rim and consciously avoiding the mid-range area. Their efforts to attack the rim also allowed them to draw fouls at a considerably high rate, as they ranked in the top five in the league in Free Throw Attempt Rate.

After the hiccup at the beginning of the season, the Jazz solidified its spot as a playoff team in the Western Conference. However, it doesn't appear that the team has a lot of room to grow. After all, most of the team's primary rotation players are limited to being complementary pieces and though Mitchell had another very good season, it's unclear if he's actually improved as an overall player. On top of this, Utah's position as a smaller market team makes it difficult to bring in any kind of major piece to alter their trajectory. With this in mind, the Jazz may have no choice but to manage their situation as they have been and keep themselves competitive using whatever means are possible. If nothing changes for the worse, then Utah should continue to be a playoff team in the Western Conference for the next few years.

Players Under Contract for 2019-20

* Age and Salary numbers are for 2019-20. See page 9 for explanation for Cap Value and RCV. A number in parentheses indicates that the value is negative.

	Age	Salary	Years Left	2018-19 Cap Value	RCV
Rudy Gobert	27	$25.01M	1	$40.56M	$61.59M
Derrick Favors*	28	$16.90M	0	$19.69M	$17.98M
Joe Ingles	32	$11.95M	1	$16.77M	$38.07M
Dante Exum	24	$9.60M	1	($3.97M)	($7.98M)
Jae Crowder	29	$7.82M	0	$14.94M	$13.36M
Kyle Korver*	38	$7.50M	0	$4.55M	$6.44M
Donovan Mitchell	23	$3.64M	Team Option	$27.99M	$56.47M
Grayson Allen	24	$2.43M	2 Team Options	($0.86M)	($5.17M)
Raul Neto*	27	$2.15M	0	$3.35M	$2.97M
Tony Bradley	22	$1.96M	Team Option	($1.13M)	($4.71M)
Georges Niang*	26	$1.65M	1	$4.66M	$3.95M
Royce O'Neale*	26	$1.62M	0	$13.50M	$12.19M

* Favors' contract for 2019-20 is guaranteed after July 6, 2019. Korver's contract for 2019-20 is partially guaranteed for **$3.40M** until July 7, 2019. Neto's contract for 2019-20 is guaranteed after July 6, 2019. Niang's contracts for 2019-20 and 2020-21 are not guaranteed. O'Neale's contract for 2019-20 is not guaranteed.

Two-Way Contracts

* In this section, listings are read: Player, Current Age, Height, Weight, College or Country

- Tyler Cavanaugh, 24, 6'9", 238, George Washington
- Naz Mitrou-Long, 25, 6'4", 218, Iowa State

2019 Free Agents

* Age and Salary numbers are for 2019-20. See page 9 for explanation for Cap Value and RCV. A number in parentheses indicates that the value is negative.

	Age	Status	Salary	2018-19 Cap Value	RCV
Ricky Rubio	29	Unrestricted	N/A	$5.51M	N/A
Thabo Sefolosha	35	Unrestricted	N/A	$1.72M	N/A
Ekpe Udoh	32	Unrestricted	N/A	$3.62M	N/A

Estimated Cap Space for 2019 Free Agency

Note: Salary cap estimated to be at $109 million for 2019-20, as of September 17, 2018.

- **$43.2 million**, maximum cap space, if Favors, Korver, Neto, Niang and O'Neale are waived
- **$18.9 million**, most likely scenario, Favors, Korver, Niang and O'Neale remain on the roster, Neto is waived

2019 Draft Picks and Future Assets until 2022

- 2019 own first round – **23rd overall**
- 2019 own second round – **53rd overall**
- 2020 own first round
- 2021 own first round
- 2021 own second round
- 2022 own first round
- 2022 own second round
- 2022 second round from San Antonio (Boris Diaw trade)

Draft Rights Held

	Year	Round	Pick
Nigel Williams-Goss	2017	2	55
Ante Tomic	2008	2	44

Offseason Recommendations

The Utah Jazz are in a position where they don't necessarily have to make a major move. After all, a lot of their core players are still under contract for next season, so their lineup will largely be intact to keep them pretty competitive if they have a relatively quiet offseason. However, Ricky Rubio is set to be a free agent and he's started for Utah for most of the last two seasons, so the team will have to decide to either bring him back or replace him. The Jazz also need to find some way to increase their overall firepower because they have struggled to score efficiently as a team and too much of the offensive load has to be shouldered by Donovan Mitchell. This introduces a conundrum because scoring and playmaking skills are not cheap on the open market and Utah is not really a destination for free agents. Because of this, small market teams are tempted to overpay for mid-tier free agents, which usually produces bad results. Specifically, these overpays lead to bloated contracts that eat up cap space and rob teams of any flexibility to maneuver, which ultimately keep them stuck in place. Therefore, finding another scoring and playmaking option is going to be difficult and will require some creativity. They could explore the trade market for an additional playmaker, but their efforts so far have come up empty. At the trade deadline, they tried to deal for Memphis' Mike Conley, but the trade talks stalled because the asking price was too steep and Conley had reservations about playing in Utah. There may other potential playmakers on the trade market this summer like Jrue Holiday or Kyle Lowry, but Utah could run into some of the same issues with those players.

With no real obvious solution for an extra dynamic playmaker, Utah's best course of action may to be to explore their options in restricted free agency. Depending on how much cap space they actually have, their ideal options would probably be Boston's Terry Rozier or Memphis' Delon Wright. After all, both are combo guards that are solid on both sides of the ball, have thrived in defensive-oriented environments and may just have some more untapped potential that could be unlocked in Utah's system. Additionally, throwing out an offer sheet to either of these players could be something of a low-risk proposition. Given that Memphis is rebuilding, they might be more inclined to match for a younger player like Wright, but their overall direction is unsettled enough where he might be attainable. Then, Boston's situation has more moving parts involved because of Kyrie Irving's free agency. Because of this, there's a chance that Utah could swoop in and get Rozier before Boston knows what's happening with Irving. If either attempt is unsuccessful, the Jazz could always circle back to Rubio or find more cost effective options on the free agent market. Then, the team could look to add shooters and versatile defenders to bolster their depth. Generally speaking, Utah is facing the dilemma that successful small market teams are going to face in this era. The team is in need of some more dynamic talent, but they may have trouble acquiring it through traditional means. If they want to reach the next level, they will have to be aggressive to creatively increase their talent level to compete with the traditional powers in the league. If they can figure some way to either acquire or manufacture another dynamic talent, they could be a serious factor in the Western Conference in the coming years. Otherwise, they will probably stay as they are and still be a consistently, competitive playoff team as long as their core is intact.

WASHINGTON WIZARDS

Season in Review

The wheels came off before this season even started for the Washington Wizards. They initially took a chance by signing Dwight Howard in the offseason, but he missed most of the season with a glute and a back injury. Then, the Wizards never really got on track because they had some early season chemistry issues, which caused them to drop some games early. Afterwards, things really took a turn for the worse when John Wall ruptured his Achilles and had complications from surgery, so he not only missed most of this past season, but he will be out for the next one as well. From there, the front office realized the severity of their situation and made several changes over the course of the season. Most notably, they dealt Otto Porter to Chicago at the trade deadline for Bobby Portis and Jabari Parker. All of this turmoil caused the Wizards to miss the playoffs and finish as a lottery team this past season.

The Wizards stayed within shouting range of the Eastern Conference playoff picture because they were still an above average offensive team, despite their injuries and personnel shuffling. This is mainly because head coach, Scott Brooks pivoted to center the offense around All-Star, Bradley Beal and his abilities as the Wizards' new primary ball handler allowed them to stay somewhat competitive this season. With Beal as the lead ball handler, the team utilized a more modernized offense. Specifically, the ball moved more from side to side and they focused more on taking higher-yield shots. As a result, the Wizards were one of the league's most effective passing teams, ranking in the top ten in Assists per Game. The emphasis on taking more efficient shots allowed them to be an effective shooting team to the point where they finished in the top ten in Effective Field Goal Percentage. Though they didn't have many players outside of Beal that could really threaten a defense consistently, they were fairly good at getting to the foul line and they actually ranked in the upper half of the league in Free Throw Attempt Rate. Additionally, the Wizards were fairly good at maintaining control of the ball because they ranked in the upper half of the league in Turnover Percentage. On the negative side, the team tended to use smaller lineups and there were a lot of moving parts overall, so the team had some difficulties on the offensive glass, and they wound up finishing near the bottom of the league in Offensive Rebound Percentage.

On defense, the Wizards' performance really took a hit because the roster changes and injuries didn't allow them to defend as a cohesive unit. As a result, they finished with one of the league's worst Defensive Efficiency ratings. The Wizards were generally susceptible to miscommunication and breakdowns in their rotations, so they allowed their opponents to get a lot of easy looks at the basket. They also weren't especially effective at taking a particular area away because they often had to cover up for their lack of rim protection, which then opened up opportunities for opponents to shoot from outside. Because of this, the Wizards really struggled with their shooting defense, as they ranked near the bottom of the league in Opponents' Effective Field Goal Percentage. Also, the constant scrambling and helping often put them out of position to the point where they were forced to commit fouls to send the opponents to the free throw line. Specifically they ranked in the bottom third of the league in Opponent Free Throw Attempts per Field Goal Attempt. Finally, the team was initially counting on Dwight Howard to serve as their rim protector, but because he missed most of the season due to injury, the Wizards were suffering on the interior. It also didn't help that they played smaller lineups to boost the offense. This caused the Wizards to be one of the league's worst defensive rebounding teams, as they ranked near the bottom of the league in Defensive Rebound Percentage. If there was a silver lining for Washington's defense, it was that the constant personnel shuffling put younger, more active bodies into the lineup. The injection of activity allowed them to be more aggressive in pressuring opponents, which helped the Wizards force turnovers at a pretty high rate. In fact, the Wizards were actually one of the best teams in the NBA at forcing turnovers, as they ranked in the top five in Opponents' Turnover Percentage this past season.

This was a lost season for the Wizards and the future doesn't appear to be much better because the franchise is going to have a difficult time building a roster with a severely injured John Wall occupying a sizeable portion of the team's salary cap. The team's front office is also unsettled because Ernie Grunfeld was fired at the end of the season. Positively speaking, the team does have an All-Star building block in place with Bradley Beal. However, his presence may not mesh with the Wizards' new reality as a possible rebuilding team, so the new front office might have to entertain the idea of dealing him. No matter what happens, the Wizards really have to formulate a plan to work around their current situation. If they can minimize the damage from Wall's potential albatross contract, they could possibly become a more sustainable and competitive team in the future. Otherwise, they could be headed on the path to a very difficult rebuild in the coming years.

Players Under Contract for 2019-20

* Age and Salary numbers are for 2019-20. See page 9 for explanation for Cap Value and RCV. A number in parentheses indicates that the value is negative.

	Age	Salary	Years Left	2018-19 Cap Value	RCV
John Wall	29	$37.80M	2 + Player Option	($8.13M)	($107.62M)
Bradley Beal	26	$27.09M	1	$19.90M	$33.51M
Ian Mahinmi	33	$15.45M	0	($10.88M)	($8.37M)
Dwight Howard	34	$5.60M	0	($2.14M)	$10.96M
Troy Brown, Jr.	20	$3.22M	2 Team Options	$2.72M	$6.16M
Tarik Phillip*	26	$1.44M	0	($0.01M)	($1.44M)

* Phillip's contract for 2019-20 is not guaranteed.

Two-Way Contracts

* In this section, listings are read: Player, Current Age, Height, Weight, College or Country

- Devin Robinson, 23, 6'8", 200, Florida

2019 Free Agents

* Age and Salary numbers are for 2019-20. See page 9 for explanation for Cap Value and RCV. A number in parentheses indicates that the value is negative.

	Age	Status	Salary	2018-19 Cap Value	RCV
Jabari Parker	24	Team Option	$20.00M	($5.74M)	($6.05M)
Tomas Satoransky	28	Restricted	N/A	$21.61M	N/A
Sam Dekker	25	Restricted	N/A	$4.06M	N/A
Bobby Portis	24	Restricted	N/A	$10.04M	N/A
Thomas Bryant	22	Restricted	N/A	$26.17M	N/A
Chasson Randle	26	Restricted	N/A	$3.64M	N/A
Jordan McRae	28	Restricted	N/A	$3.21M	N/A
Trevor Ariza	34	Unrestricted	N/A	$2.92M	N/A
Jeff Green	33	Unrestricted	N/A	$19.45M	N/A

Estimated Cap Space for 2019 Free Agency

Note: Salary cap estimated to be at $109 million for 2019-20, as of September 17, 2018.

- **$19.8 million**, most likely scenario, Parker's option is not picked up, Phillip is waived

2019 Draft Picks and Future Assets until 2022
- 2019 own first round – **9th overall**
- 2020 own first round
- 2021 own first round
- 2022 own first round

Draft Rights Held

	Year	Round	Pick
Issuf Sanon	2018	2	44
Aaron White	2015	2	49

Offseason Recommendations

The Wizards have a little bit of cap space to work with, but they have so many outgoing free agents that their flexibility is going to be limited in filling out the roster. They will probably be able to get a Disabled Player Exception because John Wall is almost certain to miss all of next season, so there may be a little extra wiggle room. However, the Wizards will have to creatively figure out how to position their team for the near future. A full-scale rebuild doesn't necessarily make sense because so many other teams in the Eastern Conference have already gotten a head start and beaten them to the bottom. On the other side, contention is probably out of the question because they simply will not have the funds to field a legitimately threatening team. Therefore, **the Wizards probably have to approach the next year or so as if they were expansion team**, except they may have some structure in place to work with because of the presence of Bradley Beal. Offensively, the team doesn't have to make major stylistic changes, as they could continue to utilize Beal as the primary ball handler and surround him with shooters and at least one competent roll man. In all likelihood, Dwight Howard will exercise his option. If he stays healthy, keeps his personal disruptions to a minimum and returns close to his typical form, he could be the effective roll man that the Wizards sorely needed to suck in defenses to create more open outside shots. Because of the variables involved with having Howard on the roster, the Wizards might be best served to hedge their bets and find an athletic rim runner prospect in the draft to serve as a temporary understudy, similar to how Clint Capela came up with the Rockets when he was initially drafted. From there, the team would bargain hunt for valuable perimeter players to complement Beal. **In an**

ideal situation, they would re-sign Tomas Satoransky as long as his price tag is reasonable to give the Wizards an excellent secondary ball mover and shooter that already has played well with Beal. If possible, **the team might benefit in the long-term by dangling Ian Mahinmi's expiring contract to possibly take on a little bit of extra money as a way to extract additional assets**. Though they are in control of all of their own first round picks for the foreseeable future, they don't have any extra assets on top of that. In fact, they may not have a second round pick until 2023, depending on what happens to the Chicago Bulls. Therefore, if they could add an extra draft pick or two in a salary dump involving Mahinmi, then those additional draft picks could give them more flexibility to maneuver and find value either for next season or in the future. Washington is in a tough situation this summer, as their team's overall direction is unclear. Given the severity of Wall's injury, it's probably best if the Wizards take more of a long-term approach because it simply wouldn't be wise to make the situation any worse than it already is by compounding matters with short-sighted moves. If they stay prudent with their decision-making and stay competitive enough, they may just be able to work around the situation and stay close to the fringes of the playoff picture in the Eastern Conference. Otherwise, if they try to force a hasty move of any kind, then they could be left with no choice but to start over and rebuild over the next few years.

2019 NBA Free Agency Projections

These are projections of an ideal contract for all of this summer's potential free agents. To get to these numbers, I used the simple projection methods that I used to calculate the future contract values in the team reports. It is a little too complicated to fully factor in all of the various salary cap conditions, so these values are more of a reflection of that player's market value in a vacuum. The listed age is that player's age as of the 2019-20 season.

Atlanta Hawks

	Age	Current Status	Ideal Contract
Justin Anderson	26	Restricted	1 year, minimum
Dewayne Dedmon	30	Unrestricted	2 year, $19.0M
Vince Carter	43	Unrestricted	1 year, minimum

Boston Celtics

	Age	Current Status	Ideal Contract
Al Horford	33	Player Option	2 years, $50.0M
Kyrie Irving	27	Player Option	3 years, maximum
Aron Baynes	33	Player Option	1 year, $5.0M
Terry Rozier	25	Restricted	4 years, $56.0M
Daniel Theis	27	Restricted	2 years, $12.0M
Brad Wanamaker	30	Restricted	1 year, minimum
Jonathan Gibson	32	Restricted	1 year, minimum
Marcus Morris	30	Unrestricted	2 years, $17.0M

Brooklyn Nets

	Age	Current Status	Ideal Contract
Shabazz Napier	28	Team Option	2 years, $10.0M
D'Angelo Russell	23	Restricted	4 years, $81.0M
Rondae Hollis-Jefferson	25	Restricted	1 year, $4.5M
Theo Pinson	24	Restricted	1 year, minimum
DeMarre Carroll	33	Unrestricted	1 year, $6.0M
Jared Dudley	34	Unrestricted	1 year, minimum
Ed Davis	30	Unrestricted	1 year, $7.0M

Charlotte Hornets

	Age	Current Status	Ideal Contract
Marvin Williams	33	Player Option	1 year, $8.0M
Michael Kidd-Gilchrist	26	Player Option	2 years, $15.0M
Frank Kaminsky	26	Restricted	2 years, $13.0M
Kemba Walker*	29	Unrestricted	3 years, maximum
Jeremy Lamb	27	Unrestricted	3 years, $47.0M
Shelvin Mack	29	Unrestricted	1 year, $3.5M

* Walker qualifies for the Supermax. The figure above values him at a typical maximum contract.

Chicago Bulls

	Age	Current Status	Ideal Contract
Ryan Arcidiacono	25	Restricted	1 year, $4.0M
Wayne Selden	25	Restricted	1 year, minimum
Walter Lemon, Jr.	25	Restricted	1 year, minimum
Robin Lopez	31	Unrestricted	1 year, $4.5M
Timothe Luwawu-Cabarrot	24	Unrestricted	1 year, minimum

Cleveland Cavaliers

	Age	Current Status	Ideal Contract
David Nwaba	27	Restricted	1 year, $3.0M
Marquese Chriss	22	Unrestricted	1 year, minimum
Channing Frye	36	Unrestricted	1 year, minimum
Nik Stauskas	26	Unrestricted	1 year, $3.0M

Dallas Mavericks

	Age	Current Status	Ideal Contract
Kristaps Porzingis	24	Restricted	2 years, $35.0M
Dorian Finney-Smith	26	Restricted	2 years, $8.0M
Maxi Kleber	28	Restricted	2 years, $11.0M
Dwight Powell	28	Unrestricted	2 years, $25.0M
Dirk Nowitzki	41	Unrestricted	1 year, minimum
J.J. Barea	35	Unrestricted	1 year, minimum
Trey Burke	27	Unrestricted	1 year, $3.5M
Devin Harris	36	Unrestricted	1 year, minimum
Salah Mejri	33	Unrestricted	1 year, minimum

Denver Nuggets

	Age	Current Status	Ideal Contract
Paul Millsap	34	Team Option	2 years, $29.0M
Trey Lyles	24	Restricted	2 years, $9.0M
Tyler Lydon	23	Unrestricted	1 year, minimum
Isaiah Thomas	30	Unrestricted	1 year, minimum

Detroit Pistons

	Age	Current Status	Ideal Contract
Glenn Robinson III	26	Team Option	1 year, minimum
Ish Smith	31	Unrestricted	1 year, minimum
Wayne Ellington	32	Unrestricted	1 year, $3.0M
Jose Calderon	38	Unrestricted	1 year, minimum
Zaza Pachulia	35	Unrestricted	1 year, minimum

Golden State Warriors

	Age	Current Status	Ideal Contract
Kevin Durant	31	Player Option	4 years, maximum
Quinn Cook	26	Restricted	1 year, $3.5M
Jordan Bell	25	Restricted	2 years, $8.0M
Klay Thompson	29	Unrestricted	2 years + Player Option, maximum
DeMarcus Cousins	29	Unrestricted	2 years, $21.0M
Jonas Jerebko	32	Unrestricted	1 year, $4.5M
Kevon Looney	23	Unrestricted	4 years, $46.0M
Andrew Bogut	35	Unrestricted	1 year, minimum

Houston Rockets

	Age	Current Status	Ideal Contract
Danuel House	26	Restricted	2 year, $7.0M
Chris Chiozza	24	Restricted	1 year, minimum
Iman Shumpert	29	Unrestricted	1 year, minimum
Gerald Green	34	Unrestricted	1 year, minimum
Austin Rivers	27	Unrestricted	1 year, $3.5M
Kenneth Faried	30	Unrestricted	1 year, $3.0M

Indiana Pacers

	Age	Current Status	Ideal Contract
Thaddeus Young	31	Unrestricted	2 years, $27.0M
Bojan Bogdanovic	30	Unrestricted	2 years, $27.0M
Darren Collison	32	Unrestricted	2 years, $27.0M
Cory Joseph	28	Unrestricted	2 years, $19.0M
Kyle O'Quinn	29	Unrestricted	1 year, minimum
Wesley Matthews	33	Unrestricted	1 year, $6.0M

Los Angeles Clippers

	Age	Current Status	Ideal Contract
Ivica Zubac	22	Restricted	3 years, $14.0M
Rodney McGruder	28	Restricted	1 year, $4.0M
Wilson Chandler	32	Unrestricted	1 year, $4.0M
Garrett Temple	33	Unrestricted	1 year, minimum
JaMychal Green	29	Unrestricted	1 year, $4.5M
Patrick Beverley	31	Unrestricted	2 years, $12.0M

Los Angeles Lakers

	Age	Current Status	Ideal Contract
Kentavious Caldwell-Pope	26	Unrestricted	2 years, $23.0M
Rajon Rondo	33	Unrestricted	1 year, minimum
Mike Muscala	28	Unrestricted	2 years, $9.0M
Lance Stephenson	29	Unrestricted	1 year, $3.5M
Reggie Bullock	28	Unrestricted	2 years, $13.0M
JaVale McGee	32	Unrestricted	1 year, $7.5M
Tyson Chandler	37	Unrestricted	1 year, minimum

Memphis Grizzlies

	Age	Current Status	Ideal Contract
Jonas Valanclunas	27	Player Option	2 years, $25.0M
Ivan Rabb	22	Team Option	2 years, 6.0M
Delon Wright	27	Restricted	3 years, $40.0M
Tyler Dorsey	23	Restricted	1 year, minimum
Justin Holiday	30	Unrestricted	2 years, $11.0M
Joakim Noah	34	Unrestricted	1 year, minimum
Tyler Zeller	30	Unrestricted	1 year, minimum

Miami Heat

	Age	Current Status	Ideal Contract
Hassan Whiteside	30	Player Option	2 years, $35.0M
Goran Dragic	33	Player Option	2 years, $23.0M
Udonis Haslem	39	Unrestricted	1 year, minimum
Dwyane Wade	38	Unrestricted	1 year, minimum

Milwaukee Bucks

	Age	Current Status	Ideal Contract
Khris Middleton	28	Player Option	3 years, $70.0M
Malcolm Brogdon	27	Restricted	4 years, $62.0M
Nikola Mirotic	28	Unrestricted	3 years, $34.0M
Brook Lopez	31	Unrestricted	2 years, $28.0M
Pau Gasol	39	Unrestricted	1 year, minimum
Tim Frazier	29	Unrestricted	1 year, minimum

Minnesota Timberwolves

	Age	Current Status	Ideal Contract
Tyus Jones	23	Restricted	3 years, $22.0M
Mitch Creek	27	Restricted	1 year, minimum
Taj Gibson	34	Unrestricted	1 year, $9.0M
Jerryd Bayless	31	Unrestricted	1 year, minimum
Anthony Tolliver	34	Unrestricted	1 year, minimum
Luol Deng	34	Unrestricted	1 year, minimum
Derrick Rose	31	Unrestricted	1 year, $6.0M

New Orleans Pelicans

	Age	Current Status	Ideal Contract
Julius Randle	25	Player Option	4 years, $76.0M
Jahlil Okafor	24	Team Option	1 year, $3.0M
Stanley Johnson	23	Restricted	1 year, minimum
Cheick Diallo	23	Restricted	1 year, $3.0M
Elfrid Payton	25	Unrestricted	1 year, $3.0M
Darius Miller	29	Unrestricted	1 year, $3.5M
Ian Clark	28	Unrestricted	1 year, minimum

New York Knicks

	Age	Current Status	Ideal Contract
Allonzo Trier	24	Team Option	3 years, $13.0M
Emmanuel Mudiay	23	Restricted	2 years, $7.0M
Luke Kornet	24	Restricted	2 years, $4.0M
Billy Garrett	25	Restricted	1 year, minimum
DeAndre Jordan	31	Unrestricted	2 years, $35.0M
Mario Hezonja	24	Unrestricted	1 year, minimum
Noah Vonleh	24	Unrestricted	3 years, $13.0M

Oklahoma City Thunder

	Age	Current Status	Ideal Contract
Patrick Patterson	30	Player Option	1 year, minimum
Nerlens Noel	25	Player Option	2 years, $13.0M
Raymond Felton	35	Unrestricted	1 year, minimum
Markieff Morris	30	Unrestricted	1 year, $5.0M

Orlando Magic

	Age	Current Status	Ideal Contract
Wesley Iwundu	25	Team Option	2 years, $7.0M
Jerian Grant	27	Restricted	1 year, $2.5M
Jarell Martin	25	Restricted	1 year, minimum
Khem Birch	27	Restricted	2 years, $4.0M
Nikola Vucevic	29	Unrestricted	2 years, $51.0M
Terrence Ross	28	Unrestricted	2 years, $19.0M
Michael Carter-Williams	28	Unrestricted	1 year, minimum

Philadelphia 76ers

	Age	Current Status	Ideal Contract
Jimmy Butler	30	Player Option	2 years, maximum
Tobias Harris	27	Unrestricted	3 years, $89.0M
J.J. Redick	35	Unrestricted	1 year, $13.5M
Boban Marjanovic	31	Unrestricted	1 year, $6.0M
Mike Scott	31	Unrestricted	1 year, $3.5M
Justin Patton	22	Unrestricted	1 year, minimum
James Ennis	29	Unrestricted	2 years, $13.0M
Furkan Korkmaz	22	Unrestricted	1 year, $2.5M
T.J. McConnell	27	Unrestricted	2 years, $11.0M
Amir Johnson	32	Unrestricted	1 year, minimum

Phoenix Suns

	Age	Current Status	Ideal Contract
Tyler Johnson	27	Player Option	2 years, $13.0M
Kelly Oubre	24	Restricted	4 years, $45.0M
Dragan Bender	22	Unrestricted	1 year, minimum
Troy Daniels	28	Unrestricted	1 year, minimum
Richaun Holmes	26	Unrestricted	2 years, 12.0M
Jamal Crawford	39	Unrestricted	1 year, minimum

Portland Trail Blazers

	Age	Current Status	Ideal Contract
Jake Layman	25	Restricted	2 years, $9.0M
Al-Farouq Aminu	29	Unrestricted	2 years, $23.0M
Rodney Hood	27	Unrestricted	2 years, $20.0M
Seth Curry	29	Unrestricted	2 years, $9.0M
Enes Kanter	27	Unrestricted	2 years, $17.0M

Sacramento Kings

	Age	Current Status	Ideal Contract
Harrison Barnes	27	Player Option	3 years, $44.0M
Willie Cauley-Stein	26	Restricted	3 years, $41.0M
B.J. Johnson	24	Restricted	1 year, minimum
Alec Burks	28	Unrestricted	2 years, $8.0M
Kosta Koufos	30	Unrestricted	1 year, minimum
Corey Brewer	33	Unrestricted	1 year, minimum

San Antonio Spurs

	Age	Current Status	Ideal Contract
Rudy Gay	33	Unrestricted	1 year, $11.0M
Dante Cunningham	32	Unrestricted	1 year, minimum
Quincy Pondexter	31	Unrestricted	1 year, minimum
Donatas Motiejunas	29	Unrestricted	1 year, minimum

Toronto Raptors

	Age	Current Status	Ideal Contract
Marc Gasol	35	Player Option	2 years, $30.0M
Kawhi Leonard	28	Player Option	3 years, maximum
Patrick McCaw	24	Restricted	1 year, minimum
Danny Green	32	Unrestricted	2 years, $24.0M
Jeremy Lin	31	Unrestricted	1 year, $3.5M
Jodie Meeks	32	Unrestricted	1 year, minimum
Eric Moreland	28	Unrestricted	1 year, minimum

Utah Jazz

	Age	Current Status	Ideal Contract
Ricky Rubio	29	Unrestricted	2 years, $23.0M
Thabo Sefolosha	35	Unrestricted	1 year, minimum
Ekpe Udoh	32	Unrestricted	1 year, minimum

Washington Wizards

	Age	Current Status	Ideal Contract
Jabari Parker	24	Team Option	1 year, $4.5M
Tomas Satoransky	28	Restricted	3 years, 29.0M
Sam Dekker	25	Restricted	1 year, $2.5M
Bobby Portis	24	Restricted	3 years, $26.0M
Thomas Bryant	22	Restricted	2 years, $15.0M
Chasson Randle	26	Restricted	1 year, minimum
Jordan McRae	28	Restricted	1 year, minimum
Trevor Ariza	34	Unrestricted	1 year, $7.5M
Jeff Green	33	Unrestricted	1 year, $7.5M

The Impact of Modern NBA Strategy on the Draft Evaluation Process

A lot has changed in the NBA over the last few years. Player empowerment and the creation of modern super-teams have caused a change in organizational thinking as it applies to team building. Also, shifts in on-court strategy have radically changed the way that players are valued in this current era. After all, the game is becoming more and more position-less and traditional roles are starting to disappear. Take current Philadelphia 76ers center, Greg Monroe for example. When he hit free agency in the summer of 2015, he was viewed as a very good, second-tier center and he was paid accordingly, signing a 3-year contract with Milwaukee for an average of over $16 million per season. To put that yearly average salary into perspective, Draymond Green re-signed with the Golden State Warriors that same summer for roughly the same amount. Unfortunately for Monroe, he was bought out at the end of his three-year deal. He has been bouncing around from various teams in the time since while playing for the veteran's minimum. The interesting thing is that this rapid devaluation of Monroe's overall utility is not really a fault of his own. His per-minute production is still close to what it was in 2015, he hasn't suffered any significant injury and he's had no substantial problems off the court. The only thing that has changed is that strategies on both sides of the ball have rendered a player like Monroe, a classic, big body, offensive-minded, back-to-the-basket center almost obsolete simply because the NBA is moving towards a faster paced game that requires a higher degree of mobility and quickness to be effective. The modern NBA strategy revolution has had an impact on the draft evaluation process because talent evaluators, me included, have had to alter their internal valuation systems on the fly to make sense of the changes in the league. With this in mind, the following is a look at how to best account for current NBA strategy shifts to make more informed evaluations on draft prospects.

To begin this deep dive, we have to get a sense of the level of preparedness of a typical NBA rookie. As a way to figure this out, I wanted to see if it's easy for a rookie to essentially hit the ground running in today's NBA. To do this, I used Basketball-Reference's Play Index tool to search for rookies that came into the league immediately after their draft year that played at least 1000 minutes or its equivalent in the case of a lockout season, had a PER at or above 15 and posted an Offensive Rating that was higher the player's Defensive Rating. I limited this search to rookies that came into the league from the 2011-12 season to last season to account for this new era of the NBA, as that coincided with the year that the Miami Heat elected to move away from using a lineup with a traditional big man and instead downshifted LeBron James and Chris Bosh to the four and five spots, respectively.

This search left me with the following 19 names.

- Kawhi Leonard
- Kenneth Faried
- Isaiah Thomas
- Anthony Davis
- Andre Drummond
- Kelly Olynyk
- Mason Plumlee
- Karl-Anthony Towns
- Kristaps Porzingis
- Willie Cauley-Stein
- Myles Turner
- Jayson Tatum
- Bam Adebayo
- John Collins
- Jarrett Allen
- DeAndre Ayton
- Jaren Jackson, Jr.
- Marvin Bagley III
- Mitchell Robinson

As you can see from the list above, the vast majority of these players are interior players. Therefore, it's safe to suggest that it's probably much easier for a young big man prospect to enter the league and immediately produce in an impactful and efficient manner. Stylistically, the big man's job description has become more simplified in this era because teams aren't using as many big-on-big post-ups as a feature of their offense. As a result, the offensive skill requirements are lower because a modern big really only has to be able to set solid screens, roll hard to the rim and finish efficiently around the basket to be effective. Then, the main challenge for a modern big man prospect is the defensive side of the ball where those prospects have to quickly grasp current rotation schemes while demonstrate the ability to protect the rim and adequately handle perimeter players on switches. Interestingly enough, the changing role of the big man in today's NBA has basically made the center spot a young man's position, as it's become increasingly more difficult for older big men with declining athleticism to remain effective. Using the same criteria as the previous list, I wanted to get a sense of the overall productivity of big men in their age-31 season or older. In 2016-17, ten older big men played at least 1000 minutes, had a PER of 15 or higher and posted an Offensive Rating higher than their Defensive Rating. In 2017-18, the number of older big men that met that specific criteria was cut in half. Then this season, the number has gone down once again, as only four older big men (Marc Gasol, JaVale McGee, Al Horford, LaMarcus Aldridge) are set to hit these basic benchmarks.

Because productive big men are now skewing younger, teams have to make sure that they get as much value as possible in a big man's early years. As a result, immediate translatability is going to become a much more important factor in evaluating young big man prospects. Now that it's easier for a young big man to come into the league and be effective right away, teams would wise to use the draft as a source for cheap production that provides them with ample surplus value to manage their cap resources more efficiently. Therefore, it doesn't make much sense to draft an unpolished big man unless that player can be stashed overseas because the team will be unnecessarily wasting cap space on a raw big man languishing at the end of the bench as well as some extra space on another market value veteran on an expensive contract to get a fraction of the value that they could have received by taking a translatable young big man prospect on a cheap rookie scale deal. With this in mind, teams have to greatly reconsider their spending practices on mid-tier veteran big men because the production from those players are now much more easily replaceable at a lower cost. For instance, last season, the Warriors employed six big men for a combined total of about $11.5 million with none of the six making more than $3.5 million. Then this season, they spent the early chunk of the season relying on three big men (Damian Jones, Kevon Looney, Jordan Bell) to provide with a combined WS/48 value of 0.162 or approximately 13.3 WS if extrapolated to a full season at a combined salary of just over $4.4 million. Because it is easier to find productive big men especially for cheap in the draft, teams should think twice about using their free agent dollars on a non-max contract veteran big man because they could probably get as much value or more by taking a big man prospect in the draft and locking him into a rookie scale contract. Essentially, the modern simplification of the big man's role in today's NBA has made taking a center a much safer bet than it was in the previous era.

On the flip side, it is now much more difficult for perimeter players to quickly transition into being efficient contributors in the current game. This is mainly because perimeter players have more responsibilities on both ends and their roles aren't as specialized as they were in the past. For example, switching has become a much greater part of NBA defenses because the better offensive teams are using more screens, motion and pick-and-rolls rather than solely relying on post-ups or isolations. Therefore, a perimeter player has to not only defend his own position, but also be able to guard smaller and bigger players due to all of the constant switching. Because a perimeter player has to defend multiple positions in any given game, it's easier to expose any flaws that player may have on the defensive side of the ball. As a result, rookie perimeter players tend to have a steeper learning curve on the defensive end. After all, the typical American college prospect doesn't regularly face NBA level competition throughout a relatively shortened college schedule, so being forced to defend different types of NBA perimeter players on a game-to-game basis over a long 82-game season can be something of an overload that can require a year or two to make the appropriate adjustments. There's also an adjustment for rookies coming into the league from international leagues overseas as well because even though they are accustomed to playing against grown men over a longer schedule, those international rookies have to adapt to facing NBA perimeter players that present greater challenges due to being in a higher class of athleticism and skill level.

On the offensive end, the immediate transition to being an efficient producer is much more difficult for a variety of reasons. For starters, the three-pointer is no longer optional and it's now a necessity, as teams are continuing to embrace optimal shot distributions to increase their scoring efficiency. Therefore, the bar to shoot at an average level of efficiency is getting higher and higher, making the learning curve for young prospects much steeper. In addition to this, the NBA is playing at an increasingly faster tempo while the pace of the college game remains much slower and more stagnant. Specifically, the average pace in Division I NCAA basketball has hovered around 68 possessions per 40 minutes (81.6 possessions per 48 minutes) while the NBA game is now being played at a pace of close to 100 possessions per 48 minutes. The international game is typically played at slower pace as well, even though they use a 24-second shot clock. Based on a simplistic estimation, the highest scoring EuroLeague teams play at a pace of around 70 to 75 possessions per 40 minutes. If you extrapolate this pace to 48 minutes, they would play around 84 to 90 possessions, which is still considerably slower than the modern NBA pace. As a result, young perimeter prospects have to get used to making their decisions at a much faster speed, which tends to lead to more mistakes early in their careers that they have to learn to overcome. To illustrate how the NBA game has changed in the last five seasons, here is a chart showing the league averages in True Shooting Percentage, Pace and Three-Point Attempts.

	ORTG	TS%	Pace	3PTA/G	3PT%
2014-15	105.6	0.534	93.9	22.4	0.350
2015-16	106.4	0.541	95.8	24.1	0.354
2016-17	108.8	0.553	96.4	27.0	0.358
2017-18	108.6	0.556	97.3	29.0	0.362
2018-19	110.4	0.560	100.0	32.0	0.355

Basically, the table above emphasizes the point that the NBA game is getting faster and the three-point shot is becoming more and more important, which drives up the bar for scoring efficiency. Because of this, young perimeter prospects are placed in a much more difficult environment to start their careers, which lengthens the time it takes for them to reach their full potential. As a result, perimeter prospects are a bit riskier now because the higher skill level requirements on both ends essentially create more ways to stunt a player's growth. Due to the greater learning curve for perimeter players, teams will have to adjust their draft strategies accordingly. Raw athleticism is less important than it was in the past because floor spacing and playmaking skills are held to a much higher premium. Therefore, prospects that can adapt quickly to the NBA game by knocking down outside shots, maintaining a team's offensive flow and playing solid enough defense have an advantage over ball dominant, raw athletes that may need to rework their entire game to adjust to the league. With this in mind, the prototypes for successful perimeter players have to be changed and evaluations need to adjusted to reflect the changes in the NBA game.

In the past, the ideal wing player archetype was an explosively athletic, isolation scorer similar to a player like Kobe Bryant or Tracy McGrady. However, the most recently successful wing players in the league right now didn't necessarily come into the league with that profile. If we look at wing players that were drafted in or after 2010 that made at least one All-Star team and primarily played either two-guard or small forward, we get a list of the following eight players.

- Gordon Hayward, 9th overall, 2010
- Paul George, 10th overall, 2010
- Klay Thompson, 11th overall, 2011
- Kawhi Leonard, 15th overall, 2011
- Jimmy Butler, 30th overall, 2011
- Bradley Beal, 3rd overall, 2012
- Khris Middleton, 39th overall, 2012
- Victor Oladipo, 2nd overall, 2013

For the most part, the players on the list were considered second-tier wing prospects in their respective draft years, as they were mostly expected to be complimentary scorers that could effectively contribute on both ends. This was even the case for Beal and Oladipo despite the fact that they both were taken in top three. However, all of the players on the list above were able to raise their ceiling because their skill sets were a better fit for today's game than the traditional isolation scorer prototype, as they could contribute in other areas and compliment other high-end players. If these recent successes are factored into draft evaluations, the ideal wing prospect would theoretically follow a career path similar to Paul George, Kawhi Leonard or Klay Thompson. Specifically, they would fill a three-and-D role as a rookie and then they would gradually build up their offensive game as they approach their prime. Developing wing prospects in this fashion makes them better equipped to adapt to the modern era where wings often have the responsibility to defend multiple positions, space the floor and provide efficient volume scoring as a bonus. Going in a more traditional development path of focusing on volume scoring first and adding the complementary parts in later has not worked out as well in recent years because the better teams in the league are playing to maximize their overall efficiency and isolation-based, volume scoring almost runs counter to current trends in basketball strategy by encouraging inefficient shot selection and stagnating ball movement. Therefore, prospects that fit the old isolation scorer prototype have to be approached with a greater degree of scrutiny because they may have a tougher time transitioning into the NBA as efficient, two-way contributors. Because wing players have more responsibilities in today's game and it's now tougher for rookies to efficiently produce, established variations of a three-and-D wing in their prime years are much more valuable than they have ever been, simply as a result of scarcity. After all, roster construction hasn't really caught up to changes in the game, so there aren't enough quality two-way wings to fill the demand. Therefore, the value of the three-and-D wing is beginning to rise significantly as a result. Players like Robert Covington and Danny Green would have spent their prime years on contracts hovering around the mid-level if they were on the open market a decade ago. Now because their skill set is scarce and much more valuable, they each make eight figures per year. In summary, wing players with two-way skills are at a much higher premium in today's game and teams would be wise to hold onto established veterans or be more aggressive in targeting prospects with this profile in the draft.

      As the modern NBA has become less reliant on isolations and post-ups, the role of the point guard has changed. In the past, teams looked for a pass-first, table setter to feed their primary scorers and run slower developing sets. However, defenses are now much smarter and exploit non-scorers by playing off them to either choke off the opponent's offensive spacing or reduce the number of available passing lanes. As a result, the point guard position is primarily an offensive role where the team's main ball handler has to be an effective scoring threat in addition to being able to make plays for his teammates. To provide some evidence, here is a list of the top ten leaders in Win Shares from the 2017-18 season among players that played a majority of their minutes at point guard.

	WS	USG%	AST%	TS%
Damian Lillard	12.6	30.6	30.9	0.594
Chris Paul	10.2	24.5	40.9	0.604
Kyle Lowry	10.2	21.7	30.9	0.598
Russell Westbrook	10.1	34.1	49.8	0.524
Ben Simmons	9.2	22.3	37.4	0.557
Stephen Curry	9.1	31.0	30.3	0.675
Kyrie Irving	8.9	31.0	30.7	0.610
Kemba Walker	8.5	27.4	27.4	0.572
Darren Collison	7.6	17.4	26.4	0.610
Jrue Holiday	7.1	23.1	24.9	0.570

At a first glance, you can see that the top point guards tend to be higher volume players that score efficiently and distribute the ball at a high rate. The only exception to this profile last season was Darren Collison, who still played a lower volume, pass-first style, but was still threatening as a scorer due to his high shooting efficiency. For the most part, the performance of the elite point guards in the league results from having dynamic scoring ability and solid playmaking skills. The old, pass-first profile for point guards is not quite as productive as it once was. To illustrate this, here is a list of regular rotational point guards from the 2017-18 season that had a Usage Percentage under 20% and an Assist Percentage above 20%.

	MP	WS	USG%	AST%	TS%
Darren Collison	2018	7.6	17.4	26.4	0.610
Fred VanVleet	1520	4.7	19.1	22.8	0.556
D.J. Augustin	1760	4.1	18.6	24.4	0.615
T.J. McConnell	1706	3.8	13.8	24.5	0.545
Rajon Rondo	1705	3.6	16.9	42.2	0.522
Jerian Grant	1686	3.3	17.4	30.1	0.528
Lonzo Ball	1780	2.0	17.4	29.2	0.444
Jarrett Jack	1548	1.2	16.7	31.3	0.489
Tyler Ulis	1658	-0.2	18.5	28.0	0.465

Aside from Collison, none of the other players on the list played more than 2000 minutes. Also, most of these guys were either backup point guards or players that split time with others. Though a pass-first point guard can be useful, that player's utility is limited simply because his skill set may be too specialized for today's game. If a player is more reluctant to shoot, he's easier to guard because he doesn't possess the proper balance between scoring and passing to keep defenders honest. A heavy passing-minded player can present his own team with a disadvantage because that player's presence can give the opponent a place to hide weaker defending, high-end scorers, which would add more firepower to the opponent. Therefore, teams probably should place less value on the traditional, pass-first point guard prototype and look for dynamic ball handlers that have relatively equal scoring and passing skills. As a result, teams have to analyze point guard prospects much more carefully because the skill level requirements are now much higher, and the position has become more important in the modern game. Because of this, relatively small factors like free throw shooting carry much more weight, as any minor seeming inconsistency may raise a red flag that could hint a lower degree of skill and lesser likelihood of translating to the NBA. For instance, if Markelle Fultz's performance doesn't improve after he addresses his shoulder issues, we could go back into past his college stats and see that a warning sign may have been staring us right in the face. Specifically, his Free Throw Percentage was just under 65%, which suggests that his stroke may not have been as consistent as it was projected to be. All of this means that a highly translatable, premium ball handler prospect has much more value in today's league because the NBA's reliance on quick ball movement and pick-and-roll play have raised the importance of the point guard role and the availability of dynamic, multi-skilled ball handlers is scarce. If a team has to pay a steep price for an elite primary ball handler in his prime, then it might be more tempting to meet that demand today than it was in the previous era. However, the scarcity of quality ball handling playmakers may lead to some drastic over-valuations, as the supply simply isn't great enough to meet the demand. As a result, teams may need to become more creative in their on-court execution to either embrace non-traditional playmakers or ramp up their ball movement to compensate for the limited supply of quality ball handlers and essentially de-centralize the traditional point guard position.

  The changes in strategy in the NBA today have altered positional roles and draft evaluation systems of any kind have to be adjusted accordingly. Because the game is much more perimeter-oriented, traditional big men are not as important as they once were, as their roles are much more specialized and the greater availability of rim running, rim protector types makes them a little more fungible in this era. Conversely, multi-skilled perimeter players are now much more valuable as their roles have become less specialized as teams continue to adopt modern offenses that rely on spacing and ball movement. As a result, the traditional isolation scorer and pass-first point guard prototypes have seen their effectiveness diminish and dynamic scoring ball handlers and three-and-D wing players have become the most productive profiles that give a team a better chance to win. With this in mind, teams have to alter their acquisition strategies to allocate the bulk of their cap dollars to higher performing perimeter players that are now harder to replace and be more selective when they give out contracts to big men, as it's easier to find adequate substitutes. If a team can appropriately manage their resources to adjust for these changes in modern basketball strategy, it has a better chance of succeeding in the long-term and possibly it could compete for championships in the future.

ANALYZING THE 2019 NBA DRAFT

Glossary of Terms and Metrics

TS% = True Shooting Percentage, a measure of shooting efficiency that accounts for field goals, threes and free throws

OREB% = Offensive Rebound Percentage, an estimate of the percentage of offensive rebounds a player grabs while he was on the floor

DREB% = Defensive Rebound Percentage, an estimate of the percentage of defensive rebounds a player grabs while he was on the floor

TRB% = Total Rebound Percentage, an estimate of the percentage of total rebounds a player grabs while he was on the floor

AST% = Assist Percentage, an estimate of the percentage of teammate field goals a player assisted while he was on the floor

STL% = Steal Percentage, an estimate of the percentage of opponent possessions that ended in a steal by the player while he was on the floor

BLK% = Block Percentage, an estimate of the percentage of opponent two-point field goal attempts that were blocked by the player while he was on the floor

TOV% = Turnover Percentage, turnovers per 100 plays

USG% = Usage Percentage, an estimate of the percentage of team plays used by a player while he was on the floor

SIMsc = Similarity Score, a metric denoting how similar a prospect is to a given historical comparable, the number is taken out of 1000. Therefore, 900 or above represents a 90% or higher degree of similarity.

College player stats are their completed career stats.

International player stats are only from this season. They are accurate as of May 1, 2019.

Measurements are either from this year's Draft Combine or the Portsmouth Invitational. Height listings for players at the combine is their Height Without Shoes plus one inch.

For an explanation of the methods used to analyze the following methods, please refer back to the introductory article on page [x]

GREEN PROSPECTS

This is the subset of the highest yield prospects in the 2019 NBA Draft.

Zion Williamson   60/65/75

College/Country	Height	Weight	Age on July 1
Duke	6'6"	280	18.986

Wingspan	Standing Reach	No Step Vert	Max Vert
N/A	N/A	N/A	N/A

Basic Stats		Advanced Stats	
GP	33	TS%	0.702
MIN/G	30.0	3PTA/FGA	0.163
PTS/G	22.6	FTA/FGA	0.467
REB/G	8.9	OREB%	12.7
AST/G	2.1	DREB%	18.0
STL/G	2.1	TRB%	15.5
BLK/G	1.8	AST%	14.9
FG%	0.680	STL%	3.9
3PT%	0.338	BLK%	5.8
FT%	0.640	TOV%	12.8
		USG%	28.6

Projected Draft Range: Top 5

Top 10 Comps (Top 20 Picks Only)

	SIMsc			Year
1	860.9	Jahlil	Okafor	2015
2	854.8	Larry	Johnson	1991
3	852.6	Elton	Brand	1999
4	840.1	Kevin	Love	2008
5	838.9	Terrence	Jones	2012
6	835.8	Clarence	Weatherspoon	1992
7	834.0	Jabari	Parker	2014
8	833.7	Stanley	Johnson	2015
9	828.9	Corliss	Williamson	1995
10	827.8	Sean	May	2005

Initially, Zion Williamson was not regarded as the top NBA prospect on Duke's roster. However, that quickly changed the moment that he stepped foot on the court this season. He immediately became the premier player in all of college basketball and he wound up sweeping every major award. This June, Williamson is almost assured to be a lock for the first overall selection in this year's draft.

Offensively, Williamson was rated as excellent in almost every situation, according to Synergy. His combination of explosive quickness and power allows him to be a dynamic threat in transition. He can either immediately start a fast break off a rebound or use his speed to run the floor. In addition to this, he excels at moving off the ball in the half court by effectively cutting, rolling to the rim in pick-and-roll situations and crashing the offensive glass to score on put-backs. Also, his wide frame allows him to set very solid screens for his teammates. When he has the ball in his hands, he can be very difficult to stop. In isolation situations, he can use his strength and very good ball handling ability to easily get to the rim to either score or draw fouls. According to Synergy, he was effective on isolations in all parts of the floor, but he displayed a strong tendency to go left and he wasn't quite as efficient when he went to his right. In the post, he mainly succeeded by bullying defenders with a simple drop step, as he didn't utilize many other moves aside from an occasional hook shot. Additionally, he tended to make all of his moves by going over his right shoulder. Therefore, he'll have to go over his other shoulder to keep defenders honest in the NBA. Furthermore, he is a very good passer with enough natural court sense to eventually become a primary ball handler in the future. His only weakness is his outside shot, as he was only rated as average in spot-up situations, according to Synergy. At the moment, his shooting is a work-in-progress. From a mechanics standpoint, he has a bit of line drive shot and his release is rather slow. This creates some timing issues, which can explain why he has some trouble repeating his stroke. After all, he only made 64% of his free throws and just under 34% of his threes. If he can clean up his mechanics to get a little more lift on his shot, he could be an even more dynamic offensive player.

Defensively, he's a good fit for today's position-less NBA. Specifically, he's displayed the ability to defend inside as well as out on the perimeter. As an interior defender, he was very good at using his strength to keep his man from establishing good position inside. Also, his leaping ability allowed him to be effective at contesting and altering shots. Additionally, he was very consistent in blocking out, which enabled him to be an excellent defensive rebounder. This season, Williamson was mainly utilized as a roaming, weak side help defender to take advantage of his superior athleticism. Because of this, he was excellent at covering his teammates' mistakes by either rotating over to block shots or jumping passing lanes to get steals. As an on-ball defender, he showed some potential because he could capably guard any position in an isolation situation. He has very good lateral mobility for a player that is as big as he is, so he was pretty effective at containing guards on switches this season. If he displayed a weakness, it was that he could get over-aggressive and sometimes he would get caught out of position either gambling or going the wrong way on a screen. If he can channel his energy in a little more disciplined manner, he could really be a complete defensive player as his career progresses.

Zion Williamson is one of the best prospects to enter the draft in recent memory and his fit for the modern NBA gives him the potential to be a once-in-a-generation player if everything breaks right. In fact, the system had difficulty finding appropriate comparables, so the rarity of his profile suggests that his ceiling could be considerably high. From there, his extremely efficient level of production at Duke suggests that he's polished enough that he could make an immediate impact in the league next season. If he lands in a positive developmental environment that can help him reach his immense potential, he could be on the path to being an elite franchise player that could eventually become an MVP candidate in the future. Even if his developmental conditions aren't ideal, his floor is still incredibly high due to his enormous level of talent. At worst, he would probably end up becoming an excellent ball handling power forward similar to a more advanced version of Blake Griffin.

Ja Morant   55/60/65

College/Country	Height	Weight	Age on July 1
Murray State	6'3"	175	19.890

Wingspan	Standing Reach	No Step Vert	Max Vert
N/A	N/A	N/A	N/A

Basic Stats		Advanced Stats	
GP	65	TS%	0.597
MIN/G	35.3	3PTA/FGA	0.536
PTS/G	18.7	FTA/FGA	0.298
REB/G	6.1	OREB%	5.0
AST/G	8.2	DREB%	14.0
STL/G	1.4	TRB%	9.8
BLK/G	0.6	AST%	43.0
FG%	0.485	STL%	2.2
3PT%	0.343	BLK%	1.8
FT%	0.810	TOV%	19.7
		USG%	27.2

Projected Draft Range: Top 5

Top 10 Comps (Top 20 Picks Only)

	SIMsc			Year
1	902.9	D.J.	Augustin	2008
2	902.4	Mike	Conley	2007
3	901.3	Dennis	Smith	2017
4	901.3	Shai	Gilgeous-Alexander	2018
5	894.5	John	Wall	2010
6	891.3	Derrick	Rose	2008
7	890.9	Trey	Burke	2013
8	890.7	Jeff	Teague	2009
9	890.3	Jonny	Flynn	2009
10	885.5	Trae	Young	2018

Ja Morant was rated high on draft boards at the start of the year, but his stock rose significantly with his excellent performance throughout his sophomore season. Over the course of the year, he established himself as one of the nation's top college players, earning honors as a consensus first team All-American and Ohio Valley Conference Player of the Year. In all likelihood, Morant will be selected early in the lottery, possibly as high as the second overall pick.

Offensively, Morant fits the profile of a modern primary ball handler because he displays excellent playmaking skills to go along with his ability to threaten defenses as a scorer. As a playmaker, he excels at finding spot-up shooters on the perimeter and hitting open teammates around the rim. At times, he can be a little careless with the ball and he'll commit his fair share of turnovers, so he'll have to address this issue at the next level. As a scorer, Morant relies on his excellent speed to blow by his man and cause the defense to collapse towards him. Because of his considerable quickness, he excelled at pushing the ball up in transition and turning the corner on pick and rolls. This season, he was very good in isolation situations, but he heavily favored his left hand. In fact, he drove left almost 69% of the time and his efficiency dropped significantly when opponents forced him to his right. Therefore, he'll have to improve his ability to go right to keep defenders honest and maximize his effectiveness in the NBA. He had the ball in his hands most of the time, but in limited opportunities, he showed a strong ability to move off the ball. Specifically, he was an excellent cutter and he was good at coming off screens. He also was very good at picking his spots to hit the offensive glass to score on put-backs. At this stage, he's more of a mid-range shooter because his long range shot is still developing. On the positive side, his very good Free Throw Percentage suggests that he has the ability to repeat his stroke. However, he's only been a break-even three-point shooter in college at this stage. This is mainly because some mechanical issues arise when he shoots from deep. Specifically, his elbow tends to flare out, which causes some inconsistencies with his release point. Also, his release is a bit slow, so he'll sometimes lose his mechanics when he has to shoot off the dribble. If he puts in the time to fix these mechanical issues, he could eventually become a solid shooter down the line.

At the other end of the floor, Morant has all of the athletic tools to be an effective defender in the NBA. He has great length and lateral quickness to go along with his explosive leaping ability. At Murray State, he was mainly used as a weak side help defender. He was very effective at using his quickness to jump passing lanes to get steals and occasionally rotate inside to block a shot. He was also a very good rebounder for a player of his size. As an on-ball defender, he was generally pretty good at staying in front of his man. He was hidden a little bit in favorable matchups, so opponents didn't test him very often. When they did, he held up quite well and he rated in the 92nd percentile at defending in isolation situations. In pick-and-roll situations, he was good at using his lateral mobility to prevent ball handlers from turning the corner. However, he tended to overplay the drive, which allowed opponents to get additional space to knock down jumpers. Additionally, Morant had a tendency to gamble a bit too much. Because of this, he was caught out of position quite a bit, especially when he had to defend a player coming off screens. Specifically, he would often try to shoot the gap to go for a steal, but when he missed, it would leave his man open for a three. When he maintained his discipline, he was very good at using his length to close out on spot-up shooters on the perimeter.

Ja Morant is the top point guard prospect in this year's draft because of his great athleticism and high level of production at the college level. At this stage, he still needs to play with more discipline on the defensive end, improve his ability to drive right and shoot more consistently from the perimeter to become the best version of himself. If he can improve in these areas, he could reach his ceiling and become a taller variation of Kemba Walker. On the other hand, his floor is high enough that he could still be an effective NBA player if he doesn't improve upon his current weaknesses. If this scenario happens, then he could still have some success as a speed-reliant point guard along the lines of a poor man's John Wall.

Jarrett Culver 55/60/65

College/Country	Height	Weight	Age on July 1
Texas Tech	6'6"	194	20.359

Wingspan	Standing Reach	No Step Vert	Max Vert
6'9.5"	8'4.5"	N/A	N/A

Basic Stats		Advanced Stats	
GP	75	TS%	0.548
MIN/G	29.5	3PTA/FGA	0.351
PTS/G	14.9	FTA/FGA	0.363
REB/G	5.6	OREB%	5.3
AST/G	2.8	DREB%	16.8
STL/G	1.3	TRB%	11.3
BLK/G	0.6	AST%	20.5
FG%	0.459	STL%	2.6
3PT%	0.341	BLK%	2.7
FT%	0.687	TOV%	13.6
		USG%	27.8

Projected Draft Range: Lottery

Top 10 Comps (Top 20 Picks Only)

	SIMsc			Year
1	922.3	D'Angelo	Russell	2015
2	917.7	Alec	Burks	2011
3	915.8	Jerome	Robinson	2018
4	914.7	Bradley	Beal	2012
5	913.0	O.J.	Mayo	2008
6	912.9	Markelle	Fultz	2017
7	912.8	Rashad	McCants	2005
8	912.6	Bob	Sura	1995
9	910.7	Ben	Gordon	2004
10	909.2	Klay	Thompson	2011

After spending his freshman season in a secondary role, Jarrett Culver emerged this season as one of the nation's top college players. He earned several honors including the Player of the Year in the Big 12 Conference and a spot as a first team consensus All-American. In addition to his individual awards, he helped lead Texas Tech to their first Final Four appearance. In all probability, Culver will come off the board somewhere in the lottery, possibly as high as the top five in this year's NBA Draft.

Culver's stock rose this season because he was one of the best defenders on the nation's best defensive team. Naturally, he projects to be a solid defender at the next level. He has all of the requisite tools because he has great lateral quickness, very long arms and explosive leaping ability. As a result, Culver has demonstrated that he's a very good on-ball ball defender that could handle different matchups and situations. Generally, he's good at using his quickness and length to stay in front of his man in isolation situations to prevent drives and also contest pull-up jumpers. He also has enough strength to push opposing players off the block in post-up situations to force them into more difficult shots. Additionally, he was an effective pick-and-roll defender because he could either fight over the screen to contain the ball handler or he could switch to take away the roll to the rim. He was also excellent at closing out on shooters in spot-up situations, although he could sometimes be a bit too aggressive, which allowed opponents to occasionally get driving lanes to the hoop. Off the ball, he was usually pretty good at chasing shooters off screens, but he did have some trouble when the shooter was coming off a screen to the right. It's been an issue in each of his two seasons at Texas Tech, so if he cleans this issue up, he could be a more complete defender. Otherwise, he really has no other weaknesses on defense. He's also very good as a weak side help defender because he can use his length to play passing lanes to get steals and he'll rotate inside to occasionally block a shot. He's a solid rebounder as well.

On offense, Culver made a fairly smooth adjustment to a larger role. In fact, according to Synergy, he was rated as good or better in almost every offensive situation. Throughout his college career, he's been very effective off the ball, as he's demonstrated a consistent ability to knock down spot-up jumpers, cut to the rim and come off screens. This season, he's improved his ball handling and playmaking skills, which have allowed him to have success in other situations. He's much better at pushing the ball up the floor to find opportunities to score in transition and his improving playmaking skills allow him to be a much more dynamic player when he has the ball in his hands in a half-court offense. He was very good at finding spot-up shooters and hitting cutters in both isolation and pick-and-roll situations. As a scorer, he was mainly effective as a driver because he was good at going either way to score at the rim or draw fouls. His outside shot was a bit streaky over the course of the season. His shooting motion shows no major mechanical flaws aside from a small hitch at the top of his release. This hasn't really affected his shooting too much at the college level because he's been pretty solid at knocking down open shots and his free throw shooting has improved enough to suggest that he can consistently repeat his stroke. On the negative side, his Three-Point Percentage dropped a bit this season because he had to take more shots under duress as his team's primary shot creator. Therefore, he could stand to improve his ability to shoot off the dribble to become a more complete shooter.

Jarrett Culver is one of the safer wing prospects in this draft because at a minimum, he could fit into a team as a complementary, three-and-D player. If he continues to improve his all-around game, he could reach his potential to become a versatile, multi-positional, two-way wing player similar to someone like Michael Finley or Khris Middleton. On the other hand, if he's not quite as dynamic as an on-ball scorer, he could still have a long career in the league because of his defensive skills and ability to hit open shots. If this scenario happens, then he could be a reliable three-and-D role player along the lines of Josh Richardson.

Other Notable Comps Not Listed Above

SIMsc		Year
924.7	Will Barton	2012
916.6	Latrell Sprewell	1992
914.1	Ricky Davis	1998
903.9	Michael Finley	1995

R.J. Barrett   55/60/65

College/Country	Height	Weight	Age on July 1
Duke	6'7"	205	19.047

Wingspan	Standing Reach	No Step Vert	Max Vert
N/A	N/A	N/A	N/A

Basic Stats		Advanced Stats	
GP	38	TS%	0.532
MIN/G	35.3	3PTA/FGA	0.338
PTS/G	22.6	FTA/FGA	0.319
REB/G	7.6	OREB%	4.8
AST/G	4.3	DREB%	17.2
STL/G	0.9	TRB%	11.2
BLK/G	0.4	AST%	23.5
FG%	0.454	STL%	1.4
3PT%	0.308	BLK%	1.2
FT%	0.665	TOV%	13.2
		USG%	32.2

Projected Draft Range: Top 5

Top 10 Comps (Top 20 Picks Only)

	SIMsc			Year
1	907.4	Jamal	Murray	2016
2	905.5	James	Young	2014
3	896.4	DeMar	DeRozan	2009
4	890.8	Bradley	Beal	2012
5	890.8	Miles	Bridges	2018
6	890.4	Rashad	Vaughn	2015
7	889.9	Adam	Morrison	2006
8	889.6	Brandon	Ingram	2016
9	889.2	D'Angelo	Russell	2015
10	888.8	Kevin	Knox	2018

R.J. Barrett began the season as the favorite to become the first overall pick, only to be overshadowed by his teammate, Zion Williamson. Even so, he established himself as an excellent prospect in his own right, as he became a consensus first team All-American in his freshman season at Duke. Most likely, he'll be selected somewhere within the first five picks of this year's draft.

Right now, Barrett's defense is ahead of his offense. Athletically, he has a solid set of tools to be an effective defender in the NBA. He has solid lateral mobility, explosive leaping ability and good enough length to give opponents trouble. At Duke, Barrett was more of a stay-at-home defender because he didn't look to go for steals or blocks. On the ball, he was very good at defending in isolation situations. In particular, he was good at taking away jumpers off the dribble and he was adept at forcing his man to take tougher shots towards the baseline on the right side of the court. He also good at fighting over the top of screens to take away outside shots in pick-and-roll situations and stay attached to shooters off the ball. Every once in a while, he would be a bit too aggressive to go over the top and he would prone to allowing the ball handler to turn the corner for an easy lane to the basket. Additionally, he was vulnerable to some lapses off the ball. Specifically, he would get caught sagging a bit too far to give his man extra space to knock down a spot-up jumper. Also, he could stand to get a little stronger because opponents had considerable success against him in post-up situations by overpowering him to get easy scores around the basket.

Offensively, Barrett was a ball dominant, high volume scorer that generally looked to attack the rim. Most of his success came from using his athleticism to break down opponents in transition and drive in isolation situations. As a driver, he displayed some interesting tendencies. He generally looked to go right but was much more effective when he drove to his left. A reason for this may be that he seems more comfortable at taking pull-up jumpers when he goes left, which helps to keep defenders honest to make his drives more effective. As his career progresses, he'll have to work on improving his ability to shoot off the dribble when he goes right to keep opposing defenses from overplaying the drive. At this stage, Barrett may have some trouble fitting into a modern NBA offense. First off, he really doesn't know how to play off the ball because he was so ball dominant in college. As a result, he wasn't especially effective when he was cutting or coming off a screen. He also isn't really a natural playmaker, so opponents could aggressively bring help to force him into tougher shots because he doesn't quite have the vision to identify an open teammate on a consistent basis. Finally, Barrett is rather inconsistent as a shooter due to a below break-even Three-Point Percentage and he also has difficulties at the free throw line. His relatively low Free Throw Percentage suggests that he has some trouble in repeating his stroke. Most notably, his shooting elbow is a bit too far away from his body, so his release point can be thrown off as a result. Also, he doesn't always stay balanced when he goes up for a shot, so his release point is negatively affected this way as well. In order for him to succeed in the NBA, he will have to consistently work to fix these issues and improve his shot. Otherwise, his future effectiveness could be limited at the next level.

Overall, Barrett has plenty of tools to become an impact player in the NBA, but he'll have to put in considerable work to fit in as a wing player in the league today. Fortunately, he's solid enough on the defensive end to make some contributions right away. If he makes strides to improve his jump shot and playmaking skills, he could reach his ceiling and become a very good scoring wing player like DeMar DeRozan. Otherwise, he could wind up being a shorter variation of Brandon Ingram, a player that can occasionally flash some brilliance but tends to have his career defined by inconsistency.

Cam Reddish   50/60/65

College/Country	Height	Weight	Age on July 1
Duke	6'8"	208	19.830

Wingspan	Standing Reach	No Step Vert	Max Vert
7'0.5"	8'9.5"	N/A	N/A

Basic Stats		Advanced Stats	
GP	36	TS%	0.499
MIN/G	29.7	3PTA/FGA	0.618
PTS/G	13.5	FTA/FGA	0.264
REB/G	3.7	OREB%	2.0
AST/G	1.9	DREB%	10.7
STL/G	1.6	TRB%	6.5
BLK/G	0.6	AST%	10.7
FG%	0.356	STL%	2.9
3PT%	0.333	BLK%	1.9
FT%	0.772	TOV%	16.5
		USG%	25.3

Projected Draft Range: Lottery

Top 10 Comps (Top 20 Picks Only)

	SIMsc			Year
1	929.4	Xavier	Henry	2010
2	909.4	Rashad	McCants	2005
3	904.8	Thaddeus	Young	2007
4	904.3	DerMarr	Johnson	2000
5	902.7	Josh	Okogie	2018
6	901.4	Paul	George	2010
7	901.0	Luol	Deng	2004
8	900.1	Jayson	Tatum	2017
9	898.9	Joe	Johnson	2001
10	895.7	Kevin	Knox	2018

Cam Reddish came into the season as a major part of Duke's highly touted freshman class. However, he got a little lost in the shuffle because the majority of the responsibilities went to Zion Williamson and R.J. Barrett. Even though Reddish's numbers took a hit because he had some struggles adjusting to a supporting role, he flashed enough potential in limited opportunities to keep his draft stock high enough to the point where he'll probably be taken somewhere in the lottery in this particular draft.

On the offensive end, Reddish's skill set wasn't a good match for his role as a supporting player. This is mainly because he's at his best when he has the ball in his hands. The problem was that he spent 87.4% of his possessions off the ball, which really went against his strengths. In the limited number of situations that he was able to play on the ball, he was pretty effective because he could either pull up for a quick jumper or get all the way to the rim on isolations or as the pick-and-roll ball handler. As a driver, he's fairly good at changing directions, but he has a very strong tendency to go left. Therefore, he'll have to work on his ability to go right to keep defenders honest at the NBA level. In a small sample, he's flashed some playmaking skills, but he's not fully polished in this area because he's limited to making simple reads. Most of his struggles this season came when he had to play off the ball. Some of this was a product of Duke's stagnant offensive system, as they didn't really use very much player or ball movement. Because of this, Reddish often was left standing around on the weak side. Therefore, he really wasn't effective at cutting or coming off screens. Additionally, the limited number of offensive touches caused him to play in a rushed or anxious manner, so he was prone to forcing up some hurried, contested shots that really hurt his efficiency. When he plays under control, he shown some promise as a shooter. The mechanics in his shooting form are fairly sound and his Free Throw Percentage suggests that his stroke is repeatable. Also, he shot very well on unguarded catch and shoot attempts this season, as he posted an Effective Field Goal Percentage of 56.9% in those situations. If he can just cut down on the number of forced shots, he could be much more efficient shooter in the NBA than he was at Duke.

Defensively, he has flashed considerable potential, but he's still a bit unpolished. From an athletic standpoint, he has all of the necessary tools. He has quick feet that allow him stay with his man along with a very long wingspan and great leaping ability. These tools allow him to be a very good weak side help defender, as he'll jump passing lanes or use his length to get deflections and steals. He's also very effective at rotating inside to block shots and he's a solid defensive rebounder. As an on-ball and team defender, he was effective most of the time, but opponents were able to use his aggressiveness against him. On the positive side, he was very good at using his length to contest shots, either on the ball in isolation situations or when he was closing out on a spot-up shooter. He was also good at fighting over screens to prevent ball handlers from taking pull-up jumpers in pick-and-roll situations. However, he would often close out a bit too aggressively, which opened up some driving lanes to allow opponents to get to the rim. In addition to this, he would also get caught trying to shoot the gap when defending shooters off screens. When he wasn't able to jump the passing lane to get a steal, he would allow his man to get an open look from outside. At the NBA level, he'll have to tone down his aggressiveness a bit to maintain his positioning. If he can stay in a better defensive position on a consistent basis, he could become a versatile defender with the tools to guard a lot of different types of players.

    Overall, Cam Reddish is a high upside prospect that could wind up being better as a pro than he was as a college player. He's still pretty unpolished at the moment, so it could take some time for him to develop. If he lands with a team that is patient enough to allow him to develop at his own speed, his tools could eventually come together to allow him to be a very good, two-way wing player with All-Star potential. If he reaches his ceiling, he'll probably follow a career path similar to Joe Johnson. Specifically, he might have some struggles when he immediately enters the league, but after a few years, he could grow into an impact player. On the other hand, if he lands in an adverse situation that stunts his growth in some way, he could still have a solid career as a complementary two-way role player along the lines of Thaddeus Young.

De'Andre Hunter   55/60/60+

College/Country	Height	Weight	Age on July 1
Virginia	6'7"	225	21.581

Wingspan	Standing Reach	No Step Vert	Max Vert
N/A	N/A	N/A	N/A

Basic Stats		Advanced Stats	
GP	71	TS%	0.606
MIN/G	26.6	3PTA/FGA	0.264
PTS/G	12.4	FTA/FGA	0.420
REB/G	4.4	OREB%	6.3
AST/G	1.6	DREB%	14.0
STL/G	0.6	TRB%	10.3
BLK/G	0.5	AST%	12.6
FG%	0.509	STL%	1.4
3PT%	0.419	BLK%	2.5
FT%	0.773	TOV%	10.2
		USG%	24.7

Projected Draft Range: Lottery

Top 10 Comps (Top 20 Picks Only)

	SIMsc			Year
1	923.9	Vince	Carter	1998
2	916.7	Kirk	Snyder	2004
3	913.6	Jason	Richardson	2001
4	913.1	Gerald	Henderson	2009
5	911.9	Tracy	Murray	1992
6	910.8	Wally	Szczerbiak	1999
7	905.3	Eric	Piatkowski	1994
8	904.8	Anthony	Bennett	2013
9	903.8	Pat	Garrity	1998
10	903.5	Calbert	Cheaney	1993

There was some speculation that De'Andre Hunter would enter last year's NBA Draft, but after suffering a broken wrist in the 2018 ACC Tournament, he chose to return to Virginia for his sophomore season. The move to return to school paid off significantly and Hunter became a critical part of Virginia's national championship team. He also earned honors the ACC's Defensive Player of the Year and his draft stock has risen to the point where he'll probably be taken somewhere in the lottery.

Hunter's primary strengths are on the defensive end of the floor. Physically, he has all of the tools to be an excellent wing defender that can capably defend multiple positions in the NBA. He's a very good athlete with long arms, quick feet and good leaping ability. He also comes from one of the nation's most disciplined defensive programs, so he's a very sound team defender. He's very active to close out on spot-up shooters on the perimeter and he's excellent at defending shooters when they are coming off screens. In addition to this, he excels at defending the pick-and-roll by either containing the ball handler or switching onto the roll man to take away the dive to the hoop. He'll also alter shots around the basket, and he maintains sound positioning that allows him to be a very good defensive rebounder. At this stage, he's more of a stay-at-home defender, so he rarely goes for steals. However, his long arms do allow him to get deflections and be disruptive to opposing ball handlers. Generally, he was effective at defending in isolation situations, but he would sometimes be a bit too aggressive to take away the outside shot, leaving him vulnerable to drives to the basket. Right now, his positives outweigh his negatives and he should be a very good defensive player in the NBA.

Offensively, Hunter is better suited for a complementary role because he was primarily used off the ball at Virginia. In fact, he was put in non-dribbling situations over 82% of the time this past season. In those situations, he was very effective because he's an advanced shooter. His Three-Point Percentage is just under 42% for his career and his free throw shooting is good enough to suggest that he's able to repeat his stroke with a good degree of consistency. He also doesn't have any real flaws in his mechanics. From a performance perspective, he was rated by Synergy as very good at coming off screens and knocking down spot-up jumpers. He was also very effective as the screener in pick-and-pop situations. In addition to his shooting, Hunter was very good at cutting to the rim to take advantage of defenders that tried to overplay his shot and he showed a great ability to pick his spots to crash the offensive boards to score on put-backs. On the ball, he had success in isolation situations because he could use the threat of his shot to set up drives to the rim. At this stage, he's more of a straight line driver because he doesn't really change directions particularly well. Additionally, he displays a fairly heavy tendency to drive to his left, so he will have to work on going right more often to keep defenders honest. Though he's a willing passer, he's not a natural playmaker because he's limited to making simple reads and making safer passes to avoid turnovers. On the positive side, he's an effective post-up player that mainly relies on overpowering smaller defenders to get scores at the rim or using his shooting ability to set up a strong face up game. He's also an excellent passer out of the post because he can easily hit spot-up shooters on the perimeter if opponents try to double team him.

De'Andre Hunter is a pretty safe bet that should become a useful, long-term NBA player. Because his skill set is best suited for a complementary role, he may not have a great deal of high-end upside. Even so, his skills are polished enough that he should make a fairly quick transition to the league and fill a role as a three-and-D wing player. If he finds the right fit, he could end up at the higher end of the three-and-D spectrum and become a team's second or third best player, similar to someone like Khris Middleton. Otherwise, if he lands in a chaotic environment that doesn't allow him to reach his full potential, he could wind up becoming a very good role player along the lines of a bigger version of Mikal Bridges from last year's draft.

Other Notable Comps Not Listed Above

SIMsc		Year
913.1	Khris Middleton	2012
902.7	Kyle Kuzma	2017

Bol Bol 50/60/60+

College/Country	Height	Weight	Age on July 1
Oregon	7'2"	208	19.622

Wingspan	Standing Reach	No Step Vert	Max Vert
7'7"	9'7.5"	N/A	N/A

Basic Stats		Advanced Stats	
GP	9	TS%	0.632
MIN/G	29.8	3PTA/FGA	.189
PTS/G	21.0	FTA/FGA	.280
REB/G	9.6	OREB%	8.7
AST/G	1.0	DREB%	29.0
STL/G	0.8	TRB%	19.2
BLK/G	2.7	AST%	9.6
FG%	0.561	STL%	1.6
3PT%	0.520	BLK%	12.4
FT%	0.757	TOV%	10.7
		USG%	33.4

Projected Draft Range: Top 20

Top 10 Comps (Top 20 Picks Only)

	SIMsc			Year
1	862.2	Eddie	Griffin	2001
2	858.8	Mohamed	Bamba	2018
3	845.1	Kevin	Durant	2007
4	824.6	Chris	Bosh	2003
5	820.7	Michael	Beasley	2008
6	818.7	Marvin	Bagley III	2018
7	817.4	Brandan	Wright	2007
8	815.8	DeAndre	Ayton	2018
9	813.3	Kris	Humphries	2004
10	812.4	John	Henson	2012

Bol Bol is the son of former NBA center, Manute Bol. Bol Bol is an interesting prospect in his own right and he was off to a great start before his season was cut short due to a foot injury. Specifically, he suffered a stress fracture to the navicular bone in his left foot. The timetable for Bol's injury is a little uncertain, as big men with his injury have sometimes taken longer to make a full recovery. Even with the injury, he flashed enough potential in his nine games at Oregon to keep his draft stock fairly high and he's expected to be off the board somewhere within the first twenty picks of the first round.

At the offensive end, Bol has a lot of skills that will allow him to succeed in the NBA. Most notably, he's an excellent outside shooter. The sample of shots is small, but he made 13 of his 25 threes this past season. He also shot a solid percentage from the free throw line, so his shooting stroke is fairly repeatable and consistent. From a mechanics standpoint, he shoots with a pretty smooth motion and he's fairly comfortable at shooting from beyond NBA three-point range. Therefore, his shot could translate fairly well if he makes a full recovery. In addition to his outside shooting, Bol is a very effective rim runner due to his incredible length and athleticism, as he's very good at cutting to the rim and running the floor in transition. He'll also crash the offensive boards to score on put-backs. His frame is rather thin at this stage, so he has some trouble holding position in the post. When he has solid position, he was a solid post-up player mainly because he could use his considerable length to shoot over the top of most defenders. He doesn't really have a lot of post moves, so he could stand to develop a few more to increase his effectiveness. However, with the way that the NBA game is played today with fewer teams using big-on-big post-ups, he may not need to do much more with his post-up game, especially if his outside shot translates. As another note, Bol is decent passing big man that can hit spot-up shooters if opponents try to double team him.

At the other end of the floor, he has a lot of the necessary tools to thrive as a rim protecting big man, but his defense is a little tough to project at this stage. This is mainly because he played in a zone heavy defensive system, so he was planted in the paint for most of his defensive possessions. He was very effective in those possessions because he's an excellent shot blocker due to his extraordinary length, solid leaping ability and great timing. These physical traits also made him a very good defensive rebounder. When he was healthy, he displayed enough lateral mobility to suggest that he could handle the switching responsibilities of a modern defense. He was very good at staying with his man in a very small number of isolation possessions and he was excellent at using his length to close out on spot-up shooters on the perimeter. Because he didn't play a lot of man defense at Oregon, he struggled in a limited number of pick-and-roll situations. Specifically, he was sometimes unsure of his rotations, so he would get caught in an in-between position and he'd either allow the ball handler to get an open jumper or the roll man would score at the rim. Additionally, he had some trouble defending in the post because he simply wasn't strong enough to prevent opponents from establishing deep position against him. Therefore, he'll have to get stronger to effectively defend the better post-up players in the NBA.

Bol Bol is one of the more intriguing prospects in this year's draft. His foot injury is serious enough to make him something of a risky pick, but the payoff could be significant if he fully recovers. If all of his best skills translate, he could develop into a younger, more athletic variation of this season's version of Brook Lopez, as he would be a rim protecting big man that could also space the floor. Otherwise, if he suffers some setbacks in his recovery or he doesn't quite reach his potential, he could still have a solid career as a rotational big man that can knock down threes and block shots.

Coby White 50/55/60+

College/Country	Height	Weight	Age on July 1
North Carolina	6'5"	191	19.370

Wingspan	Standing Reach	No Step Vert	Max Vert
6'5"	8'1.5"	N/A	N/A

Basic Stats		Advanced Stats	
GP	35	TS%	0.556
MIN/G	28.5	3PTA/FGA	0.525
PTS/G	16.1	FTA/FGA	0.293
REB/G	3.5	OREB%	1.3
AST/G	4.1	DREB%	11.3
STL/G	1.1	TRB%	6.4
BLK/G	0.3	AST%	24.4
FG%	0.423	STL%	2.0
3PT%	0.352	BLK%	1.3
FT%	0.800	TOV%	15.7
		USG%	26.9

Projected Draft Range: Lottery

Top 10 Comps (Top 20 Picks Only)

	SIMsc			Year
1	930.1	D'Angelo	Russell	2015
2	929.1	Stephon	Marbury	1996
3	926.8	Brandon	Knight	2011
4	912.2	William	Avery	1999
5	911.7	Ben	Gordon	2004
6	911.4	Trey	Burke	2013
7	911.3	Malik	Monk	2017
8	911.2	Jerome	Robinson	2018
9	909.0	Cameron	Payne	2015
10	907.4	Jerryd	Bayless	2008

At the start of the season, Coby White wasn't viewed as the top prospect on North Carolina's roster. However, his steady play as the team's full-time starting point guard made him one of the top players on one of the nation's best teams. As a result, he earned honors as a second team All-ACC performer and his stock has shot up to the point where it's likely that he'll be taken early in the first round of this year's draft, possibly in the lottery.

Offensively, White has displayed a lot of skills that could allow him to be effective as a point guard in the NBA. Particularly, he was pretty good as the ball handler in pick-and-roll situations this past season at North Carolina. He showed sound playmaking skills because he was good at hitting the roll man and he could consistently find shooters on the perimeter or cutters off the ball. He also could use his natural quickness to turn the corner to score at the rim. His speed also allowed him to be effective as a driver in isolation situations. However, he has trouble going to his left, so he'll have to improve upon this to prevent opponents from exploiting this potential weakness. Next, White has a fairly good outside shot. His motion has no real mechanical issues and his stroke is pretty repeatable, which is evidenced by the fact that he made 80% of his free throws. He's a solid three-point shooter that made threes at a rate just over 35%, but he's much better in catch and shoot situations than he is at taking shots of the dribble. This season, he was excellent in catch and shoot situations overall because he could consistently knock down spot-up jumpers and he could come off screens. Off the dribble, he had some trouble making shots because he would rush his motion at times, which would throw off his balance. As a result, he was rated as being below average at taking dribble jumpers in pick-and-roll situations and this tendency to rush his shot caused him to miss a lot of trail threes in transition. Additionally, he had a tendency to be a little too hyper overall. This caused him to be a bit out of control in pushing the ball in transition and he would sometimes over-penetrate to take wild shots in heavy traffic. He also was a little bit turnover prone as well. If he can rein in his activity level and stay under control, he could fix these issues to become a much more effective offensive player in the NBA.

At the defensive end, White has the potential to be a solid defender, but he needs to break some bad habits. From a physical tools standpoint, he could hold up fairly well because he has good lateral quickness and solid leaping ability. His arms aren't especially long, but he's taller than most point guard prospects, so he could adequately handle wing players if it's necessary. On the ball, he was very good at containing his man in isolation situations because he had the quickness to stop drives to the basket and he was consistent at contesting the outside shots. He was also good at staying attached to shooters that were coming off screens. In addition to this, he was a very good weak side help defender that would play passing lanes to get steals and he's a solid rebounder for his size. On the negative side, he has a tendency to gamble a bit, which caused him to be out of position quite a bit. As a result, he would either be late to close out on shooters on the perimeter or he would close too aggressively to open up a driving lane. He would also get caught in an in-between position when he was defending the high pick-and-roll, so he was unable to prevent opposing ball handlers from turning the corner or pulling up for a jumper. When he was in decent position in pick-and-rolls, he would overplay the drive by sagging a bit too far under the screen, which made him vulnerable to allowing open shots on the outside. At the NBA level, White will have to be more disciplined with his rotations and work on his abilities as a team defender. If he makes the necessary adjustments, he could eventually develop into a decent defensive player in the NBA.

Overall, Coby White is an interesting prospect that could play both guard spots at the NBA level. The system rates him as extremely similar to D'Angelo Russell and if everything breaks right, he could turn into a similar player. To do so, he'll have to learn to play under control on a consistent basis, improve his ability to use his left hand and be a more disciplined position defender. If these weaknesses don't improve as his career progresses, he could still be a solid point guard in the league because of his shooting and playmaking skills. If this worst-case scenario were to occur, he could be a useful combo guard like Brandon Knight before he suffered his various injuries.

Romeo Langford   50/55/60+

College/Country	Height	Weight	Age on July 1
Indiana	6'6"	210	19.682

Wingspan	Standing Reach	No Step Vert	Max Vert
6'11"	8'7"	N/A	N/A

Basic Stats		Advanced Stats	
GP	32	TS%	0.542
MIN/G	34.1	3PTA/FGA	0.316
PTS/G	16.5	FTA/FGA	0.491
REB/G	5.4	OREB%	4.8
AST/G	2.3	DREB%	12.8
STL/G	0.8	TRB%	8.9
BLK/G	0.8	AST%	14.2
FG%	0.448	STL%	1.3
3PT%	0.272	BLK%	2.7
FT%	0.722	TOV%	12.2
		USG%	26.1

Projected Draft Range: Top 20

Top 10 Comps (Top 20 Picks Only)

	SIMsc			Year
1	924.8	James	Young	2014
2	923.6	DeMar	DeRozan	2009
3	918.6	Bradley	Beal	2012
4	918.3	Austin	Rivers	2012
5	914.6	James	Anderson	2010
6	912.9	Josh	Okogie	2018
7	912.1	Andrew	Wiggins	2014
8	909.1	Gerald	Henderson	2009
9	904.8	Ben	McLemore	2013
10	903.6	Miles	Bridges	2018

Romeo Langford came into the season as a highly touted prospect. Last year, he was a McDonald's All-American and he was expected to only be at Indiana for one season. He was Indiana's leading scorer this past season and he was productive enough to earn honors as a second team All-Big-Ten player. His stock stayed throughout the season and he will probably be off the board within the first twenty picks of this year's draft.

Offensively, Langford is primarily a slashing wing player that aggressively looks to attack the basket. He's most effective with the ball in his hands as either an isolation player or as a pick-and-roll ball handler. He mainly relies on his quickness and athleticism to beat his man off the dribble to score at the rim or draw fouls. His off-the-dribble game isn't fully polished at this stage because he has trouble driving to his left. Therefore, he'll need to improve in this area to prevent defenders from sitting on his right hand. He also isn't really a natural passer or playmaker, as he's limited to making simple, pre-programmed reads. If he was driving into unanticipated extra traffic, he wasn't able to locate an open teammate and he would try to get bailed out the officials by throwing his body into opposing defenders to try to get a foul call. It worked to some extent in college, but he may not get these kinds of calls in the NBA. Therefore, he'll have to improve his court vision to be a more effective driver at the NBA level. In addition to his driving abilities, he was effective in a few other areas. The sample of possessions is limited, but he was good at taking advantage of size mismatches by posting up smaller guards to either bully them inside with a drop step or face up to drive by them. He also displayed a pretty good ability to move without the ball, as he was an effective cutter and he had a good sense of knowing when to pick his spots to hit the offensive glass to score on put-backs. On the negative side, his outside shooting still needs considerable work. He wasn't especially efficient from the field for a number of reasons. First off, he was prone to taking a lot of ill-advised, contested shots, so he could stand to improve his shot selection. Secondly, he has a slight pause at the top of his shooting motion, which causes some timing issues that throw off his balance and the release of his shot. Over the course of his career, he'll have to make a mechanical adjustment to make his release more consistent. Fortunately for him, his free throw shooting is solid enough to suggest that he can adequately make necessary the changes to develop a reliable and repeatable stroke in the future.

At the defensive end, Langford has the tools to be effective, but he's not quite a finished product right now. He was hidden in favorable matchups at Indiana because he was tested too often, so he'll have to adjust to defending much better opponents. Physically, he has all of the requisite tools. He moves very well laterally, and he has explosive leaping ability to go along with a sizeable wingspan. In the few situations where he was tested, he held up quite well. Specifically, he was good at using his quickness to prevent opponents from driving to the basket in isolation and pick-and-roll situations. He had a slight tendency to overplay the drive, so he was prone to giving up an occasional pull-up jumper. As a weak side defender, he was good at using his leaping ability and length to rotate inside to block shots. He was also a solid defensive rebounder as well. In off ball situations, he had some struggles. He would be prone to bouts of ball watching, so he would sometimes be late to close out on spot-up shooters. Other times, he would close out too aggressively, and he would allow his man to get an easy driving lane to the rim. In addition to this, he wouldn't always fight through screens, so opposing shooters were able to free themselves up for shots much more easily against him. If he ends on a team with more sound defensive structure, he has a better chance of dropping these bad habits to become a better overall defender. Otherwise, his potential could be somewhat limited if he's only a middling defender.

Romeo Langford has a lot of tools to eventually be a successful wing player in the future, but he'll have to improve his shooting and defense to fit into today's NBA. His game right now isn't especially polished, so the team that takes him will have to be patient to allow him to grow at his own speed. If everything breaks right and he makes the necessary improvements on both ends of the floor, he could develop into an impactful perimeter scorer along the lines of a slightly bigger version of Jamal Murray. Otherwise, he could wind up becoming a solid rotational wing player that provides some supplementary scoring as either a borderline or high-end bench player similar to someone like Tim Hardaway, Jr.

Other Notable Comps Not Listed Above

SIMsc		Year
904.6	Tim Hardaway, Jr.	2013
902.2	Kevin Knox	2018

Darius Garland   50/55/60

College/Country	Height	Weight	Age on July 1
Vanderbilt	6'2"	175	19.427

Wingspan	Standing Reach	No Step Vert	Max Vert
N/A	N/A	N/A	N/A

Basic Stats		Advanced Stats	
GP	5	TS%	0.657
MIN/G	27.8	3PTA/FGA	0.426
PTS/G	16.2	FTA/FGA	0.296
REB/G	3.8	OREB%	1.6
AST/G	2.6	DREB%	13.7
STL/G	0.8	TRB%	7.7
BLK/G	0.4	AST%	25.7
FG%	0.537	STL%	1.7
3PT%	0.478	BLK%	1.5
FT%	0.750	TOV%	19.6
		USG%	27.9

Projected Draft Range: Lottery

Top 10 Comps (Top 20 Picks Only)

	SIMsc			Year
1	899.3	Brandon	Knight	2011
2	898.2	Stephon	Marbury	1996
3	883.2	Malik	Monk	2017
4	876.1	Trey	Burke	2013
5	870.6	Collin	Sexton	2018
6	866.8	Eric	Bledsoe	2010
7	863.0	Malik	Beasley	2016
8	862.5	Jamal	Crawford	2000
9	862.3	D'Angelo	Russell	2015
10	860.9	Ben	McLemore	2013

Darius Garland came into this season as a heralded recruit, as he was the only incoming freshman to make the SEC's preseason all-conference team. His season got off to a great start, but it was cut short when he tore the meniscus in his left knee in late November. He missed the rest of the season and he's spent the last few months preparing for the upcoming draft. His stock wasn't affected too much, and he'll probably be taken at some point in the lottery.

Garland showed the most promise on the offensive end of the floor in his limited game action. He only really played one game against an opponent from a major conference, but he flashed enough skill to suggest that he could be a solid offensive player in the league. This is mainly because his most translatable skill is his shooting. He has a smooth, repeatable stroke that allowed him to shoot very efficiently at Vanderbilt, posting an Effective Field Goal Percentage of 63.9%. He also made almost 48% of his threes in a small sample of attempts. He was able to make outside shots in a variety of ways. He could knock down spot-up jumpers, come off screens and hit pull-up threes as a pick-and-roll ball handler. In general, he's an excellent pick-and-roll player because he can leverage the threat of his shot to also get to the rim. He's also a willing playmaker with great court vision, although it didn't necessarily translate into assists at Vanderbilt because his teammates had trouble making shots. At times, he would try to do too much by attempting to make complicated passes, so he was prone to throwing the ball away. This can explain why his turnover rate was somewhat high in his limited game action. As a negative, Garland didn't appear to be overwhelmingly quick when he was healthy, and he had some difficulty beating defenders off the dribble in isolation situations. Therefore, it's unclear if he will develop into a dynamic scorer at the NBA level.

As a defender, Garland looked to be more of a team defender than an individual defender in the few games that he played. His physical tools aren't particularly ideal because he has a thin frame, his arms are on the shorter side and he isn't really an explosive leaper. However, he does have solid enough lateral quickness to stay with opposing point guards. He wasn't tested at all in isolation situations at Vanderbilt, but he was an effective pick-and-roll defender. In particular, he was good at fighting through screens to take away the outside shot and he was quick enough to prevent ball handlers from turning the corner. He was more of a stay-at-home defender because he really didn't get blocks or steals. On the other hand, he generally maintained solid defensive positioning, which allowed him to be a good rebounder for his size. A lot of times, Vanderbilt hid him off the ball by having him guard a stationary spot-up shooter. He would consistently close out on the shooters, but his lack of length still allowed opponents to shoot over the top of him. Therefore, he'll have to figure out a way to improve his defense to a point where he won't be a target for opposing offenses.

Darius Garland is a skilled prospect that should be able to handle the offensive responsibilities of the modern point guard position. If he makes a full recovery from his meniscus injury, he'll still have to improve his defense to allow him to be an impact player in the league. If everything breaks right, he could be another variation of Trae Young from last year's draft. Most likely, he'll wind up becoming a borderline starting point guard or a higher-end rotational player due to his lack of explosive athleticism. In the most probable scenario, he could develop into a good outside shooting playmaker similar to someone like Mo Williams.

Keldon Johnson — 50/55/60

College/Country	Height	Weight	Age on July 1
Kentucky	6'6"	216	19.721

Wingspan	Standing Reach	No Step Vert	Max Vert
6'9.25"	8'8"	N/A	N/A

Basic Stats		Advanced Stats	
GP	37	TS%	0.559
MIN/G	30.7	3PTA/FGA	0.316
PTS/G	13.5	FTA/FGA	0.414
REB/G	5.9	OREB%	5.5
AST/G	1.6	DREB%	16.4
STL/G	0.8	TRB%	11.3
BLK/G	0.2	AST%	10.6
FG%	0.463	STL%	1.5
3PT%	0.381	BLK%	0.6
FT%	0.703	TOV%	11.8
		USG%	22.8

Projected Draft Range: Top 20

Top 10 Comps (Top 20 Picks Only)

	SIMsc			Year
1	934.5	James	Young	2014
2	933.6	DeMar	DeRozan	2009
3	916.4	Kevin	Knox	2018
4	912.8	Austin	Rivers	2012
5	907.7	Tobias	Harris	2011
6	907.5	Quentin	Richardson	2000
7	907.2	Luol	Deng	2004
8	907.2	Justise	Winslow	2015
9	905.6	Malik	Beasley	2016
10	905.0	Gerald	Henderson	2009

Keldon Johnson was expected to be among the latest one-and-done players from Kentucky, as he came into school as a heralded recruit and a McDonald's All-American. He played well in his freshman season, earning honors as the SEC's Rookie of the Year and he was named as a second team All-SEC player as well. Because of his solid performance, Johnson elected to forego his final three years of eligibility and he'll probably be taken early in the first round, possibly somewhere in the lottery.

Johnson's main strengths are on the defensive end of the floor, as he was rated by Synergy as being good or better in every defensive situation this past season. Physically, he has all of the tools to become a valuable multi-positional defender in the NBA. He has very good lateral mobility to go along with great length and solid leaping ability. These tools allowed him to be a very good defender in isolation situations, as he could stay with his man to stop drives and he could use his length to bother shots on the perimeter. In addition to this, he showed enough functional strength to effectively guard bigger players in the post when he was caught on a switch. Specifically, he could push opposing players off the block to prevent them from getting deep position and his length made it tough for his man to shoot over him. He was also a very good, stay-at-home team defender as well. He didn't really take unnecessary gambles to go for steals or blocks and he was usually in a very good defensive position, which enabled him to be a good rebounder. He would consistently close out on shooters on the perimeter and he was generally good at fighting through screens to either stay attached to a shooter off the ball or contain the ball handler in pick-and-roll situations. As a slight negative, he tended to overplay the drive a bit, so he would sometimes give his man extra space to take an outside shot. It didn't really affect his defense very much at Kentucky because he would close these gaps with his length and superior athleticism. He's not going to have the same advantages in the NBA, so he will have clean up this little issue to be a more complete defender. Even so, his positives greatly outweigh this negative and he's probably going to develop into a solid defensive player at the NBA level.

Offensively, Johnson projects to be more of a complementary player because he was mainly used off the ball. In fact, non-dribbling situations accounted for 95.4% of his offense, according to Synergy. He was pretty effective in these possessions because he's a very good shooter, as he made just over 38% of his threes. His mechanics are pretty sound, and his stroke is pretty repeatable. This season, he established that he could knock down catch-and-shoot spot-up jumpers. Then, if defenders were too aggressive in closing out on him, he could use straight-line drives to score at the rim or draw fouls. In addition to being a good spot-up shooter, he was pretty good at shooting off screens. He was a little bit better at coming off to his left than he was when he was coming off a screen to the right. Furthermore, he's a willing passer, but he's not a natural playmaker because he can only make simple reads and safe passes on the perimeter. On the negative side, Johnson's upside is limited by his lack of ideal ball handling skills. As a result, he struggles to create his own shot off the dribble. In a small number of possessions on isolations or as the ball handler in the pick-and-roll situations, he really had trouble getting all the way to the basket. Therefore, he's not likely to be a primary scorer at the NBA level.

Overall, Keldon Johnson projects to be a solid three-and-D wing player that could guard multiple positions and knock down perimeter shots. If he significantly improves his ball handling, he may be able to unlock some additional upside. However, it's more likely that he'll have a long career as a pretty good complementary role player along the lines of a better shooting version of Justise Winslow or a shorter variation of Luol Deng.

Other Notable Comps Not Listed Above

SIMsc		Year
915.2	Lance Stephenson	2010
905.5	Arron Afflalo	2007

YELLOW PROSPECTS

NCAA Guards

Carsen Edwards

50/50/50

College/Country	Height	Weight	Age on July 1
Purdue	6'0"	199	21.304

Wingspan	Standing Reach	No Step Vert	Max Vert
6'6"	7'10.5"	28.5"	34.0"

Basic Stats		Advanced Stats	
GP	108	TS%	0.547
MIN/G	29.4	3PTA/FGA	0.496
PTS/G	17.8	FTA/FGA	0.295
REB/G	3.4	OREB%	1.6
AST/G	2.5	DREB%	11.3
STL/G	1.2	TRB%	6.7
BLK/G	0.2	AST%	17.7
FG%	0.412	STL%	2.3
3PT%	0.368	BLK%	0.8
FT%	0.817	TOV%	12.1
		USG%	32.3

Projected Draft Range: Late 1st to 2nd Round

Top 10 Comps (All Drafted Players)

	SIMsc			Year
1	916.6	Shawn	Respert	1995
2	914.1	Cory	Carr	1998
3	912.4	Gary	Harris	2014
4	905.1	Richard	Hamilton	1999
5	904.9	Voshon	Lenard	1994
6	904.5	Guillermo	Diaz	2006
7	903.4	Marcus	Thornton	2009
8	902.9	Khalid	El-Amin	2000
9	902.9	Stephen	Curry	2009
10	902.9	Steve	Logan	2002

Carsen Edwards participated in last year's NBA Draft Combine before he ultimately withdrew to return for his junior season at Purdue. This season, Edwards established himself as one of the best players in college basketball, as he was named as a second team consensus All-American and first team All-Big Ten performer. In addition to these honors, he had a very strong showing in the NCAA Tournament, as he broke the single-tournament record for most made three-pointers with 28. As a result, he's very likely to be taken at some point in this year's draft with the possibility that he could even be a first round pick.

As it was alluded to earlier, Edwards stands out because he's an excellent shooter that has maintained a high level of efficiency as his volume has increased. His ability to handle additional volume allows him to make shots on and off the ball. Starting with the latter, he's a threat off the ball because he can knock down spot-up jumpers and run off screens. At this stage, he's much better at coming off the screen to his left and has some trouble when he comes off the right side. He will have to get better at coming off to the right to be a more dynamic off ball threat. On the ball, he's very good at taking quick pull-up jumpers in isolation situations and he can make defenders pay if they go under the screen in pick-and-roll situations. Even though he isn't explosively quick, he leverages the threat of his shot to get driving lanes to the basket. He has been effective at driving both ways, but his efficiency is significantly higher when he drives left. Right now, Edwards plays with a heavy score-first mindset and he is not really a natural playmaker. Specifically, he rarely looks to pass and when he does, he lacks the court vision to do more than make simple passes. Therefore, he might not be a good fit as a traditional point guard. However, teams have become more receptive to running their offense through non-traditional ball handlers. If he lands on a team with a bigger playmaker, he could be useful in a role as an undersized scoring guard.

Defensively, Edwards was hidden in favorable matchups at Purdue, so he needs to improve significantly to defend NBA caliber players. He wasn't tested a whole lot, but he had some struggles in the few situations where opponents decided to go at him. He was about average in isolation situations, according to Synergy. This is mainly because he lacks some of the ideal physical tools. He does have long arms for his size, but he is a bit lacking in lateral quickness and he's only about an average leaper. Therefore, he tended to give up scores because quicker guards could drive by him and taller players could find room to shoot over him. As a weak side help defender, he's not really a dynamic threat because he's only about an average rebounder and he's not much of a shot blocking threat. However, he can play passing lanes to pick up timely steals. On the positive side, he plays with a high effort level and he's a decent team defender that's generally in the proper position. As a result, he'll consistently close out on spot-up shooters on the perimeter and he's pretty good at fighting over screens to prevent ball handlers from turning the corner in pick-and-roll situations. He has some trouble chasing shooters off screens because he can sometimes get caught trying to shoot the gap. If he works on staying at home more, he could fix this issue and be a little more effective on the defensive end.

      Carsen Edwards is a prospect that would been stuck in between positions in the past. However, the league is becoming more position-less, so he has a much better chance of finding a role in today's NBA. His ability to make shots could allow him to find a spot in a team's rotation fairly quickly, but his upside is limited by his potential limitations as a defender. If he can improve his defense to avoid being a liability, he could improve his career prospects and take on a greater role in the future. Most likely, he'll have a solid career as a scoring guard off the bench similar to Marcus Thornton.

Ty Jerome   50/50/50

College/Country	Height	Weight	Age on July 1
Virginia	6'5"	194	21.984

Wingspan	Standing Reach	No Step Vert	Max Vert
6'4"	8'2"	26.0"	31.5"

Basic Stats		Advanced Stats	
GP	105	TS%	0.558
MIN/G	26.4	3PTA/FGA	0.508
PTS/G	9.6	FTA/FGA	0.181
REB/G	3.0	OREB%	1.4
AST/G	3.7	DREB%	12.7
STL/G	1.2	TRB%	7.2
BLK/G	0.0	AST%	28.0
FG%	0.435	STL%	3.0
3PT%	0.392	BLK%	0.2
FT%	0.788	TOV%	13.9
		USG%	21.9

Projected Draft Range: Late 1st to 2nd Round

Top 10 Comps (All Drafted Players)

	SIMsc			Year
1	921.7	Jevon	Carter	2018
2	916.6	William	Avery	1999
3	906.4	Jalen	Brunson	2018
4	902.7	Dee	Brown	2006
5	899.8	Acie	Law	2007
6	899.6	Brooks	Thompson	1994
7	899.4	Chris	Herren	1999
8	899.0	Aaron	Holiday	2018
9	898.9	Jeff	McInnis	1996
10	897.7	Andy	Rautins	2010

Ty Jerome was one of the top players on Virginia's national championship team. Not only did he have a strong showing in the NCAA Tournament, he was a highly productive player all season long, as he was a second team, All-ACC performer this year. After being a very consistent two-year starter at one of the nation's top programs, Jerome decided to forego his final year of eligibility to enter this year's draft. He's likely to be taken at some point in the draft with a chance that he could go in the first round.

At Virginia, Jerome showed that he was a skilled offensive player with very good shooting and passing skills. He is one of the most consistent shooters in this year's draft because he has a compact stroke that he can easily repeat. He shoots just over 39% on his threes for his career and interestingly enough, his Three-Point Percentage increased in conference play. In fact, he made just over 42% of his threes in conference play for his career, which is significant because the ACC is one of toughest conferences in college basketball. Anyway, his sound mechanics allow him to excel at making spot-up jumpers and hitting shots on the move when he comes off screens. He also can make defenders pay if they go under the screen in pick-and-roll situations. Additionally, Jerome is a solid playmaker with the vision to find shooters on the perimeter and hit the roll man in pick-and-roll situations. Because Virginia plays a notoriously methodical offense, Jerome is extremely safe with the ball, so he'll rarely commit turnovers. On the negative side, he's not really a dynamic ball handler and he's not especially quick. Therefore, he has difficulty in creating his own offense. To be specific, he wasn't very effective in isolation situations because he can't really create enough separation to get his shot off and he doesn't really change directions well when he drives. He also has difficulty driving right, so opponents often gave him trouble by sitting on his left hand. At this stage, he's better suited to playing a complementary role in the NBA.

At the other end of the floor, Jerome was a very effective defensive player even though he lacks the ideal physical tools. After all, he has relatively short arms and he's not really an explosive athlete, so he plays much smaller than his actual height. Despite these physical limitations, he defended well in almost every situation. One of the reasons for this is that he comes from one of the best defensive programs in the country, so he's a very good team defender that makes sound rotations. Therefore, he'll consistently close out to contest perimeter shots and he's very good at staying attached to shooters that are coming off screens. He's also an excellent pick-and-roll defender that can fight over the screen to prevent the ball handler from turning the corner and he can adequately switch to guard the roll man. In general, he was pretty good as an on-ball defender. He was very good in isolation situations because he would actively pressure his man and funnel him into either help inside or into the inefficient mid-range area to take a lower percentage shot. He also showed some functional strength because he could decently hold position against bigger players in the post in a switch situation. Finally, though he was more of a stay-at-home defender, he was good at picking his spots to play passing lanes to get steals and he's a solid for rebounder his size.

Ty Jerome is a fairly safe prospect that should find a spot in the league as a complementary role player because his skills on both ends of the floor. As a result, his floor is pretty high, but his ceiling is limited because he lacks the athleticism and ball handling skills to develop into a more dynamic player. Even so, he should be able to carve out a long-term career as a player that could play both guard spots, make plays and knock down outside shots. In all likelihood, he'll wind up being a player similar to someone like Roger Mason.

Shamorie Ponds   45/45/50

College/Country	Height	Weight	Age on July 1
St. John's	6'1"	180	21.005

Wingspan	Standing Reach	No Step Vert	Max Vert
6'3.5"	8'0.5"	29.0"	37.0"

Basic Stats		Advanced Stats	
GP	96	TS%	0.555
MIN/G	35.2	3PTA/FGA	0.394
PTS/G	19.5	FTA/FGA	0.345
REB/G	4.5	OREB%	3.4
AST/G	4.3	DREB%	10.9
STL/G	2.3	TRB%	7.1
BLK/G	0.2	AST%	25.8
FG%	0.437	STL%	3.7
3PT%	0.328	BLK%	0.7
FT%	0.840	TOV%	11.0
		USG%	27.7

Projected Draft Range: 2nd Round

Top 10 Comps (Second Rounders Only)

	SIMsc	First Name	Last Name	Year
1	925.3	Eddie	House	2000
2	920.6	Patty	Mills	2009
3	913.5	Nick	Van Exel	1993
4	906.7	Erick	Green	2013
5	905.0	Tyler	Harvey	2015
6	903.9	Henry	Williams	1992
7	903.8	Terrence	Rencher	1995
8	903.3	Moochie	Norris	1996
9	902.6	Guillermo	Diaz	2006
10	898.4	Chris	Smith	1992

Shamorie Ponds entered last year's draft, but he later withdrew and returned for his junior season at St. John's. This season, he built upon an already productive college career because he was named as a first team All-Big East performer for the second consecutive year. With nothing left to prove at the college level, he decided to enter the draft for good and he'll probably be selected somewhere in the second round.

Offensively, Ponds was mainly used as a scoring guard and was the focal point of his team's offense. He had great success in this role because he could use crafty moves to get to the basket in isolation situations even though he doesn't really have explosive quickness. He also was good at hitting floaters or pull-up jumpers if there was extra traffic at the rim. In addition to his success as a one-on-one player, he was a very good pick-and-roll ball handler because he could either turn the corner to score at the rim or take the outside jumper if his defender went under the screen. He has some untapped potential as a shooter. Mechanically, his stroke is pretty sound, and his high free throw percentage suggests that it's very repeatable. However, his shot selection was fairly questionable, and he was prone to taking a lot of contested shots. As a result, his shooting percentages fluctuated a bit and his efficiency was a bit inconsistent. If he learns to take better shots, his shooting could improve, and he can be more effective overall. Ponds has shown that he can play without the ball. This season, he was very good at knocking down spot-up jumpers and he could effectively run off screens. The sample was a bit small, but in limited opportunities, he showed that he could be a pretty good cutter off the ball, and he would selectively crash the offensive glass to score on put-backs. On the negative side, he's not really a natural playmaker because he plays with a heavy score-first mindset and he's a bit lacking in court vision. Primarily, he doesn't really look to make interior passes, so he's limited to making simple passes to shooters on the perimeter. Therefore, he might not be able to handle point guard responsibilities in the NBA and he might be better suited to being a complementary scoring guard off the bench.

At the defensive end, Ponds was pretty effective even though he lacks the ideal physical tools. He's at a bit of an athletic disadvantage because he's a shorter guard that has relatively short arms. He compensates for these limitations because he's a solid leaper and he has fairly good lateral mobility. He also plays aggressively, and he'll actively pressure his man on the ball. He also could stay in front of his man and he was usually in a position to contest shots. As a result, he was very good at defending in isolation situations this season. The constant pressure he applied helped him force his man into committing turnovers. He was also good at playing passing lanes, so he collected steals at a high rate. In addition to this, he was a decent rebounder for his size. In general, he was a very effective team defender because he would close out on perimeter shooters and fight over screens to contain pick-and-roll ball handlers. Most of the time, he would stay attached to shooters that were coming off screens. However, he would occasionally be too aggressive to shoot the gap and his man could get free for an open shot. There's some concern that he may not be able to handle taller players on switches, but he was effective enough at defending in post-up situations to possibly ease some of those questions. To be specific, he showed a decent amount of functional strength to prevent bigger players from pushing him around inside and they had to take tougher shots as a result.

Overall, Shamorie Ponds has been productive enough at both ends to suggest that he could find a place in the NBA. He will have to make a few key adjustments to stick in the league on a long-term basis. Namely, he'll have to adjust to not being in a primary offensive role and he'll have to show that he can handle the switching responsibilities in a modern defensive scheme. If everything breaks his way and he fully adapts his game to fit the modern NBA, he could carve out a career as a solid rotational guard that could defend, make plays and hit timely outside shots similar to someone like Patrick Beverley. Otherwise, his offensive skills and solid enough defense could allow him to be solid backup guard along the lines of somebody like Patty Mills or Eddie House.

Tremont Waters   40/45/50

College/Country	Height	Weight	Age on July 1
LSU	5'11"	172	21.471

Wingspan	Standing Reach	No Step Vert	Max Vert
6'2.25"	7'9.5"	30.5"	40.5"

Basic Stats		Advanced Stats	
GP	66	TS%	0.551
MIN/G	32.7	3PTA/FGA	0.468
PTS/G	15.6	FTA/FGA	0.341
REB/G	3.1	OREB%	1.1
AST/G	5.9	DREB%	9.7
STL/G	2.5	TRB%	5.4
BLK/G	0.1	AST%	33.9
FG%	0.423	STL%	4.3
3PT%	0.340	BLK%	0.4
FT%	0.807	TOV%	18.4
		USG%	26.1

Projected Draft Range: 2nd Round to Undrafted

Top 10 Comps (Second Rounders Only)

	SIMsc			Year
1	940.8	Pierre	Jackson	2013
2	915.1	Tyson	Wheeler	1998
3	914.1	Nick	Calathes	2009
4	914.1	Moochie	Norris	1996
5	913.6	Patty	Mills	2009
6	912.6	Anthony	Goldwire	1994
7	907.4	Steve	Henson	1990
8	903.2	Elliot	Perry	1991
9	900.4	Gabe	Pruitt	2007
10	900.0	Mo	Williams	2003

Tremont Waters tested the draft waters last year, but he later withdrew and returned for his sophomore season at LSU. He led his team in scoring for the second straight year and he was one of the most productive players in the SEC, earning honors as a first team all-conference performer. He entered this year's draft and has retained the option of returning to LSU. However, he's given an indication that he may stay in the draft for good. If this is the case, then he may be a second round pick this year.

On offense, Waters served as LSU's primary shot creator, but he will have to adapt to a complementary role in the NBA. He was overextended a bit in college because he doesn't quite have the quickness to handle a high volume role. He had some trouble beating his man off the dribble in isolation situations and he often was forced to take a lot of tough shots late in the shot clock that hurt his efficiency. Therefore, he might benefit from being in a complementary role that reduces his responsibilities and scales back his volume. This could allow him to play more to his strengths in the NBA. He's a solid shooter when he can just operate in the flow of an offense. He has smooth, repeatable mechanics that allow him to knock down spot-up jumpers and occasionally shoot off screens. He's also a very good pick-and-roll player because he can make defenders pay for going under the screen and he can use the screen to turn the corner to score in the paint. In addition to this, he's a solid playmaker with pretty good court vision that enables him to hit the roll man inside or find shooters on the perimeter. He also is good at taking care of the ball because his Assist-to-Turnover ratio is almost at 2.4 for his career, so he should be able to handle point guard duties at the NBA level.

Defensively, Waters is always going to be limited because he's a sub-six footer with relatively short arms. Therefore, he's going to be targeted by taller players on switches at the NBA level, so the team that takes him probably has to find ways to hide him on favorable matchups. Even so, he has been effective enough as a defender in college to suggest that he may not be a major defensive liability in his pro career. This is mainly because he plays with a high level of effort and shows a fairly sound understanding of defensive rotations. On the ball, he held up quite well and was very good at defending in isolation situations. He relied on his solid lateral quickness to stay front of his man and he would actively pressure his man to force turnovers. He could also opportunistically play passing lanes as well, so he collected steals at a pretty high rate. He was also a fairly solid team defender, as he would consistently close out to contest perimeter shots and he was good at fighting over screens to prevent ball handlers from turning the corner in pick-and-roll situations. He wasn't really asked to defend in any other situations, so it's uncertain if he can handle bigger players on post-ups or chase shooters around screens. If he can demonstrate some ability to defend in these situations at the next level, he could become adequate enough to stay on the floor for longer stretches.

Tremont Waters' offensive skills are solid enough to allow him to find a roster spot in the NBA. However, he will have to figure out a way to compensate for his physical limitations on the defensive end. He may need to spend at least a season in the G-League to prove that he can guard higher level players. If he becomes at least a decent defender, he could eventually fill a role as a backup point guard that can space the floor and make plays similar to someone like Patty Mills.

Luguentz Dort   40/45/50

College/Country	Height	Weight	Age on July 1
Arizona State	6'4"	222	20.200

Wingspan	Standing Reach	No Step Vert	Max Vert
6'8.5"	8'3.5"	32.5"	38.0"

Basic Stats		Advanced Stats	
GP	34	TS%	0.518
MIN/G	31.5	3PTA/FGA	0.409
PTS/G	16.1	FTA/FGA	0.481
REB/G	4.3	OREB%	4.4
AST/G	2.3	DREB%	10.0
STL/G	1.5	TRB%	7.3
BLK/G	0.2	AST%	15.1
FG%	0.405	STL%	2.7
3PT%	0.307	BLK%	0.8
FT%	0.700	TOV%	15.8
		USG%	27.9

Projected Draft Range: Late 1st to 2nd Round

Top 10 Comps (All Drafted Players)

	SIMsc			Year
1	925.8	James	Cotton	1997
2	909.4	Lance	Stephenson	2010
3	908.3	Khris	Middleton	2012
4	907.6	P.J.	Tucker	2006
5	906.5	Justise	Winslow	2015
6	905.9	Stanley	Johnson	2015
7	903.7	Dion	Glover	1999
8	901.6	Bobby	Simmons	2001
9	900.9	Eric	Gordon	2008
10	900.4	Kirk	Snyder	2004

Luguentz Dort was one of the best high school players in Canada before he enrolled at Arizona State. In his freshman season, he established himself as one of the best players in the Pac-12 Conference by earning a spot on the all-conference second team in addition to being named Pac-12 Freshman of the Year. He elected to enter this year's draft, but he has retained the option of returning for another season at Arizona State. If he stays in the draft, he probably will be taken at some point and he could potentially go as high as the first round.

Defensively, Dort has the potential to guard multiple positions, but he needs to polish up his overall awareness. Physically, he has the ideal tools because he has good lateral quickness to go along with a fairly long wingspan and solid leaping ability. He also is very strong for his size, so he's able to guard bigger players. Because of his physical tools, he excelled as an on-ball defender this season. He showed the quickness to stay with smaller guards and his length enabled him to contest outside shots. He was also very good at applying pressure to his man, so he could force turnovers or get steals. In addition to this, he was a solid rebounder for his size. As a team defender, he had his struggles. First off, he tended to gamble a bit too much, so he was often out of position. He would sometimes get caught trying to shoot the gap when shooters were coming off screens, so when he missed a steal opportunity, he would leave his man open on the perimeter. He also tended to wander into the paint off the ball, which made him late to close out on shooters outside. Additionally, he had trouble defending pick-and-rolls because he was often caught in an in-between position. Therefore, he was sometimes slow to fight over the screen, which allowed the ball handler to turn the corner. Other times, he would go too far under the screen to give up an open jump shot. He will have work hard to learn NBA defensive concepts and rotation schemes to find a long-term fit in the league.

On offense, Dort is a ball dominant scorer that will likely need to adjust his game to fit into a team's rotation. He was mainly used as a pick-and-roll ball handler and had some success because he could turn the corner to get to the rim. He also was a solid passer that could hit the roll man or find open shooters outside. However, he's not really a natural playmaker because he plays with a heavy score-first mindset and he can only make simple reads. He can also be a bit out of control, so he is prone to committing his fair share of turnovers. He was fairly inefficient in isolation situations because he doesn't really have explosive quickness and he struggles to change directions off the dribble. Therefore, he would often try to crash his body into defenders to try to draw fouls when he was driving. This strategy worked most of the time, but when it didn't, it just led to a lot of missed shots in heavy traffic. He also had a heavy tendency to go right, so defenders could easily sit on his strong hand to force him into difficult shots. The main concern for him at this stage is that he's not really a great outside shooter. His mechanics are a little funky because he has a bit of a hitch at the top of his release that causes some timing issues. As a result, opponents can play off him to disrupt the flow of his team's offense, so he will have to work on his shot to avoid being a spacing liability in the NBA. As a final note, he had some skills off the ball, as he was a good cutter and he would run hard down the floor to score in transition.

       Luguentz Dort has some athletic potential, but he will have to adapt to fit into a role in today's NBA. He has the tools to succeed on the defensive end and his pick-and-roll ball handling skills can translate into the league. However, he needs to learn NBA defensive concepts and his shot needs to improve significantly, so he could benefit from spending at least a season in the G-League. If he makes the necessary improvements to his game, he could develop into a decent combo guard off the bench that can defend multiple positions and provide some complementary scoring similar to Austin Rivers.

Kyle Guy   40/40/45

College/Country	Height	Weight	Age on July 1
Virginia	6'2"	168	21.888

Wingspan	Standing Reach	No Step Vert	Max Vert
6'4.5"	7'11.5"	30.5"	36.5"

Basic Stats		Advanced Stats	
GP	106	TS%	0.572
MIN/G	29.1	3PTA/FGA	0.555
PTS/G	12.5	FTA/FGA	0.158
REB/G	3.0	OREB%	1.9
AST/G	1.6	DREB%	10.7
STL/G	0.7	TRB%	6.5
BLK/G	0.0	AST%	11.9
FG%	0.433	STL%	1.6
3PT%	0.425	BLK%	0.2
FT%	0.806	TOV%	9.0
		USG%	23.8

Projected Draft Range: 2nd Round to Undrafted

Top 10 Comps (Second Rounders Only)

	SIMsc			Year
1	906.9	Joe	Young	2015
2	904.7	Tyler	Harvey	2015
3	898.8	Andrew	Goudelock	2011
4	896.1	Marcus	Denmon	2012
5	889.9	Rodney	Monroe	1991
6	889.9	Louis	Bullock	1999
7	888.8	Nick	Van Exel	1993
8	887.7	A.J.	Guyton	2000
9	884.1	Henry	Williams	1992
10	883.1	Derrick	Dial	1998

Kyle Guy is one of the more accomplished college players in this year's draft. He was a first team All-ACC selection for the last two years and he was a critical part of Virginia's national championship team. In fact, he was named the NCAA Tournament's Most Outstanding Player this past season. He initially entered the draft to test the waters, but he elected stay for good with a strong showing in this year's NBA Draft Combine. If he is taken in this year's draft, he will likely be a second round pick.

In his three years at Virginia, Guy has established himself as highly skilled offensive player. He was mainly used as an undersized two guard, so he best fits a team with a taller non-traditional ball handler. If he can find the right fit, he could help a team because he's one of the best shooters in the draft. He's made 42.5% of his threes against top-flight college competition and he makes shots in a variety of ways. He's an extremely reliable spot-up shooter and he constantly runs off screens to free himself without the ball. He also can quickly set up in transition to knock down a trail three. Occasionally, he can make a step-back jumper, but he has less success at shooting off the dribble. This is primarily because he's not overwhelmingly quick, so he can't really use the threat of a drive to give himself enough separation. When he was successful driving, it was mostly because defenders were overplaying his shot. In these situations, he was able to score on straight-line drives to the basket, although he has a heavy tendency to go left. He was sometimes used as a pick-and-roll ball handler. Opposing defenses often had to keep a man attached to him because of his great outside shot, so he mostly looked to keep the ball moving by making simple passes to the roll man. Though he's a smaller player, he can pick his spots to grab timely offensive rebounds to score on an occasional put-back. His only real negative on offense is that he floats on the perimeter a bit too much, so he won't always cut to the rim if defenders stay up on him.

As a defender, he's doesn't really look the part because his arms are somewhat short, and he only has around average lateral quickness. On the other hand, he's a better than average leaper, so he has enough athleticism to hold up against NBA guards. He also compensates for his physical limitations through strong defensive awareness and a high effort level. As a result, he was an effective defender in one-on-one isolation situations this season because he could play angles to stop drives or funnel his man into help. He was also active to apply pressure to either force turnovers or make his man take tougher shots. Overall, he was a pretty solid team defender. He would consistently close out on spot-up shooters and he was generally pretty good at fighting through screens to either contain pick-and-roll ball handlers or stay attached to shooters off the ball. He also was fairly good at rotating over from the weak side to draw charges. Virginia played a highly disciplined style of defense, so like his teammates, Guy didn't really roam very much, and he was more of a stay-at-home defender. He didn't really get blocks or steals, but he stayed in solid rebounding position, which made him a fairly good rebounder for his size.

Kyle Guy is a lower ceiling prospect because he doesn't fit a traditional position and he doesn't have the dynamic athleticism to be a high-end starter. However, his advanced shooting skills give him a high enough floor to suggest that he could contribute right away as a situational specialist. If he lands with a team that can play to his strengths, he could carve out a role as a shooting specialist off the bench similar to someone like Seth Curry. Otherwise, if he goes through some adverse circumstances, he could be headed for a lucrative career in one of the higher end European leagues.

Other Notable Comps Not Listed Above

SIMsc		Year
922.9	Troy Hudson	1997
903.7	Seth Curry	2013

Jordan Poole   35/40/45

College/Country	Height	Weight	Age on July 1
Michigan	6'5"	191	20.033

Wingspan	Standing Reach	No Step Vert	Max Vert
6'6.75"	8'3.5"	27.5"	35.5"

Basic Stats		Advanced Stats	
GP	75	TS%	0.576
MIN/G	22.7	3PTA/FGA	0.572
PTS/G	9.4	FTA/FGA	0.261
REB/G	2.2	OREB%	0.8
AST/G	1.4	DREB%	10.2
STL/G	0.8	TRB%	5.6
BLK/G	0.2	AST%	11.9
FG%	0.434	STL%	2.2
3PT%	0.370	BLK%	0.9
FT%	0.831	TOV%	11.8
		USG%	22.2

Projected Draft Range: 2nd Round to Undrafted

Top 10 Comps (Second Rounders Only)

	SIMsc			Year
1	916.1	Von	Wafer	2005
2	914.5	Doron	Lamb	2012
3	911.8	Sviatoslav	Mykhailiuk	2018
4	910.1	Tyler	Dorsey	2017
5	908.3	Daniel	Gibson	2006
6	904.8	Kim	English	2012
7	902.7	Marcus	Denmon	2012
8	900.2	Josh	Selby	2011
9	898.3	Curtis	Blair	1992
10	897.2	Jodie	Meeks	2009

Jordan Poole had his moments as a bench player for Michigan in his freshman season. Most notably, he hit a buzzer-beating three-pointer in the 2018 NCAA Tournament to help his team advance to the Sweet Sixteen. Then this season, he played pretty well in his first year as a full-time starter. His performance was solid enough for him to gain the notice of a few scouts and he elected to enter this year's draft. At this point, he's given every indication that he'll remain in the draft and not return to Michigan. If he's selected in this year's draft, he'll probably be a second round pick.

Defensively, Poole has the potential to defend both guard spots at the NBA level. Though his arms are about average in length, he's a taller guard with good lateral quickness and solid leaping ability. He's also a pretty disciplined defender that maintains sound positioning. As a result, he was a very good defender in isolation situations this season because he was excellent at staying in front of his man to stop drives and he was usually in position to contest shots. He also held up pretty well against bigger players in post-up situations because he had enough functional strength to hold position on the block to make his man take a tougher shot. As a team defender, he was generally pretty good. He played effective pick-and-roll defense by getting over the screen to prevent the ball handler from turning the corner and he could occasionally switch to take away the roll man as well. He also was good at keeping track of his man off the ball because he would usually be in position to close out in a spot-up situation. His only weak point on defense was that he had trouble covering shooters off screens, as he tended to get caught on the screen and his man could easily get free for a shot. If he cleans up this issue and learns to do a better job of fighting through screens off the ball, he could become a sound NBA-level defender.

On offense, Poole projects to be a complementary role player. He was mainly used off the ball at Michigan this season and this type of role plays into his strengths. In particularly, he's a pretty good overall shooter. His stroke is consistently repeatable, and he shows no major mechanical flaws. Because of this, his percentages have held steady even though his role has changed over the course of two seasons. He's been most effective at making spot-up jumpers, but he's also shown an ability to shoot on the move. He was mostly good at shooting off screens, although he was much better at coming off to his left. At the moment, his skill set doesn't allow him to be an effective shot creator at the NBA level because he's only about average ball handler and he struggles to get all the way to rim on drives. Therefore, he wasn't really effective on isolations this past season. He was a little better as a pick-and-roll ball handler, but his success was due to his ability to make perimeter shots when defenders went under the screen and his willingness to make simple passes if a shot wasn't available. As a final note, he moves fairly well without the ball because he can effectively make a backdoor cut if defenders overplay his shot and he'll run hard down the floor to score in transition.

Though Jordan Poole is still a pretty young prospect, his ceiling is limited because he lacks the necessary ball handling skills to become a primary shot creator at the NBA level. Even so, he could become a useful rotational player in the future due to his outside shooting and his ability to possibly defend both guard spots. If he gets an opportunity to play a consistent number of minutes, he could develop into a complementary rotational guard like E'Twaun Moore. Otherwise, he may have to grind his way through the G-League for a season or two to find the right fit. In a worst-case scenario, he could have a short stint in the league a two-way player before he spends the bulk of his career overseas or in the G-League.

Quinndary Weatherspoon 35/40/45

College/Country	Height	Weight	Age on July 1
Mississippi State	6'4"	207	22.805

Wingspan	Standing Reach	No Step Vert	Max Vert
6'9"	8'4"	31.0"	38.0"

Basic Stats		Advanced Stats	
GP	131	TS%	0.585
MIN/G	31.2	3PTA/FGA	0.345
PTS/G	15.4	FTA/FGA	0.356
REB/G	5.2	OREB%	5.4
AST/G	2.4	DREB%	13.3
STL/G	1.5	TRB%	9.4
BLK/G	0.4	AST%	15.5
FG%	0.480	STL%	2.8
3PT%	0.368	BLK%	1.2
FT%	0.788	TOV%	15.1
		USG%	24.8

Projected Draft Range: 2nd Round to Undrafted

Top 10 Comps (Second Rounders Only)

	SIMsc			Year
1	946.2	Sindarius	Thornwell	2017
2	939.4	Danilo	Pinnock	2006
3	937.0	Nate	Erdmann	1997
4	936.3	Charles	O'Bannon	1997
5	934.1	Keith	Bogans	2003
6	932.9	Darrun	Hilliard	2015
7	929.8	Toby	Bailey	1998
8	929.1	Davon	Reed	2017
9	928.3	Willie	Green	2003
10	927.5	Lavor	Postell	2000

Quinndary Weatherspoon declared for last year's draft, but he elected to withdraw to return to Mississippi State for his senior season. He established himself as one of the SEC's most productive players, as he earned honors as a first team all-conference performer this past season. He also had a very strong showing at this year's Portsmouth Invitational, and he landed a spot on the All-Tournament team. If he's taken in this year's draft, he will likely go somewhere in the second round.

On offense, Weatherspoon was a primary scorer at Mississippi State, but his skill set may be better suited for a complementary role in the NBA. He had some difficulty creating shots for himself in isolation situations. Occasionally, he could beat his man with a straight-line drive. However, his ball handling wasn't quite good enough to allow him to change directions, and he struggles to drive to his right. He was better as a ball handler in pick-and-roll situations because he could use the screen to give himself an extra step to get to the basket or he could step behind it to knock down a perimeter jumper. He also showed that he can make simple reads to find open teammates as well. His main strength is his solid outside shooting. His shooting mechanics were a little funky when he first came into college, but he's reworked his mechanics to give himself a smooth, repeatable motion. As a result, he's become a fairly good overall three-point shooter that can knock down spot-up jumpers and occasionally come off screens. At this stage, he's much better at coming off a screen to his left and he has some difficulty going the other way. He's also effective at moving without the ball because he's pretty good at making back-door cuts to exploit defenders that overplay his shot and he'll run hard down the floor to score in transition.

Defensively, he has the potential to defend both guard spots at the NBA level because he's a taller guard with solid physical tools. In particular, he has long arms to go along with good lateral quickness and solid leaping ability. These physical abilities allow him to be very effective at guarding perimeter players on the ball. He was good at defending in isolation situations because he was quick enough to consistently stay with his man and he could apply pressure either force a turnover or contest shots. Also, his length and functional strength allowed him to effectively defend inside if he was switched onto a bigger player in the post. In addition to being a good on-ball defender, he was an active help defender that could rebound fairly well for his size and play passing lanes to get steals. At times, he would be a little too aggressive in going for steals. Specifically, he would tend to get caught trying to shoot the gap when defending a shooter coming off a screen, which allowed his man to get free for an open jumper. That issue aside, he was generally a solid team defender. He was pretty good at defending pick-and-rolls, as he would usually fight over the screen to contain ball handlers and he could occasionally switch to take away the roll man. He was also consistent to close out on perimeter shooters in spot-up situations.

Quinndary Weatherspoon has the potential to develop into a useful role player in the NBA. His game is fairly polished, so he's not too far away from being able to contribute to a team's rotation. If he gets the right opportunity to play, he could carve out a role as a rotational shooter that could defend both guard spots similar to someone like E'Twaun Moore. Otherwise, he'll have to grind it out in the G-League for a season or two before he finds a home in the league. In the worst-case scenario, he could still have a solid career in professional basketball, but he would probably be playing overseas instead of being in the NBA.

Other Notable Comps Not Listed Above

SIMsc		Year
919.6	Roger Mason	2002
918.9	Joe Harris	2014

Jaylen Nowell 35/40/45

College/Country	Height	Weight	Age on July 1
Washington	6'4"	202	19.978

Wingspan	Standing Reach	No Step Vert	Max Vert
6'7.25"	8'2"	32.0"	38.5"

Basic Stats		Advanced Stats	
GP	70	TS%	0.563
MIN/G	33.5	3PTA/FGA	0.257
PTS/G	16.1	FTA/FGA	0.279
REB/G	4.6	OREB%	3.6
AST/G	2.9	DREB%	12.9
STL/G	1.2	TRB%	8.3
BLK/G	0.3	AST%	19.3
FG%	0.476	STL%	2.0
3PT%	0.396	BLK%	0.8
FT%	0.789	TOV%	16.0
		USG%	26.0

Projected Draft Range: 2nd Round to Undrafted

Top 10 Comps (Second Rounders Only)

	SIMsc			Year
1	937.8	Willie	Green	2003
2	926.7	Gilbert	Arenas	2001
3	917.7	Roger	Mason	2002
4	916.5	Shelvin	Mack	2011
5	916.0	E'Twaun	Moore	2011
6	914.0	Chase	Budinger	2009
7	913.6	Marcus	Williams	2007
8	911.5	Jordan	Clarkson	2014
9	909.4	James	Cotton	1997
10	909.4	Daniel	Hamilton	2016

Jaylen Nowell had a breakout year in his sophomore season at Washington. He was the leading scorer on the Pac-12's best regular season team, so he earned honors as the Pac-12's Player of the Year. After initially being on the fence about his decision to either stay in the draft or return to school, he eventually decided to forego his remaining two years of eligibility to remain in the draft pool. Most likely, he will be taken in the second round, although he's been mentioned as a possibility for the late first round.

At this stage, Nowell has shown that he's a pretty skilled offensive player. He's been an effective scorer over the course of his two seasons at Washington because he's a very good perimeter shooter. He really shot the ball well from behind the three-point line this season, as he made 44% of his threes. He was most effective as a catch and shoot player because he was excellent at knocking down spot-up threes and he was generally good at coming off screens. As a tendency note, he was much better at coming off a screen to his left than he was at coming off to the right. He might be better suited for a complementary role because he had some trouble making jump shots off the dribble. On the positive side, he was fairly good as a driver in general because he handles the ball pretty well, so he could use shifty movements to change directions and get to the rim. He also was a willing passer that could kick the ball to an open shooter if he was in heavy traffic. However, he plays with more of a score-first mindset, so he's not likely to be a point guard at the NBA level. He's a pretty dynamic player in transition because he could push the ball up court to either set up his teammates or score himself. He also runs hard down the floor without the ball to fill lanes or quickly get set for a trail three. On the other hand, he tends to stand idly on the perimeter when he doesn't have the ball in a half-court offense, so he won't always look to cut if defenders try to crowd him off the ball.

On defense, he's much harder to project because he has spent his entire career playing in a zone defense. This is a different situation from his teammate, Matisse Thybulle because Nowell has only played for Mike Hopkins, so there really isn't a lot of data to provide any hints as how his defense could translate into the NBA. From an athleticism standpoint, he could theoretically hold up against either guard spot because he has fairly long arms to go along with decent leaping ability and solid lateral quickness. However, it's unclear if these tools can translate into effective on-ball defense. He also is going to have learn man-to-man defensive concepts from scratch, so there might be an initial adjustment period while he tries to grasp NBA rotation schemes. The only real area that can be assessed is his abilities as a help defender. He played more of a complementary role in Washington's zone defense because Thybulle served as their primary roamer. Therefore, Nowell stayed mostly in his area. He was fairly effective at his using length to jump passing lanes to get steals and he was a solid defensive rebounder for his size.

Jaylen Nowell is an intriguing prospect because he could potentially be a decent scoring guard. However, his defensive skills are very raw and prospects that have come out of zone-dominant college systems have historically not translated into effective NBA defenders. This makes him something of a risky prospect. If he can spend a season or two in the G-League to learn NBA defensive concepts and become at least an adequate man defender, he could reach his ceiling and fill a role as a scoring guard off the bench similar to someone like Jordan Clarkson. Otherwise, he could end up being a fringe player that shuttles back and forth from the end of a roster to the G-League or he could wind up overseas for most of his career.

Ky Bowman   35/40/45

College/Country	Height	Weight	Age on July 1
Boston College	6'2"	181	22.038

Wingspan	Standing Reach	No Step Vert	Max Vert
6'7"	8'2"	N/A	N/A

Basic Stats		Advanced Stats	
GP	98	TS%	0.550
MIN/G	35.5	3PTA/FGA	0.428
PTS/G	16.9	FTA/FGA	0.284
REB/G	6.4	OREB%	2.6
AST/G	3.9	DREB%	17.6
STL/G	1.3	TRB%	10.1
BLK/G	0.3	AST%	22.9
FG%	0.433	STL%	2.1
3PT%	0.388	BLK%	1.1
FT%	0.762	TOV%	16.3
		USG%	25.9

Projected Draft Range: 2nd Round to Undrafted

Top 10 Comps (Second Rounders Only)

	SIMsc			Year
1	930.9	Olivier	Hanlan	2015
2	924.3	Guillermo	Diaz	2006
3	922.4	JamesOn	Curry	2007
4	920.1	Nigel	Williams-Goss	2017
5	918.1	Chris	Smith	1992
6	915.4	Patrick	Beverley	2009
7	914.9	A.J.	Guyton	2000
8	914.8	Isaiah	Canaan	2013
9	914.2	Corey	Williams	1992
10	912.4	Henry	Williams	1992

Ky Bowman declared for the 2018 NBA Draft, but he later withdrew to return to Boston College for his junior season. He was Boston College's leading scorer this past season and he became one of the most productive players in the ACC. Because of his high level of play, he was named as a second team, All-ACC performer this season. If a team picks him in this year's draft, he will probably be taken at some point in the second round.

Bowman was used as a primary ball handler in college, but he might have to transition to playing as a complementary player in the NBA. This is mainly because he had trouble driving to the basket in isolation situations. Though he has a decently quick first step, he doesn't always get by his man because opponents can sit on his right hand to force him to go left where he's not nearly as effective. He also has trouble finishing shots inside and his Two-Point Percentage has declined in every season. He's better as a pick-and-roll ball handler because he can use the screen and the threat of his shot to give himself an extra step to turn the corner. On the negative side, opposing defenses can trap him to limit some of his effectiveness on pick-and-rolls because he's not a true playmaker. He has shown the ability to hit the roll man, but he lacks the natural court vision to do anything except make simple reads and safer passes. His main strength is that he's been an excellent outside shooter throughout his career. His stroke is smooth and repeatable, so his percentages have been fairly consistent. He mainly thrives as a spot-up shooter because he's at his best when can set his feet. He's had some trouble shooting on the move because he's only about average at shooting off screens. He's good at coming off a screen to his right, but he struggles when he has to come off to his left. He will have to improve in this area to be a more dynamic shooter in the NBA. In other areas on offense, his athleticism makes him a threat in transition because he's good at quickly pushing the ball up court and he can occasionally finish plays above the rim. He also has been an effective cutter in a limited number of possessions because he can go back-door if defenders overplay his shot.

On defense, Bowman is somewhat limited due to his smallish size. Though he has solid lateral quickness and leaping ability, he has some physical limitations because he's a smaller guard with relatively short arms. At the next level, he could be targeted by bigger players on switches. To some extent, he was already a target for opposing offenses at Boston College because he had some trouble guarding his man in isolation situations. He was actually solid at keeping his man in front of him, but due to his size and length disadvantages, opponents were able to shoot over him. This was also the case when he was trying to close out on perimeter shooters. He would usually be in position on closeouts, but a taller shooter would still get a fairly clean look by shooting over the top of him. His usage in the NBA may be limited, and there's a chance that he might only be able to play against other small guards. At Boston College, he has shown that he may not be a complete liability because he was an effective team defender. Most notably, he was very good at fighting through screens to either stay attached to a shooter off the ball or contain the ball handler in a pick-and-roll situation. He also was a very good rebounder for his size, and he was active to play passing lanes to pick up steals.

Ky Bowman has a chance to find a spot in the league because there's a high demand for efficient outside shooting in the NBA. At worst, he could hang on the fringes as a specialist along the lines of Isaiah Canaan. However, if he plans on sticking as a long-term rotational player, he may have to spend at least a season in the G-League to figure out a way to compensate for his size disadvantage on the defensive end. If things break favorably and he becomes at least an adequate defender, he could find a spot in somebody's rotation as an undersized shooter off the bench similar to Daniel Gibson. Otherwise, he might end up spending a large chunk of his career overseas or in the G-League.

Other Notable Comps Not Listed Above

SIMsc		Year
908.0	Daniel Gibson	2006
903.4	Aaron Brooks	2007

Jaylen Hands 35/40/45

College/Country	Height	Weight	Age on July 1
UCLA	6'3"	180	20.381

Wingspan	Standing Reach	No Step Vert	Max Vert
6'5.5"	8'1"	N/A	N/A

Basic Stats		Advanced Stats	
GP	64	TS%	0.533
MIN/G	28.3	3PTA/FGA	0.460
PTS/G	12.1	FTA/FGA	0.298
REB/G	3.8	OREB%	1.9
AST/G	4.4	DREB%	12.0
STL/G	1.2	TRB%	7.2
BLK/G	0.2	AST%	28.8
FG%	0.409	STL%	2.2
3PT%	0.373	BLK%	0.6
FT%	0.762	TOV%	18.3
		USG%	23.4

Projected Draft Range: 2nd Round to Undrafted

Top 10 Comps (Second Rounders Only)

	SIMsc			Year
1	929.6	Mo	Williams	2003
2	922.3	Marcus	Taylor	2002
3	913.2	A.J.	Price	2009
4	909.0	Jerome	Allen	1995
5	905.2	Jeff	McInnis	1996
6	904.9	Moochie	Norris	1996
7	904.2	Nick	Calathes	2009
8	903.8	Kenny	Satterfield	2001
9	903.7	JamesOn	Curry	2007
10	903.0	Nigel	Williams-Goss	2017

Jaylen Hands participated in last year's NBA Draft Combine, but he elected to withdraw from last year's draft to return for another season at UCLA. Because Aaron Holiday left for the NBA, Hands assumed a role as the team's full-time point guard. He went on to have a very good season and he was one of the better players in the Pac-12 Conference, earning a spot as a second team all-conference performer this year. He decided to put his name in the draft pool once again, but this time, he is not expected to return for another season in college. If he's taken in this year's draft, he will likely be a second round pick.

On offense, Hands projects to be a game managing backup point guard. This is mainly because he lacks the explosive athleticism to be a primary scorer in the NBA. He had some trouble beating his man off the dribble because he couldn't really turn the corner on pick-and-rolls and opponents tended to sit on his left hand to force him into tougher shots to his right. He had some success at driving in isolation situations, but this is mainly because he had previously knocked down a few outside shots to cause his defender to overplay his shot. Along those lines, his shooting is his primary strength. His mechanics are fairly sound, and he can consistently repeat his stroke. He's been a very good three-point shooter in college because he can knock down spot-up threes and shoot off screens. He had solid playmaking skills because he plays with more of a pass-first mentality and he has decent court vision. Therefore, he'll consistently hit the roll man in pick-and-roll situations, and he can find shooters outside. He'll also push the ball up court quickly to set up teammates in transition. He takes more of a safe approach, so he'll generally avoid turnovers by making lower risk passes.

Hands' defense is a bit tougher to project because UCLA played in a zone defense for a majority of their possessions. In the other possessions where the team played man defense, he was hidden most of the time and wasn't given a lot of tough assignments to test his skills. With this in mind, Hands has to make a big leap on the defensive end to make it in the NBA. Physically, he doesn't quite have an ideal set of tools. He does have a better than average vertical leap and decent lateral mobility, but his arms aren't especially long. UCLA played more man defense the season before and he wasn't effective as an on-ball defender. He struggled in a small sample of isolation situations because he would often allow his man to blow by him with very little resistance. He also has a small frame, so opposing players had some success in overpowering him to the basket. He was a little bit better as a team defender because he was good at fighting over screens to contain the pick-and-roll ball handler. However, he had problems defending in other areas. He would lose track of his man off the ball, so he would be late to close out on a shooter or he wouldn't always get through a screen. He also would get caught trying to shoot the gap when his man was coming off a screen as well. On the positive side, he made some plays as a help defender because he would jump passing lanes to get steals and he was a decent defensive rebounder for a player of his size.

Jaylen Hands has a chance to land on an NBA roster because of his shooting. However, he's so far away defensively that he'll probably need to spend some time in the G-League to learn NBA defensive concepts. There's a strong possibility that he may end up having a short career in the NBA and it's highly probable that he'll spend the majority of his time either overseas or in the G-League. If his defense improves to at least an adequate level, he could develop into a situational shooting backup point guard like Damon Jones.

Other Notable Comps Not Listed Above

SIMsc		Year
923.4	Damon Jones	1997

Terence Davis 35/40/45

College/Country	Height	Weight	Age on July 1
Ole Miss	6'4"	192	22.126

Wingspan	Standing Reach	No Step Vert	Max Vert
6'8.75"	8'5"	29.5"	34.0"

Basic Stats		Advanced Stats	
GP	121	TS%	0.543
MIN/G	24.3	3PTA/FGA	0.421
PTS/G	12.5	FTA/FGA	0.269
REB/G	4.9	OREB%	5.3
AST/G	2.1	DREB%	17.2
STL/G	1.2	TRB%	11.2
BLK/G	0.6	AST%	18.4
FG%	0.445	STL%	2.7
3PT%	0.339	BLK%	2.6
FT%	0.717	TOV%	14.8
		USG%	27.0

Projected Draft Range: 2nd Round to Undrafted

Top 10 Comps (Second Rounders Only)

	SIMsc			Year
1	940.3	Chris	Robinson	1996
2	918.5	Cuttino	Mobley	1998
3	912.8	David	Young	2004
4	912.7	Roberto	Bergersen	1999
5	911.6	Kevin	Lynch	1991
6	910.7	Chris	Carr	1995
7	910.4	Daniel	Ewing	2005
8	910.3	Nate	Erdmann	1997
9	907.5	Kim	English	2012
10	906.8	E'Twaun	Moore	2011

After seeing limited action in his freshman year, Terence Davis has had a solid college career as a three-year starter at Ole Miss. As a senior, he developed into one of the most productive players in his conference, earning honors as a second team All-SEC performer this season. He had a strong showing at this year's Portsmouth Invitational, as he was named to the All-Tournament team. If he's selected in this year's draft, he'll likely be a second round pick.

In all likelihood, Davis is probably going to be a complementary player in the NBA. He was in a primary role at Ole Miss, but he was rarely put in isolation situations. He had trouble getting quality shots off in a one-on-one situation because he's only an average ball handler and he lacks an explosive first step. He had much more success as a pick-and-roll ball handler because he could use the screen to get an extra step to turn the corner. If defenders tried to go under the screen to take away the drive, then he could make them pay by pulling up for a jumper. He also showed solid playmaking skills, as he showed the court vision to either hit the roll man, find open perimeter shooters or make passes to cutters inside. He's been willing to take outside shots throughout his career, but this season has been the only one where he was an above average three-point shooter. His stroke is more consistent from mid-range because he has shot free throws well. However, he has struggled from long range throughout his career because there's a lot of movement in his lower body that throws off his balance. His shot can be a bit streaky as a result. Also, the excessive motion in his lower half makes him better suited for a stationary spot-up role because he has trouble shooting on the move. He showed some ability to come off screens this season, but he was only effective at coming off a screen to his left. He was much worse when he had to come off a screen to his right. Because he was inconsistent as a shooter, opponents could sometimes play off of him to take away any opportunities to cut to the rim. On the positive side, he was a threat to score in transition because he was very good at running hard down the floor on the wings and he could use his athleticism to finish plays above the rim. He also was good at picking his spots to crash the offensive boards to score on put-backs.

Defensively, Davis has the potential to guard multiple positions in the NBA. From a physical standpoint, he's a taller guard that has the length and leaping ability to handle bigger wing players and he has enough lateral mobility to stay with quicker guards on the perimeter. Therefore, he was good at defending isolations on the perimeter, as he tended to stay in front of his man, apply pressure and actively contest shots. He was also very active as a help defender because he would aggressively play passing lanes to collect steals at a high rate, rotate from the weak side to occasionally block shots and he was a very good rebounder for his size. For the most part, he was a solid team defender because he was very good at fighting through screens to either contain the ball handler on pick-and-rolls or stay attached to a shooter off the ball. He would generally close out on perimeter shooters in spot-up situations. He showed excellent recovery speed when his man hesitated on the catch because he would typically shut down a drive or a pull-up jumper off the dribble. However, a decisive opponent could take advantage of Davis' over-aggressiveness and tendency to gamble. At times, he would close out a bit too hard, so his man could get a driving lane to the basket. Other times, he would get caught of position trying to go for a big play, which caused him to be late on a closeout. Additionally, he was also prone to committing cheap fouls by being a little too aggressive. If he plays a little more under control, he could be a solid defensive player at the NBA level.

Terence Davis is a lower ceiling prospect that could eventually develop into a decent rotational combo guard that defends multiple positions and provides secondary ball handling. At this point, his game isn't polished enough to fit into a rotation immediately because his shooting is still a bit inconsistent. Therefore, he could benefit from getting some additional seasoning in the G-League for at least a season. If his outside shooting becomes more consistent, he could carve out a role as a backup combo guard similar to someone like Willie Green. Otherwise, he'll likely spend the bulk of his career in the G-League or overseas.

Other Notable Comps Not Listed Above

SIMsc		Year
901.1	Willie Green	2003

Kerwin Roach   35/40/45

College/Country	Height	Weight	Age on July 1
Texas	6'5"	175	22.685

Wingspan	Standing Reach	No Step Vert	Max Vert
6'6"	8'2.5"	N/A	N/A

Basic Stats		Advanced Stats	
GP	128	TS%	0.526
MIN/G	27.6	3PTA/FGA	0.365
PTS/G	11.0	FTA/FGA	0.437
REB/G	3.7	OREB%	2.8
AST/G	2.9	DREB%	12.6
STL/G	1.3	TRB%	7.7
BLK/G	0.3	AST%	21.8
FG%	0.431	STL%	2.7
3PT%	0.341	BLK%	1.0
FT%	0.649	TOV%	17.4
		USG%	23.8

Projected Draft Range: 2nd Round to Undrafted

Top 10 Comps (Second Rounders Only)

	SIMsc			Year
1	931.7	Kevin	Pritchard	1990
2	929.6	Alvin	Williams	1997
3	928.1	Daniel	Ewing	2005
4	925.0	John	Celestand	1999
5	924.9	Joey	Wright	1991
6	911.3	Phil	Henderson	1990
7	911.0	Isaiah	Cousins	2016
8	908.9	Sir'Dominic	Pointer	2015
9	907.6	Tyshawn	Taylor	2012
10	905.6	Jerome	Allen	1995

Kerwin Roach entered last year's draft, but he later withdrew to return for his senior season at Texas. After recovering from an injury to his meniscus and serving an early suspension for violating team rules, he put up a fairly strong performance this season and he was named as the MVP of this year's NIT. If he's taken in this year's draft, he will likely be a second round pick.

At this stage, Roach projects to be a complementary player at the next level. At Texas, he was used in a primary scoring role, but he doesn't have the skills to be effectively play this way in the NBA. He was only about average in isolation situations this past season. Though he could draw fouls at a high rate, he had trouble getting all the way to basket because he's only an average ball handler that struggles to change directions. He also has a heavy tendency to go left and is much worse at driving right, so defenders can sit on his strong hand to force him into a tougher shot. On the positive side, he was more effective as the ball handler in pick-and-roll situations. He showed solid playmaking skills that allowed him to either hit the roll man, find open shooters on the perimeter or pass to cutters off the ball. He also was good at using the screen to give him an extra step to turn the corner and score at the rim. Defenders did have some success going under screens because his jump shot is still a work-in-progress. He struggles to repeat his stroke because though he's been an average three-point shooter over the last two seasons, he still shoots free throws at a rate below 70%. Mechanically, he has a slight hitch in his motion that causes his release point to be a bit inconsistent. If he fixes his motion to give him a consistently repeatable stroke, he could become an effective shooter. He was fairly good from mid-range at knocking down spot-up jumpers and in a small sample size, he could come off screens. As an additional positive, he has pretty good overall athleticism, so he was a dynamic player in transition that could push the ball up the floor and finish plays above the rim. Because Texas' offense was a bit too simplistic, there really wasn't a lot of movement off the ball. As a result, he would often stand idly on the perimeter and rarely looked to cut to the basket.

Defensively, he has some potential because he has the physical tools to defend both guard spots. He's a taller guard that has good enough lateral quickness to handle the smaller, quicker players and he has enough length and leaping ability to take on bigger wing players. His performance in isolation situations wasn't great because he comes from a system that encourages gambling and over-aggressive play. As a result, Roach would get caught reaching in, which would open up a lane for his man to drive by him. He also was a bit foul prone as well. When he stayed fairly disciplined, he did show that he could stay with his man and actively contest shots. He also held up pretty well in the post against bigger players on switches, as he had enough strength to hold his position and his length allowed him to force his man into a tough shot. As a team defender, he was pretty effective overall. He would fight through screens to either contain the ball handler in pick-and-roll situations or stay attached to a shooter off the ball. He was also good at closing out on shooters in spot-up situations as well. Finally, he was pretty active off the ball as a help defender because he was very good at playing passing lanes to get steals and he's a fairly good rebounder for his size.

Kerwin Roach is a prospect that could find a fit in the league as a defensive guard that could also serve as a secondary ball handler. He's not quite ready to be an NBA rotation player at this point because his outside shot is still somewhat inconsistent. He may need to play in the G-League for a year or so to show that he can consistently knock down enough shots to avoid being a liability on offense. If his jump shot improves to allow him to be at least be an average shooter, he could be a rotational combo guard similar to someone like Tyler Johnson. Otherwise, he could end up being a game managing backup point guard at the end of a roster like Royal Ivey.

Other Notable Comps Not Listed Above

SIMsc		Year
922.7	Tyler Johnson	2014
911.5	Kent Bazemore	2012

Chris Clemons   35/40/45

College/Country	Height	Weight	Age on July 1
Campbell	5'10"	186	21.940

Wingspan	Standing Reach	No Step Vert	Max Vert
6'2"	7'7.5"	N/A	N/A

Basic Stats		Advanced Stats	
GP	130	TS%	0.594
MIN/G	34.1	3PTA/FGA	0.531
PTS/G	24.8	FTA/FGA	0.373
REB/G	4.5	OREB%	1.7
AST/G	2.6	DREB%	14.0
STL/G	1.6	TRB%	8.0
BLK/G	0.4	AST%	18.9
FG%	0.444	STL%	2.8
3PT%	0.363	BLK%	1.2
FT%	0.852	TOV%	10.7
		USG%	36.1

Projected Draft Range: 2nd Round to Undrafted

Top 10 Comps (Second Rounders Only)

	SIMsc			Year
1	893.1	Louis	Bullock	1999
2	892.0	Henry	Williams	1992
3	883.4	Tyler	Harvey	2015
4	881.9	Marcus	Thornton	2009
5	880.8	Eddie	House	2000
6	880.5	Scoonie	Penn	2000
7	879.6	Myron	Brown	1991
8	874.7	Kyle	Hill	2001
9	872.9	Travis	Diener	2005
10	871.5	Bimbo	Coles	1990

Chris Clemons entered last year's draft, but later withdrew to return for his senior season at Campbell University. He capped off an extremely productive college career by leading the nation in scoring and earning MVP honors at the 2019 Portsmouth Invitational. Though he spent his four years playing in a smaller conference, his production was high enough to potentially make him a selection in this year's draft. If a team takes him, they will likely do so in the second round.

Clemons was a dynamic offensive player throughout his college career, and he thrived in a ball dominant role. He used his fluid ball handling skills, solid quickness and deep shooting range to consistently create shots. As a result, he was excellent as an isolation player because he could either pull-up for a jumper or drive to the basket. He even has the explosiveness to finish a few plays above the rim. He was also pretty effective as a pick-and-roll ball handler because he could turn the corner or step behind the screen to make an outside shot. On the downside, he's not a natural playmaker because of his heavy score-first mentality and he has a tendency to over-dribble, so opponents could give him trouble at the NBA level by trapping him in pick-and-roll situations. In addition to his on-ball skills, he shown the ability to play without the ball. For starters, his outside shooting should allow him to be a good floor spacer. He's comfortable shooting from NBA range and he can hit shots in a variety of ways. Particularly, he can knock down spot-up jumpers and he can come off screens to complement his ability to shoot off the dribble. He's also good at pulling up for trail threes in transition as well. Going further, he also is effective at cutting to the basket if defenders overplay his shot and in a small sample, he's shown a willingness to sneak inside to score on an occasional put-back.

At the defensive end, Clemons' effectiveness is always going to be somewhat limited due to his height. He has the physical tools to play a little bigger than his size because he's a good leaper and he has a longer than average wingspan. He also has quick feet and solid functional strength for a smaller player. Surprisingly, he held up quite well when opponents tried to target him on post-ups this season. He took a fairly aggressive approach by actively getting into feet of his opponent, so he forced his man to take uncomfortable shots inside. He was also good at fighting over screens to contain ball handlers in pick-and-roll situations. Additionally, he was an active help defender on the weak side because he was good at jumping passing lanes to get steals and he was a fairly good rebounder for his size. From a negative standpoint, he had a tendency to gamble a bit too much, so he would sometimes get caught trying to shoot the gap when he was chasing a shooter off screens, which allowed his man to get free for an open look. He also would reach in a bit too much in an isolation situation, so his man could blow by him if he didn't get the steal. Finally, he also tended to sag off his man a bit too much, which made him late to close out in spot-up situations.

Chris Clemons may be skilled enough to fit into a modern NBA offense, but he'll need to figure out a way to compensate for his physical limitations on defense to find a long-term fit in a team's rotation. He could benefit by spending at least a season in the G-League to improve as a defender and adjust to a higher level of competition. If he sticks in the league, he could be a scoring guard off the bench similar to someone like Eddie House. Otherwise, he could be headed for a fairly lucrative career overseas.

John Konchar   35/40/45

College/Country	Height	Weight	Age on July 1
IPFW	6'5"	200	23.277

Wingspan	Standing Reach	No Step Vert	Max Vert
6'8"	8'6.5"	N/A	N/A

Basic Stats		Advanced Stats	
GP	133	TS%	0.643
MIN/G	35.2	3PTA/FGA	0.340
PTS/G	15.5	FTA/FGA	0.372
REB/G	8.6	OREB%	7.6
AST/G	4.2	DREB%	20.4
STL/G	2.0	TRB%	14.0
BLK/G	0.6	AST%	20.9
FG%	0.556	STL%	3.2
3PT%	0.416	BLK%	1.8
FT%	0.697	TOV%	13.3
		USG%	19.2

Projected Draft Range: 2nd Round to Undrafted

Top 10 Comps (Second Rounders Only)

	SIMsc			Year
1	912.4	Fred	Hoiberg	1995
2	899.6	Khyri	Thomas	2018
3	895.3	Shake	Milton	2018
4	892.3	Jimmy	King	1995
5	885.6	Bruce	Brown	2018
6	884.3	Brian	Oliver	1990
7	883.9	Lamar	Patterson	2014
8	881.8	Charles	O'Bannon	1997
9	881.7	Jerome	Allen	1995
10	880.8	Darington	Hobson	2010

John Konchar has put up some impressive numbers as a four-year starter at Purdue-Fort Wayne. For the last two seasons, he's led the Summit League in almost every assist and steal metric. He also was named as a first team All-Summit League performer this season. Because he spent his career playing in a mid-major conference and he's coming off an uneven showing at the Portsmouth Invitational, there's a chance that he may go undrafted. If he's picked in this year's draft, he'll probably be taken in the second round.

Konchar was his team's primary scoring option this season, but his skill set is more suited for a complementary role. He's been an excellent shooter throughout his career, as he's made just under 42% of his threes for his career. He was a lower volume player in his first three seasons, so he's mainly a standstill shooter at this stage. He's most effective when he takes spot-up threes. He can also make quick no dribble jumpers in isolation situations and he can knock down outside shots if his defenders go under the screen on pick-and-rolls. He's not quite as good at shooting on the move because he has trouble staying balanced when he comes off a screen. He'll need to work on coming off screens in order to be a more dynamic shooter in the NBA. As his career progressed, he was asked to handle the ball more. He was effective at driving in isolation situations because he could leverage his shooting ability to get straight-line drives to the rim. However, his ball handling is only about average, and he doesn't really change directions well. He also has a heavy tendency to drive left, so defenders can sit on his strong side to force him into tougher shots. He was better as a pick-and-roll ball handler because he could use the screen to get an extra step to the basket. He also showed very good playmaking skills because he would consistently make solid reads to either hit the roll man, find perimeter shooters or pass to cutters inside. His Assist Percentage has increased in each of his four years in college. Additionally, he moves fairly well off the ball. He's adept at going backdoor to score on cuts to the rim if defenders overplay his shot and he'll run hard down the floor to either get layups or shoot open trail threes in transition.

Defensively, Konchar needs significant improvement to become an adequate defender. Physically, he has some limitations. Even though he has decent leaping ability and an average wingspan, he doesn't have great lateral mobility. As a result, he has difficulty guarding perimeter players on the ball. He was below average at defending in isolation situations because he lacked the foot speed to consistently keep his man in front of him. He also had his struggles in defending the ball handler in pick-and-roll situations. He was usually a step slow to fight over the screen, which allowed his man to turn the corner. Other times, he would over-compensate by going under the screen, but he would give his man space to get a clean look for an outside shot. On the positive side, he was more effective as a help defender because he could jump passing lanes to get steals at a very high rate, he was a very good defensive rebounder and he would occasionally rotate from the weak side to block a shot. However, he had a tendency to gamble a bit too much, so he would be out of position to close out on shooters in spot-up situations. When he was disciplined, he did a solid job of staying attached to shooters that were coming off screens.

John Konchar has a chance to land on an NBA roster because of his shooting ability, but his defense could make him a liability. Therefore, he'll need to play at least a season in the G-League to figure out some way to become at least an adequate defender to stay on the court for long stretches. If his skill set stays as is, he will probably be headed for a fairly lucrative career overseas. On the other hand, if his defense comes around, he may able to stick as a shooting specialist similar to someone like Fred Hoiberg.

Amir Hinton   35/40/45

College/Country	Height	Weight	Age on July 1
Shaw	6'5"	190	22.375

Wingspan	Standing Reach	No Step Vert	Max Vert
N/A	N/A	N/A	N/A

Basic Stats		Advanced Stats	
GP	81	TS%	0.617
MIN/G	36.2	3PTA/FGA	0.246
PTS/G	25.7	FTA/FGA	0.545
REB/G	6.0	OREB%	N/A
AST/G	3.1	DREB%	N/A
STL/G	2.3	TRB%	N/A
BLK/G	0.7	AST%	N/A
FG%	0.504	STL%	N/A
3PT%	0.331	BLK%	N/A
FT%	0.855	TOV%	N/A
		USG%	N/A

Projected Draft Range: 2nd Round to Undrafted

Top 10 Comps (Second Rounders Only)

	SIMsc			Year
1	926.4	Steve	Rogers	1992
2	919.0	Ronald	Murray	2002
3	916.4	Lucious	Harris	1993
4	908.8	Ricky	Minard	2004
5	907.1	Terrence	Rencher	1995
6	904.7	Marcus	Brown	1996
7	897.7	Rodney	Buford	1999
8	897.5	Shawn	Harvey	1996
9	896.4	Frankie	King	1995
10	895.4	Lawrence	Moten	1995

Amir Hinton is looking to be the first Division II player to be selected in the draft since 2005. He started his college at Lock Haven, where he became the fastest player in PSAC history to reach 1000 career points. He transferred to Shaw University after his redshirt sophomore season to play for former journeyman guard Flip Murray. In his only season at Shaw, he led all of Division II in scoring and he was named as the CIAA Player of the Year. If he's picked in this year's draft, he'll likely be a second round pick.

Offensively, Hinton thrived in a high volume role as his team's primary shot creator. He was mainly used as a pick-and-roll ball handler and he excelled at scoring in those situations. He was able to use his fluid ball handling skills and above average quickness to turn the corner to get to the rim or step behind the screen to hit a pull-up jumper. He was also good at beating his man off the dribble in isolation situations, but due to the fact that he played against a lower level of competition, opponents were unable to expose his main weakness. Specifically, he mainly looks to drive left and isn't quite as effective when he goes right. He'll have to improve his ability to drive right to prevent defenders from sitting on his strong hand at the next level. Additionally, he was good at pushing the ball up the floor in transition to either score at the rim or set up his teammates. At this stage, he's not really a natural playmaker because he plays with a very heavy score-first mindset and he is a bit lacking in court vision. He's able to reliably make kick-out passes to perimeter shooters but he struggles to find open players on the interior. Also, he isn't really a polished shooter right now. From a mechanics standpoint, he has a smooth, repeatable motion overall, which is evidenced by his high free throw percentage. However, he struggles to consistently make shots from long range because his percentages for his career are just below break-even. Some of this is shot selection related because he is prone to taking a lot of contested shots under duress. Another reason why his Three-Point Percentage is lower is that he has trouble shooting on the move, as he isn't as effective at coming off screens. Therefore, he might be better in a spot-up role in the NBA. As a final note, he has decent awareness off the ball because he was pretty effective as a cutter.

On defense, Hinton needs to improve significantly to stick in the league long-term. He has the physical tools to be at least a decent defender because he has a fairly long wingspan to go along with solid lateral quickness and leaping ability. However, he wasn't really an effective overall defender this past season. This is a concern because he was facing a much lower level of competition, so the jump up to the NBA could make his potential deficiencies even greater. His effort on the defensive end was a bit lacking because he didn't seem to be especially engaged on defense. On the ball, he would easily allow his man to get by him for drives to the hoop in isolation situations. He also wouldn't really fight over the screen to contain the ball handler in pick-and-roll situations, so they would easily turn the corner. He was a little better as a team defender because he was fairly good at staying attached to shooters coming off screens and he would close out on in spot-up situations. On the downside, he tended to close out a bit too aggressively, so he was prone to biting pump fakes to allow his man to get an easy lane to the basket. On the positive side, he was an active help defender on the weak side because he was a pretty good rebounder for his size and he would jump passing lanes to get steals at a high rate, but he sometimes had a tendency to gamble a bit too much.

      Amir Hinton's high scoring output could make him an intriguing prospect despite the fact that he was facing a lower level of competition. On the flip side, he's a bit risky because his defense is under-developed, and he needs to significantly improve to reach a level where he can comfortably guard NBA level players. As it stands now, he would benefit from spending at least a year or two in the G-League to adjust to playing with other talented players and learn NBA defensive concepts. If he makes the necessary improvements, he could carve out a role in the league as a backup combo guard like his former coach, Flip Murray. Otherwise, he's probably going to spend the majority of his career overseas or in the G-League.

YELLOW PROSPECTS

NCAA 2 - 3 Wings

Nickeil Alexander-Walker　　　　　　　　50/55/55

College/Country	Height	Weight	Age on July 1
Virginia Tech	6'5"	204	20.827

Wingspan	Standing Reach	No Step Vert	Max Vert
6'9.5"	8'6"	N/A	N/A

Basic Stats		Advanced Stats	
GP	67	TS%	0.582
MIN/G	29.9	3PTA/FGA	0.448
PTS/G	13.5	FTA/FGA	0.306
REB/G	4.0	OREB%	2.5
AST/G	2.7	DREB%	13.4
STL/G	1.4	TRB%	8.3
BLK/G	0.5	AST%	18.7
FG%	0.464	STL%	2.8
3PT%	0.383	BLK%	2.4
FT%	0.763	TOV%	16.1
		USG%	24.6

Projected Draft Range: Mid to Late 1st Round

Top 10 Comps (First Rounders Only)

	SIMsc			Year
1	933.9	Donte	DiVincenzo	2018
2	933.2	Jacob	Evans	2018
3	929.6	Latrell	Sprewell	1992
4	927.0	Ben	Gordon	2004
5	926.7	O.J.	Mayo	2008
6	925.6	Klay	Thompson	2011
7	922.6	Rashad	McCants	2005
8	920.7	D'Angelo	Russell	2015
9	920.0	Bradley	Beal	2012
10	919.7	Xavier	Henry	2010

Nickeil Alexander-Walker entertained the idea of entering last year's draft, but he opted to return for his sophomore season at Virginia Tech. The decision to stay paid off and he became Virginia Tech's leading scorer this past season. He also earned a spot as a third team All-ACC performer as well. Because of his increased production at one of the nation's toughest conferences, Alexander-Walker's stock rose high enough that he'll probably be taken at some point in the first round of this year's draft.

Offensively, Alexander-Walker projects to fill a role as a ball moving, complementary wing player. In his two years at Virginia Tech, he's established himself as a very good shooter. It takes a him an extra split second for him to get fully set, but when he sets up, he shoots with very good balance and a smooth release. As a result, his career Three-Point Percentage is just over 38% and he excels at knocking down spot-up jumpers. He's also good at making outside shots if defenders go under the screen when he handles the ball in pick-and-roll situations. In general, he was a very good pick-and-roll player overall because the threat of his shot allowed him to turn the corner and get to the rim. Also, his playmaking skills improved dramatically to make him a much more effective player. In fact, his Assist Percentage was more than twice as high as it was last season. These improved passing skills allowed him to consistently hit the open roll man or find shooters on the perimeter. Additionally, he's fairly good at moving without the ball, as he'll run the floor in transition, and he can pick his spots to cut to the rim. However, the extra load time in his shooting motion doesn't allow him to have a quick enough release to effectively shoot off screens. He'll have to work on his ability to shoot on the move or else he'll probably just be a stationary spot-up shooter in the NBA. As another negative, he's not really a great ball handler at this stage, so he has trouble creating his own shot without a screen. He really struggles to change directions and he can be rather predictable. Specifically, he drove to his left over 78% of the time this past season and he wasn't especially effective in those possessions. Therefore, it's not likely that he'll become a primary scorer at the NBA level.

At the defensive end, he's more of a team defender at this stage. He was mainly used as a roaming weak side help defender that could jump passing lanes to get steals, occasionally rotate inside to block a shot and grab defensive rebounds. He was also sound enough from a positioning standpoint to stay close enough to his man to consistently be able to contest spot-up jumpers. In addition to this, he was good at fighting through screens to stay attached to shooters. He was also a solid pick-and-roll defender that generally kept ball handlers from turning the corner. However, on occasion, he would go a little too far under the screen and give his man some extra space to take a pull-up jumper. In the few times where an opponent actually tested him on the ball, he had some struggles. Though he has very long arms and jumps fairly well, he's a little stiff in his lateral mobility. As a result, opponents can get by him in isolation situations. He also isn't particularly strong, so he was vulnerable against post-ups inside because bigger players could simply overpower him to get to the rim. He'll have to find some way to avoid being a liability on the defensive end, or else he'll top out as a situational role player.

Nickeil Alexander-Walker has a chance to stick in the NBA because his best skill, shooting is highly valued in today's NBA. However, his upside is limited by the fact that he isn't polished as an on-ball defender and he struggles to create his own offense. Out of these two weaknesses, it's much more important for him to improve his on-ball defense. If he can become an adequate defender, he could fill a role as a ball moving, complementary shooter similar to someone like Gary Harris. Otherwise, he could become a rotational shooter off the bench like a taller version of Randy Foye.

Other Notable Comps Not Listed Above

SIMsc		Year
916.2	Mike Dunleavy	2002
915.5	Jim Jackson	1992
912.6	Arron Afflalo	2007
910.5	Rodney Stuckey	2007
907.6	Gary Harris	2014

Tyler Herro 50/55/55

College/Country	Height	Weight	Age on July 1
Kentucky	6'6"	192	19.444

Wingspan	Standing Reach	No Step Vert	Max Vert
6'3.25"	8'4.5"	N/A	N/A

Basic Stats		Advanced Stats	
GP	37	TS%	0.580
MIN/G	32.6	3PTA/FGA	0.419
PTS/G	14.0	FTA/FGA	0.231
REB/G	4.5	OREB%	1.6
AST/G	2.5	DREB%	13.9
STL/G	1.1	TRB%	8.2
BLK/G	0.3	AST%	15.2
FG%	0.462	STL%	2.0
3PT%	0.355	BLK%	1.1
FT%	0.935	TOV%	11.8
		USG%	21.4

Projected Draft Range: Top 20

Top 10 Comps (First Rounders Only)

	SIMsc			Year
1	917.5	Malik	Monk	2017
2	916.0	Cory	Joseph	2011
3	912.2	Malik	Beasley	2016
4	909.7	Joseph	Forte	2001
5	909.6	Luke	Kennard	2017
6	898.7	Jeremy	Lamb	2012
7	898.5	Wayne	Ellington	2009
8	897.0	Jordan	Crawford	2010
9	896.7	Ben	McLemore	2013
10	896.1	Jamal	Murray	2016

Tyler Herro initially was committed to go to Wisconsin, but he changed his mind and spent his freshman season at Kentucky. He was very productive this past season, as he ranked 5th in the SEC in Win Shares and was named as a second team All-SEC player as well. He elected to forego his remaining three years to stay in this year's draft and he'll probably come off the board somewhere in the first round with a chance to possibly be taken somewhere in the lottery.

Right now, Herro is one of the best shooting prospects in this year's draft. He was a fairly efficient overall shooter, but he shows the potential to be even better in the NBA. Mechanically, he has a smooth release and he's excellent at repeating his stroke. The latter is evidenced by the fact that he made 93.5% of his free throws this past season. Situationally, he excelled at knocking down catch-and-shoot spot-up jumpers and making trail threes in transition. He had a slight tendency to force up some unnecessary contested shots, so his percentages weren't as high as they could be. If he improves his shot selection, he could be a much more efficient shooter at the next level. In addition to cleaning up some shot selection issues, he needs to improve his ability to shoot on the move. At this stage, Herro is very good at making shots when he's clearly facing his target. However, he wasn't as effective when he was coming off screens. Specifically, he couldn't really turn his body quick enough to properly get set and immediately release his shot. Therefore, he'll have to continue to work on this skill to become a more dynamic shooter in the NBA. As for his other skills, he wasn't really asked to create his own shot very much at Kentucky, but he was fairly solid at driving to the basket in a small sample of possessions. This is mainly because he could utilize the threat of his shot to bait opponents into overplaying him to open up lanes to the basket. He's more of a straight-line driver right now because he's not really quick to change directions. He's also not really a natural passer or playmaker because he can only make simple reads. With this in mind, he's better suited to a complementary role and he's not likely to be a primary scorer at the NBA level.

At the defensive end, he needs considerable work to improve and he'll have to be hidden a bit in his early years. He's more of a team defender at this stage because he lacks some of the physical tools to effectively guard NBA players on the ball. In particular, though he has solid leaping ability, he's a bit lacking in lateral quickness and he has relatively short arms. Because of these limitations, he had some struggles in on-ball situations this season, as opponents could either drive by him or take quick pull-up jumpers to shoot over the top of him. On the positive side, he plays with a pretty high motor and he's solid at maintaining proper defensive positioning. He's pretty consistent in blocking his man out, so he's a fairly good rebounder for his size. He'll also fight through screens to stay attached to shooters when they are coming off screens and he's very good at closing out to contest spot-up jumpers.

Based on his shooting skills, Tyler Herro could stick in the league for a long time as a specialist. However, if he has higher aspirations, he'll need to figure out some way to be an effective enough defender to stay on the floor for long stretches. He also could stand to improve his ball handling to make him a more dynamic offensive player. If this best-case scenario occurs and he makes significant improvement in these areas, he could be a very good complementary scorer similar to a better shooting variation of Jeremy Lamb. In all likelihood, he'll have a long-term career as a shooting specialist off the bench similar to someone like Wayne Ellington.

Chuma Okeke 50/50/55

College/Country	Height	Weight	Age on July 1
Auburn	6'8"	230	20.868

Wingspan	Standing Reach	No Step Vert	Max Vert
N/A	N/A	N/A	N/A

Basic Stats		Advanced Stats	
GP	72	TS%	0.584
MIN/G	25.5	3PTA/FGA	0.424
PTS/G	9.9	FTA/FGA	0.269
REB/G	6.3	OREB%	10.5
AST/G	1.5	DREB%	17.8
STL/G	1.3	TRB%	14.0
BLK/G	1.0	AST%	11.3
FG%	0.481	STL%	2.8
3PT%	0.389	BLK%	4.9
FT%	0.703	TOV%	13.3
		USG%	18.5

Projected Draft Range: Late 1st to 2nd Round

Top 10 Comps (Picks Outside the Top 20)

	SIMsc			Year
1	920.1	Justin	Jackson	2018
2	904.6	Branden	Dawson	2015
3	902.6	Tyler	Lydon	2017
4	900.8	Vincent	Yarbrough	2002
5	898.6	Justin	Anderson	2015
6	898.1	Norman	Powell	2015
7	894.7	Donte	Greene	2008
8	894.1	Matt	Bonner	2003
9	888.9	Justin	Harper	2011
10	887.6	Demetris	Nichols	2007

Chuma Okeke's draft stock was steadily rising over the course of the year due to his strong play in both the regular season and the NCAA Tournament. However, he suffered a setback when he tore his left ACL in a Sweet 16 matchup against North Carolina. Even though it typically takes at least a year to recover from this injury, he elected to enter this year's draft. He still has the option of returning to school, but if he remains in the draft, he probably will be taken at some point after the first twenty picks.

Offensively, Okeke's skill set is best suited for a complementary role because he's primarily been a lower volume player at Auburn. In fact, non-dribbling situations accounted for 96.6% of his offense this season. He was pretty effective in his role because he's a very good outside shooter that made almost 39% of his threes for his career. He has a smooth and repeatable release and that allows him to be very good at making spot-up jumpers and he can efficiently hit trail threes in transition. At this stage, he's more of a stationary shooter because he struggles to shoot on the move, as he wasn't especially good at coming off screens. On the positive side, he moves pretty well without the ball in other situations. He's good at cutting to the rim if opponents overplay his shot and he can pick his spot to crash the offensive boards to score on put-backs. He'll also run hard down the floor to pick up points in transition. He was occasionally used as a post-up player and he was fairly effective in limited opportunities. He doesn't really have a lot of advanced moves, so he mainly looked to either take a quick face up jumper or bully a smaller opponent around the rim. Additionally, he's a willing passer that can occasionally hit cutters or find shooters on the perimeter. However, he's not really a natural playmaker because he's limited to making lower risk passes. On the negative side, he really isn't effective at creating his own shot. He was actually effective in isolation situations, but he mainly looked to take quick no dribble jumpers. He really struggled to drive because he isn't overly quick, and he lacks the dynamic ball handling skills to change directions. Also, he almost exclusively looks to drive left. According to Synergy, he didn't drive right in any possession this season. Therefore, he's limited to being a catch and shoot player at the NBA level.

On the defensive end, Okeke does a lot of things well, but still needs to improve in a few areas to become a reliable defender at the NBA level. At Auburn, he was mainly used as a roaming, weak side help defender and he was pretty good in this role. He could use his considerable length to play passing lanes to get steals and rotate inside to block shots. He's also a pretty good rebounder for his size and he's generally good at blocking his man out. Though he isn't overwhelmingly explosive, he was an effective on-ball defender in isolation situations. This is mainly because his feet are quick enough to stay in front of his man and his length allows him to actively contest shots. He has some potential as a pick-and-roll defender because he could effectively cover the roll man.

However, he tended to go too far under screens, so he would give the ball handler additional space to take outside shots. He tended to sag into the paint in general because he would be late to close out on perimeter shooters. Additionally, he had trouble defending in the post because he would sometimes get caught reaching in or he would bite on fakes. He gambles a bit too much in general, so he could stand to improve his discipline to stay in better position defensively. If he can make this adjustment, he could play more to his strengths and be at least an adequate defender in the NBA.

      Chuma Okeke has a little bit more risk attached to his profile because of his knee injury. If he makes a full recovery, he still needs to become a more disciplined defender to become a rotation player in the NBA. He also could stand to improve his ability to shoot on the move because his offensive potential is limited to being a stationary spot-up shooter at the moment. Most likely, if he's completely healthy and his position defense improves, he could become a spot-up shooting, three-and-D wing player along the lines of a bigger variation of Jae Crowder.

Nassir Little   45/50/55

College/Country	**Height**	**Weight**	**Age on July 1**
North Carolina	6'6"	224	19.384

Wingspan	Standing Reach	No Step Vert	Max Vert
7'1.25"	8'8.5"	31.0"	38.5"

Basic Stats		Advanced Stats	
GP	36	TS%	0.551
MIN/G	18.2	3PTA/FGA	0.190
PTS/G	9.8	FTA/FGA	0.366
REB/G	4.6	OREB%	9.2
AST/G	0.6	DREB%	16.8
STL/G	0.5	TRB%	13.0
BLK/G	0.5	AST%	6.1
FG%	0.480	STL%	1.5
3PT%	0.269	BLK%	3.3
FT%	0.770	TOV%	13.0
		USG%	25.1

Projected Draft Range: Top 20

Top 10 Comps (Top 20 Picks Only)

	SIMsc			Year
1	935.5	Tobias	Harris	2011
2	916.1	Luol	Deng	2004
3	909.5	Anthony	Bennett	2013
4	909.0	Jason	Richardson	2001
5	901.0	Jabari	Parker	2014
6	898.6	Trey	Lyles	2015
7	895.5	Kevin	Knox	2018
8	894.6	Austin	Croshere	1997
9	893.5	Kawhi	Leonard	2011
10	892.8	Kelly	Oubre	2015

Nassir Little came into this season as one of the nation's most heralded recruits. However, he spent most of his freshman season coming off the bench for North Carolina. He was only able to showcase his skills in short bursts, but even in relatively limited opportunities, he displayed enough potential to keep his draft stock fairly high. He elected to forego his remaining years of eligibility to enter this year's draft and he'll most likely be taken somewhere within the top twenty picks in the first round.

At this stage, his defense is ahead of his offense. Physically, he has all of the necessary tools to succeed as a defender in the NBA. He has quick feet, extremely long arms and he's an explosive leaper. These attributes allowed him to be a very good one-on-one perimeter defender, as he really excelled at defending drives in isolation situations. He was very good at fighting over the screen to contain ball handlers in pick-and-roll situations. On the weak side, he was fairly effective. He didn't really look to go for steals, but he would be a threat to rotate inside to occasionally block a shot and he was an excellent defensive rebounder. As a team defender, he's a bit lacking in awareness. Some of this is a product of North Carolina's defensive scheme, as they tended to encourage over-aggressive play and unnecessary gambling. Because of this, he was out of position quite a bit. He would usually get caught wandering into the paint or he'd overplay a passing lane. This made him very vulnerable to losing track of the roll man in pick-and-roll situations and allowing a perimeter shooter to get free for an open look. His tendency to sag into the paint also allowed spot-up shooters to get additional space to get clean looks at the rim. Therefore, it would be best for him to be taken by a team that has a sound defensive structure in place. That way, he would have a better chance of breaking these bad habits, which would allow him to utilize his physical tools more effectively to defend in a way that's more conducive to team success.

At the offensive end, he is still rather unpolished and has a long way to go to become an effective wing player in the NBA. On the positive side, he's aggressive, athletic and he plays with a high motor, which allows him to do a lot of damage around the basket, especially off the ball. He was very effective as a cutter and he was very good at running the floor to pick up scores in transition. In addition to this, he was a very good offensive rebounder that could crash the glass to score on put-backs. His aggressive play allowed him to draw fouls at a high rate. On the downside, he struggled with the ball in his hands. At this stage, he's not a natural playmaker and he's not especially dynamic as a ball handler. Therefore, he had trouble scoring off the dribble in college because he couldn't really change directions and he had a heavy tendency to drive left. He also wouldn't look to pass out of traffic, so if he was in a crowd inside, he would just try to force up a tough, low percentage shot. On top of this, he really struggled to shoot from outside, as he shot below 30% from behind the three-point line. He was a pretty good free throw shooter, but he had trouble translating that stroke to a longer range shot. This is mainly because he has some mechanical hitches in his jump shot. Primarily, he doesn't always square his shoulders and his elbow would flare out, which cause some inconsistencies in his release point. He will need to put in considerable work to fix his mechanics and develop an adequate enough shot to be a rotational player in the NBA.

Nassir Little's athleticism suggests that he could have untapped potential, but he needs to improve his shooting and defense to become a legitimate rotational player in the NBA. His profile is a bit risky because there are a lot of variables in play. If he lands in a chaotic situation, he could end up in a spot similar to Stanley Johnson, where he's a young player with a lot of tools, but with an unclear understanding of how to use them. Most likely, he could develop into a defensive specialist along the lines of Andre Roberson. If everything breaks right and he improves on both sides of the ball, he could fill a three-and-D role as a player similar to Justise Winslow.

Cameron Johnson   50/50/50

College/Country	Height	Weight	Age on July 1
North Carolina	6'8"	205	23.329

Wingspan	Standing Reach	No Step Vert	Max Vert
6'10"	8'7"	N/A	N/A

Basic Stats		Advanced Stats	
GP	135	TS%	0.600
MIN/G	25.4	3PTA/FGA	0.565
PTS/G	11.2	FTA/FGA	0.241
REB/G	4.1	OREB%	4.8
AST/G	1.8	DREB%	12.5
STL/G	0.8	TRB%	8.7
BLK/G	0.3	AST%	13.0
FG%	0.456	STL%	1.7
3PT%	0.405	BLK%	1.1
FT%	0.817	TOV%	9.9
		USG%	19.6

Projected Draft Range: Late 1st to 2nd Round

Top 10 Comps (Picks Outside the Top 20)

	SIMsc			Year
1	936.2	Romain	Sato	2004
2	933.6	C.J.	Wilcox	2014
3	927.3	Davon	Reed	2017
4	925.8	Reggie	Bullock	2013
5	925.6	Damyean	Dotson	2017
6	921.7	Demetris	Nichols	2007
7	921.2	Eddie	Lucas	1999
8	920.6	Pat	Connaughton	2015
9	920.5	Rodney	Hood	2014
10	919.8	Adam	Haluska	2007

Cameron Johnson is a fifth-year senior that spent his first three years at Pittsburgh before transferring to North Carolina. After being a role player for most of his college career, Johnson took on more responsibilities this season and he had a considerable amount of success. He was named as a first team All-ACC performer in his final collegiate season. As a result, he will probably be taken at some point in this year's draft with a chance that he could go as high as the late first round.

Offensively, Johnson projects to be a complementary player because he's spent the bulk of his career in a lower volume role. He also wasn't really asked to create shots for himself this season, as non-dribbling situations accounted for 90.6% of his offense, according to Synergy. He generally thrived in these situations because he's an excellent outside shooter that has made over 40% of his threes for his career. Mechanically, he has a smooth and compact release that allows him to consistently knock down spot-up jumpers. He's also excellent at coming off screens and hitting trail threes in transitions. In addition to this, he's good at making quick pull-up jumpers when defenders go under the screen in pick-and-roll situations and he has a quick release that allows him to shoot no dribble jumpers when he's isolated on his defender. As another positive, he moves well without the ball because he'll roll hard to the rim as the screener in pick-and-rolls and he's good at cutting to the rim if opponents overplay his shot. At this stage, he's primarily a catch and shoot player because his playmaking skills are limited to making low risk passes on the perimeter. He's also not especially quick and he's not really a fluid ball handler, so he's not a dynamic shot creator. He rarely looks to drive and he's not particularly effective either. He's mostly a straight-line driver that really isn't shifty enough to change directions. He also has a strong tendency to go right and struggles when he has to go left.

Defensively, Johnson is a polished prospect that has the potential to be a valuable multi-positional defender in the NBA. This season, he excelled in virtually every area, as he was rated as being good or better in every defensive situation, according to Synergy. Despite the fact that he doesn't really possess explosive athleticism, he has enough physical tools to defend NBA players because he has fairly long arms, moves his feet fairly well and plays with a high motor. He's also a disciplined, stay-at-home defender, so he's rarely out of position. This allows him to be a pretty good on-ball defender because he'll actively contest jumpers and he can generally stay in front of his man. He's also an excellent pick-and-roll defender that can prevent ball handlers from turning the corner and he can switch to stop the roll man. In addition to this, he's an excellent team defender that will fight through screens, close out on perimeter shooters and occasionally take charges. His stay-at-home style doesn't really allow him to make many plays on the weak side, so he really doesn't get blocks or steals. However, he will consistently block out his man, so he's a fairly solid defensive rebounder.

Cameron Johnson doesn't have a lot of high-end upside because he's an older prospect that will be 23 on draft day. Therefore, it's not likely that he'll make a significant leap in his development to improve upon his weaknesses. Even so, his polished outside shooting and ability to guard multiple positions could allow him to fit into an NBA rotation very quickly. Most likely, he'll have a solid career as a complementary, three-and-D wing player similar to Reggie Bullock.

Dylan Windler   50/50/50

College/Country	Height	Weight	Age on July 1
Belmont	6'7"	196	22.773

Wingspan	Standing Reach	No Step Vert	Max Vert
6'10"	8'8.5"	29.0"	37.5"

Basic Stats		Advanced Stats	
GP	128	TS%	0.663
MIN/G	29.4	3PTA/FGA	0.487
PTS/G	13.2	FTA/FGA	0.340
REB/G	7.8	OREB%	6.9
AST/G	2.0	DREB%	22.7
STL/G	1.0	TRB%	15.3
BLK/G	0.8	AST%	12.2
FG%	0.541	STL%	1.9
3PT%	0.406	BLK%	2.6
FT%	0.761	TOV%	14.2
		USG%	19.9

Projected Draft Range: Late 1st to 2nd Round

Top 10 Comps (All Drafted Players)

	SIMsc			Year
1	923.5	Carrick	Felix	2013
2	919.9	Davon	Reed	2017
3	919.8	Mikal	Bridges	2018
4	917.1	Dwayne	Morton	1994
5	914.1	Lavor	Postell	2000
6	912.6	Jake	Layman	2016
7	912.5	Josh	Richardson	2015
8	908.2	Markel	Brown	2014
9	906.6	Rod	Grizzard	2002
10	905.6	James	Ennis	2013

Dylan Windler was one of the most productive seniors in college basketball this season, but his performance was overshadowed to an extent by the fact that he was in the same conference as Ja Morant. Even so, Windler established himself as a very good prospect in his own right, as he's been a solid three-year starter that improved every year that he's been in college. He was also one of his conference's best players, earning a spot as first team all-OVC player this season. As a result, he is very likely to be taken at some point in this year's draft and could possibly go as high as the first round.

Windler stands out because he's one of the most consistent shooters in this year's draft. After struggling with his shot as a freshman, he's made just over 42% of his threes over the last three seasons. From a mechanical standpoint, he shoots with a smooth release that he can repeat consistently. Because of this, he can knock down spot-up jumpers and he's excellent at quickly squaring himself up when coming off screens. He's also very good at hitting trail threes in transition and he's an effective screener in pick-and-pop situations. In addition to his shooting, he moves very well off the ball because he excels at taking advantage of defenders that overplay his shot by cutting hard to the rim. In fact, he was rated by Synergy as being in the 97th percentile at per-possession scoring on plays that ended with a cut this season. He also was very good at picking his spot to crash the offensive glass to score on put-backs. On the ball, his skills are a bit limited. On the positive side, he's a solid pick-and-roll ball handler because he can leverage the threat of his shot to turn the corner and get to the rim. He's also a willing passer that can make simple passes to either an open roll man or the occasional shooter on the perimeter. However, he isn't especially quick and he's about average as a ball handler. He also struggles to efficiently make shots when he drives right. Even though he was effective in isolation situations in college, he may not have the same success in the NBA against a better class of athletes.

Defensively, Windler has the chance to at least be adequate. He has a solid set of physical tools, as he has good leaping ability to go along with fairly long arms and decently quick feet. He also plays with a high effort level and he tends to make sound rotations. He wasn't tested a whole lot, but in a small sample of isolation possessions, he defended quite well. This is mainly because he had the quickness to stay with his man and he could use his length to contest shots. In general, he was pretty good as a team defender. He was excellent in pick-and-roll situations, as he would fight over the screen to contain the ball handler and he could effectively switch to cover the roll man. He was also very good at staying attached to shooters when they were coming off screens and he was generally in position to close out on spot-up shooters. On occasion, he had a tendency to sag a little too far into the paint, so he would sometimes be late on his closeouts. As a weak side defender, he was pretty effective because he was an excellent defensive rebounder and he was good at making timely rotations to block shots. He would also occasionally play passing lanes to get steals as well. On the negative side, he isn't particularly strong. Because of this, bigger players gave him trouble in the post, as they had some success bullying him inside for scores. Therefore, he could stand to get a little stronger to prevent himself from being targeted on post-ups in the NBA.

    Dylan Windler is a pretty polished prospect that is solid enough on both ends to fit into a rotation fairly quickly. Because he played most of his game against mid-major competition, it's uncertain if his defense will translate. Even if it doesn't, he still could stick in the league as a shooting specialist like Eric Piatkowski. However, his performance against major conference competition in college suggests that some of his defense is likely to carry over to the NBA. If that ends up being the case, he could develop into a solid complementary role player similar to a better shooting variation of Josh Hart.

Louis King   45/50/50

College/Country	Height	Weight	Age on July 1
Oregon	6'8"	195	20.236

Wingspan	Standing Reach	No Step Vert	Max Vert
7'0.25"	8'8.5"	N/A	N/A

Basic Stats		Advanced Stats	
GP	31	TS%	0.552
MIN/G	30.4	3PTA/FGA	0.450
PTS/G	13.5	FTA/FGA	0.232
REB/G	5.5	OREB%	5.4
AST/G	1.3	DREB%	16.0
STL/G	0.9	TRB%	10.9
BLK/G	0.2	AST%	9.0
FG%	0.435	STL%	1.7
3PT%	0.386	BLK%	1.0
FT%	0.785	TOV%	14.5
		USG%	25.0

Projected Draft Range: Late 1st to 2nd Round

Top 10 Comps (All Drafted Players)

	SIMsc			Year
1	918.0	Rod	Grizzard	2002
2	912.0	Jayson	Tatum	2017
3	911.1	Malachi	Richardson	2016
4	909.7	Daequan	Cook	2007
5	909.5	Nick	Young	2007
6	909.4	Andrew	Wiggins	2014
7	908.6	Terrence	Ross	2012
8	907.7	Donte	Greene	2008
9	906.5	Dontae'	Jones	1996
10	905.5	Kevin	Knox	2018

Louis King came into this season as a heralded recruit, as he was a McDonald's All-American in 2018. He became Oregon's leading scorer after Bol Bol's injury and his solid overall play landed him a spot on this season's Pac-12 All-Freshman team. He has decided to test the draft waters this year. If he elects to stay in the draft, he is probably going to be taken somewhere outside the top twenty, but he could rise higher if he performs well in workouts.

Offensively, King shows considerable promise because his blend of shooting and athleticism could allow him to be at least be a solid complementary player in the NBA. This season, he shot the ball very efficiently because he displayed fairly good shot selection to go along with his consistent ability to make shots. Mechanically, his motion is mostly sound, especially from the waist up. He has a smooth release, gets good extension on the follow through, but he tends to kick his legs out during his initial jump. At times, he'll get thrown off balance, but his mechanics from his upper body and his percentages are solid enough where this isn't a major issue. Anyway, he's a very good catch and shoot player, as he can knock down spot-up jumpers and shoot off screens. He's also effective as the screener on pick-and-pop plays. At this stage, he's a young player that's still learning how to move without the ball. On the plus side, he has a good idea of when to pick his spots to crash the offensive boards to score on put-backs. However, he tends to get caught standing idly on the perimeter, which makes him less effective as a cutter. He's also better suited for a complementary role because he's not an especially dynamic ball handler or playmaker. He was effective at driving in college, but that was mainly because defenders were overplaying his shot. In those situations, he was able to get to the rim by using straight-line drives. He doesn't change directions particularly well or have a quick initial first step. Additionally, he's not a natural playmaker because he doesn't look to pass very often, and he can only make simple passes. Therefore, King is not likely to be much of a shot creator at the NBA level.

At the defensive end, King has the tools to become a solid defender, but still needs to polish his skills to defend at an NBA level. Physically, he has the potential to guard multiple positions because he has solid lateral quickness to go along with long arms and pretty good leaping ability. He played more of a stay-at-home style, so he didn't really get blocks or steals, but he was a good defensive rebounder. He flashed a lot of potential as an on-ball defender and he was pretty effective at guarding players in isolation situations this season. This is mainly because he could use his length to contest shots, and he was quick enough to keep his man in front of him. Despite his thin frame, he showed some wiry strength that allowed him to be a solid post defender. This enabled him to hold position on the block to force his man into taking a tougher shot. At this point, he still needs work as a team defender. Positively speaking, he consistently closed out on perimeter shooters in spot-up situations. In other situations, he sometimes appeared to be lost. Some of this attributed to a rapid mid-season change in Oregon's defensive strategy. At the start of the season, Oregon primarily played a zone defense, but after Bol Bol's injury, the team switched to man-to-man. Because of this sudden switch, the team didn't really work out a clear plan for its rotation scheme. King ended up struggling at defending pick-and-rolls because the team couldn't settle on a distinct coverage. He also was used as a four, so he didn't really have to chase perimeter shooters off screens. Therefore, he has to work to learn NBA coverages and defensive schemes to reach his full potential on defense.

Louis King is a fairly young prospect with the potential to become a valuable three-and-D wing player. Right now, his offense isn't too far off, but he still needs to build up his awareness on the defensive end to handle some of the more complex elements of NBA defense. If he can grasp these concepts quickly, then he could carve out a long-term career as a complementary, three-and-D role player similar to someone like Terrence Ross. Otherwise, he may need to spend a season in the G-League to get some seasoning before he becomes a reliable rotational player.

Talen Horton-Tucker   40/45/50

College/Country	Height	Weight	Age on July 1
Iowa State	6'4"	235	18.597

Wingspan	Standing Reach	No Step Vert	Max Vert
7'1.25"	8'7"	N/A	N/A

Basic Stats		Advanced Stats	
GP	35	TS%	0.488
MIN/G	27.2	3PTA/FGA	0.416
PTS/G	11.8	FTA/FGA	0.230
REB/G	4.9	OREB%	2.9
AST/G	2.3	DREB%	16.7
STL/G	1.3	TRB%	10.2
BLK/G	0.7	AST%	16.2
FG%	0.406	STL%	2.8
3PT%	0.308	BLK%	2.7
FT%	0.625	TOV%	12.4
		USG%	26.2

Projected Draft Range: Late 1st to 2nd Round

Top 10 Comps (Picks Outside the Top 20)

	SIMsc			Year
1	897.4	Lance	Stephenson	2010
2	888.7	Jordan	Hamilton	2011
3	878.3	Khris	Middleton	2012
4	877.4	P.J.	Hairston	2014
5	872.3	Dontae'	Jones	1996
6	871.4	Donte	Greene	2008
7	869.2	Von	Wafer	2005
8	868.7	Kyle	Singler	2011
9	867.7	Abdel	Nader	2016
10	866.8	Daequan	Cook	2007

Talen Horton-Tucker is one of the youngest prospects in this year's draft because he doesn't turn 19 until late November. In addition to being younger than most draft prospects, he was fairly productive this season and he was good enough to earn a spot on the Big 12 All-Freshman team. It's highly probable that he'll be in this year's draft for good, but he has left the door open for a return to Iowa State if he suffers a setback during the workout process. If he stays in the draft, he will likely be taken at some point after the first twenty picks.

In the past, a lot of teams would not have known what to do with a player with Horton-Tucker's unique body type. As the league becomes more position-less, his physical attributes will allow him to find a fit, at least on the defensive side of the ball. From a physical standpoint, he has all of the tools to be a versatile defender that can capably guard multiple positions. He has solid lateral mobility to go along with a very long wingspan and solid leaping ability. His stockier build also allows him to have the strength to handle bigger players inside. As a result, he was a pretty good overall defender in one-on-one situations. As it was mentioned earlier, he could use his strength to push his man off the block in post-up situations and he had more than enough length to force his man into taking tough, contested shots. Also, when he was isolated on the perimeter, he was quick enough to stay in front of his man, apply pressure and contest shots. In addition to being a good on-ball defender, he made a lot of plays as a weak side help defender. He was a pretty good rebounder that would consistently block out. He also could rip balls away from opponents or play passing lanes to get steals and he would occasionally rotate inside to block a shot. Going further, he was a very good team defender as well. He would typically be in the right position, as he would consistently close out on perimeter shooters and he was adept at fighting through screens to either stay attached to shooters coming off screens or contain ball handlers in pick-and-roll situations. He wasn't asked to cover the roll man very often, but when he did, he was pretty effective at taking away the immediate basket area. In fact, he didn't allow a score to a roll man in a very small sample of possessions this season.

Offensively, Horton-Tucker is not quite as advanced as he is on defense. At this stage, he's a bit of a one-dimensional scorer that relies on using his strength to bully smaller defenders to the basket on drives, so he was mainly effective in isolation and dribble hand-off situations. His only other offensive strength as a scorer was that he would aggressively crash the offensive boards to score on put-backs. On the plus side, he has some playmaking skills that allow him to find open shooters on the perimeter or hit cutters inside. He also tends to take pretty good care of the ball because his turnover rate is fairly low. However, his offensive effectiveness is negatively affected by the fact that he's an inefficient shooter. For starters, his shot selection is spotty because he'll tend to force up a lot of contested shots that hurt his efficiency. He also has some inconsistencies in his release because he doesn't always get full extension, especially when he's shooting from long range. This can explain why he struggles to repeat his shooting motion, which is evidenced by the fact that his Free Throw Percentage is below 70% and he's a below break-even three-point shooter. In order to find a place in a team's rotation, he will have to improve to become at least an adequate shooter. As another negative, he tends to get caught standing around on the perimeter. Because of this, he isn't especially effective as a cutter and he can't really run off screens either.

Talen Horton-Tucker is an interesting prospect that could provide a team with some value due to his defensive versatility. However, he isn't polished enough on offense to be a long-term rotation player right now. He will have to grow as an outside shooter to turn into more than just being a defensive specialist. If he shot comes around, he could become a solid rotational, three-and-D wing player like Jae Crowder. Otherwise, he might be just be a defensive specialist at the end of a roster similar to somebody like Abdel Nader.

Ignas Brazdeikis 40/45/50

College/Country	Height	Weight	Age on July 1
Michigan	6'7"	221	20.477

Wingspan	Standing Reach	No Step Vert	Max Vert
6'9.25"	8'6"	N/A	N/A

Basic Stats		Advanced Stats	
GP	37	TS%	0.573
MIN/G	29.6	3PTA/FGA	0.351
PTS/G	14.8	FTA/FGA	0.369
REB/G	5.4	OREB%	4.6
AST/G	0.8	DREB%	16.1
STL/G	0.7	TRB%	10.5
BLK/G	0.5	AST%	6.1
FG%	0.462	STL%	1.5
3PT%	0.392	BLK%	1.7
FT%	0.773	TOV%	8.8
		USG%	26.1

Projected Draft Range: Late 1st to 2nd Round

Top 10 Comps (Picks Outside the Top 20)

	SIMsc			Year
1	921.9	Jumaine	Jones	1999
2	910.1	DeShaun	Thomas	2013
3	905.3	Dwayne	Bacon	2017
4	904.6	Jordan	Hamilton	2011
5	898.9	Ryan	Anderson	2008
6	898.9	Terrico	White	2010
7	898.6	Da'Sean	Butler	2010
8	897.2	James	Cotton	1997
9	897.0	Kyle	Singler	2011
10	897.0	Donte	Greene	2008

Ignas Brazdeikis came in as one of the best high school players in Canada and he made a quick adjustment to college basketball. In his first season at Michigan, he led the team in scoring, and he was the Big Ten's Rookie of the Year. He also earned a spot on the All-Big Ten second team as well. He entered his name in this year's draft, but he still has the option to return to Michigan. Unless he has a poor performance in his workouts, he'll probably stay in the draft. Most likely, he will be selected at some point after the first twenty picks.

Offensively, Brazdeikis could add some value as a complementary player because he's a pretty good shooter. At this stage, he's more of a stand-still shooter, but he's been pretty effective in this role. He excels at knocking down spot-up jumpers and he's very good at popping out as the screen on pick-and-pop plays. Occasionally, he can step behind the screener as a pick-and-roll ball handler to hit an outside shot if his man goes too far under the screen. Mechanically, his motion is pretty sound from the waist up, but he tends to kick out his legs when he goes up for a jumper. This doesn't allow him to be as effective at shooting on the move. He wasn't as good at coming off screens because he had trouble getting his feet into a set position. Therefore, he'll need to learn how to shoot off screens in order to become a dynamic part of a team's offense. As another positive note, he's also pretty good at making backdoor cuts to exploit defenders that overplay his shot. His primary weakness is that he isn't really a shot creator. He isn't especially effective as a driver because he's lacking in quickness and he's only about an average ball handler. Instead of getting all the way to the rim, he would attempt to seek out contact to draw fouls. This worked at the college level, but it unclear if this strategy would work against better athletes in the NBA. Also, he's not really much of a playmaker because he sticks to playing a catch and shoot style. If he passes, he mainly looks to make low-risk passes to avoid turnovers.

On defense, he finds a way to be effective even though he doesn't quite have all of the physical tools. His lateral movements are a little on the stiff side and his arms are only about average in length for a player of his size. He also isn't particularly explosive as an athlete, as his vertical leap is roughly around average. Even so, he plays a disciplined stay-at-home style and he's fairly good at playing angles to keep himself in position. This season, he was actually very effective at defending players in isolation situations. He kept his man in front of him and he would consistently be in a solid position to contest shots. On the negative side, he's a bit lacking in strength. In situations where he was switched onto a bigger player, they had some success in pushing him around inside on post-ups. For the most part, he was a solid team defender. He was good at closing out on perimeter shooters in spot-up situations and he would consistently stay attached to shooters that were coming off screens. He was also a fairly solid pick-and-roll defender, as he could switch to take away a roll to the rim and he was generally good at fighting over the screen to contain the ball handler. However, every once in a while, a quicker guard could turn the corner and blow by him. As it was alluded to earlier, he didn't really look to help off his man to go for steals or blocks. This also meant he was typically in solid rebounding position. As a result, he would usually box his man out, which made him a solid defensive rebounder.

Even though he's on the younger side of the spectrum, Ignas Brazdeikis profiles as a complementary role player in the NBA. His strengths may be polished enough where he could step into a rotation fairly quickly. Most likely, he'll wind up being a rotational spot-up shooter that plays adequate enough defense by making sound rotations and being in the right spots similar to someone like Jonas Jerebko. In a worst-case scenario, he could still have a role in the NBA as a situational shooting specialist along the lines of a poor man's Ryan Anderson.

Matisse Thybulle — 40/45/50

College/Country	Height	Weight	Age on July 1
Washington	6'5"	200	22.326

Wingspan	Standing Reach	No Step Vert	Max Vert
N/A	N/A	N/A	N/A

Basic Stats

GP	135
MIN/G	29.4
PTS/G	9.2
REB/G	3.1
AST/G	2.0
STL/G	2.4
BLK/G	1.3
FG%	0.429
3PT%	0.358
FT%	0.782

Advanced Stats

TS%	0.550
3PTA/FGA	0.520
FTA/FGA	0.210
OREB%	3.4
DREB%	8.4
TRB%	5.9
AST%	12.8
STL%	4.7
BLK%	4.9
TOV%	18.2
USG%	17.0

Projected Draft Range: Late 1st to 2nd Round

Top 10 Comps (All Drafted Players)

	SIMsc			Year
1	900.4	Laron	Profit	1999
2	894.2	Jeff	Trepagnier	2001
3	889.2	Kevin	Lynch	1991
4	889.2	Josh	Richardson	2015
5	887.1	Darnell	Mee	1993
6	884.9	Francisco	Garcia	2005
7	882.0	Sir'Dominic	Pointer	2015
8	880.7	Danny	Green	2009
9	879.7	Daniel	Ewing	2005
10	875.7	Scott	Burrell	1993

Matisse Thybulle has been a productive four-year starter at Washington. His production has spiked in the last two years and he's established himself as one of the nation's best defensive players. He has been named as the Pac-12's Defensive Player of the Year for the last two seasons and he received the 2019 Naismith Defensive Player of the Year as the best defender in all of college basketball. His defensive reputation has helped his stock to the point where he will be picked at some point in this year's draft with a chance that he could go in the first round.

As it alluded to earlier, Thybulle has considerable potential as a defender, but he's spent the last two seasons playing almost exclusively in a zone defense. His coach at Washington, Mike Hopkins was a longtime former assistant at Syracuse, so he employed the same 2-3 zone scheme. Thybulle really thrived in this system because he could take advantage of his physical tools to be an excellent weak side roamer. Physically, he's a pretty athletic player with good lateral quickness, long arms and some explosive leaping ability. These attributes allowed him to excel at rotating inside to block shots and he led the nation in almost every steal metric this past season. He's also a decent defensive rebounder. In his first two seasons, he did play a lot of man defense. In those years, he was a little better as a team defender than he was at guarding on the ball. As a team defender, he would consistently close out in spot-up situations and he would stay attached to shooters that were coming off screens. He was also effective at fighting over screens to contain pick-and-roll ball handlers. On the ball, he had the quickness to stay with his man to stop the drive, but he would often overplay it, which gave his man space to pull-up for a jumper. If he works on his ability to apply pressure to his man on the ball, he could realize his defensive potential to become a solid wing defender in the league.

Offensively, Thybulle was used as a low volume, spot-up shooter throughout his career. This season, non-dribbling situations accounted for 90.6% of his offense, according to Synergy. Therefore, it's highly likely that he'll be a lower volume, complementary player in the NBA. He's been a decent catch and shoot player in college because he has a compact, repeatable stroke. His release is a bit slow, so he tends to rush his shot if a defender is close to him. Because of this, he's much better when he's wide open. He also isn't quick to set up with his feet, so he has trouble shooting on the move. He couldn't really shoot off screens, so he may be better suited to being a stationary spot-up shooter. If he's making his shot, he can use his quickness to take advantage of defenders that overplay his shot to get to the rim on straight-line drives, but he can't really create his own shot because his ball handling skills are not especially advanced. As a result, he doesn't really change directions and he almost exclusively tries to drive left, so defenders can force him into difficult shots by sitting on his strong hand.

Off the ball, he tends to float on the perimeter, so he doesn't really look to cut to the basket. However, he does have a good idea of when to pick his spots to go to the offensive boards to score on put-backs. He plays with a pass-first mindset, so he will hit the open man to pick up assists, but he doesn't have natural court vision, so he's limited to making simple reads. Also, he can sometimes be a little careless with the ball, which makes him a bit turnover prone.

Matisse Thybulle is a lower ceiling prospect that could be valuable as a three-and-D wing player in the NBA. He'll have to prove himself as an on-ball defender and he'll need to improve his offensive skills to show that he can be more than just a stationary spot-up shooter. In all probability, his defense should translate to allow him to carve out a role as a defensive specialist that can occasionally knock down an outside shot. He'll likely follow a career path similar to someone like Wesley Johnson if he sticks in the league.

Admiral Schofield   40/45/50

College/Country	Height	Weight	Age on July 1
Tennessee	6'5"	241	22.255

Wingspan	Standing Reach	No Step Vert	Max Vert
6'9.75"	8'6.5"	30.0"	34.0"

Basic Stats		Advanced Stats	
GP	132	TS%	0.556
MIN/G	24.9	3PTA/FGA	0.373
PTS/G	11.9	FTA/FGA	0.222
REB/G	5.3	OREB%	5.7
AST/G	1.3	DREB%	17.6
STL/G	0.7	TRB%	11.9
BLK/G	0.4	AST%	10.9
FG%	0.458	STL%	1.6
3PT%	0.387	BLK%	1.6
FT%	0.763	TOV%	11.8
		USG%	24.2

Projected Draft Range: Late 1st to 2nd Round

Top 10 Comps (Picks Outside the Top 20)

	SIMsc			Year
1	922.2	Matt	Bonner	2003
2	914.6	Georges	Niang	2016
3	911.2	Justin	Harper	2011
4	911.1	Abdel	Nader	2016
5	906.6	Lazar	Hayward	2010
6	903.8	Erik	Murphy	2013
7	903.2	Dillon	Brooks	2017
8	902.1	Sam	Jacobson	1998
9	902.0	Rico	Hill	1999
10	901.3	Morris	Peterson	2000

Admiral Schofield entered last year's draft, but he later withdrew and returned to Tennessee for his senior season. In his final season in college, he established himself as one of the SEC's most productive players and he earned honors as a first team, All-SEC performer. His excellent track record increased his stock to the point where he'll probably be taken at some point after the first twenty picks in this year's NBA Draft.

On offense, Schofield projects to be a complementary wing player because he wasn't really a shot creator in college. This season, he spent 88.6% of his offensive possessions in non-dribbling situations, so he'll likely be a role player on offense. Even so, he could thrive in this kind of role. His outside shooting has improved every year to the point where he made just under 42% off his threes this season. He was mainly a stationary catch and shoot player that could knock down spot-up jumpers, hit trail threes in transition and make shots as the screener on pick-and-pop plays. He really doesn't shoot on the move or off the dribble. He had problems setting his feet quickly when he was coming off screens, so he tended to miss more in these situations. He was good at making jumpers in isolation situations, but the bulk of them were no dribble jumpers where he took the shot before his man could contest. In addition to being a solid outside shooter, he was effective at moving without the ball because he plays with a high motor. Because he plays with a lot of energy, he'll roll hard to the rim on pick-and-rolls and he's very good at cutting if opponents overplay his shot. He also will run the floor in transition to pick up point around the basket and he'll actively crash the offensive glass to score on put-backs. He was fairly effective on drives in isolation situations, but he could only score on straight-line drives. He's not really a great ball handler and he doesn't change directions particularly well. Also, he has a strong tendency to go right, so defenders can sit on his strong hand to make him take tougher shots. Additionally, he can post up smaller players because he could use his strength advantage to bully them inside to get scores around the basket. He's not really a natural playmaker at this stage, so he's limited to making simple reads and safer passes.

Defensively, he has the potential to become effective defender, but his skills aren't quite polished at the moment. Physically, he has all of the necessary tools because he has a pretty long wingspan to go with some explosive leaping ability and solid lateral mobility. These physical attributes allowed him to be a pretty good on-ball defender in isolation situations because he was quick enough to stay with his man, he would aggressively apply pressure and he would actively contest shots. He also made a lot of plays on the weak side as a help defender, as he would rotate inside to occasionally block shots and he would play passing lanes to pick up steals. He was also a pretty good defensive rebounder that usually blocked his man out. On the downside, he wasn't nearly as effective as a team defender. Positively speaking, he was very good at fighting through screens to stay attached to shooters. However, he had some trouble in other areas because he was either not especially sound in his rotations or he would play a little too aggressively. He struggled as a pick-and-roll defender because he was typically caught in an in-between position. At times, he would give up a wide open outside shot by sagging too far into the paint. Other times, he would over-compensate by hedging too far to give up either an opening to the roll man inside or a lane for the ball handler to split the pick-and-roll. His tendency to hang back into the paint also made him late to close out on perimeter shooters, so he was prone to giving up some open looks outside. Finally, he had some difficulty defending players in the post because he tended to bite on fakes, and he was prone to picking up cheap fouls. Therefore, he'll have to become a more disciplined defender in order to become a long-term player in the league.

Admiral Schofield has some of the basic skills to develop into a role player in the NBA. His ceiling isn't especially high because he's on the older side of the spectrum. However, he could become a useful three-and-D player if he improves his defensive discipline and maintains his outside shooting efficiency. If things break right for him, he could turn into a decent rotational combo forward like Mike Scott. Otherwise, he could wind up either becoming a fringe player or he may end up spending most of his career overseas or in the G-League.

Kevin Porter Jr.   40/45/50

College/Country	Height	Weight	Age on July 1
USC	6'5"	213	19.159

Wingspan	Standing Reach	No Step Vert	Max Vert
6'9"	8'7"	27.0"	34.0"

Basic Stats		Advanced Stats	
GP	21	TS%	0.559
MIN/G	22.1	3PTA/FGA	0.433
PTS/G	9.5	FTA/FGA	0.293
REB/G	4.0	OREB%	4.8
AST/G	1.4	DREB%	15.0
STL/G	0.8	TRB%	10.0
BLK/G	0.5	AST%	12.0
FG%	0.471	STL%	2.1
3PT%	0.412	BLK%	2.6
FT%	0.522	TOV%	17.9
		USG%	23.3

Projected Draft Range: Mid to Late 1st Round

Top 10 Comps (First Rounders Only)

	SIMsc			Year
1	895.3	Daequan	Cook	2007
2	895.2	Justise	Winslow	2015
3	894.1	Antoine	Wright	2005
4	885.5	Jason	Richardson	2001
5	876.1	Xavier	Henry	2010
6	873.7	Donte	DiVincenzo	2018
7	871.3	Bradley	Beal	2012
8	867.9	Jayson	Tatum	2017
9	867.1	Gerald	Wallace	2001
10	866.9	Kareem	Rush	2002

Kevin Porter, Jr. came into this season as a heralded recruit. His freshman year didn't quite go as expected, as he mostly came off the bench for USC. He also missed most of the season due to a quadriceps injury and an indefinite suspension for "personal conduct issues." Despite these setbacks, he flashed enough potential in a limited number of minutes to keep his draft stock fairly high. In all likelihood, he could be taken in the first round of this year's draft.

Porter has the tools to become a solid defender in the NBA, but he hasn't really been tested very much. Physically, he's quite gifted and he has the necessary athletic tools. He has good lateral quickness to go along with great leaping ability and a long wingspan. He was solid at roaming as a weak side help defender because he could play passing lanes to get steals, rotate inside to occasionally block shots and he was a solid rebounder. His tendency to roam hurt him when he was chasing shooters off screens because he could get caught shooting the gap to go for a steal. In general, he was solid as a team defender because he would consistently close out on perimeter shooters and he would fight over screens to contain ball handlers in pick-and-roll situations. At this stage, his ability to play on-ball defense is uncertain. He was rarely matched up against an opponent that could test him either on the perimeter or in the post. Theoretically, he may have some unseen abilities to defend on the on-ball because he's been pretty solid at defending in other situations and he has great physical tools. However, there is not a lot of hard evidence at the moment, so he may need to prove himself in workouts to show that he can defend NBA-caliber players on the ball.

Offensively, he projects to be a complementary player because his game is still unpolished. On the plus side, his great athleticism allowed him to be an excellent transition player because he could push the ball quickly up court and finish plays above the rim. He also has some potential as a shooter because he made over 41% of his threes this season. However, his stroke is still inconsistent, as he made below 60% of his free throws. His shooting motion needs to be a tweaked a bit because he tends to kick out his feet to throw him off balance and his off hand is positioned on top of the ball, which causes an awkward rotation. He can somewhat shoot off the dribble because he was fairly good at making pull-up jumpers off the pick-and-roll. However, he struggled at driving in general. He had a tendency to over-penetrate, which made him a bit turnover prone because he would sometimes either lose the ball in traffic or throw the ball away trying to pass. He also had a heavy tendency to go right, so opponents could sit on his strong hand to force him into low percentage shots. He was willing to pass at times, but he isn't a natural enough playmaker to anything beyond making safe, simple passes on the perimeter. Off the ball, he flashed some ability to be effective as a cutter, but he doesn't do it very often and he'll tend to float on the perimeter a bit too much.

Kevin Porter, Jr. is a young prospect with a lot of athletic upside. At the moment, his defense is ahead of his offense, so he might be able to adjust to playing in an NBA defensive scheme fairly quick. However, his offensive game may be so raw that he would benefit from spending at least a season in the G-League to improve the consistency of his shooting and improve his overall feel for the game. If his offense comes around, he could turn into a solid rotational, three-and-D wing player similar to Justise Winslow. Otherwise, he could wind up being a situational defensive specialist along the lines of Ruben Patterson.

Kezie Okpala   40/45/50

College/Country	Height	Weight	Age on July 1
Stanford	6'8"	210	20.175

Wingspan	Standing Reach	No Step Vert	Max Vert
7'1.75"	8'10.5"	30.5"	37.0"

Basic Stats		Advanced Stats	
GP	52	TS%	0.521
MIN/G	30.8	3PTA/FGA	0.213
PTS/G	13.9	FTA/FGA	0.504
REB/G	4.8	OREB%	4.4
AST/G	1.9	DREB%	12.7
STL/G	1.0	TRB%	8.7
BLK/G	0.5	AST%	12.4
FG%	0.440	STL%	1.8
3PT%	0.336	BLK%	1.7
FT%	0.674	TOV%	16.8
		USG%	25.2

Projected Draft Range: Late 1st to 2nd Round

Top 10 Comps (All Drafted Players)

	SIMsc			Year
1	939.8	Jared	Jeffries	2002
2	931.1	Al-Farouq	Aminu	2010
3	918.5	Josh	Okogie	2018
4	905.3	Quincy	Miller	2012
5	904.8	Bobby	Simmons	2001
6	903.2	Andrew	Wiggins	2014
7	902.8	Lamar	Odom	1999
8	901.1	Ansu	Sesay	1998
9	900.4	Jeff	Green	2007
10	900.1	Paul	George	2010

After being in a complementary role in his freshman year, Kezie Okpala took on more responsibilities for Stanford this season. He ended up becoming one of the most productive players in the Pac-12, earning a spot on the All-Pac-12 first team. He decided to forego his final two years of eligibility to enter this year's draft. He will probably be taken at some point in the draft with a chance to go in the first round.

At this stage, Okpala is more of a volume scorer and he hasn't really been overly efficient over the course of his career. Though his Three-Point Percentage has improved this season, his shooting is still a question mark right now. His stroke is pretty inconsistent, as he almost has two different shooting motions. His mechanics in the flow of a game are a little better because he'll release the ball at the top of his motion, and he gets decent extension. However, his stroke at the free throw line is unusual because he has something of a low shot put release. Therefore, he had trouble making free throws, as his percentage is below 70% for his career. As a result of his inconsistent shooting, opponents can play off him to reduce his effectiveness as a driver. He also had trouble in isolation situations because he primarily looks to go left, so opponents can sit on his strong hand to force him into tougher shots. Additionally, he can be a little turnover prone and he'll tend to stand idly on the perimeter off the ball. On the plus side, he was a solid pick-and-roll player this season. His quickness allows him to turn the corner and he will hit enough pull-up jumpers to keep defenders honest. He also was a willing passer that could effectively hit the roll man. Moreover, he stands out because he's a good athlete that plays an energetic style. This makes him a dynamic transition player that will run hard down the floor and finish plays above the rim. He also is pretty aggressive to crash the offensive glass to score on put-backs.

At the defensive end, Okpala was mostly ineffective even though he is very gifted from a physical standpoint. Athletically, he possesses all of the ideal tools because he has a very long wingspan to go along with great leaping ability and pretty quick feet. However, according to Synergy, he was rated as being average or worse in every situation in man defense this season. He was only effective when Stanford played in a zone because he could roam and defend an area. He was decent as a weak side help defender because he could rebound, play passing lanes to get deflections and occasionally rotate inside for a block. In most situations, he had considerable difficulties. In isolation situations, he tended to bite hard on an opponent's first move, so it was easier for them to use a counter-move to get an open look. His tendency to bite on the first move also hurt him as a post defender because opposing players could use fakes to get easy scores inside. He was a little better in pick-and-roll situations because he would fight over the screen to contest outside shots, but he was usually too aggressive at coming over the top. This allowed the ball handler to easily turn the corner to score inside. Off the ball, he would often lose track of his man. Therefore, he would be late to close out in spot-up situations or he would go the wrong way when chasing a shooter off a screen.

Kezie Okpala has great athleticism, but his skills are bit raw at this stage, so it may take him a while to become a viable rotation player. He needs to spend at least a season in the G-League to learn NBA defensive schemes and become a more consistent shooter. If he doesn't improve significantly, he could spend the bulk of his career either overseas or in the G-League. If everything breaks right and his overall game improves, he could become a rotational, three-and-D wing player similar to someone like Dahntay Jones.

Miye Oni 35/45/50

College/Country	Height	Weight	Age on July 1
Yale	6'5"	206	21.907

Wingspan	Standing Reach	No Step Vert	Max Vert
6'10.75"	8'4.5"	30.5"	38.5"

Basic Stats		Advanced Stats	
GP	87	TS%	0.547
MIN/G	31.7	3PTA/FGA	0.465
PTS/G	15.0	FTA/FGA	0.286
REB/G	6.2	OREB%	3.1
AST/G	3.3	DREB%	18.7
STL/G	0.9	TRB%	11.2
BLK/G	1.0	AST%	19.9
FG%	0.428	STL%	1.5
3PT%	0.356	BLK%	3.4
FT%	0.777	TOV%	15.7
		USG%	25.8

Projected Draft Range: 2nd Round to Undrafted

Top 10 Comps (Second Rounders Only)

	SIMsc			Year
1	923.2	Rod	Grizzard	2002
2	919.1	Khris	Middleton	2012
3	917.9	Carrick	Felix	2013
4	917.7	Malik	Hairston	2008
5	917.2	Davon	Reed	2017
6	915.0	Lavor	Postell	2000
7	912.8	Charles	O'Bannon	1997
8	912.6	Roger	Mason	2002
9	910.2	Josh	Richardson	2015
10	907.9	Marcus	Williams	2007

Miye Oni is looking to be the first Ivy League player drafted since Jerome Allen from Penn was taken in 1995. Oni comes in with a pretty solid pedigree, as he was named as the Ivy League's Player of the Year this season. His performance at Yale earned him an invite to this year's NBA Draft Combine, so there's a decent chance that he could be picked in this year's draft. If he is selected, he will likely be a second round pick.

Oni has the potential to develop into a very good defender in the NBA. His physical skills are pretty close to ideal, as he has a pretty long wingspan to go along with fairly explosive leaping ability and solid lateral quickness. Even though he mostly played against a lower level of competition, he was a solid on-ball defender in college. He excelled at defending one-on-one in isolation situations because he was quick enough to stay with his man and he would actively contest shots. He also held up pretty well as a post defender because he had enough functional strength to hold inside position and he had the length to make it tougher on his man to shoot. He also was a solid help defender because he could rotate from the weak side to block a shot or two, use his length to get deflections and he was a good rebounder for his size. As a team defender, he was generally pretty good because he would consistently close out hard on perimeter spot-up shooters and he was good at staying attached to shooters coming off screens. He had some problems defending in pick-and-roll situations because he would often go too far under the screen, which made him prone to giving his man too much space to shoot a jumper. This issue may be more of a problem with his team's defensive scheme, so if he plays in a more aggressive, switching-oriented scheme, he could be more effective overall defender.

On offense, he was his team's primary scoring option, but he might be better suited for a complementary role at the NBA level. He did well in isolation situations this season because he had the quickness and athleticism to drive by his man and finish a lot of plays above the rim. However, he had some struggles as a pick-and-roll ball handler. On the plus side, he has decent playmaking skills that allowed him to make simple reads to either hit the roll man or find shooters on the outside. However, he had trouble shooting off the dribble, so he tended to miss a lot of pull-up jumpers. Because of this weakness, defenders were able to sag into the paint to clog his driving lanes and force him into taking tougher shots. Therefore, his relative inability to shoot off the dribble might make him a better fit for a complementary role as a secondary ball mover and spot-up shooter. A role like this could play more to his strengths because he was very good in transition, as he would quickly push the ball up court to either set up his teammates or get layups for himself. He was also an excellent spot-up shooter that has been an above average three-point shooter throughout his career. His percentages fluctuated a bit on a year-to-year basis because he takes a slight pause at the top of his motion, which causes him to have an inconsistent release point at times. If he tweaks his motion to rectify this little issue, he could be an even more efficient shooter at the NBA level. His work off the ball still needs some work because he doesn't really shoot well on the move and he will sometimes stand idly on the perimeter. He has some trouble shooting off screens because he isn't quick to get his feet set, so his balance can be thrown off. At other times, he'll tend to stand still on the perimeter off the ball, so he doesn't always look to cut or go to the basket to pursue an offensive rebound. At the next level, he will have to improve his ability to move off the ball to fit into the demands of a modern NBA offense.

Miye Oni is an intriguing prospect because his combination of athleticism, defense and outside shooting ability. He's not quite a finished product at this moment because he will have to adjust to playing against a higher level of competition, so he could benefit from some additional seasoning in the G-League. If he sticks in the league, he could develop into a useful rotational, three-and-D wing player along the lines of somebody like Raja Bell or Arron Afflalo. Otherwise, he could be headed for a solid career overseas.

Other Notable Comps Not Listed Above

SIMsc		Year
913.9	Raja Bell	1999
907.1	Arron Afflalo	2007
904.5	Danny Green	2009

Aubrey Dawkins   40/40/45

College/Country	Height	Weight	Age on July 1
UCF	6'6"	205	24.148

Wingspan	Standing Reach	No Step Vert	Max Vert
N/A	N/A	N/A	N/A

Basic Stats		Advanced Stats	
GP	99	TS%	0.609
MIN/G	23.1	3PTA/FGA	0.515
PTS/G	9.7	FTA/FGA	0.208
REB/G	3.2	OREB%	4.2
AST/G	0.8	DREB%	11.9
STL/G	0.6	TRB%	8.2
BLK/G	0.2	AST%	7.1
FG%	0.475	STL%	1.6
3PT%	0.422	BLK%	1.1
FT%	0.819	TOV%	10.6
		USG%	20.8

Projected Draft Range: 2nd Round to Undrafted

Top 10 Comps (Second Rounders Only)

	SIMsc			Year
1	945.1	Eddie	Lucas	1999
2	932.4	Jabari	Bird	2017
3	926.4	Damyean	Dotson	2017
4	913.7	Demetris	Nichols	2007
5	912.3	Melvin	Levett	1999
6	909.4	Romain	Sato	2004
7	908.7	Gary	Collier	1994
8	906.5	Steve	Novak	2006
9	904.7	Adam	Haluska	2007
10	903.9	Sviatoslav	Mykhailiuk	2018

Aubrey Dawkins started his career at Michigan, but he transferred after his sophomore year and he sat out the 2016-17 season due to transfer rules. He was set to start his career at UCF last year, but he missed the entire 2017-18 season due to a season-long shoulder injury. He made a full recovery this year and he ended up becoming one of the most productive players in the AAC this past season. He also had a very strong showing in UCF's NCAA Tournament loss against Duke. There's a chance that he could be picked in this year's draft and if he's taken, he'll likely go somewhere in the second round.

Dawkins has established himself as a reliable outside shooter throughout his career. He was able to maintain his high level of efficiency in a larger role at UCF by making over 40% of his threes this season. He has a very quick release that allows him to excel as a catch and shoot player. He was excellent at coming at screens and he was very good at knocking down spot-up jumpers. He also could make quick no dribble jumpers on isolations and he could step behind the screen if his man went too far under in a pick-and-roll situation. He was good in general at moving without the ball because he could effectively cut to the rim to complement his great shooting abilities. He showed some ability to drive to the basket and use crafty finishes to score inside. However, he's not explosively quick and his ball handling skills aren't dynamic enough to allow him to quickly change directions. He also has a bit of tendency to favor his left hand on drives. Therefore, it's not likely that he will be a shot creator at the NBA level and he's better suited for a complementary role. Also, he's not really a natural playmaker because he can only make simple reads and safe passes.

At the other end of the floor, Dawkins projects to be a solid overall wing defender. He has all of the ideal physical tools because he has solid leaping ability to go along with a fairly long wingspan and good lateral quickness. Because of his athletic tools, he was a pretty good on-ball defender. In isolation situations, he was quick enough to stay with his man and he would actively apply pressure to either force a turnover to get an occasional steal or contest a shot. At UCF, he often shared the court with Tacko Fall, who was almost always anchored in the paint. This meant that he rarely had to guard a bigger player in the post in a switch situation. In a small sample of post-up possessions, he was solid because he had enough to strength to hold position and his length allowed him to force his man into a more difficult shot. In addition to being good at defending on the ball, he was an excellent team defender that made sound rotations. He didn't really take unnecessary gambles and mainly stayed home on his man. He would also consistently close out on spot-up shooters and fight through screens to either stay attached to a shooter off the ball or contain the ball handler in pick-and-roll situations. He was also very consistent at blocking out his man, which made him a pretty good rebounder for his size.

Aubrey Dawkins is a lower ceiling prospect because he'll be 24 on draft day, making him one of the oldest prospects in this draft. Despite his age, his relatively polished skill set could allow him to fit into a team's rotation as a complementary, three-and-D wing player like Reggie Bullock if his strengths fully translate. In another scenario, it's very possible that he could end up becoming a shooting specialist similar to someone like Anthony Morrow. Otherwise, in a worst-case scenario, he could be headed overseas for a fairly lucrative career.

Other Notable Comps Not Listed Above

SIMsc		Year
948.4	Anthony Morrow	2008

DaQuan Jeffries   35/40/45

College/Country	Height	Weight	Age on July 1
Tulsa	6'5"	216	22.170

Wingspan	Standing Reach	No Step Vert	Max Vert
6'11.25"	8'8"	N/A	N/A

Basic Stats		Advanced Stats	
GP	85	TS%	0.631
MIN/G	23.6	3PTA/FGA	0.372
PTS/G	9.9	FTA/FGA	0.358
REB/G	5.0	OREB%	7.3
AST/G	1.2	DREB%	15.8
STL/G	0.8	TRB%	11.8
BLK/G	1.1	AST%	10.8
FG%	0.530	STL%	1.8
3PT%	0.377	BLK%	5.2
FT%	0.770	TOV%	13.8
		USG%	19.6

Projected Draft Range: 2nd Round to Undrafted

Top 10 Comps (Second Rounders Only)

	SIMsc			Year
1	898.6	Bill (Henry)	Walker	2008
2	896.3	Matt	Steigenga	1992
3	894.4	Chris	Carr	1995
4	890.9	Carrick	Felix	2013
5	888.7	Dillon	Brooks	2017
6	888.4	Bryan	Bracey	2001
7	886.5	Erik	Murphy	2013
8	885.7	Khris	Middleton	2012
9	884.7	Landry	Fields	2010
10	884.3	Lavor	Postell	2000

DaQuan Jeffries started his career at Oral Roberts, but then he transferred to Tulsa after brief one-year stop at Western Texas Community College. He's coming off a solid senior season, as he landed a spot on the All-AAC third team. After the season, he won the 2019 College Slam Dunk Contest and he had a very strong showing at this year's Portsmouth Invitational, earning a spot on the All-Tournament team. His recent performance may have built up his stock to make him a viable draft candidate. If he is taken in this year's draft, he could be selected as a second rounder.

Right now, his offensive skill set is best suited for a complementary, catch and shoot role in the NBA. This season, non-dribbling situations accounted for 86.3% of his offensive possessions, according to Synergy. He also wasn't especially effective at creating his own offense off the dribble as either an isolation player or as a pick-and-roll ball handler because he does not handle the ball well. Therefore, he had a lot of difficulty getting all the way to the rim. He was mainly looking to seek out contact to draw fouls and he was fairly effective at doing so at the college level. He was much better when he was off the ball because his high motor allows him to make hustle plays and he's a solid outside shooter. He was very good at moving without the ball in a half-court offense. He would usually cut hard to the rim and he aggressively crashed the offensive boards to score on put-backs. He was also a dynamic player in transition because he had the athleticism to finish plays above the rim in addition to having the high motor to quickly run up the court to fill a lane. Throughout his college career, he's been a pretty good outside shooter, making just under 38% of his threes. His stroke is compact and repeatable, which enables him to be very good at making spot-up threes. He also flashed some ability to shoot off screens and he was solid at making trail threes in a small sample size.

At the defensive end, Jeffries has the potential to be a solid defender that has the capability to guard multiple positions in the NBA. He has great physical tools, as he has solid lateral mobility to go along with very long arms and explosive leaping ability. Due to his high level of athleticism, he was pretty effective as an on-ball defender. Opposing players had trouble driving by him in isolation situations because he had the quickness to stay with them and his length allowed him to actively contest shots. He was also accustomed to guarding bigger players in the post and he held up pretty well. This is mainly because he has solid strength to hold position inside, which allowed him to force his man into taking a tougher shot. Tulsa played a lot of zone this season, so he didn't defend a lot of pick-and-rolls and he didn't have to cover anyone coming off a screen. There's a chance that he may be unpolished as a team defender at this stage. In a small sample of pick-and-rolls, he was an effective defender because he flashed the ability to contain the ball handler and stop the roll man from getting easy points inside. He also was very good at closing out on perimeter shooters in spot-up situations. He made some plays as a help defender because he was very good at rotating from the weak side to block shots and he was a solid defensive rebounder. However, he did have a tendency to be over-aggressive, so he was prone to committing cheap fouls.

DaQuan Jeffries may still have a little more room to grow because he is slightly younger than the average senior, as he'll still be 21 on draft day. At the moment, his skill set is well suited for a role as a rotational three-and-D wing player, but he could benefit from some additional seasoning in the G-League to learn NBA defensive schemes. He may have to grind it out on the fringes of the league in his early years, but he could eventually land a spot on a roster and he could possibly become a rotation player. If things break favorably for him, he could develop into a solid role player like Taurean Prince. Otherwise, if he's unlucky, he could spend most of his career in the G-League or overseas.

Terance Mann   35/40/45

College/Country	Height	Weight	Age on July 1
Florida State	6'6"	205	22.701

Wingspan	Standing Reach	No Step Vert	Max Vert
6'7.75"	8'5"	32.5"	38.5"

Basic Stats		Advanced Stats	
GP	140	TS%	0.602
MIN/G	25.9	3PTA/FGA	0.180
PTS/G	9.4	FTA/FGA	0.421
REB/G	5.1	OREB%	8.5
AST/G	1.9	DREB%	13.6
STL/G	0.8	TRB%	11.1
BLK/G	0.2	AST%	13.7
FG%	0.552	STL%	1.7
3PT%	0.327	BLK%	1.0
FT%	0.670	TOV%	14.8
		USG%	17.2

Projected Draft Range: 2nd Round to Undrafted

Top 10 Comps (Second Rounders Only)

	SIMsc			Year
1	932.6	Chris	Carrawell	2000
2	930.6	Chandler	Parsons	2011
3	927.1	Jud	Buechler	1990
4	925.0	Lavor	Postell	2000
5	924.4	Maarty	Leunen	2008
6	918.6	Jeffery	Taylor	2012
7	918.1	Malcolm	Lee	2011
8	915.0	Charles	O'Bannon	1997
9	913.2	Davon	Reed	2017
10	910.8	Tyrone	Wallace	2016

Terance Mann started his career as a backup to Malik Beasley and Dwayne Bacon. After Beasley left for the NBA, Mann became a solid three-year starter at Florida State. Even though he's been a role player throughout his career, he flashed enough potential to participate in the Portsmouth Invitational and he was later invited to this year's NBA Draft Combine. He didn't quite stand out too much at Portsmouth, so there's a chance that he could go undrafted. If he's picked in this year's draft, he will probably be taken in the second round.

Mann stands out because he's been a solid defender throughout his college career. His physical tools are close to ideal because he's an outstanding leaper that has very good lateral mobility. His arms are relatively short for his size, but he makes up for his lack of length by playing with high energy. Therefore, he's been very good at defending on the ball in isolation situations because he has the quickness to stay with his man and he'll aggressively apply pressure to force a tough shot. He also has solid strength that allows him to occasionally guard bigger players in the post. He was generally good at holding position and getting into the feet of his man to make him take a more difficult shot. Stylistically, he was more of a stay-at-home, position defender, so he rarely looked to gamble to go for steals or blocks. When he did try to make plays on the weak side, he was pretty opportunistic and the turnovers he forced usually led to transition offense. He was also a solid rebounder for his size. As a team defender, he was mostly good because he would fight through screens to either contain pick-and-roll ball handlers or stay attached to shooters off the ball. However, he tended to wander into the paint off the ball, so he was often late to close out on perimeter shooters in spot-up situations. This issue is fairly minor and in the right scheme, it could be fixed to allow him to be a solid wing defender in the NBA.

As it was alluded to earlier, Mann has been a lower volume role player throughout his career, so it's likely that he'll be in a similar role in the NBA. He wasn't really a shot creator in college because he doesn't quite have the ball handling skills to be an effective driver. He had trouble getting all the way to the basket in pick-and-roll and isolation situations. To compensate for his relative inability to blow his man, he often had to crash into defenders to try to draw fouls and he got to the free throw line frequently as a result. He was a willing passer, but he wasn't really a natural playmaker because he was limited to making simple reads. As a catch and shoot player, he was much more effective as a stationary spot-up shooter. This season, his shooting improved tremendously, as he shot 39% on his threes and he made 79% of his free throws. However, his career percentages are much lower, so it's uncertain if his shooting will stay consistent at the next level. On the positive side, his mechanics appear to be much smoother than they were in his earlier years. If he keeps working on his shot, he could be an effective floor spacer in the NBA. Off the ball, his very high motor allowed to be pretty effective. He would cut hard to the rim in half-court situations and his athleticism allowed him to be a dynamic threat in transition, as he could finish plays above the rim. As a final note, he was also aggressive to crash the offensive boards to score on put-backs.

Terance Mann has a chance to develop into a decent role player at the NBA level. He's not fully polished at the moment, so he could use an extra season in the G-League to prove that he can be a reliable outside shooter. Right now, he projects to be a defensive specialist at the end of the roster similar to a player like Tyrone Wallace. If he establishes himself as at least an average three-point shooter, he could develop into a decent rotational, three-and-D wing player like Sterling Brown.

Kris Wilkes 35/40/45

College/Country	Height	Weight	Age on July 1
UCLA	6'7"	209	20.781

Wingspan	Standing Reach	No Step Vert	Max Vert
6'10.75"	8'7"	27.5"	35.0"

Basic Stats		Advanced Stats	
GP	66	TS%	0.535
MIN/G	30.7	3PTA/FGA	0.437
PTS/G	15.5	FTA/FGA	0.311
REB/G	4.8	OREB%	4.5
AST/G	1.7	DREB%	11.9
STL/G	0.7	TRB%	8.4
BLK/G	0.5	AST%	10.9
FG%	0.436	STL%	1.2
3PT%	0.343	BLK%	1.7
FT%	0.664	TOV%	10.1
		USG%	25.1

Projected Draft Range: 2nd Round

Top 10 Comps (Second Rounders Only)

	SIMsc			Year
1	950.0	Terrico	White	2010
2	929.6	Marcus	Williams	2007
3	914.8	Malik	Hairston	2008
4	914.5	Dwayne	Bacon	2017
5	906.8	Joe	Crawford	2008
6	905.8	Davon	Reed	2017
7	902.9	Chase	Budinger	2009
8	902.6	Da'Sean	Butler	2010
9	902.0	Allen	Crabbe	2013
10	901.3	Jermaine	Taylor	2009

Kris Wilkes was a participant in the last year's draft combine, but he chose to withdraw his name to return for his sophomore season at UCLA. He led the team in scoring this season and he established himself as one of the better players in the Pac-12 Conference, as he landed a spot on the All-Pac-12 second team. He chose to enter the draft once again and he still has the option to go back to UCLA for another year. However, he's made indications that he'll probably stay in the draft. If he's taken, he'll probably be a second round pick.

On offense, Wilkes projects to be a complementary wing player. He wasn't really used as a shot creator this season because he was put in a non-dribbling situation 93.6% of the time, according to Synergy. He was most effective at using his great athleticism to be a dynamic threat in transition, as he could push the ball up court to finish a lot of plays above the rim. He also was good at cutting in a half-court set to get lobs at the rim. He was solid as a spot-up shooter this season, but he's much more comfortable at taking shots from mid-range. He's shot threes at just over a break-even percentage and his stroke isn't especially consistent, as he shoots free throws at a rate below 70%. From a mechanics standpoint, he has a few moving parts in his shooting motion because he tends to lean his upper body back and he'll also kick out his legs a bit as well. Because of his current motion, he's only really able to be a stand-still shooter at this point, as he struggled to keep his feet set when he shoots on the move. With this in mind, he will have to work on his footwork to maintain some more balance to become a more reliable long range shooter at the next level. In the small sample of possessions where he was asked to handle the ball, he had some success as a driver. However, he could only score on straight-line drives because he's only about an average ball handler and he almost exclusively looks to drive right. As a result of the latter, defenders could give him trouble by taking away his strong hand to force him to take tougher shots the other way. Additionally, he doesn't really have many playmaking skills because he rarely looks to pass, and he's limited to making simple reads.

As a defender, Wilkes is somewhat tough to project because he played in a zone defense for most of this season. On the other hand, he has flashed enough potential the season before to suggest that he might be able to transition into being a defender at the NBA level. Physically, he has all of the requisite tools. He's an explosive leaper that has fairly long arms and solid lateral mobility. These athletic traits allowed him to be a solid on-ball defender last season, as he showed that he could generally stay with his man to stop drives and he was active to contest shots. There's a possibility that he could have trouble at defending bigger players on switches because his frame is still rather thin, so he may be vulnerable to being pushed around inside in those situations. In his two years at UCLA, he's been fairly solid as a team defender because he mainly looks to stay at home on his man and he rarely tries to roam to pursue steals or blocks. He was pretty effective at fighting through screens to either stay attached to shooters off the ball or contain the ball handler in a pick-and-roll situation. Usually, he was pretty good at closing out on spot-up shooters. However, he could sometimes be a bit too aggressive, so his man could either get to the rim or get space to pull-up for a jumper. Finally, though he jumps high and tends to play with solid positioning, he's only a middling defensive rebounder because he doesn't always block his man out.

Kris Wilkes has the athleticism to compete in the NBA, but his overall game is still unpolished. He'll need to become a more consistent outside shooter and defender to earn a spot in a team's rotation. Because it's unlikely that he'll return to school for another year, he'll need to get some additional seasoning in the G-League. If his game shows the necessary improvement over the next year or two, he could develop into an energetic defensive specialist that has the capability of knocking down a few outside shots similar to a taller variation of Norman Powell. Otherwise, he could end up spending the bulk of his career in the G-League or overseas.

Charles Matthews 35/40/45

College/Country	Height	Weight	Age on July 1
Michigan	6'6"	195	22.625

Wingspan	Standing Reach	No Step Vert	Max Vert
6'9.5"	8'7"	29.5"	37.5"

Basic Stats		Advanced Stats	
GP	111	TS%	0.519
MIN/G	24.1	3PTA/FGA	0.253
PTS/G	9.1	FTA/FGA	0.382
REB/G	4.1	OREB%	6.1
AST/G	1.4	DREB%	13.9
STL/G	0.7	TRB%	10.1
BLK/G	0.4	AST%	11.9
FG%	0.464	STL%	1.8
3PT%	0.308	BLK%	1.9
FT%	0.576	TOV%	14.2
		USG%	22.8

Projected Draft Range: 2nd Round to Undrafted

Top 10 Comps (Second Rounders Only)

	SIMsc			Year
1	938.4	Lavor	Postell	2000
2	934.4	Landry	Fields	2010
3	932.7	Jamie	Watson	1994
4	928.9	Dwayne	Morton	1994
5	923.4	Chris	Douglas-Roberts	2008
6	923.0	Malik	Hairston	2008
7	921.7	Davon	Reed	2017
8	920.8	Sammy	Mejia	2007
9	920.5	Markel	Brown	2014
10	916.5	Dijon	Thompson	2005

Charles Matthews started his career at Kentucky, but he transferred to Michigan after his freshman season. He sat out the 2016-17 season due to transfer rules, but at Michigan, he became a solid two-year starter. His production this season was slightly down from what it was a year ago, but he elected to enter this year's draft anyway. There's a chance that he could go back to school for another season, but he's given every indication that he'll remain in the draft pool. If he's taken, he'll probably be picked in the second round.

Matthews has a chance to make it to the NBA because he's been a very good defender at the college level. His defense could translate to the next level because he's a good athlete with solid physical tools. He has quick feet, long arms and he's a fairly explosive leaper. He also plays with a high motor, so all of these traits made him an excellent on-ball perimeter defender. Opponents had trouble driving by him in isolation situations and he was aggressive to apply pressure to contest shots or force turnovers. Stylistically, he was more of a stay-at-home defender because he rarely looked to roam off the ball to go for steals or blocks, but occasionally, he would use his length to get deflections. He usually maintained pretty solid positioning and he was consistent in blocking out his man, so he was a fairly good defensive rebounder at Michigan. He was generally a good team defender because he was good at fighting over screens to contain the ball handler in pick-and-roll situations and he would aggressively close out on perimeter shooters in spot-up situations. At times, he would be prone to closing out too hard, which gave his man a lane to get to the rim. His only real weak area was that he had trouble staying attached to shooters when they were coming off screens. Typically, he would either get caught on the screen or he would try to go under it. Both approaches were problematic because he tended to allow his man to get open looks. He'll have to improve his ability to get through screens to transition into becoming a reliable defender at the next level.

Offensively, he has to make a lot of improvements to his game in order to become an NBA level contributor. At this stage, he's not really a great shooter because he shoots at a below break-even percentage and he's made less than 60% of his free throws in his college career. His stroke is inconsistent because he has a hitch at the top of his release, which causes some timing issues. As a result, he struggles to knock down open spot-up jumpers. In addition to his shooting issues, he wasn't especially effective as a driver as either a pick-and-roll ball handler or isolation player because he's only about an average ball handler and he doesn't have a very quick first step. He had trouble getting all the way to the rim, so he often looked to crash into defenders to draw fouls. Moreover, he doesn't have great playmaking skills, but he can make simple reads and he'll avoid committing turnovers. His primary offensive value is his energetic play because he'll get a lot of scores on hustle plays. He's fairly dynamic in transition because he'll run hard down the floor and finish plays above the rim. He's also aggressive to crash the offensive boards to score on put-backs and he'll make hard flex cuts to get layups inside.

Charles Matthews is a lower ceiling prospect that could fill a role as a defensive specialist. His offensive game is still raw, so he'll need to spend at least a season or two in the G-League to develop his jump shot to being at least passable. Because his offense needs considerable work, there's a good chance that he would spend the majority of his career either in the G-League or overseas. If his shot comes around, he could carve out as a career as a situational defensive specialist like Quinton Ross.

Other Notable Comps Not Listed Above

SIMsc		Year
921.7	Quinton Ross	2003

Markis McDuffie   35/40/45

College/Country	Height	Weight	Age on July 1
Wichita State	6'9"	202	21.816

Wingspan	Standing Reach	No Step Vert	Max Vert
6'9.25"	8'9"	N/A	N/A

Basic Stats		Advanced Stats	
GP	129	TS%	0.551
MIN/G	24.8	3PTA/FGA	0.406
PTS/G	11.8	FTA/FGA	0.404
REB/G	4.4	OREB%	6.4
AST/G	1.1	DREB%	13.3
STL/G	0.9	TRB%	9.9
BLK/G	0.2	AST%	9.1
FG%	0.428	STL%	2.1
3PT%	0.340	BLK%	1.0
FT%	0.791	TOV%	11.2
		USG%	24.1

Projected Draft Range: 2nd Round to Undrafted

Top 10 Comps (Second Rounders Only)

	SIMsc			Year
1	938.1	Rod	Grizzard	2002
2	920.3	Marcus	Liberty	1990
3	919.7	Landry	Fields	2010
4	919.6	Dan	Langhi	2000
5	918.7	Lavor	Postell	2000
6	917.7	Demetris	Nichols	2007
7	916.8	Norman	Powell	2015
8	916.7	Da'Sean	Butler	2010
9	916.3	Dijon	Thompson	2005
10	915.3	Davon	Reed	2017

Markis McDuffie tested the draft waters a year ago, but he elected to withdraw his name to return to Wichita State for his senior season. This season, he established himself as one of the better players in the American Athletic Conference, as he earned honors as a second team all-conference performer. His draft stock has been up and down over the course of the year, so there's a chance that he may go undrafted. If he's taken in this year's draft, he'll likely be a second round pick.

At this stage, McDuffie's defense is ahead of his offense. He's flashed the potential to be a versatile wing defender at the NBA level. From a physical standpoint, he has the necessary tools because he has fairly long arms to go along with solid lateral quickness and good leaping ability. He's a pretty good on-ball defender as a result. He was effective at guarding players in isolation situations because he could stay with his man and he could use his length to contest shots. Despite having a relatively thin frame, he held up fairly well against bigger players in post-up situations. He showed enough functional strength to hold position inside to force his man in taking a tougher shot. He was more of a stay-at-home, position defender, so he didn't look to go for blocks or steals, although he was a pretty solid defensive rebounder. He had his ups and downs as a team defender. On the positive side, he was generally good at fighting over the screen to contain ball handlers in pick-and-roll situations. However, he had trouble guarding the roll man, especially on pick-and-pop plays, as he would typically sag into the paint to give his man extra space to shoot. He also tended to have some lapses off the ball because he would sometimes be late to close out on shooters and he could get caught on screens. With this in mind, he'll have to improve his overall defensive awareness to become a more complete defender at the next level.

Offensively, he still has some room for improvement. It's likely that he'll have to play a complementary role because he wasn't really used as a shot creator in college. In fact, non-dribbling situations accounted for 93% of his offense this season, according to Synergy. The reason for this is that he's a below average ball handler and he doesn't really have a great first step. He also has a heavy tendency to drive right, so defenders can easily sit on his strong hand to force him into tougher shots. He doesn't have a lot of playmaking skills either because he's limited to making safe, simple passes. He's much better as a catch and shoot player at this stage. He was fairly good at hitting spot-up jumpers and coming off screens, but he did most of his damage from mid-range. His mechanics are a little funky because he tends to kick out his legs, which throws him off balance. The extra movement makes him inconsistent from long range, as he's only been a break-even three-point shooter throughout his career. To improve as a shooter, he will need to focus on staying on balance to allow him to have a more consistent release on his three-point shot. Finally, McDuffie is fairly good at moving without the ball. He was generally good at cutting to the basket and he would actively crash the offensive glass to score on put-backs. He also was a pretty dynamic threat in transition because he would run hard down the floor and use his athleticism to finish plays above the rim.

Markis McDuffie is fairly young for a senior, so there may still be some extra room for growth. His game isn't polished yet, so he could benefit from some additional seasoning in the G-League. Ideally, he would work on becoming a more consistent three-point shooter and defender. If he make the necessary adjustments to improve in these areas, he could eventually develop into a rotational, three-and-D wing player similar to someone like a taller variation of Norman Powell. Otherwise, he could wind up spending the bulk of his career overseas or in the G-League.

Caleb Martin 35/40/45

College/Country	Height	Weight	Age on July 1
Nevada	6'6"	200	23.756

Wingspan	Standing Reach	No Step Vert	Max Vert
N/A	N/A	N/A	N/A

Basic Stats		Advanced Stats	
GP	139	TS%	0.555
MIN/G	28.5	3PTA/FGA	0.593
PTS/G	13.6	FTA/FGA	0.344
REB/G	4.5	OREB%	3.4
AST/G	1.9	DREB%	13.9
STL/G	1.0	TRB%	8.7
BLK/G	0.6	AST%	12.8
FG%	0.414	STL%	2.0
3PT%	0.359	BLK%	2.1
FT%	0.725	TOV%	10.4
		USG%	23.9

Projected Draft Range: 2nd Round to Undrafted

Top 10 Comps (Second Rounders Only)

	SIMsc			Year
1	945.5	Romain	Sato	2004
2	937.4	Adam	Haluska	2007
3	929.3	Davon	Reed	2017
4	924.1	Da'Sean	Butler	2010
5	922.9	Kim	English	2012
6	918.5	Keith	Bogans	2003
7	915.5	Jabari	Bird	2017
8	914.8	Kyle	Singler	2011
9	914.3	Nate	Erdmann	1997
10	914.3	E'Twaun	Moore	2011

Caleb Martin's background is very similar to his twin brother, Cody. They both started their career at N.C. State before transferring to Nevada for their junior season. The twins also entered last year's draft only to withdraw and return for another season at Nevada. Caleb Martin has been pretty productive in his last two seasons, as he was the Mountain West Conference's Player of the Year in 2017-18 and he earned honors as a first team all-Mountain West performer this past season. If he is selected in this year's draft, he will probably go somewhere in the second round.

Martin's profile on the defensive end is very similar to his twin brother. In fact, their physical measurements are essentially identical. This means that Caleb Martin projects fairly well from a tools standpoint because he has a fairly long wingspan, good lateral quickness and decent leaping ability. His athleticism allowed him to be a very effective defender on the ball. He was good at defending in isolation situations because he generally stayed with his man, applied pressure and contested shots. He also showed some functional strength to handle bigger players in the post on switches by effectively holding position inside to force his man into some tough shots. Stylistically, Martin was a little more of a stay-at-home defender, so he was a little more disciplined than his brother was as a team defender. He was more consistent at staying in position to close out on perimeter shooters and he excelled at fighting over screens to contain ball handlers in pick-and-roll situations. The only flaw in his defensive profile was that he tended to get caught trying to shoot the gap when covering shooters off screens. If he missed a steal attempt, he would often allow his man to get an open look from outside. As a help defender, he was pretty similar to his brother because he would also jump passing lanes to get steals, occasionally rotate from the weak side to block a shot and he was a solid defensive rebounder.

On offense, Martin was Nevada's primary scoring option, as he led the team in scoring this past season. He mainly relied on his outside shooting to set up the rest of his game. His stroke doesn't have any real distinct mechanical flaws, but he's a bit more comfortable shooting from mid-range than he is from long range. His percentage on threes has fluctuated on a year-to-year basis, so he could stand to improve his consistency. As a shooter, he's better when his feet are set, so he mainly thrives on making spot-up jumpers. He's shown some ability to shoot off screens, but he's much better at coming off a screen to his right and he struggles going the other way. He was effective as an isolation player because he could quickly shoot a no dribble jumper, or he could beat an over-aggressive defender on a straight-line drive. He does tend to drive left on a more frequent basis, so he could stand to improve his ability to go right to keep defenders honest. Additionally, he was a very good pick-and-roll ball handler because he could use the screen to get an extra step to turn the corner and he showed solid playmaking abilities. If the drive wasn't available, he would look to pass and he was good at either hitting the roll man, locating shooters on the perimeter or passing to cutters off the ball. On the downside, defenders had some success at going under screens because he isn't quite as good at shooting off the dribble, so he missed a lot of pull-up jumpers. Finally, he was fairly good at moving off the ball. In a small sample of possessions, he was effective at cutting to the rim if an opponent overplayed his shot and he was fairly good at picking his spots to crash the offensive glass to score on put-backs.

Caleb Martin is a prospect that doesn't have a whole lot of high-end upside because he's on the older side of the spectrum, as he'll be 23 on draft day. Even so, his game isn't too far away from being ready to possibly make an NBA roster. The only thing that's holding him back is that his outside shooting is still rather inconsistent. If he can improve his shot to at least an average level, he could carve out a career as a backup, three-and-D wing player like Danuel House. Otherwise, he could end up spending the bulk of his career overseas or in the G-League.

Other Notable Comps Not Listed Above

SIMsc		Year
921.7	Danuel House	2016
917.2	Quinton Ross	2003

Cody Martin 35/40/45

College/Country	Height	Weight	Age on July 1
Nevada	6'6"	192	23.756

Wingspan	Standing Reach	No Step Vert	Max Vert
6'10.25"	8'6.5"	28.0"	35.5"

Basic Stats		Advanced Stats	
GP	122	TS%	0.558
MIN/G	28.9	3PTA/FGA	0.178
PTS/G	9.7	FTA/FGA	0.365
REB/G	4.6	OREB%	5.4
AST/G	3.6	DREB%	12.0
STL/G	1.3	TRB%	8.8
BLK/G	0.8	AST%	22.5
FG%	0.501	STL%	2.5
3PT%	0.325	BLK%	3.0
FT%	0.689	TOV%	16.0
		USG%	17.8

Projected Draft Range: 2nd Round to Undrafted

Top 10 Comps (Second Rounders Only)

	SIMsc			Year
1	917.0	Kadeem	Allen	2017
2	914.5	Alvin	Williams	1997
3	913.8	James	White	2006
4	912.3	Josh	Richardson	2015
5	912.3	Bruce	Brown	2018
6	909.2	Sammy	Mejia	2007
7	906.7	Sir'Dominic	Pointer	2015
8	905.0	Kyle	Weaver	2008
9	901.5	DeAndre	Liggins	2011
10	901.0	Michael	Gbinije	2016

Cody Martin along with his twin brother, Caleb entered last year's draft, but ultimately chose to withdraw to return to Nevada. He started his career at N.C. State, but he transferred to Nevada after his sophomore season. At Nevada, he established himself as one of the Mountain West Conference's best players, as he was named as the conference's Defensive Player of the Year in 2018 and he made the all-conference third team this season. If a team takes him in this year's draft, he'll likely be picked in the second round.

As it was alluded to earlier, Martin was a very good defender in college and his defense could translate to the NBA. He has solid physical tools, as he has good lateral quickness to go along with a fairly long wingspan and decent leaping ability. His athleticism allowed him to be a very good on-ball defender. In isolation situations, he generally stayed with his man and he was active to contest shots. He also held up fairly well against bigger players in the post because he had enough functional strength to push his man off the block to force a tougher shot. In addition to being good on the ball, he was very active as a help defender. He was very good at jumping passing lanes to get steals and he would also rotate from the weak side to block shots. He was also a solid defensive rebounder as well. He had his ups and downs as a team defender. On the plus side, he was effective at getting through screens to stay attached to shooters off the ball. He would mostly close out in spot-up situations, but he could sometimes get caught ball watching. As a result, he would sometimes be late on a few closeouts. He was mostly a solid pick-and-roll defender because he was good at preventing his man from turning the corner. However, he tended to go under screens, which made him prone to giving up open looks on the perimeter. If Martin learns to be more disciplined when making his rotations, he could be a sound defender in the NBA.

On offense, Martin took on a lot of ball handling duties and more or less, he operated as his team's point guard. From a stylistic standpoint, he's been a low volume, pass-first player throughout his career, so his playmaking abilities are his best skill. He's been good in transition at pushing the ball up the floor to find teammates on the break or score at the rim. He also is pretty good at kicking the ball out to shooters on the perimeter if the defense collapses. As a scorer, he mainly looks to drive to the rim. He has a decent quickness and solid ball handling ability that allows him to beat his man off the dribble. Because of this, he was good in isolation situations and he could turn the corner as a pick-and-roll ball handler. On the downside, he has shown a strong tendency to favor his right side when driving, so he may need to work on going more to his left to prevent opponents from sitting on his strong hand. He's fairly good at moving without the ball because he's been an effective cutter and he can pick spots to crash the offensive boards to score on put-backs. He doesn't really come off screens because his shot is still developing. His stroke is fairly consistent from mid-range and he has become a much better free throw shooter in his two years at Nevada. However, it's uncertain if he can be counted on to knock down threes. His Three-Point Percentage was slightly above average this season, but he's been close to a break-even three-point shooter for most of his career. The mechanics on his shot aren't noticeably flawed, so he may just need to get some more repetitions to get accustomed to taking more long range shots to be a better fit for a modern NBA offense.

Cody Martin will be 23 on draft day, so he is something of a lower ceiling prospect. Even though he's on the older side of the spectrum, his game still isn't fully polished, and he could stand to spend a season in the G-League to learn NBA defensive concepts and improve his outside shooting. At this stage, he fits the profile of a fringe defensive specialist similar to somebody like DeAndre Liggins. If he makes the necessary improvements to his game, he could stick in the league as a backup wing along the lines of Corey Brewer. Otherwise, he's likely to spend the bulk of his career in the G-League or overseas.

Jaylen Hoard   35/40/45

College/Country	Height	Weight	Age on July 1
Wake Forest	6'8"	213	20.255

Wingspan	Standing Reach	No Step Vert	Max Vert
7'0.75"	8'9.5"	N/A	N/A

Basic Stats		Advanced Stats	
GP	31	TS%	0.519
MIN/G	30.2	3PTA/FGA	0.160
PTS/G	13.1	FTA/FGA	0.383
REB/G	7.6	OREB%	9.0
AST/G	1.5	DREB%	19.6
STL/G	0.6	TRB%	14.0
BLK/G	0.6	AST%	12.3
FG%	0.458	STL%	1.2
3PT%	0.226	BLK%	2.5
FT%	0.717	TOV%	16.6
		USG%	24.6

Projected Draft Range: 2nd Round to Undrafted

Top 10 Comps (Second Rounders Only)

	SIMsc			Year
1	923.3	Justin	Jackson	2018
2	913.8	Quincy	Miller	2012
3	908.0	Marcus	Williams	2007
4	905.4	Sean	Lampley	2001
5	904.9	Randy	Holcomb	2002
6	902.4	Travis	Leslie	2011
7	897.0	Devin	Ebanks	2010
8	896.3	Sherron	Mills	1993
9	895.7	Luc Richard	Mbah a Moute	2008
10	893.4	Stanley	Robinson	2010

Originally born in France, Jaylen Hoard started his career with the French athlete institute, INSEP when he signed a two-year contract with them in 2015. He later moved to play high school basketball in North Carolina before arriving at Wake Forest for this season. He posted solid numbers in his freshman season and built up enough stock to get an invite to this year's NBA Draft Combine. Though he still has the option of returning to Wake Forest, he's made an indication that he'll probably remain in the draft. If he is selected in this year's draft, he will most likely be a second round pick.

On offense, Hoard was mainly utilized as a higher volume scorer that got a lot of his points by aggressively attacking the basket. He was effective at getting to the rim as either the ball handler in pick-and-roll situations or as an isolation player. He also played a high motor style and he was willing to absorb contact, so he drew fouls at a fairly high rate. On the downside, his ball handling isn't especially advanced at this stage. He's primarily a straight-line driver and he mainly looks to go right. He struggles when he's forced to go to his left, so defenders could sit on his strong hand to force him to take tough shots. Though he can occasionally hit the roll man on pick-and-rolls, he isn't really a playmaker because he rarely looks to pass. This makes him prone to over-dribbling and forcing up difficult shots in traffic. On the plus side, his high motor allows him to score on hustle plays, as he'll crash the offensive glass to get points off put-backs and he'll run hard down the floor to get dunks in transition. At this stage, he's far away from being a reliable offensive contributor in the NBA because he really struggles to make outside shots. He has difficulty getting a consistent release point from long range because he has a hitch and a pause at the top of his release that causes some timing issues. As a result, his Three-Point Percentage was well below break-even this season and he struggled to make outside shots in virtually every situation. He's a little more comfortable from mid-range because he shoots a solid percentage at the free throw line, so there may be some potential for him to eventually become an adequate shooter in the future.

As a defender, he's still pretty unpolished even though he has the physical tools to guard NBA players. Specifically, he has a long wingspan to go along with solid lateral mobility and fairly explosive leaping ability. However, Hoard struggles to translate these tools into effective defense. He was only about average as an on-ball perimeter defender this season, according to Synergy. He showed enough quickness to stay with his man to stop drives, but he tended to drop a little too far back, which gave his man extra space to take an uncontested pull-up jumper. He also was sometimes tasked to guard bigger players in the post, but he had difficulties defending them inside because he didn't quite have the strength to hold position and he tended to bite on fakes to give up easy scores inside. As a team defender, he was a bit of a mixed bag. On the plus side, he would consistently close out on perimeter shooters and in pick-and-roll situations, he was good at taking away the roll man. On the other hand, he would tend to sag into the paint, which made him prone to leaving the ball handler open on the perimeter. He also had a tendency to get caught on screens as well. He was decent as a help defender because he could occasionally rotate from the weak side to block shots and he could use his length to get deflections. Finally, he was consistent to block out his man, so he was a pretty good defensive rebounder this season.

Jaylen Hoard is still a raw prospect at this stage because he simply doesn't shoot or defend well enough to fit into an NBA rotation. With this in mind, he'll probably need to spend at least a season or two in the G-League to improve his overall game. His profile is pretty risky because there's a considerable chance that he could wind up spending most of his career in either the G-League or overseas. If things break favorably and he adapts his game to become more of a three-and-D wing, he could develop into a fringe rotational energy player similar to someone like Luc Mbah a Moute.

Tyus Battle 35/40/45

College/Country	Height	Weight	Age on July 1
Syracuse	6'6"	210	21.770

Wingspan	Standing Reach	No Step Vert	Max Vert
N/A	N/A	N/A	N/A

Basic Stats		Advanced Stats	
GP	103	TS%	0.537
MIN/G	35.4	3PTA/FGA	0.406
PTS/G	16.0	FTA/FGA	0.351
REB/G	2.8	OREB%	1.6
AST/G	2.1	DREB%	7.2
STL/G	1.3	TRB%	4.4
BLK/G	0.2	AST%	13.4
FG%	0.417	STL%	2.2
3PT%	0.335	BLK%	0.8
FT%	0.803	TOV%	10.7
		USG%	24.4

Projected Draft Range: 2nd Round to Undrafted

Top 10 Comps (Second Rounders Only)

	SIMsc			Year
1	939.7	Chase	Budinger	2009
2	928.2	Adam	Haluska	2007
3	920.1	Romain	Sato	2004
4	919.1	Bracey	Wright	2005
5	914.5	Terrico	White	2010
6	912.4	Jodie	Meeks	2009
7	911.9	Michael	Redd	2000
8	911.6	Lucious	Harris	1993
9	911.4	Darius	Johnson-Odom	2012
10	910.5	Rickey	Paulding	2004

Tyus Battle entered last year's draft but elected to withdraw his name to return for his junior season at Syracuse. He had another solid season overall and he made one of the All-ACC teams for the second consecutive year. However, his stock took a bit of hit because he struggled with his efficiency during conference play this season. If he's taken in this year's draft, he'll likely go somewhere in the second round.

On offense, Battle projects to be a complementary player in the NBA. He was utilized as a high usage shot creator, but his effectiveness in this role was only about average. This is mainly because he doesn't possess an especially quick first step and he's only about average as a ball handler. Therefore, he had some trouble getting all the way to the rim on drives in general. He also tends to go left when he drives, so defenders can sit on his strong side to force him into taking tougher shots. A lot of his success as a shot creator was dependent on his ability to make pull-up jumpers. He was able to use a screen to create space for himself as a pick-and-roll ball handler, but he had trouble freeing himself in isolation situations. In the NBA, he'll have to play off the ball. His outside shot is still a work-in-progress. He's comfortable taking spot-up jumpers from mid-range and he can repeat his stroke at the free throw line. However, he sometimes has a hitch in his motion that doesn't allow him to maximize distance, so he's been a below break-even three-point shooter for the last two seasons. Also, he has trouble getting his feet set on the move, so he doesn't have a strong ability to come off screens. If he can square away his mechanics, he'll likely end up being a stationary spot-up shooter in the league. Off the ball, he has a bit of a tendency to stand idly on the perimeter because he rarely looks to cut to the rim. On the positive side, he has great athleticism that allows him to be a dynamic threat in transition, as he'll run quickly down the floor and finish plays above the rim. Finally, he's a willing passer that has improved his Assist Percentage in every season, but his playmaking skills are only about average because he's limited to making simple reads.

Battle's defensive potential is uncertain because he's spent his entire career playing in a zone defense. Historically, players from Syracuse have had difficulty adjusting to playing defense in the NBA, so his defensive skills have to be built from the ground up. From an athletic standpoint, he has the tools to possibly become a decent defender. Specifically, he has a fairly long wingspan and he has solid lateral mobility to go along with some fairly explosive leaping ability. With these tools, he could physically handle the duties of defending perimeter players on the ball. He also has shown some decent functional strength, so he might be able to handle interior players on switches in the future. The issue with playing in a zone dominant scheme is that he isn't especially familiar with NBA level defensive concepts. Therefore, he could struggle against teams that employ a complex, pace-and-space system that puts him into a lot of screen or pick-

and-roll actions. He also isn't accustomed to blocking out a man when a shot goes up, so he's a below average rebounder for his size. On the positive side, he was fairly good at using his length to play passing lanes to come up with steals, although his Steals Percentage declined in each of his three seasons.

Tyus Battle's game doesn't really fit today's NBA, so he's a bit of a project even though he'll be 21 on draft day. At this point, he needs to spend at least a season or two in the G-League to learn how to play man defense and fix his shooting mechanics to become an adequate three-point threat. If everything breaks right and his game improves significantly, he could carve out a role as a situational, fringe rotation, three-and-D wing player along the lines of Keith Bogans. Most likely, he could spend the bulk of his career either in the G-League or overseas.

Other Notable Comps Not Listed Above

SIMsc		Year
907.1	Shelvin Mack	2011
904.6	Keith Bogans	2003
902.8	Allen Crabbe	2013

YELLOW PROSPECTS

NCAA Combo Forwards

P.J. Washington   50/55/55

College/Country	Height	Weight	Age on July 1
Kentucky	6'7"	230	20.855

Wingspan	Standing Reach	No Step Vert	Max Vert
7'2.25"	8'10.5"	N/A	N/A

Basic Stats		Advanced Stats	
GP	72	TS%	0.577
MIN/G	28.3	3PTA/FGA	0.159
PTS/G	12.9	FTA/FGA	0.619
REB/G	6.6	OREB%	9.0
AST/G	1.7	DREB%	17.4
STL/G	0.8	TRB%	13.5
BLK/G	1.0	AST%	11.8
FG%	0.521	STL%	1.7
3PT%	0.384	BLK%	4.2
FT%	0.632	TOV%	14.8
		USG%	23.3

Projected Draft Range: Mid to Late 1st Round

Top 10 Comps (First Rounders Only)

	SIMsc			Year
1	927.2	Rondae	Hollis-Jefferson	2015
2	920.9	Jared	Jeffries	2002
3	918.3	Cody	Zeller	2013
4	916.9	Jarell	Martin	2015
5	913.5	Michael	Kidd-Gilchrist	2012
6	913.2	Jeff	Green	2007
7	912.2	Bill	Curley	1994
8	911.9	Michael	Bradley	2001
9	909.0	Dickey	Simpkins	1994
10	906.5	Derrick	Williams	2011

P.J. Washington initially declared for last year's draft, but he decided to go back to Kentucky for his sophomore season. The decision to return worked out well for him because he was Kentucky's leading scorer and he was one of the most productive overall players in the SEC this past season. He ranked third in the SEC in Win Shares and he was a first team all-SEC selection. As a result of his highly productive season, his draft stock rose to the point where he'll probably be taken somewhere in the first round.

Defensively, Washington projects to be a player that could guard multiple positions in the NBA. He started his career as an interior player, and he has the physical tools to play bigger than his actual size. In particular, he has a very long wingspan and he possesses a great deal of functional strength. This allows him to be a very good post defender, as he'll push his man off the block and use his length to alter shots. He also maintains sound positioning and he consistently will box his man out, so he's a pretty good rebounder. In addition to this, he's a very good help defender because he can block shots and he uses his active hands to get deflections or rip the ball away from opponents to get steals. He also has solid lateral mobility, which allows him to be a very good pick-and-roll defender. He's very good at preventing the roll man from getting easy scores around the rim and he has quick enough feet to contain ball handlers on switches. At this stage, he's still adjusting to playing on the wing. Therefore, his one-on-one defense is still a bit unpolished and he was prone to giving up a few scores in isolation situations. On the positive side, he was very good at contesting outside shots in general. However, he had a tendency to overplay the outside shot, which made him vulnerable to giving up a drive to the basket. He was much better at containing drivers that were going right, but less successful against players that drove left. If he cleans up this minor issue, he could be an excellent defender in the NBA.

At the offensive end, his game improved significantly, and he showed that he could fit into an offense as a modern NBA wing. As it was mentioned earlier, he was primarily an interior player in his freshman year, but he made considerable improvements to his outside shooting this past season. Specifically, he made over 42% of his threes this season after only making less than 24% of these shots the season before. He was mainly able to knock down threes in spot-up opportunities and as the screener in pick-and-pop situations. On the other hand, he still shoots free throws at less than a 70% rate, so his stroke isn't necessarily repeatable at this point. He also has a pause at the top of his release, so he will have to keep working on his shot to stay consistent at the NBA level. As for his other skills, he was able to maintain his strengths as an inside player. He was a very good rim runner that could roll or cut to the rim. He was also good at running the floor in transition and crashing the offensive glass to score on put-backs. Additionally, he was a pretty effective post player that mainly relied on a quick drop step and an occasional hook shot. He was also a willing passer that could hit cutters and find open shooters on the perimeter. As a weakness, he's not really a dynamic ball handler, so it's not likely that he'll be able to create shots. He also wasn't especially effective in isolation situations, so he's better suited for a complementary role.

This season, P.J. Washington showed that he can adapt his game to fit into an evolving NBA. His production suggests that he could fit into a rotation fairly quickly. If he continues to progress as a shooter, he could be a valuable combo forward that guards multiple positions and spaces the floor, similar to someone like Marcus Morris. Otherwise, his defense is polished enough that he could still stick in the league for a long time. If his shooting isn't as a consistent in the NBA, he could wind up being a multi-positional defensive specialist along the lines of Michael Kidd-Gilchrist.

Other Notable Comps Not Listed Above

SIMsc		Year
906.2	Marcus Morris	2011
904.4	Larry Nance, Jr.	2015

Brandon Clarke   50/55/55

College/Country	Height	Weight	Age on July 1
Gonzaga	6'8"	207	22.781

Wingspan	Standing Reach	No Step Vert	Max Vert
6'8.25"	8'6"	34.0"	40.5"

Basic Stats		Advanced Stats	
GP	98	TS%	0.643
MIN/G	27.8	3PTA/FGA	0.026
PTS/G	14.5	FTA/FGA	0.429
REB/G	7.7	OREB%	11.7
AST/G	1.9	DREB%	19.6
STL/G	1.0	TRB%	15.7
BLK/G	2.3	AST%	14.4
FG%	0.639	STL%	2.0
3PT%	0.250	BLK%	8.7
FT%	0.618	TOV%	11.6
		USG%	22.4

Projected Draft Range: Top 20

Top 10 Comps (Top 20 Picks Only)

	SIMsc			Year
1	882.8	Ed	O'Bannon	1995
2	879.3	Antawn	Jamison	1998
3	879.3	Shane	Battier	2001
4	878.1	Josh	Childress	2004
5	878.0	Vince	Carter	1998
6	877.2	John	Wallace	1996
7	876.4	Ryan	Humphrey	2002
8	876.1	Donyell	Marshall	1994
9	874.9	Wesley	Johnson	2010
10	874.9	Cherokee	Parks	1995

Brandon Clarke played his first two seasons at San Jose State. He was a productive player there, as he was a first team All-Mountain West performer in 2017. He moved up to Gonzaga this season and immediately became an impact player. He was named as the West Coast Conference's Defensive Player of the Year and he was on the All-WCC first team. As a result of his high level of production, his draft stock rose significantly to the point where he'll probably taken somewhere within the first twenty picks in the first round.

As it was alluded to earlier, Clarke stands out because of his excellent play on the defensive end of the floor. In the past, a player like him would have been in-between positions. But in today's position-less NBA, Clarke could be a valuable defender that's capable of guarding multiple positions. First off, he plays much bigger than his actual size because he has fairly long arms and he has a lot of functional strength. These physical skills allow him to be an effective post defender against taller players because he can hold position on the block and use his length to contest shots. He's a very good weak side help defender in general because he's an excellent shot blocker and rebounder. He is also active with his hands, as he'll rip balls away from opponents to get steals or play passing lanes to deflect wayward passes. Additionally, he's a solid pick-and-roll defender that can prevent rolls to the rim and he can capably switch to contain the ball handler. He can sometimes be a little too aggressive on his switches, so he'll occasionally open up a driving lane to the basket. In general, he showed that he can hold his own in situations where he has to defend on the perimeter. He was pretty good in isolation situations because he has solid lateral quickness to stay in front of his man and he's also very aggressive to contest shots. From there, he's a very good team defender that makes sound rotations, as he'll close out on shooters in spot-up situations and he'll fight through screens. He hasn't shown very many weaknesses at the college level, so he should be able to make a quick adjustment to the NBA on the defensive side of the ball.

Clarke was an excellent offensive player in college, but he may have to adapt his game to fit the modern NBA. At this stage, he's essentially a rim running big man in a wing player's body. He might be able to get away with being a small-ball five if he shows that he can consistently defend NBA big men. However, it may not be best for him to exclusively play inside if he wants to have a long career in the league. After all, the extra pounding that comes with guarding much bigger players could put more wear and tear on his body, which could make him more vulnerable to injury or it could cause him to age a bit faster. Anyway, he's polished in his strong areas. As it was hinted at earlier, he is an excellent rim runner that plays with an extremely high motor. Therefore, he really excels at cutting or rolling to the rim and he'll run hard down the floor to get buckets in transition. He also will aggressively crash the offensive boards to get second chances and score on put-backs. In the half court, he was effective as a post player, but he mainly relied on his strength and energy to bully smaller opponents around the rim. He didn't really have much variety in his moves and he only looked to use a quick drop step to score inside. On the positive side, he was a decent post passer that could find open shooters on the perimeter and occasionally hit cutters. He also thrived in short to mid-range isolation situations, but he was more of a straight-line driver in college. He didn't really change directions especially well and he had a heavy tendency to go left. Right now, his biggest weakness is his jump shot. It's improved a little bit at Gonzaga, but he still can't really repeat his stroke and his shooting motion has a slight hitch at the top of his release. As a result, he can't really shoot with a great deal of range, as he's a little more comfortable from mid-range at this point in his development. If he gradually improves his shot to expand his range to at least the corners, he could enhance his versatility by playing a wing position in addition to playing inside.

Brandon Clarke is a unique prospect in this year's draft. In years past, teams may not have known what to do with him, but his ability to defend inside and out makes him a good fit for a modern NBA defense. He's polished enough on defense to be at least a rotational player in the league next season. However, his career prospects will depend on the development of his perimeter shot. If he improves his outside shooting to at least a credible level, he could become an effective multi-positional interior player along the lines of a poor man's Pascal Siakam. Otherwise, if his shot doesn't come around, he could still be valuable for his defense and he could develop into a solid interior player that provides energy and defensive versatility like Taj Gibson.

Rui Hachimura   45/50/50

College/Country	Height	Weight	Age on July 1
Gonzaga	6'8"	234	21.392

Wingspan	Standing Reach	No Step Vert	Max Vert
N/A	N/A	N/A	N/A

Basic Stats		Advanced Stats	
GP	102	TS%	0.629
MIN/G	19.7	3PTA/FGA	0.095
PTS/G	12.1	FTA/FGA	0.474
REB/G	4.4	OREB%	6.8
AST/G	0.8	DREB%	17.4
STL/G	0.6	TRB%	12.6
BLK/G	0.5	AST%	7.5
FG%	0.607	STL%	1.7
3PT%	0.316	BLK%	2.6
FT%	0.746	TOV%	10.9
		USG%	26.9

Projected Draft Range: Top 20

Top 10 Comps (Top 20 Picks Only)

	SIMsc			Year
1	920.9	Anthony	Bennett	2013
2	914.4	Antawn	Jamison	1998
3	908.9	Marcus	Morris	2011
4	907.7	Austin	Croshere	1997
5	906.9	Pat	Garrity	1998
6	900.5	Jason	Richardson	2001
7	898.5	Lamond	Murray	1994
8	898.3	Marcus	Fizer	2000
9	896.6	Kelly	Olynyk	2013
10	896.5	Ed	O'Bannon	1995

After spending his first two years as a bench player, Rui Hachimura stepped into a larger role this season at Gonzaga. In his first full season as a starter, he became one of the most productive players in the country, earning honors as the West Coast Conference's Player of the Year and as a consensus first team All-American. He elected to forego his final year of eligibility to enter this year's draft and he's likely to come off the board somewhere within the first twenty picks.

Hachimura was an excellent offensive player for Gonzaga this season and he was rated by Synergy as being very good or better in almost every situation. He was mainly used as an interior player because he mainly looked to use his athleticism and high motor to attack the basket. He's excellent in rim running situations because he can use his long arms and good leaping ability to finish plays above the rim. This allows him to excel as the roll man on pick-and-rolls and as a cutter off the ball. He also runs hard down the floor to pick up points in transition and he'll aggressively crash the offensive boards to score on put-backs. He was pretty good in post-up situations, but he didn't show much of a back-to-the-basket game. He mainly looked to face his man up and use his quick first step to beat his man to the rim. When he tried to play with his back to the basket, he could only use a drop step to score and he didn't really have any other moves beyond that. He was good as an isolation player, but he mainly looked to put his head down and bully his way to the rim. He's not really a dynamic ball handler, so he can't really change directions. He also has a heavy tendency to go left and struggles to drive to his right. He didn't really look to take jump shots, but he may have some potential as a shooter. He's been a good free throw shooter over the two seasons, and he was pretty good at making spot-up mid-range jumpers this season. He has a pretty fluid stroke and doesn't show many mechanical flaws. Therefore, he may be able to expand his range in the future. Finally, he's a willing passer that can find open perimeter shooters, but he's not really a true playmaker, as he's limited to making low risk passes.

Defensively, he has a long way to go even though he has excellent physical tools. From an athletic standpoint, he has the potential to eventually become a solid defender because he moves fairly well laterally and has long arms to go along with a good vertical leap. Because of these physical attributes, he's an effective weak side help defender. He's a good rebounder and he can use his length to block shots. He also plays with active hands, so he'll play passing lanes or rip balls away to get steals. At this stage, he's more polished as an interior defender. He was pretty good at defending post-ups because his good functional strength allowed him to hold position on the block to force his man into taking tougher shots. In most other areas on defense, he still needs to improve significantly. On the plus side, he was very good at closing out on shooters in spot-up situations. However, there were several areas where he struggled. He had problems defending on-the-ball in isolation situations because he was often a bit over-aggressive and he would usually bite on an opponent's first move, which would set up an easier counter-move. He also had a lot of difficulties defending pick-and-rolls. He would often get confused with his coverage and he get caught in an in-between position. As a result, he wasn't especially effective at covering the roll man or containing the ball handler. Because the pick-and-roll is such a staple in most modern offenses, Hachimura's struggles in these situations could limit his playing time in the NBA. He'll have to quickly figure out a way to at least be adequate or else, he'll be limited to being a situational player in the league.

Rui Hachimura is an interesting prospect that could someday develop into a useful complementary combo forward in the NBA. Right now, he's still not a finished product because it's uncertain if he can adapt to defending in an advanced NBA scheme. If he can quickly pick up NBA defensive concepts and expand his shooting range, he could be a solid complementary player that could play both forward spots, make energetic plays inside and occasionally knock down an outside jumper. If this scenario were to happen, he could develop into a variation of Marcus Morris. Otherwise, he could wind up becoming of fringe rotation player in the league.

Dedric Lawson   40/45/50

College/Country	Height	Weight	Age on July 1
Kansas	6'8"	233	21.748

Wingspan	Standing Reach	No Step Vert	Max Vert
7'2.25"	8'11.5"	N/A	N/A

Basic Stats		Advanced Stats	
GP	101	TS%	0.539
MIN/G	33.1	3PTA/FGA	0.197
PTS/G	18.2	FTA/FGA	0.416
REB/G	9.9	OREB%	10.0
AST/G	2.5	DREB%	21.9
STL/G	1.2	TRB%	16.1
BLK/G	1.6	AST%	16.0
FG%	0.455	STL%	2.1
3PT%	0.332	BLK%	5.2
FT%	0.757	TOV%	13.4
		USG%	28.5

Projected Draft Range: 2nd Round

Top 10 Comps (Second Rounders Only)

	SIMsc			Year
1	931.7	Trey	Thompkins	2011
2	917.8	Brett	Roberts	1992
3	913.7	Sam	Clancy	2002
4	912.1	Jason	Sasser	1996
5	905.4	DeMarco	Johnson	1998
6	903.1	Nick	Fazekas	2007
7	901.9	Mike	Muscala	2013
8	901.2	Lawrence	Roberts	2005
9	900.2	Jermareo	Davidson	2007
10	895.6	Justin	Jackson	2018

Dedric Lawson was a productive two-year starter at Memphis before he transferred to Kansas. After sitting out last season due to transfer rules, he built upon his success in his previous stop by being one of the most productive players in the Big 12 Conference. He ranked second in the conference in Win Shares and he earned honors as a first team All-Big 12 performer this season. He chose to forego his final year of eligibility to enter this year's draft and it's likely that he'll be taken somewhere in the second round.

In the past, a player like Lawson would have been caught in between positions because he's basically a big man in a wing player's body. However, the game has changed, so he might able to provide value as a defender that could guard multiple positions. He plays below the rim because he doesn't jump very high, but he has decent lateral mobility to go along with a long wingspan. His mobility and length allow him to be pretty effective as an on-ball defender because he was quick enough to stay in front of his man in isolation situations and he would consistently contest shots. He was generally good at defending post-ups because his solid functional strength allows him to hold position inside, but he tended to shade his man too far over the middle, which created openings for his man on the baseline. As a team defender, he was pretty solid overall. He was very good at fighting through screens to stay attached to shooters and he would consistently close out in spot-up situations. His pick-and-roll defense didn't look quite as good because Kansas employed a lot of drop coverages to keep him in the paint. Because of this, he was very good at stopping the roll man, but he was never in position to cover the ball handler. In a modernized NBA defense, he would be asked to switch and his success in isolation situations suggests that he might be able to handle these responsibilities. Finally, Lawson was also effective as a weak side help defender because he was a good shot blocker and rebounder. He was pretty good at playing passing lanes or ripping balls away from his man to get an occasional steal.

Offensively, he'll have to adapt to playing more like a wing player to fit into today's NBA. He was primarily used as a post-up player and he was very effective in these situations. However, he didn't use a lot of advanced post moves and mainly looked to use his energy to score on quick drop steps. His energy does allow him to be effective as a rim runner because he's a very good cutter off the ball and he's good on rolls to the rim in pick-and-roll situations. He's also very active on the offensive glass, so he'll get extra possessions and he'll score on put-backs. As another positive, he's been a very good passer throughout his career, so he can find shooters on the perimeter and hit cutters inside. He's been pretty efficient overall as a shooter, but a little inconsistent from three-point range. He has a repeatable stroke from mid-range, and he's been a pretty good free throw shooter over the course of his career. His release is a little slow, so he has some difficulty in catch and shoot situations, so he can rush his shot at times, especially from long range. This can explain why his Three-Point Percentage has fluctuated from year-to-year. He shot much better this year, so if he improves his ability to make catch and shoot threes, his solid performance in spot-up situations could carry over in the NBA.

Dedric Lawson is an older prospect that doesn't really a have particularly high ceiling. However, he's solid enough at both ends to eventually become a rotation player in the NBA. He will have to modify his game a bit to fit into the league. If he shows that he can consistently knock down outside shots and defend a variety of positions, he could carve out a role as a mobile rotational player that either play as a bigger wing player or as an undersized big man. If he sticks in the league, he could develop into a less explosive, better shooting variation of Larry Nance, Jr. Otherwise, he could be headed for a fairly lucrative career overseas.

Other Notable Comps Not Listed Above

SIMsc		Year
914.8	Larry Nance, Jr.	2015

Grant Williams   40/45/50

College/Country	Height	Weight	Age on July 1
Tennessee	6'7"	240	20.584

Wingspan	Standing Reach	No Step Vert	Max Vert
6'9.75"	8'8.5"	26.0"	31.5"

Basic Stats		Advanced Stats	
GP	104	TS%	0.591
MIN/G	28.9	3PTA/FGA	0.097
PTS/G	15.7	FTA/FGA	0.621
REB/G	6.5	OREB%	9.7
AST/G	2.1	DREB%	15.3
STL/G	0.9	TRB%	12.7
BLK/G	1.5	AST%	14.8
FG%	0.516	STL%	1.7
3PT%	0.291	BLK%	6.0
FT%	0.758	TOV%	13.7
		USG%	26.5

Projected Draft Range: Late 1st to 2nd Round

Top 10 Comps (Picks Outside the Top 20)

	SIMsc			Year
1	913.4	Byron	Houston	1992
2	892.5	Chris	Owens	2002
3	892.0	Mario	Bennett	1995
4	890.4	Richard	Hendrix	2008
5	888.0	Othella	Harrington	1996
6	887.9	Kenny	Thomas	1999
7	883.8	Ansu	Sesay	1998
8	882.8	Josh	McRoberts	2007
9	882.1	Justin	Reed	2004
10	881.3	Reggie	Smith	1992

Grant Williams is one of the more accomplished college players in this year's draft pool. He was selected as the SEC's Player of the Year for the second straight year and he was a first team consensus All-American this season. With nothing left to prove at the college level, he has chosen to give up his final year of eligibility to enter the draft. In all probability, he will be picked at some point after the first twenty picks of the draft.

In the past, Williams could have fit into a rotation as a slightly undersized traditional power forward, but that role no longer exists in today's NBA. Therefore, he'll have to adjust his game to find a fit in the league. He's already taken some steps to move forward. His jump shot really doesn't extend out to three-point range, but his mechanics have become much more consistent from mid-range. His free throw shooting has also improved considerably, as he shot almost 82% from the foul line this past season, which suggests that his stroke is fairly repeatable. In games, he was pretty good at knocking down spot-up jumpers or hitting shots as the screener on pick-and-pop plays. Most likely, he'll be the same kind of stationary shooter if he extends his range in the future. In general, he's a high motor player that uses his energetic play to excel off the ball. As a result, he's a good cutter and he'll roll hard to the rim in pick-and-roll situations. He'll also run the floor to pick up points in transition and he'll crash the offensive boards to score on put-backs. He was effective in isolation situations mainly because he could use his strength to overpower weaker defenders to get straight-line drives to the basket. He really isn't a dynamic ball handler and doesn't really change directions very well. He also has a heavy tendency to go left, so defenders may be able to force him into tougher shots by sitting on his strong hand. He was mainly used as a post-up player and he was excellent in these situations in college. He was often stronger than his defenders, so he mostly looked to overpower them with quick drop steps to the basket. He really didn't have to use a lot of advanced post moves, so his post-up skills might be more useful if smaller players are switched onto him. Finally, his passing has improved in each season and he's been able to keep his turnovers at a fairly low rate. His playmaking skills are fairly solid, and they allow him to find shooters on the perimeter or make interior passes to cutters.

Defensively, Williams has the tools to adapt to being a versatile player, but he has to fix some bad habits. Physically, he has all of the desired attributes because he has solid lateral mobility to go along with a fairly long wingspan and above average leaping ability. His athletic tools have allowed him to make plays on the weak side, as he can block shots, get deflections or the occasional steal and grab defensive rebounds. He can be a bit a little too aggressive at times, so he's prone to picking up cheap fouls. At Tennessee, he was mainly anchored inside, so he stayed mostly around the basket. He was effective as a post defender because his strength allowed him to keep his man off the block and he could use his length to alter shots. He also showed some ability to defend isolations on the perimeter. His feet were quick enough to stay front of his man to stop the drive, but he tended to drop into the paint a bit too much, which opened up space for his man to get free for pull-up jumpers. At this stage, he has some trouble grasping rotations and defensive schemes, so he was inconsistent as a team defender. On the plus side, he was good at closing out on spot-up shooters and he was effective at hedging on pick-and-rolls to contain the ball handler. However, he would sometimes hedge out too far, which made him vulnerable to leaving the roll man open inside. He also had a lot of difficulty defending dribble hand-offs, as he would stay attached to the screener, which would allow the guard to turn the corner much more easily. He'll need to land on a team with a disciplined defensive structure to gain a little more awareness and be a better fit for a modern defense.

Grant Williams is a highly skilled prospect that is going to have to figure out a way to fit into a different role at the NBA level. It may take him some time to make the necessary changes to his game, so it could be a benefit for him to spend at least a season either in the G-League or overseas to adjust. Specifically, he'll have to become at least an average outside shooter on offense and he'll have to demonstrate the ability to comfortably defend on the perimeter as well as grasp modern defensive concepts. If he can add those skills to his game, he could fit into a rotation as a rotational player that can guard multiple positions and knock down spot-up jumpers similar to someone like P.J. Tucker. Otherwise, he could wind up spending the bulk of his career playing overseas or in the G-League.

Isaiah Roby   35/40/45

College/Country	Height	Weight	Age on July 1
Nebraska	6'8"	214	21.405

Wingspan	Standing Reach	No Step Vert	Max Vert
7'1"	8'10"	32.5"	35.5"

Basic Stats		Advanced Stats	
GP	97	TS%	0.555
MIN/G	23.9	3PTA/FGA	0.248
PTS/G	8.1	FTA/FGA	0.429
REB/G	5.5	OREB%	7.3
AST/G	1.5	DREB%	17.6
STL/G	0.8	TRB%	12.5
BLK/G	1.6	AST%	12.2
FG%	0.476	STL%	2.0
3PT%	0.336	BLK%	6.7
FT%	0.702	TOV%	17.9
		USG%	18.9

Projected Draft Range: 2nd Round

Top 10 Comps (Second Rounders Only)

	SIMsc			Year
1	911.3	Derrick	Brown	2009
2	907.8	Ray	Spalding	2018
3	907.1	James	Gist	2008
4	905.9	Robert	Dozier	2009
5	901.7	Eddie	Elisma	1997
6	894.6	Dwight	Powell	2014
7	894.6	J.R.	Koch	1999
8	894.5	Andrew	DeClercq	1995
9	894.3	Chimezie	Metu	2018
10	892.2	Dominic	McGuire	2007

Isaiah Roby has been a relative late bloomer. He spent his first two years at Nebraska as a reserve and he became a full-time starter for the first time this past season. His solid all-around play allowed him to get the attention of NBA scouts and he landed an invite to the draft combine. At this year's combine, he played well enough in the scrimmages to boost his stock to the point where he'll likely stay in the draft. In all probability, he will be taken at some point in the second round.

Offensively, his skill set fits into a complementary role. Over the course of his three seasons at Nebraska, he's been a lower volume player. He really doesn't have the ability to create his own shot because he was not very effective in isolation situations. He's only about an average ball handler and he's not overwhelmingly quick, so he has trouble getting all the way to the rim. Also, he almost exclusively looks to drive to his left and he really struggles to go right. Typically on drives, he tends to crash into opposing defenders to try to draw fouls. Sometimes this strategy works, but other times, it causes him to miss wildly inside. He was effective as a post-up player, but he mainly looked to back down smaller opponents to score on simple drop steps. This season, he was much more effective off the ball. His shooting improved to the point where he could capably knock down spot-up mid-range shots and made threes at a break-even rate. His stroke is still not consistent because he made less than 70% of his free throws. His motion is a bit long, so he has trouble when he has to quickly release a shot. As a result, he can't really shoot on the move and at this stage, he's limited to being a stationary shooter. If he's making his shot, he can play off his defender's aggressiveness by making hard cuts to the rim off the ball. He also will crash the offensive glass to get extra shot attempts for his team and he'll run the floor to fill lanes in transition. As a final note, he's a willing passer that can make some plays to either hit cutters inside or kick the ball out to an open shooter.

On defense, Roby was a solid rim protector because he could use his very long wingspan and good leaping ability to block shots at a high rate. He was very good at rotating from the weak side to block or alter shots around the rim. In fact, he was rated in the 90th percentile at defending around the basket in non-post-up situations, according to Synergy. In addition to being able to block shots, he was a good help defender in general because he could rip balls away from opposing players inside to get steals and he was a solid defensive rebounder. On the downside, he had a tendency to play a bit too aggressive on defense. He would often commit a lot of cheap fouls in the post because he tended to bite on fakes, or he would go up too wild on a block attempt. This over-aggression hurt him on the perimeter in isolation situations because he would often be too anxious to contest a jumper, so his man could use pump fakes to get an easy driving lane. He was a bit of a mixed bag as a team defender. On the positive side, he was very good at taking away the roll man on drop coverages in pick-and-roll situations. However, ball handlers were consistently able to drive by him because he didn't quite have the lateral quickness to stay with them. Off the ball, he tended to sag into the paint a bit too much, so he was sometimes late to close out on a perimeter shooter. In general, he'll need to significantly improve his perimeter defense to fit into today's NBA.

Isaiah Roby is a prospect that will need to adjust his game to become a long-term NBA player. Therefore, it might be beneficial for him to spend at least a season in the G-League to improve his perimeter defense and shooting. With the way the league is trending, he could take one of two paths to becoming a rotation level player. If he proves that he can hold up against bigger body centers, he could be an undersized, rotational energy big man like Jordan Bell. Otherwise, he'll need to develop into at least a break-even three-point shooter to carve out a role as a wing player. If he sticks as a wing, he could be rotational combo forward that can defend multiple positions and occasionally make an outside shot similar to someone like JaMychal Green.

Other Notable Comps Not Listed Above

SIMsc		Year
917.3	JaMychal Green	2012

Eric Paschall   35/40/45

College/Country	Height	Weight	Age on July 1
Villanova	6'7"	254	22.655

Wingspan	Standing Reach	No Step Vert	Max Vert
6'11.75"	8'7.5"	33.0"	38.0"

Basic Stats		Advanced Stats	
GP	137	TS%	0.574
MIN/G	29.6	3PTA/FGA	0.407
PTS/G	12.3	FTA/FGA	0.352
REB/G	5.1	OREB%	6.4
AST/G	1.5	DREB%	14.3
STL/G	0.7	TRB%	10.4
BLK/G	0.5	AST%	10.1
FG%	0.468	STL%	1.5
3PT%	0.331	BLK%	2.0
FT%	0.765	TOV%	15.3
		USG%	22.3

Projected Draft Range: 2nd Round

Top 10 Comps (Second Rounders Only)

	SIMsc			Year
1	917.1	Matt	Freije	2004
2	909.8	DaJuan	Summers	2009
3	905.8	Mario	Austin	2003
4	903.9	Matt	Bonner	2003
5	899.5	Justin	Jackson	2018
6	899.4	Jake	Layman	2016
7	898.5	Mike	Scott	2012
8	897.5	Kyle	Singler	2011
9	897.2	Ryan	Gomes	2005
10	894.7	Alec	Peters	2017

Eric Paschall started his college career at Fordham, but he transferred to Villanova after his freshman year. He redshirted during Villanova's national championship run in 2016 and he was a starter on their national championship team in 2018. After Villanova lost four players to the NBA, he ascended into a primary role this season as a senior and he became one of the most productive players in the Big East, earning honors as a first team All-Big East performer. His stock stayed fairly high throughout and he'll likely be taken at some point in the second round in this year's draft.

At Villanova, Paschall showed promise as a player that could defend multiple positions at the NBA level. He has solid physical tools because he has quick feet that allow him to move well laterally. He also has an above average wingspan to go along with decent leaping ability and solid functional strength. These physical traits have helped him become a very good on-ball perimeter defender that can consistently stay with his man, apply pressure and contest shots. He also has been fairly good post defender because he's strong enough to hold position inside and his length enables him to force his man to take tough shots. He's been a solid team defender throughout his career, but his performance in this area was negatively affected by all of the changes in personnel. With experienced teammates, he could stick to playing more of a stay-at-home role. In this role, he was pretty good at fighting through screens, closing out on perimeter shooters and defending pick-and-rolls. However, this season, he had to help more because his younger teammates were still learning the team's defensive coverages. The team really didn't have a reliable rim protector, so he would try help into the paint. Because of this, he was sometimes late to close out on an outside shooter. Other times, the on-court communication wasn't as strong as it was in the past, so sometimes, he would get caught on a screen to allow an open perimeter jumper. For the most part, he's been a disciplined defender that could be effective in the right system. As a final note, he's been a solid defensive rebounder throughout his career.

On offense, he showed significant improvement across the board and he was pretty effective in a primary role. In fact, he was rated as being good or better in almost every offensive situation, according to Synergy. He was used as a shot creator this season, but he's probably going to be a complementary player in the NBA. He was effective as pick-and-roll ball handler and as an isolation player because he could use his strength to bully his way to the basket on drives. However, he's only about an average ball handler and he doesn't change directions particularly well. He also struggles to shoot jumpers off the dribble, so defenders can back off him when he drives. Additionally, he's limited in his ability make plays for others because he can really only make simple reads. Off the ball, he's very effective because he plays with a high motor. Therefore, he'll roll hard to the rim as the screener on pick-and-rolls and he's good at cutting off the ball. He'll also run hard down the floor to pick up scores in transition and he'll actively crash the offensive boards to score on put-backs. His outside shooting has improved over the last two seasons to the point where he's an average three-point shooter. At this stage, he's much more comfortable as a spot-up shooter because his mechanics don't allow him to be very consistent when he shoots on the move. Specifically, he tends to kick out his legs when he goes up for a shot, so he's not always balanced. Because of this, he has some trouble shooting off screens, especially when he's coming off a screen to his right. On the positive side, he's much better at coming off a screen to his left.

Eric Paschall has the chance to develop into a solid role player in the NBA. His defense might be good enough to fit into a rotation, but he still needs to become a more consistent outside shooter. If he can become at least an average three-point shooter, he could stick in the league as a versatile defender that could guard perimeter and interior players similar to a variation of a player like James Johnson. Otherwise, he may end up spending most of his career overseas or in the G-League.

Other Notable Comps Not Listed Above

SIMsc		Year
905.8	James Johnson	2009

Jalen McDaniels   35/40/45

College/Country	Height	Weight	Age on July 1
San Diego State	6'9"	192	21.414

Wingspan	Standing Reach	No Step Vert	Max Vert
7'0.25"	8'9.5"	29.5"	33.5"

Basic Stats		Advanced Stats	
GP	67	TS%	0.565
MIN/G	27.9	3PTA/FGA	0.140
PTS/G	13.2	FTA/FGA	0.358
REB/G	7.9	OREB%	8.7
AST/G	1.5	DREB%	23.1
STL/G	1.0	TRB%	16.0
BLK/G	0.5	AST%	12.1
FG%	0.504	STL%	2.0
3PT%	0.298	BLK%	2.2
FT%	0.758	TOV%	13.1
		USG%	24.2

Projected Draft Range: 2nd Round

Top 10 Comps (Second Rounders Only)

	SIMsc			Year
1	927.1	Marcus	Liberty	1990
2	905.8	Damone	Brown	2001
3	903.9	Hamidou	Diallo	2018
4	903.5	Chris	Carr	1995
5	902.6	Ron	Ellis	1992
6	902.5	Mark	Sanford	1997
7	898.4	Ben	Bentil	2016
8	898.0	Travis	Leslie	2011
9	896.6	Tremaine	Fowlkes	1998
10	895.0	Dwayne	Morton	1994

Jalen McDaniels redshirted to start his career and then went on to play two seasons at San Diego State. This season, McDaniels was one of the most productive players in the Mountain West Conference, earning honors as a second-team all-conference performer. He entered this year's draft and still has the option to return to school for another year. However, his return to San Diego State is unlikely after he had a fairly strong showing at this year's NBA Draft Combine. Most likely, he will be selected at some point in the second round.

At this stage, McDaniels' skills are more advanced on defense. He has the physical tools to succeed as a defender in the NBA because he has a fairly long wingspan to go along with good lateral mobility and solid leaping ability. This type of athletic profile could allow him to be effective in a modern defense because he's generally been solid at guarding pick-and-rolls. He's good at using his length and leaping ability to protect the rim and cover the roll man. He also has the lateral quickness to switch onto the ball handler. However, he has a tendency to go too far under the screen, which makes him prone to giving up open outside shots. In most situations, he's been a good defender. He's pretty effective as an on-ball defender because he can stay with perimeter players in isolation situations. He also does a good job of applying pressure to opposing ball handlers and contesting shots. Despite his very thin frame, he defended well in a small sample of post-ups. This is mainly because he had enough functional strength to hold position and his length allowed him to alter shots inside. Additionally, he's a very active help defender that will rotate from the weak side to block shots. He'll also jump passing lanes to get steals and he's a very good defensive rebounder. Finally, McDaniels is a solid team defender that will fight through screens and close out on spot-up shooters.

On offense, he's stuck in between positions because he's essentially a rim running big man in a wing player's body. A role as a rim runner plays to his strengths because as it was mentioned earlier, he has the athleticism to finish plays above the rim. In a half-court set, he's very effective as the roll man in pick-and-roll situations and he cuts hard to the rim off the ball. He's also very good at coming off a screen to curl to the basket to score on running dunks and he'll actively crash the offensive boards to score on put-backs. He'll generally run hard down the floor to fill a lane in transition, but he can sometimes play a bit out of control and he'll rush a shot trying to go full speed. From a skill standpoint, he's still a bit raw. He was only about average at scoring on isolations. Though he's fairly quick, he's only about an average ball handler and he predominantly drives to his left. Therefore, defenders can sit on his left hand and force him to take difficult shots. He's not particularly effective as a post-up player because his thin frame doesn't allow him to establish deep position to get quality shots inside. His shooting has improved a little bit from the season before, but it's still a work-in-progress. His form is mostly good, but he doesn't always follow through on the release and he will sometimes kick out his legs to throw off his balance. He'll need to continue to work on his shot to drill these bad habits out of his system. If he puts in the work, he could eventually develop into a decent shooter in the future. On a positive note, he's a pretty good passer that will kick the ball out to open perimeter shooters or make short area interior passes to hit cutters.

As an overall prospect, Jalen McDaniels is something of a risky prospect because he may have some character issues, as he's the subject of multiple invasion of privacy lawsuits based on a couple of questionable incidents from his time in high school. If the allegations in these lawsuits are true, then he may not be worth the risk. However, if his name is cleared in some way, then teams might be able to move on and they could look at him as an NBA prospect. On basketball skills alone, McDaniels is an interesting prospect because he could provide a team with some defensive versatility. His offensive game is still unpolished, and he doesn't quite fit a specific role. His skills might be better suited for an interior role, but he'll need to fill out a little more to play against bigger NBA players on a regular basis. If he takes this career path and shows that he carry some extra weight, he develop into a rotational rim runner that can defend multiple positions similar to someone like Kevon Looney. Otherwise, he'll need to become at least a passable shooter to hold down a rotation spot. If he develops as a wing player, he'll likely be a situational defensive specialist like DeMarre Carroll.

Robert Franks   35/40/40

College/Country	Height	Weight	Age on July 1
Washington State	6'7"	240	22.534

Wingspan	Standing Reach	No Step Vert	Max Vert
N/A	N/A	N/A	N/A

Basic Stats		Advanced Stats	
GP	111	TS%	0.592
MIN/G	23.6	3PTA/FGA	0.443
PTS/G	12.2	FTA/FGA	0.313
REB/G	4.7	OREB%	5.6
AST/G	1.5	DREB%	17.3
STL/G	0.3	TRB%	11.6
BLK/G	0.6	AST%	13.4
FG%	0.467	STL%	0.8
3PT%	0.378	BLK%	2.9
FT%	0.829	TOV%	15.6
		USG%	26.3

Projected Draft Range: 2nd Round to Undrafted

Top 10 Comps (Second Rounders Only)

	SIMsc			Year
1	915.0	Matt	Bonner	2003
2	911.6	Darius	Miller	2012
3	910.0	Abdel	Nader	2016
4	902.3	Georges	Niang	2016
5	899.4	George	King	2018
6	896.7	Justin	Harper	2011
7	896.5	Donny	Marshall	1995
8	896.2	Romero	Osby	2013
9	896.1	DaJuan	Summers	2009
10	895.3	Erik	Murphy	2013

Robert Franks has been a late bloomer as a college player. After not playing a whole lot in his first two years at Washington State, he worked his way into the starting lineup and he eventually played well enough as a junior to be named as the Pac-12's Most Improved Player in 2017-18. He later declared for last year's draft, only to withdraw his name to return for his senior season. He improved upon his season from a year ago to become one of the Pac-12's most productive players, earning honors as a first team, All-Pac 12 selection. If he's picked in this year's draft, he'll likely be a second round pick.

Franks' production dramatically improved from where it was in his first two seasons because he's established himself as an excellent shooter. He's made just over 40% of his threes, and a little over 85% of his free throws over the last two seasons. The reason for this is that he has a smooth stroke that allows him to excel in every half-court shooting situation. As a result, he's been an excellent spot-up shooter that can also come off screens and pop out as the screener on pick-and-pop plays. He can also step behind the screen as the ball handler on pick-and-rolls to knock down shots if the defender goes too far under. Off the ball, he's solid at going backdoor to cut to the rim if defenders try to crowd him and he'll crash the offensive boards to score on an occasional put-back. On the downside, he doesn't really run the floor in transition, so his motor may not always be on high. He did have the ball in his hands quite a bit this season, but he's not really suited for a shot creator role in the NBA. He was effective as a straight-line driver on isolations and as a pick-and-roll ball handler, but he predominantly drove to his left. He rarely looked to drive to his right, and he doesn't quite have the quickness or ball handling skills to consistently beat NBA defenders. He also could score on post-ups at the college level, but his moves were limited. He mainly looked to either face his man up or use a quick drop step to bully a smaller defender to score inside. He also was really only effective on the left block. Finally, he's a willing passer, but he's limited to making simple reads to avoid turnovers.

On the defensive end, Franks needs to improve significantly in order to fit into a role in the NBA. From a physical standpoint, he doesn't quite have all of the necessary tools. He does have a long wingspan, but he's a below the rim athlete that also is a bit stiff in his lateral movements. As a result, he had trouble staying with his man as an on-ball perimeter defender, as they would generally blow by him on isolation drives with very little resistance. His effort level on defense wasn't especially high, so he wasn't too effective as a team defender. He had difficulties defending pick-and-rolls because he wasn't able to stop the ball handler from turning the corner or prevent the roll man from getting an easy look inside. He also was often late to close out on perimeter shooters, so he gave up a lot open outside shots. Because of his relative inability to play perimeter defense, he may have to be repurposed as an undersized interior player. He was actually a solid post defender because his strength allowed him to hold position inside and he was good at using his considerable length to contest shots. He could occasionally block shots on the ball or rotate from the weak side. He was also a pretty good defensive rebounder as well.

Even though Robert Franks is a lower ceiling prospect due to his age and athletic limitations, he still has a chance to crack an NBA roster because he has a very valuable plus-level skill. However, he will have to figure out a way to play enough defense to be a long-term fit as a rotation player in the league. If he can improve his defense to a passable level, he could carve out a career as a situational shooting specialist like Matt Bonner. In all likelihood, he could still have a future in professional basketball, but he'll probably be playing overseas.

YELLOW PROSPECTS

NCAA Big Men

Charles Bassey   50/50/55

College/Country	Height	Weight	Age on July 1
Western Kentucky	6'10"	239	18.674

Wingspan	Standing Reach	No Step Vert	Max Vert
7'3.5"	9'1.5"	29.0"	33.0"

Basic Stats		Advanced Stats	
GP	34	TS%	0.673
MIN/G	31.4	3PTA/FGA	0.067
PTS/G	14.6	FTA/FGA	0.477
REB/G	10.0	OREB%	11.0
AST/G	0.7	DREB%	24.6
STL/G	0.8	TRB%	18.1
BLK/G	2.4	AST%	5.1
FG%	0.627	STL%	1.5
3PT%	0.450	BLK%	8.7
FT%	0.769	TOV%	20.9
		USG%	22.1

Projected Draft Range: Late 1st to 2nd Round

Top 10 Comps (All Drafted Players)

	SIMsc			Year
1	925.9	Derrick	Favors	2010
2	899.8	Tony	Mitchell	2013
3	898.6	Noah	Vonleh	2014
4	892.3	Stephen	Zimmerman	2016
5	891.9	Jarrett	Allen	2017
6	888.7	Chris	Bosh	2003
7	886.4	Wendell	Carter, Jr.	2018
8	885.2	J.J.	Hickson	2008
9	884.5	Jordan	Mickey	2015
10	882.1	Jakob	Poeltl	2016

Charles Bassey was actually supposed to be a senior in high school this year, but he reclassified to the class of 2018 and decided to play his freshman season at Western Kentucky. This season, he was one of the most productive players in Conference USA, as he was named as a first team all-conference performer and he earned honors as Conference USA's Defensive Player of the Year. He hasn't hired an agent at this point, so he has left his options open and could possibly return to school if things don't go well for him in the draft process. If he stays in the draft, he'll probably be taken at some point. Most likely, he will either be taken late in the first round or at some point in the second round.

As it was alluded to earlier, Bassey excels at the defensive end of the floor and shows promise as a rim protector at the NBA level. He's an excellent shot blocker because he has a long wingspan, solid leaping ability and he possesses great timing. Therefore, he can block shots on the ball in the post and he can rotate from the weak side. From a position defense standpoint, he can use his strength to push his man off the block to maintain his position inside and force him into tougher shots. He's also very consistent at blocking out, which allows him to be an excellent defensive rebounder. Additionally, he's good at ripping balls away from his man to get steals or use his length to deflect passes. Western Kentucky mainly used as a drop coverage in pick-and-roll situations, so he primarily looked to stay attached to the screener. He was effective at doing so because he generally took away the roll to the rim and he was usually in position to close out on pick-and-pop plays. He wasn't really asked to hedge or switch onto the ball handler in college and he's a little stiff in his lateral movements. As a result, NBA offenses could target him on switches because he may have some trouble defending quicker players in space. If he works on his perimeter defense to at least be able to handle a guard for a few dribbles, he could make himself valuable and stay on the floor for long stretches. Otherwise, he might be better suited for a situational role in the NBA.

Offensively, Bassey can fit into a modern offense because he's an excellent rim running big man. He sets very solid screens and plays with a high motor. His leaping ability also allows him to finish a lot of plays above the rim. These attributes allow him to be very effective as the roll man in pick-and-roll situations and as a cutter off the ball. He'll also run hard down the floor in transition and he'll actively crash the offensive glass to score on put-backs. He was a very good post-up player this season at Western Kentucky. However, he was playing in a smaller, mid-major conference, so he didn't have to use a lot of advanced post moves. He really just relied on his size and athleticism advantages to overpower weaker opponents around the rim. On the positive side, he has a soft touch inside that allows him to finish plays very efficiently and his aggressiveness allows him to draw fouls at a high rate. He also makes free throws at almost a 77% rate, so his stroke is fairly repeatable, and he doesn't show any real mechanical flaws in his motion. He hasn't really had to take many jump shots in college, but he might be able to at least be effective from mid-range at the moment. If his free throw shooting stays consistent, he may have some potential to eventually extend his range to beyond the three-point line to make himself a more valuable player in the long-term. As a negative, his passing needs work. Though he's willing to make the extra pass, he's not always on target and his inaccuracy makes him pretty turnover prone. If he can work on making cleaner passes, he could become a more dynamic offensive player in the future.

In general, Charles Bassey is an intriguing prospect because he could fit into a rotation spot right now. Big men in the NBA are getting increasingly younger, so his abilities as a rim runner and rim protector could allow him to provide a team with considerable surplus value if he stays in the draft and plays on a rookie contract. If he improves his outside shot, he could enhance his long-term career prospects and grow into a solid starting level big man. Most likely, he can just play to his strengths and fill a valuable role as an energetic, rim running, shot blocking big man similar to someone like Jakob Poeltl or a bigger version of Jarrett Allen.

Bruno Fernando   50/50/55

College/Country	Height	Weight	Age on July 1
Maryland	6'10"	237	20.877

Wingspan	Standing Reach	No Step Vert	Max Vert
7'3.25"	9'2"	29.5"	33.5"

Basic Stats		Advanced Stats	
GP	64	TS%	0.638
MIN/G	26.4	3PTA/FGA	0.027
PTS/G	12.0	FTA/FGA	0.493
REB/G	8.7	OREB%	10.8
AST/G	1.4	DREB%	26.3
STL/G	0.5	TRB%	19.1
BLK/G	1.6	AST%	11.4
FG%	0.595	STL%	1.2
3PT%	0.308	BLK%	6.6
FT%	0.763	TOV%	19.7
		USG%	23.1

Projected Draft Range: Mid to Late 1st Round

Top 10 Comps (First Rounders Only)

	SIMsc			Year
1	947.3	Jason	Smith	2007
2	926.5	Jakob	Poeltl	2016
3	926.0	Domantas	Sabonis	2016
4	912.0	Meyers	Leonard	2012
5	911.8	Tony	Battie	1997
6	911.3	Wendell	Carter, Jr.	2018
7	907.1	Anthony	Avent	1991
8	904.0	LaPhonso	Ellis	1992
9	903.6	Chris	Kaman	2003
10	902.7	Clifford	Rozier	1994

Bruno Fernando participated in last year's NBA Draft Combine, but he later withdrew from the draft and elected to return to Maryland for his sophomore season. His production improved from the year before and he established himself as one of the best players in his conference, earning honors as a first team All-Big Ten performer in 2018-19. His stock shot up and he's likely to be selected somewhere in the first round in this year's draft.

Offensively, Fernando profiles as a rim runner at the NBA level. He has solid leaping ability and long arms, so he's able to finish plays above the rim. He also plays with a high motor, so he'll roll hard to the rim on pick-and-rolls and he'll run the floor in transition. He's also an excellent cutter off the ball as well. On top of this, he's very active on the offensive boards, so he'll either get second chance opportunities for his team or he'll score himself on put-backs. His post-up game has improved a bit and he was pretty effective throughout the season. He mainly relied on his strength to bully weaker opponents inside, so he didn't really have to use a lot of advanced post moves. Most of his post-up scores came from either quick drop steps or an occasional hook shot. He did show improvement as a passer, as his Assist Percentage increased by a rate of more than double what was the previous season. However, he's still not quite polished at passing because his passes would sometimes be a little off target, which would lead to a few turnovers. He also struggles to make interior passes to cutters, so he is a little more comfortable making safer plays by kicking the ball out to shooters on the perimeter. His shooting has steadily improved, but his shot is still a work-in-progress. On the positive side, he's become a very consistent free throw shooter and he can comfortably make shots from the mid-range area. His stroke is pretty repeatable and shows no major mechanical flaws. On the other hand, he's still not quite comfortable at shooting threes, so he will have to work to extend his range at the NBA level. Fortunately for him, he has a pretty solid base to work from, so in a few years, he could eventually transition into becoming a stretch big at the next level.

On defense, Fernando has flashed the potential to become a solid rim protector in the NBA. As it was mentioned earlier, he has solid physical tools, as he has a solid vertical leap and considerable length. These traits allow him to be a very good shot blocker. He has some issues with timing overall, so he was a bit foul prone, especially in his freshman year. He's cut down on his foul rate this season, but it hasn't always translated into effective interior defense. At times when he's approaching foul trouble, he'll tone down his aggressiveness to the point where he'll easily allow opponents to get scores inside. In situations when fouls aren't really a factor, he was a solid interior defender. Particularly, he was good at defending post-ups because he could use his strength to hold position on the block and he would alter shots with his length. He also would consistently block out, which allowed him to be an excellent defensive rebounder.

In addition to this, he excelled at closing out on perimeter shooters in spot-up situations. As a negative, he's a bit lacking in lateral quickness, so he has some struggles defending in space. Even though Maryland used a lot of drop coverages to keep him inside, he had some difficulties in stopping the roll man from getting looks around the basket. Also, opposing perimeter players could also exploit his lack of lateral mobility on switches to generate quality shots. As his career progresses, Fernando will have to work on his perimeter defense to allow him to play longer stretches. Otherwise, he'll just be a situational rim protector in the NBA.

Bruno Fernando has enough polish to fit into an NBA rotation right away due his rim running skills and decent interior defense. At this stage, he's limited to being a big-on-big situational player because he hasn't shown that he has the necessary mobility to handle the responsibilities of a modern switching NBA defense. Most likely, he'll become a rotational rim runner that would be highly valuable in his early years by giving his team some added surplus value. In the most likely scenario, he'll develop into a player that is similar to Thomas Bryant. If things break the right way, he could turn into a higher end rotational rim running big man along the lines of Domantas Sabonis.

Other Notable Comps Not Listed Above

SIMsc		Year
913.4	Thomas Bryant	2017

Jaxson Hayes — 45/50/55

College/Country	Height	Weight	Age on July 1
Texas	6'11"	219	19.107

Wingspan	Standing Reach	No Step Vert	Max Vert
7'3.5"	9'2.5"	27.0"	34.5"

Basic Stats		Advanced Stats	
GP	32	TS%	0.739
MIN/G	23.3	3PTA/FGA	0.000
PTS/G	10.0	FTA/FGA	0.592
REB/G	5.0	OREB%	8.7
AST/G	0.3	DREB%	16.3
STL/G	0.6	TRB%	12.5
BLK/G	2.2	AST%	2.6
FG%	0.728	STL%	1.5
3PT%	0.000	BLK%	10.6
FT%	0.740	TOV%	11.8
		USG%	17.2

Projected Draft Range: Top 20

Top 10 Comps (Top 20 Picks Only)

	SIMsc			Year
1	886.6	Zach	Collins	2017
2	871.3	John	Collins	2017
3	868.9	Karl-Anthony	Towns	2015
4	856.1	Marquese	Chriss	2016
5	855.4	Jaren	Jackson Jr.	2018
6	854.7	Larry	Sanders	2010
7	854.6	Cedric	Simmons	2006
8	847.5	Duane	Causwell	1990
9	844.0	Marcus	Haislip	2002
10	841.3	Steven	Hunter	2001

Jaxson Hayes comes from an interesting background. He grew by almost a foot from his freshman year in high school to his senior year and he comes from an athletic family. His father was an NFL tight end and his mother was a former college basketball player. Hayes didn't start the season as a possible one-and-done candidate, but he quickly became one of the best players in the Big 12 Conference, as he was named Big 12 Rookie of the Year and he earned honors as a second team all-conference performer. As a result, his stock rose to the point where he'll likely be taken somewhere in the first round, probably within the first twenty picks of the draft.

On offense, Hayes is a highly efficient, rim running big man. He made almost 73% of his shots because they were almost all inside the restricted area. He was also to utilize his great leaping ability and very long wingspan to finish plays above the rim. In addition to possessing great tools, he also plays with a high motor. As a result, he excelled as a cutter and as the roll man in pick-and-roll situations. He was very good at running hard down the floor to pick up buckets in transition and he was very active to crash the offensive boards to score on put-backs. He was pretty good on post-ups this season, but he mainly looked to use his athleticism to jump over opponents inside. He didn't show a lot of advanced moves, as he mostly relied on using a quick drop step and the occasional hook shot to score in the post. As a negative, he's almost exclusively a catch and finish type of player because he rarely looks to pass and he's not really an advanced ball handler. Therefore, he's not really suited to handle a primary scorer because he's not able to create additional shots. He's also not really a shooter at this stage. He does make his free throws consistently, so he might have some potential to develop a decent shot in the future. However, he doesn't look to take jump shots in a game situation, so he will need to add a jump shot of some kind to diversify his offensive game. Otherwise, his offensive utility is going to be limited at the NBA level.

Defensively, Hayes has a lot of potential, but he needs to break some bad habits to become an effective rim protector in the NBA. As it was mentioned, he has great physical tools because he was long arms and quick feet to go along with his great vertical leap. Because of his tools, he's an excellent shot blocker that blocks shots both on the ball in the post and when rotating from the weak side. He's also a good defensive rebounder and he'll use his length to poke balls away to get deflections. Additionally, he has solid mobility that allows him to effectively cover the roll man in pick-and-roll situations. On the downside, he plays a bit too undisciplined and he's had some struggles at defending in space. In general, he can be a bit too wild on defense because he'll tend to wildly go for blocks and lose his positioning. Some of this is system related, as Texas' Havoc Press system tends to encourage over-aggressive play and constant gambling. Even in situations where he has decent positioning, he'll try too hard to make a big play and it usually leads to a lot of fouls. Opponents can also use his over-aggression against him to bait into committing early to either get a wide open layup or draw a foul on him. As a result, he was only rated as average at defending around the basket in non-post-up situations, according to Synergy. Also, he tended to get caught in an in-between spot when he had to defend on the perimeter. In isolation situations, he tended to overplay the drive by sagging too far off his man, which gave his man additional space to shoot. Other times, when he was closing out on a perimeter shooter, he would close too aggressively, and he would open up a driving lane to the rim. In general, Hayes will have to learn to make clean rotations and play under control. If he can improve in these areas, his defensive skills could translate into the league. Otherwise, he might be limited to playing a situational role if his skill set stays as is.

Jaxson Hayes has a lot of athletic upside, but he still needs to fine tune his game to reach a level close to his ceiling. If he can make the appropriate adjustments to improve his defensive discipline to better handle NBA rotations and switches, he could become a dynamic rim running big man like John Collins. Otherwise, he could have a decent career as a situational rim runner like Chris Wilcox.

Daniel Gafford   45/50/50

College/Country	Height	Weight	Age on July 1
Arkansas	6'10"	238	20.748

Wingspan	Standing Reach	No Step Vert	Max Vert
7'2.25"	9'2"	N/A	N/A

Basic Stats		Advanced Stats	
GP	67	TS%	0.626
MIN/G	25.5	3PTA/FGA	0.000
PTS/G	14.3	FTA/FGA	0.595
REB/G	7.4	OREB%	11.1
AST/G	0.7	DREB%	21.4
STL/G	0.7	TRB%	16.3
BLK/G	2.1	AST%	6.0
FG%	0.635	STL%	1.6
3PT%	0.000	BLK%	10.0
FT%	0.562	TOV%	12.9
		USG%	25.0

Projected Draft Range: Late 1st to 2nd Round

Top 10 Comps (All Drafted Players)

	SIMsc			Year
1	922.8	Rasheed	Wallace	1995
2	919.4	Jakob	Poeltl	2016
3	916.3	Damian	Jones	2016
4	916.3	Tony	Battie	1997
5	914.1	DeVon	Hardin	2008
6	912.0	Dale	Davis	1991
7	908.1	LaMarcus	Aldridge	2006
8	906.8	Richaun	Holmes	2015
9	904.0	Samaki	Walker	1996
10	899.8	Dan	Gadzuric	2002

Daniel Gafford was mentioned as a potential first round pick last year, but he elected to return for his sophomore season at Arkansas. He built upon his solid freshman year to become one of the best players in the SEC, earning honors as a first team all-conference performer this season. He was a bit out of sight, out of mind this year because his team didn't qualify for the NCAA Tournament. As a result, his stock isn't quite as high as it was last year. Even so, he's likely to be taken at some point in this year's draft and could be off the board in the first round.

At the defensive end, Gafford has the potential to be an effective rim protector in the NBA. He has all of the necessary tools, as he's a great leaper and he has long arms to go along with decent lateral mobility. Because of his length and athleticism, he's an excellent shot blocker that posts a pretty high blocks rate. He can block shots on the ball in the post and he's strong enough to hold position on the block to force his opponent into tougher shots. He's also excellent on the weak side because his length allows him to cover a lot of ground to rotate over for blocks. He also can occasionally play passing lanes to pick up steals and he's an excellent rebounder. On the downside, he can be a bit too aggressive, so he's prone to picking up cheap fouls. He's shown some ability to defend on the perimeter because he was excellent in a small sample of isolation possessions. He generally has quick enough feet to stay with perimeter players and his long arms allow him to be effective at contesting jumpers. Therefore, he has the potential to handle the switching responsibilities in the NBA. However, he needs to improve significantly as a team defender. Some of his struggles may have been system related because he was almost exclusively parked in the paint, even though Arkansas primarily played man defense. Because he wasn't always in great position, he gave up a lot of space to perimeter shooters in spot-up situations to give them wide open looks at the basket. He also struggled in a small sample of pick-and-roll possessions, as he would often get caught hedging a little too far to leave the roll man open around the basket. Because he still needs to learn how to make proper rotations, he will need to land on a team with a sound defensive structure to break his bad habits and become a more effective overall defender. Otherwise, he may be limited to being a situational backup.

Offensively, Gafford fits the role of a rim running big man. As it was mentioned earlier, he can jump fairly high and has long arms, so he's able to finish a lot of plays above the rim. His vertical abilities allow him to be very effective as a roll man in pick-and-roll situations and as a cutter off the ball. He's also very good at crashing the offensive glass to score on put-backs and he'll run hard down the floor in transition. He's been pretty effective as a post-up player at Arkansas. However, he mainly relies on his athleticism to out-jump defenders around the rim and he doesn't really have a lot of advanced post moves. He primarily looks to use a quick drop step with an occasional hook shot thrown in every once in a while. He is mainly a catch and finish player at this stage because he isn't a great shooter or passer. He struggles to make free throws, as his career percentage is below 60%. His stroke is inconsistent because he doesn't quite get full extension on his release, which makes his shot a flat line drive with very little touch. Therefore, he'll need to work on his mechanics to get more arc into his shot to give him a better chance to improve from the free throw line. He showed a greater willingness to pass this season, but he's not especially accurate with his passes. As a result of being off target, his turnover rate spiked considerably. Therefore, he may only be suited for a simplified role at the next level.

Overall, Daniel Gafford has a lot of athletic upside, but his skill set may be limited to a situational role in the NBA. On the plus side, his athleticism, shot blocking skills and rim running abilities should allow him to find a spot on an NBA roster for a while. However, he will need some considerable work to learn defensive rotations and adapt to playing defense at the NBA level. Also, he could stand to improve his overall offensive skill level to be more than a just player that scores around the basket. If his defensive awareness doesn't improve, he could be a situational rim runner at the end of the roster like Jordan Hill. Otherwise, if he makes the necessary adjustments, he'll likely develop into a solid rotational big man along the lines of Tony Battie.

Mfiondu Kabengele   40/45/50

College/Country	Height	Weight	Age on July 1
Florida State	6'10"	256	21.879

Wingspan	Standing Reach	No Step Vert	Max Vert
7'3"	9'1.5"	28.0"	35.5"

Basic Stats		Advanced Stats	
GP	71	TS%	0.580
MIN/G	18.3	3PTA/FGA	0.182
PTS/G	10.3	FTA/FGA	0.558
REB/G	5.3	OREB%	12.6
AST/G	0.3	DREB%	20.1
STL/G	0.5	TRB%	16.4
BLK/G	1.2	AST%	3.4
FG%	0.498	STL%	1.6
3PT%	0.374	BLK%	7.5
FT%	0.724	TOV%	11.6
		USG%	26.9

Projected Draft Range: Late 1st to 2nd Round

Top 10 Comps (All Drafted Players)

	SIMsc			Year
1	907.2	Ed	Stokes	1993
2	904.7	Loren	Meyer	1995
3	903.1	Joe	Vogel	1996
4	901.1	Scott	Haskin	1993
5	898.3	Lonny	Baxter	2002
6	897.1	Michael	Doleac	1998
7	894.8	Marcus	Haislip	2002
8	894.4	DeVon	Hardin	2008
9	893.2	John	Collins	2017
10	891.1	Tyler	Zeller	2012

Mfiondu Kabengele redshirted in his first year at Florida State and has spent the last two seasons in a bench role. Even so, he's been highly productive in this role and he was named as the ACC's Sixth Man of the Year this season. He also had a strong showing in this year's NCAA Tournament, so his stock was high enough that he elected to declare for this year's draft. He still has the option to return for another season at Florida State, but he's given every indication that he'll stay in the draft. He's likely to be taken at some point in the draft and could possibly be a first round pick.

On offense, he's an intriguing prospect because he showed that he could be effective as a rim runner and as a stretch big. First off, he has the ideal athletic profile for a rim running big man because he can use his long arms and great leaping ability to finish plays above the rim. He also plays with a high motor, so he'll run hard down the floor in transition to score at the basket and he's very good at cutting off the ball or rolling to the rim in pick-and-roll situations. He'll also actively crash the offensive boards to score on put-backs as well. He's also been a pretty good outside shooter that has been improving the consistency in his shot. He's always been a solid three-point shooter, but he struggled to make free throws in his freshman season. This year, his Free Throw Percentage has improved by more than 10%, so his stroke is much more repeatable now. His motion is fairly sound mechanically, which allows him to be very good as a stationary shooter. He excels at knocking down open spot-up threes and he's good at popping out on pick-and-pop plays. He also is a threat to make trail threes in transition as well. On the downside, he's almost exclusively a catch and shoot or catch and shoot finish player because he doesn't handle the ball, pass or post up well. He can be chased off his shot if a defender closes out on him hard because his ball handling skills aren't polished enough to allow him to drive to the rim. He also rarely looks to pass, and he doesn't have the court vision to do anything other than make a safe pass to avoid a turnover. Additionally, he doesn't have a lot of reliable post moves to score with his back to the basket, so he can only use a quick drop step to score in post-up situations.

Defensively, he has the potential to be a decent rim protector. As it was mentioned earlier, he has the length and leaping ability to protect the rim at the NBA level. He was also an excellent shot blocker in college because he could get blocks on the ball and he can rotate from the weak side. He also was excellent at defending around the basket in general because his presence caused opponents to hesitate inside and he was good at altering shots. In addition to being a good shot blocker, he was a very good defensive rebounder. He could also use his strength to hold position on the block to force tough shots in post-up situations. He also flashed the ability to defend on the perimeter because he was pretty good at staying with quicker players on switches. As a team defender, he's still something of a work-in-progress. For the most part, he was fairly good at closing out on perimeter shooters. However, he had a tendency to sag into the paint, which made him prone to giving his man an open look on the outside. He also had trouble defending pick-and-rolls because he would drop too far inside, which made him vulnerable to giving the ball handler room to take a pull-up jumper or leave the pop man open on a pick-and-pop play. As another negative, he tends to play a little too aggressively, so he tends to get into foul trouble quite a bit.

Mfiondu Kabengele's game could be a good fit for today's NBA if his strengths translate. At this point, he's still a bit unpolished because he hasn't seen a lot of game action over the last two seasons. Therefore, he could benefit from a little bit of extra seasoning in the G-League. In a best-case scenario where everything comes together for him, he could develop into a player similar to John Collins, as he would provide a team with a rim runner that could also space the floor and provide some additional interior defense. If his development stalls a bit, he still has enough skill to carve out a role as a rotational stretch big along the lines of somebody like Marreese Speights.

Naz Reid   40/45/50

College/Country	Height	Weight	Age on July 1
LSU	6'10"	256	19.847

Wingspan	Standing Reach	No Step Vert	Max Vert
7'3.25"	9'1"	26.0"	32.5"

Basic Stats		Advanced Stats	
GP	34	TS%	0.544
MIN/G	27.2	3PTA/FGA	0.230
PTS/G	13.6	FTA/FGA	0.351
REB/G	7.2	OREB%	10.5
AST/G	0.9	DREB%	19.2
STL/G	0.7	TRB%	14.9
BLK/G	0.7	AST%	6.2
FG%	0.468	STL%	1.5
3PT%	0.333	BLK%	2.8
FT%	0.727	TOV%	16.6
		USG%	26.4

Projected Draft Range: Late 1st to 2nd Round

Top 10 Comps (All Drafted Players)

	SIMsc			Year
1	908.9	Johnny	O'Bryant	2014
2	908.3	Isaac	Austin	1991
3	908.2	Maurice	Taylor	1997
4	906.8	Dontonio	Wingfield	1994
5	903.8	Nikola	Vucevic	2011
6	897.4	Jerome	Moiso	2000
7	896.0	Chad	Gallagher	1991
8	895.1	Diamond	Stone	2016
9	894.3	Brian	Cook	2003
10	892.5	Linas	Kleiza	2005

Naz Reid entered LSU with a decorated reputation out of high school, as he was named as a McDonald's All-American in 2018. He made an impact as a starter in his first year and he was productive enough to land a spot on the SEC's All-Freshman team. His performance this season allowed him to flash enough potential to keep his draft stock fairly high. The door is technically open for him to return to LSU for another season. However, if he stays in the draft, he will probably be taken at some point with a chance that he might be picked as high as the first round.

On the defensive end, Reid projects to be a solid interior defender in the NBA even though his physical tools aren't completely ideal. He isn't a particularly explosive leaper and he only has average lateral quickness, but he compensates for these shortcomings with his considerable length and solid positioning. As a result, he was effective at defending around the basket. On post-ups, he used his strength to hold position on the block and his long arms allowed him to force his man into tougher shots. He also could block shots on the ball and rotate over from the weak side. In addition to his ability to defend shots around the rim, he was a pretty good defensive rebounder and he would occasionally poke balls away to get deflections. On the other hand, he tended to play a bit wildly, so he was prone to committing cheap fouls inside. He really excelled as a team defender this season, particularly in pick-and-roll situations. He was very good at preventing the roll man from getting easy shots inside and he could hedge out to contain the ball handler. He would also consistently close out on shooters on the perimeter as well. The primary concern on defense for Reid is that he could be exposed if he's caught on a switch on the perimeter. He wasn't especially effective in isolation situations because opponents could exploit his lack of lateral quickness to drive to the basket. Therefore, he will have to improve his perimeter defense to at least an adequate level or else he could end up being a situational backup for the majority of his career.

Offensively, Reid has the potential to develop into a stretch big, but his skills are still unpolished at the moment. He only shot a break-even percentage on threes this season, but his shooting improved as the season progressed. In fact, he shot just over 38% on threes during conference play, so he has shown signs that his shot may be improving. Mechanically, his motion is smooth and fairly repeatable, which is evidenced by his very good free throw shooting. However, his release is a bit slow and his shot is more of set shot. Therefore, he has some trouble getting clean shots away when defenders are closing on him. He also really doesn't set his feet very quickly, so he had some trouble making shots as the screener on pick-and-pop plays. On the positive side, he has a fairly good motor and makes plays as a rim runner. He's effective as a cutter off the ball and he's very active to crash the glass to score on put-backs. He wasn't asked to roll to the rim very often, but in a small sample of possessions, he would roll hard to score inside. Negatively speaking, he's not really a great passer and he's more of a below the rim player that has trouble finishing inside. As a result of the latter, he had difficulties as a post-up player this season. He also really didn't have many effective moves to score either.

Naz Reid is an interesting young prospect that could develop into a big man that could knock down threes and provide some interior defense. He's not quite a finished product at this stage because he needs to improve his ability to make catch and shoot threes and play perimeter defense. He may need to spend at least a season in the G-League to make the proper adjustments. If he pans out, he could develop into a solid backup stretch big similar to someone like Marreese Speights.

Jontay Porter   40/45/50

College/Country	Height	Weight	Age on July 1
Missouri	6'11"	210	19.625

Wingspan	Standing Reach	No Step Vert	Max Vert
7'0"	9'1.5"	N/A	N/A

Basic Stats		Advanced Stats	
GP	33	TS%	0.567
MIN/G	24.5	3PTA/FGA	0.462
PTS/G	9.9	FTA/FGA	0.437
REB/G	6.8	OREB%	7.7
AST/G	2.2	DREB%	23.2
STL/G	0.8	TRB%	16.0
BLK/G	1.7	AST%	19.6
FG%	0.437	STL%	2.1
3PT%	0.364	BLK%	7.3
FT%	0.750	TOV%	18.0
		USG%	22.5

Projected Draft Range: Late 1st to 2nd Round

Top 10 Comps (Picks Outside the Top 20)

	SIMsc			Year
1	869.4	Stephen	Zimmerman	2016
2	865.1	Ray	Spalding	2018
3	862.2	Donnell	Harvey	2000
4	856.1	James	Gist	2008
5	856.1	P.J.	Brown	1992
6	851.5	Tommy	Smith	2003
7	848.4	Jamal	Sampson	2002
8	848.3	Derrick	Brown	2009
9	846.6	Gerald	Wallace	2001
10	845.9	Quincy	Miller	2012

Jontay Porter entered the draft last year after having a solid freshman season where he earned a spot on the SEC All-Freshman team, but he chose to return for his sophomore season at Missouri. Unfortunately, he's had a string of bad luck since then, as he missed all of this season after he tore the ACL and MCL in his right knee in a scrimmage in October. Later in March, he tore his ACL again while rehabbing, so the timetable for his recovery is unclear at this moment. If he stays in the draft, he's displayed enough potential last season for a team to take a chance on him with a draft pick at some point after the first twenty selections.

When he was healthy, Porter showed that he could potentially fill a role as a stretch big in the NBA. He shot an above average percentage on threes in his freshman season and his mechanics were sound enough that he could extend his range to the NBA three-point line if he makes a full recovery. He was mainly a stationary shooter because he was most effective at knocking down spot up jumpers and he was very good as the screener on pick-and-pop plays. He was an effective post-up player, but he didn't really use a lot of advanced moves. He mainly looked to bully weaker defenders around the basket and score with a quick drop step. In general, he's a pretty good passer that gets assists at a higher rate than most big men. He's good at hitting cutters and he's solid at finding open shooters on the perimeter. In a small sample, he had success in isolation situations. However, he isn't a great ball handler and he mainly scored on straight-line drives to the rim. He also almost exclusively drives right, so he'll have to work on going left to keep defenders honest. As a negative, he tends to float on the perimeter, and he doesn't really look to move without the ball. Therefore, he doesn't really look to cut off the ball and he's not really effective on the offensive boards. He also doesn't always run hard down the floor, so he's not really a factor in transition. If he heals from his injuries, he will have to work on being a bit more well-rounded. Otherwise, he will end up being a situational spot-up shooting stretch big at the NBA level.

Porter has some defensive potential even though he doesn't quite have ideal physical tools. This was the case before he suffered his injuries, so he could be a bit more limited now. He's probably going to have to be a below the rim player if he recovers, so his shot blocking abilities are not going to be as great as they were when he was healthy. Even so, he has pretty good timing to make up for a relatively short wingspan. He also maintains solid positioning around the basket, so he could still be a decent rim protector in a slightly diminished state. He was also an excellent rebounder that would consistently box out his man. On the ball, he was a very good post defender because he could rely on his strength to hold position inside and force his man to take tougher shots. In addition to being a solid post defender, he was pretty good at defending isolations on the perimeter. This is mainly because he could use his good lateral mobility to stay in front of his man and he would actively contest shots. Negatively speaking, he tended to struggle as a team defender. On the plus side, he was fairly good at closing out on spot-up shooters. However, he had trouble guarding pick-and-rolls. He was often caught in an in-between position, so he wouldn't always be in a spot to stop the roll man and quicker guards could blow by him on switches. He also had a tendency to sag too far into paint and go under screens, which allowed shooters to get open looks off screens. Finally, he was sometimes a bit too wild, so he was prone to committing fouls at a fairly high rate.

Like his brother, Michael Porter, Jr. from last year's draft, Jontay Porter is a risky prospect because of his significant injury history. It may take him a while to fully recover, but if that happens, he still needs to improve his defense to become a consistent rotational player in the NBA. If his defense comes around, he could develop into a rotational three-and-D big man along the lines of a taller variation of JaMychal Green. Otherwise, he could end up being a situational stretch big at the end of the roster like Anthony Tolliver, but a few inches taller.

Tacko Fall   35/40/45

College/Country	Height	Weight	Age on July 1
UCF	7'6"	289	23.556

Wingspan	Standing Reach	No Step Vert	Max Vert
8'2.25"	10'2.5"	N/A	N/A

Basic Stats		Advanced Stats	
GP	115	TS%	0.679
MIN/G	23.0	3PTA/FGA	0.001
PTS/G	10.1	FTA/FGA	0.571
REB/G	7.7	OREB%	13.9
AST/G	0.4	DREB%	22.6
STL/G	0.2	TRB%	18.6
BLK/G	2.4	AST%	4.8
FG%	0.740	STL%	0.6
3PT%	0.000	BLK%	11.3
FT%	0.432	TOV%	21.9
		USG%	21.5

Projected Draft Range: 2nd Round to Undrafted

Top 10 Comps (Second Rounders Only)

	SIMsc			Year
1	791.3	Jerome	Jordan	2010
2	791.2	Charles	Claxton	1994
3	784.6	Ruben	Boumtje-Boumtje	2001
4	770.8	A.J.	Hammons	2016
5	769.9	Hamady	N'Diaye	2010
6	758.8	Anthony	Pelle	1995
7	757.8	Todd	MacCulloch	1999
8	755.0	DeAndre	Jordan	2008
9	751.2	Jason	Jennings	2002
10	751.2	Aaron	Gray	2007

Tacko Fall previously entered the 2017 NBA Draft, but he later withdrew to return to UCF. After going through an injury-plagued junior season, he rebounded this year to have a strong showing as a senior. He was one of his conference's top players, earning a spot as a third team All-AAC performer this season. His size and efficient production could allow him to be taken in the second round in this year's draft.

In the past, Fall would have been valued more due to his immense size, as he's been the tallest player in college basketball for the last three seasons. His combination of extreme height, considerable length and body width allows him to be effective at protecting the rim and clogging the paint. He's an excellent overall shot blocker as a result, as he led the AAC in every shot blocking metric this season. In addition to being able to block shots, he's an excellent defensive rebounder because his height and length enable him to grab the ball almost immediately off the rim. For the bulk of his career, UCF kept him parked in the paint, even in man defense. They used a lot of extreme drop coverages to hide his relative immobility. Therefore, he didn't really defend in a lot of different situations, so it's unclear if he can handle playing in an NBA defense. On the positive side, he was excellent at taking away the roll man in pick-and-roll situations because of his rim protection abilities. However, he had struggles in the few situations where he was asked to move his feet. In post-up situations, opponents had success facing him up to either get quality shots inside or cause him to commit fouls. Also, he generally had difficulty staying on the floor in college, so he may be limited to playing against other big body centers.

Offensively, he was extremely effective because his size makes him a very good rim runner that sets solid screens. As a result, he'll roll hard to the rim on pick-and-rolls and he's very good at cutting to the rim off the ball. He also will aggressively crash the offensive boards, which allows him to exploit his height advantage by grabbing balls out of the air without jumping to immediately score on put-backs. He's a bit of a plodder, so he struggles to run the floor, which doesn't make him much of a factor in transition. He was very effective as a post-up player because his size allowed him to get really deep position inside. Because he could set up almost right at the rim, he really didn't have to use post moves, so he could just quickly lay the ball in or dunk it. Dunks and layups accounted for the bulk of his offense at UCF, so this can explain why he's currently the NCAA's career leader in Field Goal Percentage. Opponents had to counter this efficiency in some way, so most of the times, they would foul him and have him shoot free throws. This strategy was fairly effective because he's not an especially skilled player at this stage. His Free Throw Percentage is below 50% for his career and his percentage has progressively gotten worse. This may be a product of over-coaching because he has a lot of things going on in his mechanics. His movements at the free throw line are extremely tentative, so his release is very inconsistent. Right now, he needs to find a way to gain enough confidence to shoot the ball in one motion to provide a coaching staff with a solid enough starting point to make small gradual improvements to his shot. In addition to struggles at the free throw line, he isn't really much of a passer, so he's limited to playing as a catch and finish player.

Tacko Fall's size and college productivity makes him an intriguing backup center prospect. However, his utility is going to be heavily limited because the NBA game is getting smaller, quicker and more perimeter-oriented. If a team gives him a chance to play in a situational role that matches him up against other big body centers, he could be an efficient per-possession backup that plays in short bursts along the lines of a poor man's Boban Marjanovic. In all probability, he could wind up spending the majority of his career overseas or in the G-League.

Nicolas Claxton   35/40/45

College/Country	Height	Weight	Age on July 1
Georgia	6'11"	217	20.205

Wingspan	Standing Reach	No Step Vert	Max Vert
7'2.5"	9'2"	N/A	N/A

Basic Stats		Advanced Stats	
GP	65	TS%	0.526
MIN/G	23.0	3PTA/FGA	0.217
PTS/G	8.4	FTA/FGA	0.649
REB/G	6.2	OREB%	9.9
AST/G	1.0	DREB%	19.2
STL/G	0.6	TRB%	14.8
BLK/G	1.9	AST%	9.1
FG%	0.457	STL%	1.5
3PT%	0.302	BLK%	8.4
FT%	0.611	TOV%	14.8
		USG%	20.2

Projected Draft Range: Late 1st to 2nd Round

Top 10 Comps (All Drafted Players)

	SIMsc			Year
1	910.3	Alex	Len	2013
2	903.7	Ed	Davis	2010
3	896.6	Jerami	Grant	2014
4	896.6	Ivan	Rabb	2017
5	893.2	Jakob	Poeltl	2016
6	892.2	Tony	Battie	1997
7	890.8	Tony	Mitchell	2013
8	888.0	Tristan	Thompson	2011
9	887.9	Stephen	Zimmerman	2016
10	886.4	Rondae	Hollis-Jefferson	2015

Nicolas Claxton came off the bench in his freshman season, but he broke out this year as a sophomore for Georgia. In his first year as a starter, Claxton led the team in scoring and rebounding. He was also one of the better players in the SEC, as he earned a spot on the all-conference second team. Initially, he entered the draft to test the waters. After a strong performance in the first combine scrimmage, it's very likely that he'll stay in the draft. He'll probably be picked at some point and he could possibly even go in the first round.

On offense, Claxton shows promise as a rim runner because he has the length and athleticism to finish a lot of plays above the rim. This season, he was very good at cutting to the rim off the ball and he would actively crash the offensive glass to score on put-backs. In transition, he produced mixed results. On the plus side, he could quickly push the ball up court off a defensive rebound to put pressure on the opposing defense. However, he tended to rush his movements, so he wouldn't be in enough control to finish shots efficiently. He also wasn't as effective as the roll man in pick-and-roll situations because his thin frame doesn't really allow him to set firm screens. As a result, he couldn't really get free on rolls to the rim because he wasn't allowing the ball handler to get separation from his defender to force a rotation. He was an effective post-up player this season, but he mainly relied on his jumping ability and quickness to score on simple drop steps. He's flashed some perimeter skills, but he's still not polished enough at any of them. He's a fairly good ball handler for a big man. In short area isolations, he's shown the ability to drive by an opposing big man to get to the rim. However, he mainly looks to drive to his right, so he can be forced into difficult shots if his defenders sits on his strong hand. He's also an unselfish player that can make a few plays, but it's best if he sticks to making simple reads. At times, he'll try to do too much by forcing a pass into heavy traffic, so he is a little bit prone to making careless turnovers. As a shooter, he can occasionally stretch the defense by hitting an outside shot, but his stroke is still pretty inconsistent at this stage. He still shoots free throws at a rate below 65% and he's a below break-even three-point shooter for his career. His mechanics aren't bad, but he has difficulty shooting with the proper touch. His shot tends to have a line drive arc and it usually comes out a little bit too strong. He'll need to learn to shoot with a softer touch to become a more efficient shooter at the next level.

Defensively, Claxton could still use some significant improvement. Physically, he has most of the tools to succeed in the NBA. As it alluded to earlier, he has fairly long arms to go along with explosive leaping ability and decent lateral mobility. However, those tools have not really translated into effective on-ball defense. He really struggled to defend players in a one-on-one situation. In an isolation situation, he was almost too aggressive for his own good because he often would bite on the first move, which allowed his man to easily set him up for either a drive to the rim or an open jumper. He also had trouble defending in the post, simply because he wasn't really strong enough to prevent his man from getting deep position inside. This allowed his man to either score or force Claxton to commit a foul. He was much better as a help defender because he could use his length and athleticism to rotate from the weak side to block shots. He could also play passing lanes to get steals and he was a fairly good defensive rebounder. Additionally, he did some solid things as a team defender because he was good at closing out on perimeter shooters and he could fight through screens to contain ball handlers in pick-and-roll situations. On the downside, he often hedged out a bit too hard on the ball handler when he was assigned to guard the roll man. As a result, he was prone to giving up easy dunks inside. He will have to work to learn defensive coverages to be more effective at the NBA level.

Nicolas Claxton is a prospect with some great athleticism, but his skill set doesn't quite fit a specific role at this time. He can make plays as a rim runner and he blocks shots, but he's not a polished enough interior defender to play as a modern rim protecting big man. On the other end, he has solid mobility and he has some perimeter skills, but none of them are polished enough for him to play as a tall wing player either. He'll need to get some additional seasoning in the G-League to develop his skills to become a rotation level contributor. His best path to becoming a long-term rotation player is for him to develop into a modern energy big man. If he sticks in the league on a long-term basis, he could be a player like Ed Davis or Tristan Thompson. Otherwise, he could spend the bulk of his career in the G-League or overseas.

Mike Daum   35/40/45

College/Country	Height	Weight	Age on July 1
South Dakota State	6'9"	245	23.668

Wingspan	Standing Reach	No Step Vert	Max Vert
N/A	N/A	N/A	N/A

Basic Stats		Advanced Stats	
GP	137	TS%	0.630
MIN/G	29.5	3PTA/FGA	0.331
PTS/G	22.4	FTA/FGA	0.465
REB/G	9.0	OREB%	8.6
AST/G	1.3	DREB%	24.9
STL/G	0.6	TRB%	17.2
BLK/G	0.6	AST%	10.2
FG%	0.504	STL%	1.1
3PT%	0.410	BLK%	2.4
FT%	0.848	TOV%	10.9
		USG%	33.9

Projected Draft Range: 2nd Round to Undrafted

Top 10 Comps (Second Rounders Only)

	SIMsc			Year
1	923.4	DeMarco	Johnson	1998
2	913.8	Matt	Freije	2004
3	896.5	Nick	Fazekas	2007
4	895.4	Mike	Scott	2012
5	895.3	Alec	Peters	2017
6	894.8	Matt	Bonner	2003
7	890.5	Junior	Burrough	1995
8	889.6	Luke	Harangody	2010
9	887.2	Keith	Hughes	1991
10	885.7	Jerome	Beasley	2003

Mike Daum is one of the most decorated mid-major conference players in this year's draft. He's put up big numbers throughout his college career at South Dakota State and he was named as the Summit League's Player of the Year for the third consecutive year. In addition to this, he was a finalist for the Wooden Award this past season. Despite his accomplishments and production, his stock isn't especially high at the moment, so there's a chance that he could go undrafted. If he is picked in the draft, he'll probably go in the second round.

Daum has some potential on the offensive end because he's been an excellent shooter throughout his career. He's maintained a high level of efficiency while being a primary scorer for his entire four-year career. His compact stroke and quick release allow him to make shots in a variety of ways, as he'll knock down spot-up jumpers, run off screens and hit trail threes in transition. He can also pop out as the screener on pick-and-pop plays. His shooting then sets up the rest of his game because he will drive hard to the rim if opponents overplay his shot. He also was very good as a post-up player because he could either face his man up or use his strength to bully a weaker defender inside. On the downside, he's not really much of a passer because he plays with a heavy score-first mentality. However, he avoids turnovers and he's able to make simple reads. At this stage, his rim running abilities aren't ideal because though he plays with a very high motor, he's a below the rim athlete. His motor allows him to make positive contributions because he'll run hard down the floor in transition and he's good at actively crashing the offensive glass to score on put-backs. His athletic limitations don't allow him to finish plays inside very efficiently. Specifically, he missed some shots around the basket when he was used as either a cutter or the roll man in pick-and-situations because he didn't quite have the lift to finish over a longer defender. Therefore, he might end up becoming more of a shooting specialist at the NBA level.

At this point, Daum doesn't really fit into a specific role on the defensive end. Though he's been used as an interior defender, he hasn't established himself as a rim protector. He didn't really block shots in volume throughout his college career and he was only about average at defending around the basket this season. Based on his performance in his senior year, he might be able to be an on-ball defender, but it's unclear if his skills would translate into the NBA because he's mostly played against a weaker level of competition. On a positive note, he has shown that he may have the mental awareness to compensate for his physical shortcomings. Though he's a bit stiff in his lateral movements, he actually was effective at containing guards on switches in isolation situations because he could stay with them for at least a few dribbles. He was also good at staying attached to the roll man in pick-and-roll situations. Additionally, his strength allowed him to hold position inside against post-ups to force his man into taking a tough shot. On the downside, he tended to sag into the paint a bit too much, so he was prone to leaving shooters open in spot-up situations. As a final note, he was an excellent defensive rebounder that would consistently block out his man.

Overall, Mike Daum is on the older side of the spectrum for a draft prospect because he'll be 23 on draft day. However, he has a chance to land on an NBA roster because his shooting gives him a plus-level skill that could allow him to make something of an immediate contribution. On the other hand, he's not quite ready to be a full-time rotation player because he'll need to prove himself on the defensive end. Therefore, he could benefit from a year of seasoning in the G-League. If his defense comes around to at least an adequate level, he could fill a role as a big shooting specialist along the lines of somebody like Matt Bonner or Mike Muscala.

Dewan Hernandez 35/40/45

College/Country	Height	Weight	Age on July 1
Miami (FL)	6'10"	233	22.559

Wingspan	Standing Reach	No Step Vert	Max Vert
7'1.75"	8'11"	30.5"	35.5"

Basic Stats		Advanced Stats	
GP	64	TS%	0.583
MIN/G	21.6	3PTA/FGA	0.013
PTS/G	8.6	FTA/FGA	0.385
REB/G	4.9	OREB%	9.5
AST/G	0.3	DREB%	17.0
STL/G	0.5	TRB%	13.3
BLK/G	0.9	AST%	2.9
FG%	0.560	STL%	1.3
3PT%	0.000	BLK%	4.5
FT%	0.675	TOV%	13.5
		USG%	20.6

Projected Draft Range: 2nd Round to Undrafted

Top 10 Comps (Second Rounders Only)

	SIMsc			Year
1	927.1	Solomon	Alabi	2010
2	917.1	Justin	Hamilton	2012
3	915.3	Joseph	Blair	1996
4	913.9	Chimezie	Metu	2018
5	913.4	Tony	Massenburg	1990
6	907.9	Jermareo	Davidson	2007
7	907.5	Richard	Manning	1993
8	905.9	James	Gist	2008
9	905.8	Alec	Brown	2014
10	902.5	Romero	Osby	2013

Dewan Hernandez played under the name Dewan Huell in his first two seasons at Miami. He entered last year's draft, but he later withdrew to return for his junior season. However, he was ruled ineligible due to his connection to a corruption scandal revolving around agent, Christian Dawkins. He was forced to sit out the entire season, but he still was invited to this year's combine. He had a strong showing in the combine scrimmages and his stock has risen to the point where a team might take a flyer on him in the second round.

On the offensive end, Hernandez thrives as a rim running big man because his long arms and above average leaping ability allow him to finish plays above the rim and he also plays with a high motor. As a result, he'll roll hard to the rim as the screener on pick-and-rolls and he'll actively crash the offensive glass to score on put-backs. He also will run hard down the floor to fill a lane to get scores in transition. He's a decent cutter as well. He was an effective post-up player in college, but he didn't really have to use a lot of advanced post moves. He mainly looked to back down weaker defenders to score on quick drop steps to the hoop. He does go up very strong, so he'll draw fouls at a fairly high rate. As a general negative, he's not especially skilled at this stage. Though he avoids committing turnovers, he rarely looks to pass, so he isn't adept at hitting cutters or kicking the ball out to shooters. His shooting range is limited to the immediate basket area. He struggles to make free throws, as his career Free Throw Percentage is below 70% and he rarely looks to take a jump shot in the flow of a game. His stroke isn't especially fluid because he seems like he's aiming. He also tends to shoot with a short armed release, so he has a line drive shot that tends to miss long. Finally, he's not a great ball handler, so he doesn't have the ability to face up and drive past defenders off the dribble.

Hernandez has flashed some potential as a rim protector, but his defense is still a bit unpolished. As it was mentioned earlier, he has solid length and leaping ability, so he's able to block shots at a high rate. However, his raw shot blocking abilities don't always translate to effective interior defense because he'll give up positioning to wildly go for blocks. He also doesn't always jump straight up, so opposing players can draw fouls on him. He's a decent help defender in general because he can also use his length to deflect passes and he's a fairly solid defensive rebounder. At Miami, he was mostly asked to defend in the paint, so he has very limited experience at defending in space. Therefore, he will face a steep learning curve to handle the switching responsibilities of a modern defensive scheme. In his role, he was a fairly effective defender. He was a good post defender because he displayed some functional strength to hold position and his length allowed him to contest shots. He also was good at guarding the roll man in drop coverages on pick-and-rolls. Finally, he would also consistently close out on shooters in spot-up situations.

Dewan Hernandez has some additional baggage to go along with his skills, so his profile is fairly risky. Before he arrived at Miami, he was arrested for assault in September of 2016. As it was stated earlier, he also missed an entire season of basketball due to his ineligibility ruling. If he overcomes his past history, he could develop into a decent backup center if he improves his overall defense. In all likelihood, he'll have to grind it out for at least a season in the G-League before he lands a spot on a team's roster. If he sticks in the league, he could be a situational banging rim runner similar to someone like Jeff Ayres. Otherwise, he could wind up spending the bulk of his career in the G-League or overseas.

Other Notable Comps Not Listed Above

SIMsc		Year
900.5	Jeff Ayres	2009

Aric Holman   35/40/45

College/Country	Height	Weight	Age on July 1
Mississippi State	6'10"	210	21.973

Wingspan	Standing Reach	No Step Vert	Max Vert
7'2.25"	9'1"	N/A	N/A

Basic Stats		Advanced Stats	
GP	124	TS%	0.594
MIN/G	21.1	3PTA/FGA	0.333
PTS/G	8.3	FTA/FGA	0.331
REB/G	5.6	OREB%	9.8
AST/G	0.8	DREB%	20.2
STL/G	0.6	TRB%	15.1
BLK/G	1.6	AST%	7.1
FG%	0.510	STL%	1.5
3PT%	0.382	BLK%	8.2
FT%	0.687	TOV%	16.2
		USG%	19.9

Projected Draft Range: 2nd Round to Undrafted

Top 10 Comps (Second Rounders Only)

	SIMsc			Year
1	926.8	James	Gist	2008
2	919.6	Ryan	Kelly	2013
3	914.9	Magnum	Rolle	2010
4	914.1	Chimezie	Metu	2018
5	910.0	Terence	Morris	2001
6	908.3	Sherron	Mills	1993
7	905.9	Kyle	O'Quinn	2012
8	905.1	Alec	Brown	2014
9	902.0	Derrick	Brown	2009
10	901.7	Richaun	Holmes	2015

At one point, Aric Holman was once thought of as a potential first round draft pick. However, he's been in and out of Mississippi State's starting lineup for the last three years and he hasn't really put up big counting numbers at any point of his college career. Even so, he's been effective enough on a per-possession basis to keep him in consideration for a selection in this year's draft. If he's picked, he'll likely go somewhere in the second round.

The NBA's premium on floor spacing could allow Holman to fit into a role as a stretch big. After struggling with his shot in his first two seasons, Holman's outside shooting has improved significantly in the last two years. In fact, he's made just over 43% of his threes over the last two seasons. His free throw shooting has also gotten better to the point where his stroke is much more repeatable than it was in the past. From a mechanics standpoint, his motion is fairly smooth, he stays on balance and gets great extension. As a result, he was an excellent spot-up shooter this season. At this stage, he's more of a stationary shooter because he isn't quite as good on the move. He was around average at making shots as the screener on pick-and-pop plays mainly because he had some trouble keeping his feet on balance while he was moving. In addition to being a solid shooter, he was a very good rim runner that would roll hard to the rim on pick-and-rolls. He also could effectively cut to the rim if opponents overplayed his shot and he would consistently run hard down the floor to get scores in transition. He was a good offensive rebounder that enabled his team to get extra possessions, but he struggled to score on put-backs because he wasn't always under control to put up a quality shot attempt. Additionally, he was below average as a post-up player because he wasn't quite strong enough to hold position on the block. Opponents were able to push him further out, which forced him to take tougher shots. He also didn't really have any kind of reliable move to allow him to consistently score on post-ups. Finally, he's not really advanced as a passer, as he can only make simple kick-outs to shooters and he struggles to make any other kinds of reads.

Defensively, he has some potential as a rim protector, but his skills are still a bit unpolished at the moment. From a physical standpoint, he has close to an ideal set of tools. He has good leaping ability to go along with fairly long arms and solid lateral mobility. His tools allow him to be pretty effective as a help defender. He's very good at rotating from the weak side to block shots and he's a pretty good defensive rebounder as well. He's also gotten better at using his length to play passing lanes and get deflections to occasionally pick-up steals. This season, he was a pretty solid on-ball defender overall. In the post, he sometimes gave up some deep positioning due to a lack of strength, but he was able to compensate for this shortcoming by using his length and timing to alter his man's shot to force misses inside. He also held up well on the perimeter in isolation situations, as he had enough mobility to consistent stay with his man and actively contest shots. As a team defender, he had some struggles. He had a lot of trouble defending pick-and-rolls because he would either lose track of the roll man to give up a score inside or he wouldn't really hedge on the ball handler. He also tended to sag too far into the paint off the ball, which made him late to close out on perimeter spot-up shooters. Therefore, he'll have to learn how to make proper rotations to be a more effective defender at the NBA level.

      Overall, Aric Holman has some potential as a rim protecting, stretch big. He's not really a finished product at the moment, so he could use at least a year in the G-League to gain some additional seasoning to improve his overall defense and shooting consistency. He also could stand to gain some strength, so he can be better equipped to guard bigger centers in the NBA. If everything breaks and he adjusts his game to fit into today's NBA, he could develop into a solid rotational stretch big similar to someone like Walter McCarty.

Bennie Boatwright   35/40/45

College/Country	Height	Weight	Age on July 1
USC	6'10"	220	22.967

Wingspan	Standing Reach	No Step Vert	Max Vert
N/A	N/A	N/A	N/A

Basic Stats		Advanced Stats	
GP	106	TS%	0.569
MIN/G	28.3	3PTA/FGA	0.541
PTS/G	14.5	FTA/FGA	0.309
REB/G	5.7	OREB%	6.1
AST/G	1.8	DREB%	16.3
STL/G	0.5	TRB%	11.3
BLK/G	0.7	AST%	12.1
FG%	0.432	STL%	1.0
3PT%	0.380	BLK%	2.4
FT%	0.759	TOV%	10.1
		USG%	24.8

Projected Draft Range: 2nd Round to Undrafted

Top 10 Comps (Second Rounders Only)

	SIMsc			Year
1	926.8	Jon	Leuer	2011
2	912.9	Tamar	Slay	2002
3	909.3	Keita	Bates-Diop	2018
4	904.8	Matt	Freije	2004
5	903.8	Da'Sean	Butler	2010
6	897.3	Kevin	Hervey	2018
7	897.2	Damone	Brown	2001
8	896.3	Rick	Rickert	2003
9	895.9	George	King	2018
10	895.5	James	Jones	2003

Bennie Boatwright has been on the radar as a prospect for the last few years, but his performance through his first three seasons was fairly inconsistent. As a senior, he's finished his college career with his best overall season and he became one of the best players in the Pac-12, earning a spot on the All-Pac-12 first team. His stock is a little down, so there's a chance that he might not be drafted. If he is taken during the draft, he'll likely be off the board at some point in the second round.

Boatwright projects to be a stretch big at the next level. He was about an average three-point shooter before this season, but his Three-Point Percentage spiked this season, as he made just under 43% of his threes. He shot better this year because he played more to his strengths. His shot selection was an issue in the past, but this season, he didn't take as many contested shots and focused more on knocking down open spot-up jumpers. He also did a solid job of making shots as the screener on pick-and-pop plays and hitting trail threes in transition. He's more of a stationary shooter at this time because he doesn't really shoot off screens or take shots off the dribble. He was an effective post-up player this season, but he didn't really showcase a lot of advanced moves. He mainly relied on quick drop steps with a fadeaway jumper mixed in. At this stage, he's a willing passer, but is limited to making simple reads. He's much more comfortable in a role where he can just either catch and shoot or catch and finish. As a rim runner, he has some potential, but his motor is not always on high. He has a tendency to float on the perimeter and he doesn't always run hard. Therefore, he doesn't really run the floor in transition for layups or roll hard to the rim in pick-and-roll situations. When he's engaged, he's effective at making back-door cuts if defenders overplay his shot and he'll opportunistically crash the offensive boards to score on put-backs. If he can be more active as a rim runner, he could do a better job of keeping defenders honest to open up some more shooting opportunities.

Defensively, he projects to be at least an adequate interior defender. He doesn't quite have the ideal tools. He has solid lateral quickness and leaping ability, but his arms are relatively short for player of his size. Therefore, he wasn't really much of a shot blocker in college and he's not likely to be much of a rim protector at the NBA level. Stylistically, he was more of a stay-at-home, position defender and he was fairly effective as an on-ball defender. In isolation situations, he was usually quick enough to stop his man from driving to the hoop, but he sometimes backed off a bit too much to give up an occasional pull-up jumper. He was also a fairly solid post defender because he had enough functional strength to hold position inside and he was active enough to contest shots. He wasn't put in a lot of pick-and-roll situations, but he showed some promise in a very small sample of possessions. Specifically, in the few times where he had to defend pick-and-rolls, he was effective at defending the roll man and switching onto the ball handler. At times, he'll lose track of his man off the ball, so he has a tendency to be late when closing out on shooters in spot-up situations. Also, he doesn't always block his man out, so he's only an above average defensive rebounder at this point.

Bennie Boatwright might get a shot to make an NBA roster because reliable shooting big men are hard to find. His upside isn't especially high because his lack of rim protection skills may make him unplayable for long stretches. It might be beneficial for him to spend a season in the G-League to find a way to compensate for his lack of length on the defensive end. If he sticks in the league, he'll likely be a shooting specialist off the bench like Matt Bonner. Otherwise, he could be headed for a solid career in one of the higher-end leagues in Europe.

Simi Shittu

35/40/45

College/Country	Height	Weight	Age on July 1
Vanderbilt	6'10"	227	19.647

Wingspan	Standing Reach	No Step Vert	Max Vert
7'1.25"	8'10"	27.0"	35.5"

Basic Stats		Advanced Stats	
GP	32	TS%	0.498
MIN/G	26.7	3PTA/FGA	0.064
PTS/G	10.9	FTA/FGA	0.539
REB/G	6.7	OREB%	6.9
AST/G	1.8	DREB%	21.2
STL/G	0.7	TRB%	14.2
BLK/G	0.5	AST%	16.5
FG%	0.468	STL%	1.4
3PT%	0.056	BLK%	2.0
FT%	0.576	TOV%	20.9
		USG%	26.3

Projected Draft Range: 2nd Round to Undrafted

Top 10 Comps (Second Rounders Only)

	SIMsc			Year
1	906.0	Sean	Lampley	2001
2	897.6	J.R.	Henderson	1998
3	892.3	Trevor	Ariza	2004
4	887.9	Randy	Holcomb	2002
5	886.4	Jamal	Sampson	2002
6	885.5	Jerami	Grant	2014
7	885.1	Jabari	Smith	2000
8	880.7	Ansu	Sesay	1998
9	880.2	Johnny	O'Bryant	2014
10	879.4	Gani	Lawal	2010

Simi Shittu came into the season as one of the top high school recruits in the country, as he was a McDonald's All-American in 2018. He was initially projected as a first round pick, but his production took a major hit after Darius Garland went down due to a torn meniscus. Even though his stock has gone down from what it was at the start of the season, he elected to enter this year's draft and announced his intentions to stay in no matter what. If he is selected, he'll likely be taken in the second round.

At the defensive end, Shittu has flashed some potential as a rim protector. He has solid physical tools, as he has long arms, quick feet that allow him to move fairly well laterally and he's an explosive athlete. These tools allow him to be a good defender around the basket, even though he doesn't block shots at a high volume. He's usually in a good position to alter shots inside and he's been solid as a post defender. He relies on some decent functional strength to hold position on the block and his length helps him force his man into tougher shots. He's also a fairly good defensive rebounder. In addition to being able to defend at the rim, he has shown that he can adequately defend on the perimeter. In a small sample of isolation situations, he held up quite well, as he showed enough quickness to stay with his man and he was active to contest shots. As a team defender, he was mostly good in these situations. He would consistently close out on perimeter shooters and he was okay as a pick-and-roll defender. He was better at guarding the roll man than he was at containing the ball handler because he often dropped back to cover the paint. On the downside, he was prone to allowing the ball handler to get additional space to shoot a quick pull-up jumper. Therefore, he will have to adjust to playing a more aggressive coverage in the NBA.

As it was alluded to earlier, Vanderbilt was counting on Darius Garland to be the team's primary shot creator, so the team had a lot of problems generating quality shots in his absence. Shittu was heavily affected by this and his efficiency suffered as a result. His skill set is best suited for a role as a rim runner because his length and leaping ability allow him to finish plays above the rim. He also plays with a high motor, so he would often roll hard to the rim on pick-and-rolls and cuts off the ball. However, he didn't get the ball at the right times because his other teammates weren't really natural playmakers. Throughout the season, Shittu often tried to do too much and he was often playing too wild to force the action. Occasionally, he could push the ball in transition to make a spectacular play, but mostly, his out of control play led to forced shots or turnovers. He can also be over-aggressive to crash the offensive boards, which made him prone to committing cheap over-the-back fouls. At this stage, he's not really much of a shooter because he rarely looks to take a shot outside the paint, and he shoots free throws at a rate below 60%. He was effective as a post-up player this season, but his success was limited to the left block. On that block, he had some variety in his moves, as he could either get to the rim with a quick drop step or he could shoot over the top of the defender with a hook shot. On the other block, he really didn't have an effective move, so he struggled to make shots from that area. Finally, he was a very willing passer because he got assists at a pretty high rate for a big man, but he wasn't always on target with his passes, which led to some turnovers.

Simi Shittu is a raw prospect at this stage. In a normal situation, it would have been ideal for him to return to Vanderbilt for some more seasoning. However, Vanderbilt's situation has become rather chaotic with many players looking to leave the program and they have just changed coaches. Therefore, Shittu may have no choice but to turn pro. Because he's pretty far away from being an NBA contributor, he'll have to spend at least a season or two in the G-League to figure out his game on offense. If everything breaks right, he could eventually develop into a situational rim running big man along the lines of Dwight Powell. Most likely, he could wind up spending the bulk of his career either in the G-League or overseas.

Ethan Happ 35/40/40

College/Country	Height	Weight	Age on July 1
Wisconsin	6'10"	235	23.151

Wingspan	Standing Reach	No Step Vert	Max Vert
N/A	N/A	N/A	N/A

Basic Stats		Advanced Stats	
GP	139	TS%	0.548
MIN/G	29.6	3PTA/FGA	0.010
PTS/G	15.3	FTA/FGA	0.422
REB/G	8.8	OREB%	10.4
AST/G	3.0	DREB%	25.3
STL/G	1.6	TRB%	17.8
BLK/G	1.1	AST%	26.0
FG%	0.544	STL%	3.3
3PT%	0.063	BLK%	4.1
FT%	0.541	TOV%	15.4
		USG%	30.1

Projected Draft Range: 2nd Round to Undrafted

Top 10 Comps (Second Rounders Only)

	SIMsc			Year
1	894.9	Draymond	Green	2012
2	891.2	Paul	Davis	2006
3	890.0	Joe	Wylie	1991
4	889.7	Dwight	Powell	2014
5	886.9	James	Augustine	2006
6	886.2	Jevon	Crudup	1994
7	883.7	Jackson	Vroman	2004
8	883.3	Josh	Grant	1993
9	881.4	Trent	Plaisted	2008
10	880.6	Goran	Suton	2009

Ethan Happ entered last year's draft, but he ultimately chose to return to Wisconsin for his senior season. This season, he was one of the most productive players in college basketball, as he was named as a second team consensus All-American and he won the Kareem Abdul-Jabbar Award for being the nation's best center. If he's taken in this year's draft, he will likely be selected in the second round.

Happ had a reputation for being a good defender in college, but it's unclear if his defense will translate at the next level. First off, he lacks the ideal athleticism to be a modern rim protector because he plays below the rim and he has relatively short arms. As a result, he doesn't really block a lot of shots in volume. He also struggled to defend around the rim in general because he didn't quite have the length to alter shots inside. His lack of length also hurt him as a post defender because opposing big men were able to shoot over him. Additionally, he's lacking in strength, so he was often pushed around inside, and he tended to allow his man to get deep position, which forced him into a lot of situations where he had to foul to prevent his man from getting an easy bucket. Furthermore, he tended to over-protect the paint, which made him prone to leaving shooters open on the perimeter in spot-up situations. On the positive side, he plays hard and has solid lateral mobility. Therefore, he's much more effective at guarding players on the perimeter. He was a pretty good pick-and-roll defender because he could either stay attached to the screener to take away a roll to the rim or quickly hedge to contain the ball handler. He also held up pretty well at guarding smaller players on switches in isolation situations. Finally, his steals rate is higher than most big men because he would actively use his hands to deflect wayward passes or rip balls away from his man inside. He also was good at boxing his man out to allow him to be a great defensive rebounder.

On offense, he has a unique profile for a big man, so it's uncertain if his style can translate into the NBA. He's limited as a rim runner because he doesn't have the length or leaping ability to make plays above the rim. He was fairly good in catch and finish situations if he was open under the basket. However, he could sometimes have trouble finishing shots inside against longer, more athletic big men. As a result, he was only about an average cutter or roll man this past season. He does play with a high motor, so he was good at crashing the offensive glass to either get second chance opportunities for his team or score on put-backs. His best skill is his passing, as he's adept at hitting cutters or finding open perimeter shooters out of the post. He even showed some ability to make plays off the dribble by making solid reads in a limited sample of possessions as a pick-and-roll ball handler. He was an effective post-up player in college, but he didn't really have a lot of variety in his moves. He mainly looked to use his strength to score on quick drop steps and he occasionally would go to an up-and-under move. He didn't have many other moves beyond that. His main weakness is that he really struggles to shoot.

His mechanics don't appear have any glaring flaws, but he lacks a natural shooting touch and his stroke isn't especially repeatable. Because of this, he's been a poor free throw shooter throughout his career, as his percentage is below 60% for his career and his Free Throw Percentage this season dropped to just under 47%. He also doesn't look to take any kind of shot beyond the immediate basket area. With this in mind, his usefulness may be limited at the NBA level because he could be a liability from a spacing and shooting efficiency perspective.

Overall, Ethan Happ has a game that doesn't quite fit the modern NBA, so he will have to make serious adjustments to become a long-term rotational player. In all likelihood, he'll have to spend a season or two in the G-League to figure out his role on defense and improve his shooting to a passable level. If everything breaks favorably for him, he could become a backup, position defending big man similar to someone like Nick Collison. Otherwise, he's likely to be headed for a fairly solid career in one of the higher-end European leagues.

Other Notable Comps Not Listed Above

SIMsc		Year
900.6	Nick Collison	2003

YELLOW PROSPECTS

Non-College Players

Four prospects from either the 2017 NBA Draft Almanac or the 2018 NBA Summer Almanac withdrew after publication. They have either entered this year's draft or are now automatically eligible for selection. They are not profiled in this edition because their grades have not really changed. The edition where the prospect was originally profiled is stated in parentheses next to the grade.

Nik Slavica, Croatia – 35/40/45 (2017)

Brian Bowen II, USA (Saginaw, MI) – 35/40/45 (2018)

Amine Noua, France – 35/40/45 (2018)

Karim Jallow, Germany – 35/40/45 (2018)

Goga Bitadze

45/50/55

College/Country	**Height**	**Weight**	**Age on July 1**
The Republic of Georgia	6'11"	250	19.948

Wingspan	Standing Reach	No Step Vert	Max Vert
N/A	N/A	N/A	N/A

Basic Stats

GP	44
MIN/G	23.5
PTS/G	13.3
REB/G	6.0
AST/G	0.8
STL/G	0.5
BLK/G	1.9
FG%	0.586
3PT%	0.387
FT%	0.667

Advanced Stats

TS%	0.622
3PTA/FGA	0.186
FTA/FGA	0.775
OREB%	9.5
DREB%	22.7
TRB%	16.0
AST%	6.9
STL%	14.4
BLK%	1.2
TOV%	9.2
USG%	23.6

Projected Draft Range: Mid to Late 1st Round

Top 10 Comps (First Rounders Only)

	SIMsc			Year
1	901.8	Marcus	Haislip	2002
2	893.1	Karl-Anthony	Towns	2015
3	889.1	Marquese	Chriss	2016
4	888.0	Scott	Haskin	1993
5	881.2	Loren	Meyer	1995
6	878.2	Alaa	Abdelnaby	1990
7	878.1	George	Zidek	1995
8	875.1	Patrick	O'Bryant	2006
9	873.5	John	Collins	2017
10	869.8	Tony	Battie	1997

Goga Bitadze entered last year's draft and was profiled in the 2018 Almanac, but he withdrew right at the June deadline. He started this season playing for Mega Bemax in the Adriatic, but he was loaned to Buducnost in December. This allowed him to play a few games in the EuroLeague and he was able to maintain his high level of production against better competition. As a result, his stock has improved to the point where he's likely to be taken in the first round, assuming he stays in the draft.

On offense, Bitadze showed the most improvement as a shooter. After having a bad outside shooting season the year before, his Three-Point Percentage climbed back up to where it was in the two years prior, as he made just 41% of his threes this season. The mechanics on his jump shot were much more consistent this season, as he shot with a balanced and compact stroke. At this stage, he's more of a stationary shooter because he's most effective at making spot-up jumpers and popping out as the screener on pick-on-pop plays. He's not completely polished as a shooter because he still shoots free throws at a rate below 70%. On the plus side, his Free Throw Percentage has increased in each of the last four seasons. From there, he's maintained his strengths as a rim running big man. Though he doesn't really have explosive athleticism, he makes a lot of plays around the basket because of his very high motor. This makes him a very good screener in the pick-and-roll game because his great hands allow him to catch tough passes in tight spaces and he consistently rolls hard to the rim. He's also an aggressive offensive rebounder that will score on a lot of put-backs. Additionally, he has a pretty soft touch, so he'll score on little hooks or floaters if he's in traffic. His post-up game is still rather simplified, as he mainly relies on quick hook shots and a few turn-around jumpers. He's playing with a much more aggressive approach, so he's playing with more of a score-first mindset. He's also been better at using his strength to score on quick drop steps, which has allowed his efficiency to improve significantly. In fact, his True Shooting Percentage was just under 66% this season. Though he's looking to score more, his passing skills are still there. If a teammate has a better shot, he will hit cutters or find shooters on the perimeter.

As a defender, he's maintained his effective play as a rim protector. Even though, he stepped up a level in competition, he's continued to block shots at a high rate. In fact, even though the sample is fairly small, his Blocks Percentage was higher in EuroLeague than it was in the Adriatic League. He was an effective shot blocker because he has pretty good timing to go along with decent length and some ability to stay vertical. He also does a fairly good job of keeping his blocks in play to allow his team to regain possession. In addition to his shot blocking abilities, he's still a very good defensive rebounder and post defender. As a rebounder, he consistently blocks out and he's aggressive to pursue the ball, which allows him to consistently maintain a high Defensive

Rebound Percentage. He has very good strength that allows him to hold position against opposing post players to force them into tougher shots. His weaknesses are still the same as they were last season. He still tends to play over-aggressively, so he'll bite on fakes inside when trying to go for a block and he's very foul prone. His foul rate increased a bit this season, so he will need to work on playing a little more under control at the NBA level. Furthermore, he still doesn't have great lateral mobility and he has some difficulties defending in space. His teams have to use a lot of drop coverages to try to cover his lack of mobility. As a result, he's unable to contain ball handlers on the perimeter or adequately guard players on switches. Therefore, he may be limited to being a situational backup that can only be used against other bigger body centers.

Goga Bitadze has improved to the point where he might not be too far away from being a rotation player in the NBA. If he can find a way to compensate for his quickness limitations, he could become a valuable rotational big man due to his rim protection, rim running and shooting skills. In a best-case scenario, he could beat this projection and possibly develop into a variation of Nikola Vucevic. Most likely, he'll develop into a solid rotational big man along the lines of somebody like Dewayne Dedmon.

Sekou Doumbouya   40/45/55

College/Country	Height	Weight	Age on July 1
France	6'9"	220	18.521

Wingspan	Standing Reach	No Step Vert	Max Vert
N/A	N/A	N/A	N/A

Basic Stats		Advanced Stats	
GP	33	TS%	0.560
MIN/G	17.0	3PTA/FGA	0.381
PTS/G	6.5	FTA/FGA	0.193
REB/G	2.9	OREB%	6.7
AST/G	0.7	DREB%	16.4
STL/G	0.7	TRB%	11.6
BLK/G	0.4	AST%	7.1
FG%	0.477	STL%	2.3
3PT%	0.299	BLK%	2.7
FT%	0.765	TOV%	17.0
		USG%	20.0

Projected Draft Range: Top 20

Top 10 Comps (Top 20 Picks Only)

	SIMsc			Year
1	907.8	Jason	Richardson	2001
2	897.6	Taurean	Prince	2016
3	886.4	Joe	Alexander	2000
4	886.3	Luol	Deng	2004
5	886.0	Kelly	Oubre	2015
6	884.1	Kevin	Knox	2018
7	879.7	Austin	Croshere	1997
8	878.3	Josh	Childress	2004
9	871.8	Tobias	Harris	2011
10	871.1	Richard	Jefferson	2001

Sekou Doumbouya is one of the youngest prospects in this draft, as he won't turn 19 until late December. He's been fairly productive playing as a professional in France, as he won the French Pro B league's Best Young Player award in 2018. This season, he moved to up to the French Pro A league by signing with Limoges CSP and he was a solid contributor off their bench. His stock has been high throughout the season, so he'll likely come off the board within the first twenty picks of the draft.

Right now, Doumbouya is more advanced at the defensive end than he is on offense. Physically, he has great tools that could allow him to be a solid defender in the NBA. He's a fairly explosive athlete with good lateral mobility and leaping skills to go along with a pretty long wingspan. These athletic tools allow him to be a very good help defender, as he'll jump passing lanes to get steals, rotate from the weak side to block shots and he's a solid defensive rebounder. He also has good strength to defend players inside, as he can hold position on the block and use his length to contest shots. At this stage, he might be best suited to playing a role as an undersized big man. He's a bit too aggressive when he defends players out on the perimeter because he'll bite on his man's first move, which allows them to easily counter for a score. He's also about average as a team defender. On the plus side, he will fight screens to stay attached to shooters off the ball. However, he gets confused in pick-and-roll defense, so he's prone to leaving a man open by not making the right rotation. Additionally, he doesn't always block out and he can be caught ball watching. As a result, he will sometimes allow his man to sneak by him to get an offensive rebound.

His offensive potential is going to depend on how a team uses him. If the team that takes him believes he's a wing player, then his overall offensive game is quite raw. He has a lot of trouble shooting the ball from outside, as his Three-Point Percentage has been below 30% over the last four seasons. From a mechanics standpoint, his motion is mostly sound because he stays on balance and he has a fairly smooth release. However, he puts an unnecessarily high arc on his three-point shot that's much harder to control, so he's prone to some bad misses. He doesn't have this unusually high arc on his free throws, so he could improve if he sticks to shooting with a consistent release. In addition to his shooting struggles, he isn't really suited to being a shot creator. He's not a great ball handler because he struggles to change directions and he isn't quite able to dribble away from heavy pressure. He's also not really a playmaker in a half-court set because he doesn't have the vision to see the whole floor. If he's repurposed as an undersized big man, he has a better chance of panning out. His athleticism and fairly high motor do allow him to be effective as a rim runner. He'll run hard down the floor in transition to finish plays above the rim. He's also a threat to score on lobs off either hard cuts away from the ball or a roll as the screener on pick-and-roll plays. He'll also crash the offensive glass to score on put-backs.

Sekou Doumbouya is an intriguing prospect because of his youth and athletic potential. His skill set is not especially polished at the moment, so the team that takes him needs to have a clear plan to help him reach his full potential. Otherwise, his career in the NBA could end up being shorter than expected. With the way the game is played right now, a switch to being an interior player could be his best chance for success. If this best-case scenario were to happen, he could develop into a solid rotational player similar to someone like Al-Farouq Aminu. If a team tries to make him a traditional wing player, his learning curve will be much steeper and it could take him several years before his skill set is advanced enough for him to be a steady rotation player. However, if he were to come out of the other side of that particular process, he may eventually develop into a variation of Jerami Grant.

Luka Samanic   35/45/50

College/Country	Height	Weight	Age on July 1
Croatia	6'11"	227	19.474

Wingspan	Standing Reach	No Step Vert	Max Vert
6'10.5"	8'11"	27.0"	38.0"

Basic Stats		Advanced Stats	
GP	48	TS%	0.568
MIN/G	18.0	3PTA/FGA	0.267
PTS/G	7.6	FTA/FGA	0.422
REB/G	4.6	OREB%	7.7
AST/G	0.9	DREB%	24.6
STL/G	0.4	TRB%	16.5
BLK/G	0.4	AST%	9.3
FG%	0.481	STL%	1.4
3PT%	0.319	BLK%	2.0
FT%	0.711	TOV%	16.4
		USG%	21.4

Projected Draft Range: Late 1st to 2nd Round

Top 10 Comps (Picks Outside the Top 20)

	SIMsc			Year
1	912.2	Chris	Crawford	1997
2	894.2	Bill (Henry)	Walker	2008
3	891.4	Quincy	Miller	2012
4	891.2	Brian	Cook	2003
5	889.4	Isaiah	Morris	1992
6	885.9	Ben	Bentil	2016
7	881.9	Rick	Rickert	2003
8	881.2	Kyle	Kuzma	2017
9	881.2	Moritz	Wagner	2018
10	881.2	O.G.	Anunoby	2017

Though Luka Samanic is 19 years old, he hasn't really been playing basketball very long because he started when he was 11. He has quickly risen through the ranks of European basketball, as he's now playing a regular rotational role for Union Olimpija in the Adriatic League. He played well enough off the team's bench to get the attention of NBA scouts. If he stays in the draft, he'll probably be taken at some point after the first twenty picks, although there's some outside chance of him possibly going in the lottery.

Offensively, Samanic is best suited for a role as a rim runner even though he doesn't quite have the ideal physical tools. His arms aren't especially long and he's not really an explosive leaper, so he plays more of a below the rim game. Even so, he has a good sense of when to go to rim and he can slip into open spaces to get easy shots around the basket, which makes him a very good cutter and roll man. He will also run hard down the floor to fill lanes in transition and he's a solid offensive rebounder that will hit the boards to score on put-backs. He's flashed some perimeter skills in short bursts, but he's not fully developed in any one of these skills at the moment. He does look to aggressively drive, but he isn't really a good enough ball handler to change directions and he's not quite quick enough to regularly beat defenders off the dribble. He shown some promise as a shooter because his shooting motion looks pretty fluid. However, he's not comfortable shooting from long distance because he's been a below break-even three-point shooter for the last three seasons. His stroke is much more consistent from mid-range, which is evidenced by the fact that he's made more than 70% of his free throws in each of the last three years, so there may be some potential for growth in the future. He also shows some potential as a passer because he's an unselfish player that generally makes the right read, but his passes aren't always on target. As a result, his passes can often get deflected or mishandled by teammates, which has made him somewhat turnover prone.

At the other end of the floor, Samanic is better at playing team defense than he is at defending players on the ball. On the positive side, he generally makes sound rotations and he's usually in the right place. Therefore, he'll be in position to close out on perimeter shooters, he'll fight through screens and he can appropriately switch to defend pick-and-rolls. His positioning allows him to be a very good defensive rebounder because he will also box his man out. He also has some ability to make plays as a help defender because he'll occasionally deflect passes or rotate from the weak side to block a shot. At this stage, he has trouble guarding players on the ball because he's athletically limited. As it was mentioned earlier, his wingspan is somewhat short for a player of his size and he isn't really an explosive athlete. Because of this, he lacks the lateral quickness to consistently keep up with perimeter players, so they will often blow by him on drives. He also isn't very strong, so he has problems guarding bigger players on post-ups. Often times, his man will push him around inside to either establish deep position or overpower him to get an easy score at the rim. His struggles at playing post defense also put him in a lot of vulnerable positions that cause him commit fouls, so it's uncertain if he's able to play for long stretches at the NBA level.

Luka Samanic is a prospect with a lot of interesting skills that could make him an effective NBA player in the future. However, he's not polished enough to fit into a team right away and it would probably be best if he were stashed overseas to get a little more seasoning. Most importantly, he will need to improve his defense to becoming at least a passable interior defender. If he makes that adjustment and becomes a more consistent outside shooter, he could reach a level close to his ceiling and turn into a poor man's version of Domantas Sabonis. Specifically, he would be a rotational rim running big man that could also provide a team with a little bit of floor spacing.

Laurynas Birutis 35/45/45

College/Country	Height	Weight	Age on July 1
Lithuania	7'0"	230	21.844

Wingspan	Standing Reach	No Step Vert	Max Vert
N/A	N/A	N/A	N/A

Basic Stats		Advanced Stats	
GP	35	TS%	0.638
MIN/G	10.9	3PTA/FGA	0.000
PTS/G	4.9	FTA/FGA	0.409
REB/G	2.1	OREB%	13.7
AST/G	0.4	DREB%	14.4
STL/G	0.1	TRB%	14.1
BLK/G	0.3	AST%	6.6
FG%	0.600	STL%	0.6
3PT%	0.000	BLK%	3.3
FT%	0.745	TOV%	18.6
		USG%	22.2

Projected Draft Range: 2nd Round to Undrafted

Top 10 Comps (Second Rounders Only)

	SIMsc			Year
1	901.1	Chimezie	Metu	2018
2	900.9	Mike	Muscala	2013
3	900.0	Jermareo	Davidson	2007
4	897.9	Alec	Brown	2014
5	895.0	Joseph	Blair	1996
6	894.5	Jon	Leuer	2011
7	893.2	Ryan	Kelly	2013
8	891.4	Cory	Jefferson	2014
9	891.0	Romero	Osby	2013
10	888.7	James	Gist	2008

Laurynas Birutis entered last year's draft but he pulled out right before the June deadline. After spending last season as the most productive player on Siauliai, a mid-tier team in the Lithuanian LKL, he moved up to playing for LKL powerhouse, Zalgiris. His playing time was greatly reduced, but he was still fairly effective in limited minutes and he held his own in a limited number of minutes in the EuroLeague. His stock is down at the moment, so there's a chance that he might not get picked. If he is selected, he'll probably be a second round pick.

Offensively, Birutis is an efficient inside scorer that excels as a rim runner. Though he's rather lumbering from a foot speed standpoint, he has enough leaping ability and length to get a lot of dunks inside. He usually gets himself into threatening spots around the basket because he sets very solid screens and he rolls hard to the rim. He plays with a pretty high motor as well. He aggressively attacks the offensive glass, so he's typically been a very good offensive rebounder throughout his career. This allows him to either score on put-backs or get additional shot opportunities for his teammates. Even though he's not a fast runner, he will consistently run hard down the floor to fill a lane in transition, which makes him effective as a trailer. He has been a solid scorer on post-ups, but he mainly relies on using his strength to bully weaker defenders inside. He really doesn't have a lot of advanced post moves and primarily uses a quick drop step to get his scores around the basket. On the plus side, he has some potential to become a decent shooter. He doesn't shoot threes right now, but he's become a solid mid-range shooter and his stroke at the free throw line has become a lot more consistent. When he takes mid-range jumpers, he shoots with a smooth, compact, left-handed release. It's also become much more repeatable in the last two years, as he's shot over 74% from the free throw line. If he continues to improve as a shooter, he may be able to extend his range in the future. As a final note, he's a decent passing big man because he makes solid reads that allow him to hit cutters and find open shooters.

On defense, he's effective at using his size to eat up space and he shows some promise as a rim protector. If he's matched up against another interior player, he usually maintains solid positioning to clog the lane and make it tougher for perimeter players to drive inside. He also is a fairly good post defender because his strength helps him hold position on the block to make his man take a tougher shot. He also does a good job of going straight up when he contests a shot inside. This allows him to either alter or block shots on the ball without fouling. Additionally, he consistently boxes his man out and aggressively pursues the ball on a miss, which has made him a pretty good defensive rebounder over the course of his career. From a negative standpoint, his lack of general mobility makes him an ill fit for today's game because he struggles to defend in space. Therefore, quicker players can beat him off the dribble and he has to be hidden in drop coverages in pick-and-roll situations. He also is very hesitant to close out on perimeter shooters. As a result, his future utility is going to be limited because it's likely that he can only play against other big body centers.

Laurynas Birutis is not quite ready to play in the NBA because he needs to prove that he can maintain a high level of productivity against elite European competition. Therefore, he would benefit from being stashed in Lithuania for at least another season or two. If he can figure out a way to compensate for his quickness limitations on defense, he could develop into a solid situational banger along the lines of Ante Zizic. On the other hand, he could also work on his outside shot to eventually expand his range to the three-point line to become a backup space eating big man that can provide some rim protection and floor spacing similar to somebody like Aron Baynes.

Darius Bazley   35/40/45

College/Country	Height	Weight	Age on July 1
USA (Cincinnati, OH)	6'9"	208	19.052

Wingspan	Standing Reach	No Step Vert	Max Vert
7'0"	8'11"	N/A	N/A

Basic Stats		Advanced Stats	
GP	N/A	TS%	N/A
MIN/G	N/A	3PTA/FGA	N/A
PTS/G	N/A	FTA/FGA	N/A
REB/G	N/A	OREB%	N/A
AST/G	N/A	DREB%	N/A
STL/G	N/A	TRB%	N/A
BLK/G	N/A	AST%	N/A
FG%	N/A	STL%	N/A
3PT%	N/A	BLK%	N/A
FT%	N/A	TOV%	N/A
		USG%	N/A

Projected Draft Range: Late 1st to 2nd Round

No Comps Available – No Stats

Darius Bazley has taken a unique approach to the draft process. He initially committed to play this past season at Syracuse, but he later chose to bypass college to spend his pre-draft year in the G-League. He then changed his plans once again after signing with agent, Rich Paul, so he elected to train on his own and spend the rest of his time as a million-dollar intern at New Balance. Most of his stock is based on his play at the high school level, where he was a McDonald's All-American in 2018. He will probably be taken at some point in this year's draft and he could possibly be off the board in the first round.

On offense, Bazley doesn't really stand out in one particular skill, except that he is a pretty explosive overall athlete. This makes him a dynamic threat in transition because he can glide easily down court and finish plays above the rim. He's also an unselfish player that can find open teammates on the break. In a half-court set, his skill set may not be suited for a primary scoring role. He's a fairly solid ball handler, but he has a pretty heavy tendency to drive to his left. Therefore, opposing defenders may have some success in sitting on his strong hand to force him into a tougher shot. He also has some struggles off the dribble because he has a little bit of a long windup in his shot, so he's not really able to get shots off quickly. When he does have space to shoot, he is fairly effective at making threes because he has a consistent release point. However, he may be limited to being a spot-up shooter at this stage. He rarely played without the ball in high school, so it's unclear if he can shoot off screens. Based on his current mechanics, it's not likely that he can quickly catch and shoot while still maintaining his balance or footwork. As a result, he'll need to learn how to shoot on the move at the professional level.

Defensively, he has the tools to develop into an effective perimeter defender, but he's still very raw at this stage. From an athletic standpoint, he has good lateral mobility to go along with a fairly long wingspan and great leaping ability. These tools allow him to be a very good vertical help defender, as he's very aggressive to come in from the weak side to either block shots or grab defensive boards. He can use his length to play passing lanes to pick up a few steals, but he tends to gamble quite a bit and he can be caught out of position. At times, he'll try to shoot the gap, but he doesn't know how to pick his spots to do this, which allows his man to get free for an open shot. He gets caught over-helping inside when he tries to go for blocks as well. Additionally, his effort level is inconsistent because he will not always run back on defense and he'll cheat off his man quite a bit. Because of his thin frame, he has trouble fighting through screens. Therefore, he could have problems defending pick-and-rolls and chasing shooters off screens at the NBA level. When he is engaged on defense, he shows solid potential as an on-ball defender. His quickness helps him stay in front of his man and he can use his length to really bother shots on the perimeter. If he can learn NBA rotation schemes and if a coach can get him to consistently play with a high level of effort, he has a chance to eventually become a decent defender in the future.

Darius Bazley is an elite athlete that has flashed a lot of different skills. However, he still hasn't put everything together and there's going to be a very steep learning curve for him to adjust to the NBA. Right now, he would be best served by spending at least a season or two in the G-League to get him acclimated to playing against a high level of competition. His development process may take several years, but if he improves his defense and shooting consistency, he could eventually carve out a role as a decent rotational, three-and-D wing player like Maurice Harkless.

Joshua Obiesie   35/40/45

	College/Country	Height	Weight	Age on July 1
	Germany	6'6"	190	19.107

Wingspan	Standing Reach	No Step Vert	Max Vert
N/A	N/A	N/A	N/A

Basic Stats		Advanced Stats	
GP	20	TS%	0.563
MIN/G	15.9	3PTA/FGA	0.396
PTS/G	6.9	FTA/FGA	0.485
REB/G	2.4	OREB%	4.3
AST/G	1.5	DREB%	15.4
STL/G	0.5	TRB%	10.0
BLK/G	0.3	AST%	14.1
FG%	0.446	STL%	1.5
3PT%	0.300	BLK%	1.8
FT%	0.735	TOV%	19.7
		USG%	22.8

Projected Draft Range: 2nd Round

Top 10 Comps (Second Rounders Only)

	SIMsc			Year
1	888.1	Malcolm	Lee	2011
2	883.0	Frank	Jackson	2017
3	877.1	Josh	Selby	2011
4	871.8	Jamaal	Franklin	2013
5	867.7	Maurice	Jeffers	2001
6	863.3	Chris	Douglas-Roberts	2008
7	861.4	DeAndre	Liggins	2011
8	859.2	Roger	Mason	2002
9	859.1	Edmond	Sumner	2017
10	856.8	James	White	2006

Joshua Obiesie played in Germany's top league for the first time this season and he played sparingly in a reserve role for s.Oliver Wurzburg. He was invited to participate in this year's Nike Hoop Summit but didn't do a whole lot in only six minutes of game action. However, he showed enough in international under-18 tournaments to get the attention of a few scouts. If he stays in the draft, he could be taken at some point in the second round.

On the offensive end, Obiesie is at his best in transition because he can quickly push the ball up court to either score himself or set up his teammates on the break. When he doesn't have the ball, he'll run hard down the floor to fill a lane. In a half-court offense, he still doesn't really stand out at any one particular skill. He has some playmaking skills and he's an unselfish player in general, so he has a decent ability to find open teammates or make an extra pass. However, he tends to be quite sloppy with the ball, which leads to him making careless passes that result in turnovers. He's an above average ball handler, but he's not suited for a primary scoring role in the NBA. This is mainly because he's not overwhelmingly quick and he tends to favor his left hand. Because of the latter, defenders have had success sitting on his strong hand to force him into a tougher, contested look. As a result, his shot selection isn't especially great because he tends to take a lot of shots under duress. He's flashed some ability to score because he will drive aggressively into contact to draw fouls. Also, he's a much better shooter from a standstill position, as he can get his feet set and stay balanced. This makes him more effective at making spot-up jumpers and he shoots a solid percentage from the free throw line. When he has to shoot on the move or take a shot off the dribble, he struggles to maintain a consistent form. If he ends up in the NBA, he may have to be repurposed as a complementary, spot-up shooter.

At the other end of the floor, he has the tools to at least be an adequate defender. He's a solid athlete with a good set of physical tools. He has fairly good lateral mobility to go along with a fairly good amount of length and decent leaping ability. He's better as a help defender at this stage because he can play passing lanes to get steals and he's a good defensive rebounder for his size. Occasionally, he'll rotate from the weak side to block a shot. In addition to his weak side help defense, he's mostly a solid team defender. He'll fight through screens to stay attached to shooters off the ball and he'll consistently close out in spot-up situations. However, he was hidden away from the action quite a bit, so he wasn't always tested in pick-and-roll situations. Therefore, his pick-and-roll defense is still uncertain at this stage. On the ball, he's about an average defender. He has the ability to stay with opposing players, but he'll sometimes shade his man the wrong way to allow a drive to the basket. Other times, he'll give up on a play and he'll either give up an open shot or commit a cheap foul. Finally, there will be a few times where he'll lose track of his man off the ball, so he's prone to giving up some backdoor cuts to the rim.

Right now, Joshua Obiesie is a few years away from developing into a reliable contributor in the NBA. He would be best served to stay in Germany for a couple of more years to get some additional seasoning to improve his overall game. If he can become a more consistent shooter and defender, he could eventually land a spot on a team's bench as a rotational combo guard that also provides some secondary ball handling. If everything breaks right and he takes the necessary time to improve his game, he could resurface in a few years as a player similar to someone like Roger Mason. Otherwise, if he tries to rush to the NBA, his career could be shorter than expected and he could wind up back in Germany or another international league.

Alen Smailagic 35/40/45

College/Country	Height	Weight	Age on July 1
Serbia	6'10"	215	18.868

Wingspan	Standing Reach	No Step Vert	Max Vert
N/A	N/A	N/A	N/A

Basic Stats		Advanced Stats	
GP	49	TS%	0.561
MIN/G	17.2	3PTA/FGA	0.242
PTS/G	8.9	FTA/FGA	0.396
REB/G	4.0	OREB%	13.0
AST/G	1.0	DREB%	12.1
STL/G	0.9	TRB%	12.5
BLK/G	0.9	AST%	8.9
FG%	0.498	STL%	2.3
3PT%	0.238	BLK%	4.9
FT%	0.664	TOV%	15.4
		USG%	22.7

Projected Draft Range: 2nd Round to Undrafted

Top 10 Comps (Second Rounders Only)

	SIMsc			Year
1	887.8	Ray	Spalding	2018
2	858.1	Rick	Rickert	2003
3	852.6	Andrae	Patterson	1998
4	849.2	Chimezie	Metu	2018
5	847.7	Quincy	Miller	2012
6	846.7	Bill (Henry)	Walker	2008
7	845.7	Mark	Sanford	1997
8	845.0	Tommy	Smith	2003
9	844.5	Chris	Crawford	1997
10	844.4	James	Gist	2008

After spending a season with a semi-professional team in the third tier Serbian Regional League, Alen Smailagic put his name in the G-League Draft at the beginning of the year. He was picked fourth overall by the South Bay Lakers, who then traded him to the Santa Cruz Warriors. He became the youngest player to ever play in the G-League and he posted solid numbers as a reserve for Santa Cruz. Due to his youth and G-League productivity, Smailagic has a chance to be selected in this year's draft. If he's picked, he'll probably go somewhere in the second round.

On offense, Smailagic mainly excels as a rim runner. He doesn't really jump high enough to finish plays above the rim, but he compensates by playing with a very high motor. He runs hard down the floor to fill lanes in transition and he's very aggressive to crash offensive boards to score on put-backs. He also sets solid screens and he'll roll hard to the rim on pick-and-rolls. At this stage, he hasn't shown many polished skills. He isn't a great ball handler, so he will lose the ball quite a bit on drives. He's shown a willingness to pass and he can occasionally find the open man. However, he struggles to make decisions under pressure, which makes him very turnover prone. He can hit an outside jumper every once in a while, but he's not an efficient shooter right now. His stroke is inconsistent because he doesn't always follow through on his release and he can sometimes lose his balance. As a result, he's a below break-even three-point shooter and he has some struggles making free throws. Finally, he has been somewhat effective as a post-up player, but his moves are very limited. Specifically, he can only use a drop step to score against smaller defenders.

Defensively, he has some potential as a rim protector because he has above average length, decent timing and an aggressive mentality. These traits allow him to block shots at a fairly high rate. When he's playing well, he does a solid job of going straight up to stay vertical when challenging shots inside. Right now, he's a little bit better as a help defender. In addition to his being able to block shots on the ball, he can rotate from the weak side and he'll actively use his hands to rip balls away to get steals. His activity also allows him to be a solid defensive rebounder. He struggles as an on-ball defender overall. In the post, he has trouble preventing his man from getting deep position, so he's prone to either allowing easy scores inside or committing cheap fouls. He may need to get stronger to improve his ability to hold position inside. He doesn't really have a whole lot of lateral mobility, so he has difficulty defending players on the perimeter. Often times, quicker players can blow by him on switches or they can easily set him up to get free for an open jumper. As a team defender, he hasn't really grasped NBA level defensive concepts because he's often confused and makes the wrong rotation.

Though Alen Smailagic has produced at a decent level in the G-League, he's still far away from being ready for the NBA. He will need to stay in the G-League for another year or so to work on his defense and add some more offensive skill. If he makes significant progress in the next few years, he could find a role in the league as a situational rim runner like Chris Wilcox. Otherwise, he could follow a career path similar to someone like Ognjen Kuzmic, where he would get a short stint in the league before he spends the rest of his career either overseas or in the G-League.

Jalen Lecque   35/40/45

College/Country	Height	Weight	Age on July 1
USA (Bronx, NY)	6'4"	185	19.049

Wingspan	Standing Reach	No Step Vert	Max Vert
6'8.5"	8'2.5"	35.0"	43.0"

Basic Stats		Advanced Stats	
GP	N/A	TS%	N/A
MIN/G	N/A	3PTA/FGA	N/A
PTS/G	N/A	FTA/FGA	N/A
REB/G	N/A	OREB%	N/A
AST/G	N/A	DREB%	N/A
STL/G	N/A	TRB%	N/A
BLK/G	N/A	AST%	N/A
FG%	N/A	STL%	N/A
3PT%	N/A	BLK%	N/A
FT%	N/A	TOV%	N/A
		USG%	N/A

Projected Draft Range: 2nd Round to Undrafted

No Comps Available – No Stats

There was a slight question if Jalen Lecque was eligible for this draft because he is just now finishing his fifth year of high school. However, he fulfilled the NCAA graduation requirements at the end of his original senior year in 2017-18, so he was granted status as a draft eligible player because he will be 19 on draft day. He was invited to this year's NBA Draft Combine, so he's gained enough interest to possibly be picked by some team, assuming he stays in the draft. He has left the option of fulfilling a commitment to N.C. State open, so he could pull out if he doesn't do well in workouts. If he remains in the draft, he will probably be a second round pick.

    Lecque's standout attribute is his extraordinary athleticism, as he possesses excellent speed and explosive leaping ability. As a result, he really excels at playing in transition because his speed allows him to push the ball up court in a hurry to either explode for emphatic dunks or set up his teammates. He's also a threat to quickly fill a lane to score on lobs off the ball. At the high school level, he was a very ball dominant scorer that relied on his speed advantage to penetrate and create offense. He's an excellent ball handler that can make moves to create extra space for himself and he has a very quick first step to allow him to beat his defender. He plays with a very aggressive mentality, so he will seek out contact to draw fouls. He plays with a pretty heavy scoring mindset, so he's more likely to shoot in heavy traffic rather than find the open man. When he does look to pass, he's really only able to make simple passes like a dump off to an interior player. He doesn't really have the court vision to see the entire court at this stage, so he can be forced into turnovers if he gets caught over-penetrating. Right now, he isn't really an effective shooter. He struggles to consistently make free throws and he isn't especially efficient with his outside shot. He does make jump shots in volume because the ball is in his hands so frequently. However, he will have to adjust to having fewer touches if he makes the jump to professional basketball. Mechanically, he tends to kick out his legs quite a bit, so he tends to take a lot of off-balanced shots. Also, he doesn't really look to quickly catch and shoot and instead he'll stop the ball to try to play more of an isolation game. He will have to fix this tendency or else, he could struggle to fit into a modern NBA offense.

His athleticism could allow him to eventually become a decent defender. As it was mentioned earlier, he has great quickness and leaping ability. In addition to these traits, he has a long wingspan and he plays with a high motor. Theoretically, he could be effective at guarding smaller players on the ball. On the other hand, he could be targeted on switches because his frame is still rather thin, which could make him vulnerable against post-ups from bigger players. He doesn't really have a lot of high-end game experience, so he will have to learn NBA defensive concepts from scratch. There could be a significant adjustment period for him while he learns pick-and-roll coverages, screen defense and opposing player tendencies. His effort level does make him a solid help defender at the high school level. He's very good at using his length and quickness to jump passing lanes to get steals. He also will occasionally rotate from the weak side to block a shot and he's a pretty good rebounder for his size. If he can adjust to guarding players that are more physically mature and quickly grasp NBA rotation schemes, his athleticism could allow him to be a solid defensive point guard in the future.

Jalen Lecque has a profile that is fairly similar to Anfernee Simons from last year's draft. Simons didn't play much at all this past season because Portland didn't have a G-League team to guarantee consistent playing time. If Lecque lands in a similar situation, his growth could be stunted because he's far away from being a contributing rotation player at this stage. Ideally, he would need to spend a minimum of one season in the G-League to get some high-end game action to improve his basketball IQ and overall skill level. In a best-case scenario where he lands with a patient organization that allows him to develop at his own speed, he could become an athletic, penetrating rotational point guard like Dejounte Murray. In a typical situation where he would be shuttled back and forth from the NBA to the G-League, he could end up following a career path similar to someone like Archie Goodwin.

Marcos Louzada Silva   35/40/45

College/Country	Height	Weight	Age on July 1
Brazil	6'5"	188	19.997

Wingspan	Standing Reach	No Step Vert	Max Vert
N/A	N/A	N/A	N/A

Basic Stats		Advanced Stats	
GP	40	TS%	0.629
MIN/G	20.5	3PTA/FGA	N/A
PTS/G	11.3	FTA/FGA	N/A
REB/G	3.0	OREB%	4.5
AST/G	1.1	DREB%	13.5
STL/G	0.8	TRB%	9.2
BLK/G	0.1	AST%	9.7
FG%	0.505	STL%	2.1
3PT%	0.423	BLK%	0.3
FT%	0.733	TOV%	11.6
		USG%	24.2

Projected Draft Range: 2nd Round to Undrafted

Top 10 Comps (Second Rounders Only)

	SIMsc			Year
1	898.2	David	Young	2004
2	886.7	Von	Wafer	2005
3	886.0	Frank	Jackson	2017
4	877.1	Gary	Collier	1994
5	872.5	Nate	Erdmann	1997
6	871.5	Voshon	Lenard	1994
7	870.8	Kevin	Lynch	1991
8	870.1	Hamidou	Diallo	2018
9	868.4	Cuttino	Mobley	1998
10	867.4	Gilbert	Arenas	2001

Marcos Louzada Silva, who also goes by the first name Didi, has played the last three years for Franca in the Brazilian NBB. At 19 years old, he's just now started to play as a rotational player, and he was effective in a limited role. He was invited to play at this year's Nike Hoop Summit, and he had an up and down showing in just about 24 minutes of game action. He was a little more impressive in the practices, so his stock could be high enough to get him drafted. If he stays in the draft, he will probably be taken in the second round.

Offensively, Louzada Silva stands out because he's a very good outside shooter, as he made 42.5% of his threes this season. His mechanics are mostly good, as he stays very balanced and he has a smooth, repeatable release. The only mechanical flaw is that his release is pretty slow, and it takes him a long time to get his shot off. At this point, he's limited to being a stationary spot-up shooter. Given the time it takes for him to release his shot, he isn't really able to quickly catch the ball and shoot it. Therefore, he really doesn't have the ability to shoot off screens. In addition to his ability to make spot-up threes, he has shown some skill at moving off the ball. He's a fairly explosive athlete that can run the floor in transition and finish plays above the rim. He also has a fairly good sense of when to make backdoor cuts if defenders overplay his shot. Right now, he's a better fit as a complementary player because he's only about an average ball handler and he doesn't have a particularly quick first step. When he looks to attack the basket, he's limited to making straight-line drives. He also doesn't quite get all the way to the rim, so he'll often seek out contact to draw fouls at a decent rate. He flashed some ability to post-up smaller players, but his moves are limited to either a quick turn-around jumper or a drop step to score inside. As a final note, he's not really much of a playmaker because he can only make simple reads to safely avoid turnovers.

As a defender, he has the tools to be effective at the NBA level, but his skills are still quite raw. Physically, he has fairly long arms to go along with solid lateral quickness and great leaping ability. He's more of a stay-at-home defender at this stage because he doesn't really look to roam on the weak side. Occasionally, he can use his length to play passing lanes to get steals. He tends to stay in solid position, so he's a fairly good defensive rebounding wing player. At this stage, he's relatively untested as an on-ball defender because the level of competition is pretty low in Brazil. In a small sample size of possessions in the Nike Hoop Summit, he held up fairly well on the defensive end against the top high school players in the United States. Generally, he showed that he was quick enough to stay with his man and he tended to be in position to contest shots. He also made fairly sound rotations to allow him to close out on perimeter shooters and fight through screens. On the negative side, he can be over-aggressive at times, so he is prone to committing a few cheap fouls.

Marcos Louzada Silva is an interesting young prospect that projects into a three-and-D role in the future. His skills aren't polished enough right now, and he hasn't seen a lot of game action against quality competition. Therefore, he needs to be stashed overseas to get a few years of additional seasoning. Ideally, he would come over to the NBA after he proves himself in one of the higher end European leagues. However, he could still benefit by honing his overall game to increase his production level in Brazil. If things break favorably and he keeps producing against an increased level of competition, he could carve out a role in the league as an athletic, rotational three-and-D wing player like Terrence Ross or a stronger variation of Terrance Ferguson.

Santiago Yusta   35/40/45

College/Country	Height	Weight	Age on July 1
Spain	6'7"	190	22.175

Wingspan	Standing Reach	No Step Vert	Max Vert
N/A	N/A	N/A	N/A

Basic Stats		Advanced Stats	
GP	24	TS%	0.616
MIN/G	14.6	3PTA/FGA	0.510
PTS/G	5.8	FTA/FGA	0.310
REB/G	2.0	OREB%	4.9
AST/G	0.8	DREB%	11.4
STL/G	0.5	TRB%	8.4
BLK/G	0.1	AST%	8.9
FG%	0.480	STL%	1.7
3PT%	0.392	BLK%	0.6
FT%	0.774	TOV%	8.8
		USG%	16.7

Projected Draft Range: 2nd Round to Undrafted

Top 10 Comps (Second Rounders Only)

	SIMsc			Year
1	890.7	Brian	Davis	1992
2	887.3	Deron	Washington	2008
3	882.0	Josh	Richardson	2015
4	881.1	David	Young	2004
5	878.5	Royal	Ivey	2004
6	878.0	Carrick	Felix	2013
7	877.0	Lavor	Postell	2000
8	876.6	Norman	Powell	2015
9	875.5	James	White	2006
10	874.7	Davon	Reed	2017

Santiago Yusta has worked his way up to being a consistent rotational player in the Spanish ACB. He's spent the last two seasons with Real Madrid, and he was part of their EuroLeague championship team in 2018. He's automatically eligible for this year's draft, as an international player that was born in 1997. Based on his performance with one of the top teams in European basketball, there's a chance that someone could take a flyer on him in the second round of this year's draft, but there's a strong possibility that he could go undrafted.

On offense, he's shown considerable improvement as a shooter this season, although the sample size is small due to the fact that he plays a lower volume role for Real Madrid. Even so, he made just over 40% of his threes this past season and he's always been a consistently good free throw shooter. He has no noticeable flaws in his shooting form, as his stroke is compact, his release is smooth, and he stays on balance. Right now, he isn't really featured in the team's offense, so he's limited to being a stationary spot-up shooter and it's unclear if he can run off screens or shoot off the dribble. He can drive to the basket a little bit if defenders overplay his shot because he's a decent ball handler that can change directions. However, he doesn't really have great quickness, so he probably won't be able to get by NBA level athletes. Though he's mostly a catch and shoot player, he does play unselfishly, and he shows a willingness to make the extra pass. He also moves pretty well off the ball and plays with a pretty high motor. Therefore, he'll run the floor in transition and he'll consistently make backdoor cuts off the ball. He's also fairly good at picking his spots to crash the offensive boards to either score on put-backs or get an extra possession for his team.

As a defender, he doesn't possess ideal tools, but he compensates for his physical limitations by playing with a high level of effort and maintaining sound positioning. As it was alluded to earlier, he's not especially quick and his wingspan is only about average for a player of his size. At the NBA level, he might have some trouble staying with more athletic wing players. However, he was a solid defender in the ACB and EuroLeague because he could play angles to stay in front of his man and his effort level allowed him to be active to pressure opposing ball handlers. He was also adept at fighting through screens to stay attached to shooters off the ball or contain ball handlers in pick-and-roll situations. Additionally, he would consistently close out on perimeter shooters in spot-up situations. Stylistically, he was more of a stay-at-home defender, so he didn't really roam on the weak side to go for steals and blocks. Occasionally, he would hustle to dive on the floor for loose balls. His solid positioning and willingness to box out made him a fairly good defensive rebounding wing player.

Santiago Yusta still isn't ready to make the jump to the NBA and he would be best served to spend some more time with Real Madrid to hone his overall game. If he works his way up into a larger role by establishing a high level of consistency with his shooting and defense, he could eventually make his way to the NBA. If he makes these improvements and things break favorably for him, he could develop into a situational, three-and-D wing player along the lines of a poor man's Joe Ingles. Otherwise, he could remain a fixture in European basketball for the bulk of his career.

Borisa Simanic — 35/40/45

College/Country	Height	Weight	Age on July 1
Serbia	6'10"	215	21.282

Wingspan	Standing Reach	No Step Vert	Max Vert
N/A	N/A	N/A	N/A

Basic Stats

GP	51
MIN/G	16.8
PTS/G	6.1
REB/G	3.0
AST/G	0.8
STL/G	0.5
BLK/G	0.8
FG%	0.493
3PT%	0.395
FT%	0.927

Advanced Stats

TS%	0.639
3PTA/FGA	0.568
FTA/FGA	0.181
OREB%	5.7
DREB%	16.8
TRB%	11.7
AST%	7.9
STL%	1.8
BLK%	5.4
TOV%	9.3
USG%	15.3

Projected Draft Range: 2nd Round to Undrafted

Top 10 Comps (Second Rounders Only)

	SIMsc			Year
1	894.2	Ryan	Kelly	2013
2	875.9	Justin	Harper	2011
3	867.3	Grant	Jerrett	2013
4	866.1	Erik	Murphy	2013
5	849.1	Damone	Brown	2001
6	847.8	James	Jones	2003
7	847.0	Keita	Bates-Diop	2018
8	847.0	Jon	Leuer	2011
9	845.6	Jake	Layman	2016
10	843.7	Danny	Green	2009

Borisa Simanic has been playing for KK Crvena Zvezda in the Adriatic League since 2014. He has been a part of a team that has won three of the last four Adriatic League championships and he's been a regular rotational player for the last two seasons. He was already on the radar after he won the Next Generation Tournament MVP in 2016 and appeared in the Nike Hoop Summit in 2017. He still has the option of pulling out of the draft in June, but if he stays in the draft, he could be a second round pick.

On the offensive end, Simanic has flashed some stretch big potential. He's made just under 39% of his threes over the last two seasons and he's become a much better free throw shooter this year. His shooting form is pretty sound, as he shoots with a compact stroke with no extra wasted motion. At this stage, he's primarily a standstill shooter because almost all of his outside shots are spot-up jumpers. On occasion, he will pop out as the screener on pick-and-pop plays. He's also a pretty good rim runner that has solid athleticism and plays with a high motor. His long reach and fairly good leaping ability allows him to finish off a lot of plays above the rim. In a half-court set, he makes strong cuts off the ball and he rolls hard to the rim on pick-and-rolls. He also will aggressively attack the offensive glass to score on put-backs. In transition, he runs hard down the floor to fill a lane to allow him to score as the trailer. Stylistically, he's basically a catch and shoot or catch and finish type of player. He is an unselfish player that can make the extra pass or find an open teammate on a simple read, but he's not a natural playmaker. He also is only about an average ball handler, so he doesn't really get all the way to the rim in an isolation situation. Finally, he isn't really much of a post-up player at this stage. His thin frame doesn't allow him to establish inside position and he doesn't really have any established moves to score inside.

Defensively, he shows some rim protection skills, but he's still unpolished at this end of the floor. As it was mentioned earlier, his long reach, solid leaping ability and decent timing allows him to block shots at a high rate. He's more of a weak side shot blocker right now because his lack of strength doesn't allow him to be as effective at blocking shots on the ball. In post defense, bigger players push him around to get into his body, so he's often left in positions where he has to foul to prevent his man from getting an easy basket. In general, he was better as a help defender because he could use his length to play passing lanes to get deflections or steals. However, he hasn't been a good defensive rebounder in his career in the Adriatic League. He doesn't always block his man out and other times, opponents will outwork him get in better rebounding position to beat him to the ball. Though he has the mobility to defend players on the perimeter, he doesn't have a good sense of how to play angles, so opposing players will find lanes to drive by him in isolation situations. He's a little better at defending pick-and-rolls because his quickness does give him some ability to switch and his shot blocking ability helps him protect the rim if he's used in a drop coverage.

Borisa Simanic has some translatable skills, but he needs some more time to put everything together. At this point, he probably needs to stay overseas for a couple more years to improve his defense and fill out from a physical standpoint. If he can make these adjustments and he continues to produce against an increasing level of competition, it may be worthwhile to bring him over to the NBA. In this scenario where his skills develop to their full potential, he could eventually become a solid rotational rim runner that can space the floor and provide some rim protection similar to a variation of D.J. Wilson.

Vanja Marinkovic   35/40/45

College/Country	Height	Weight	Age on July 1
Serbia	6'6"	195	22.474

Wingspan	Standing Reach	No Step Vert	Max Vert
N/A	N/A	N/A	N/A

Basic Stats

GP	45		TS%	0.546
MIN/G	28.3		3PTA/FGA	0.516
PTS/G	12.2		FTA/FGA	0.320
REB/G	2.4		OREB%	1.3
AST/G	1.8		DREB%	9.7
STL/G	0.5		TRB%	5.6
BLK/G	0.1		AST%	11.5
FG%	0.411		STL%	1.0
3PT%	0.352		BLK%	0.5
FT%	0.752		TOV%	11.8
			USG%	21.4

(Right column header: Advanced Stats)

Projected Draft Range: 2nd Round to Undrafted

Top 10 Comps (Second Rounders Only)

	SIMsc			Year
1	911.9	Jabari	Bird	2017
2	899.6	Kevin	Lynch	1991
3	898.9	Svialoslav	Mykhailiuk	2018
4	887.2	Frank	Jackson	2017
5	886.7	Davon	Reed	2017
6	886.0	Joe	Crawford	2008
7	884.5	Josh	Richardson	2015
8	883.2	Shan	Foster	2008
9	882.3	David	Young	2004
10	880.7	Kim	English	2012

Vanja Marinkovic has been playing for Partizan Belgrade in the Adriatic League since 2013. He's gradually been working his way up to become to a key part of their team, as he's been a starter for the last two seasons. As an international player that was born in 1997, he's automatically eligible for this year's draft and he's built up enough stock to be considered for selection. If a team decides to pick him, he will most likely be a second round pick.

On the offensive end, Marinkovic stands out because he's been a pretty consistent outside shooter over the last three seasons. He shoots with deep range and his shooting mechanics are very sound. As a result, he's very good at making spot-up threes and he's shown some ability to come off screens. He also can quickly make long pull-up jumpers as well. On the downside, his shooting efficiency has decreased as his volume has increased. One reason for this is that he's picking up some bad habits by forcing up some more rushed, contested shots than he has in his previous years as a role player. The other reason is that he's not really to suited to being a primary shot creator. Though he can handle and pass a little bit, he doesn't quite have the quickness to beat defenders off the dribble on a regular basis. His dribble game is really predicated on his shooting. If his shot is falling, defenders are more prone to being over-aggressive to close out on him, which allows him to get an extra step to the basket. If he goes cold, then defenders back off a little bit and he can be baited into taking a bad shot or two. On the positive side, his passing has improved over the last couple of seasons. He's shown a greater willingness to hit the roll man inside and kick the ball out to open shooters on the perimeter. Finally, he has some solid leaping ability, so he can finish plays above the rim in transition.

On defense, Marinkovic needs to improve significantly because he could be a liability if his skills stay as is. From a physical tools standpoint, he is pretty limited because his arms are only average in length and his lateral mobility is fairly adequate. He can jump a little bit, which allows him to make an occasional chase-down block in transition. However, he's not especially active as a help defender. He doesn't really get steals, blocks or defensive rebounds at a high rate. Also, his effort level can run hot and cold. There will be times where he can be lackadaisical by not always running hard down the floor to get back on defense and he can be late to close out on perimeter shooters. When he's engaged, he can play good enough defense. He doesn't gamble and generally maintains sound positioning, so he'll stay attached to shooters off the ball. As an on-ball defender, he's decent at playing angles to either keep his man in front of him or funnel him into help. If a coach can consistently get him to play hard on the defensive end, he could improve enough to avoid being a major liability at the NBA level.

Shooting is in high demand, so a prospect like Vanja Marinkovic has some appeal. However, he will have to break some bad habits by improving his shot selection and by making a more concerted effort to become a better defender. Because he still needs to make some additional improvements in his game, it would best for him to be stashed overseas until he proves that he's ready. If he puts the work to adapt his game to fit into the NBA, he could resurface as a situational shooting specialist like Anthony Morrow. Otherwise, he'll remain overseas to continue a productive career in international basketball.

Deividas Sirvydis 35/40/45

College/Country	Height	Weight	Age on July 1
Lithuania	6'8"	195	19.058

Wingspan	Standing Reach	No Step Vert	Max Vert
N/A	N/A	N/A	N/A

Basic Stats

GP	47
MIN/G	15.1
PTS/G	5.4
REB/G	2.1
AST/G	0.8
STL/G	0.4
BLK/G	0.1
FG%	0.453
3PT%	0.370
FT%	0.778

Advanced Stats

TS%	0.568
3PTA/FGA	0.719
FTA/FGA	0.222
OREB%	4.4
DREB%	14.5
TRB%	9.5
AST%	9.0
STL%	1.7
BLK%	0.4
TOV%	10.1
USG%	17.2

Projected Draft Range: 2nd Round

Top 10 Comps (Second Rounders Only)

	SIMsc			Year
1	876.6	Frank	Jackson	2017
2	870.9	Hamidou	Diallo	2018
3	862.1	Sviatoslav	Mykhailiuk	2018
4	860.1	Sean	Higgins	1990
5	854.4	Von	Wafer	2005
6	850.9	Terrico	White	2010
7	849.2	Marcus	Liberty	1990
8	849.1	Davon	Reed	2017
9	848.2	Demetris	Nichols	2007
10	847.6	DeAndre	Daniels	2014

Deividas Sirvydis made his debut in the Lithuanian LKL in May of 2017 when he was 16 years old. He shuttled back and forth from Lietuvos Rytas' junior team to the senior team the following year. At the junior level, he was named as the Next Generation Tournament MVP in 2018. This season, he established himself as a regular for the senior team and his production has boosted his stock to the point where he's being considered for selection in this draft. If he stays in the draft, he will likely be a second round pick.

In his games with the senior team, Sirvydis is utilized in a lower volume role. He was pretty effective this season because he's a pretty good shooter that has sound mechanics. As a result, he will consistently knock down spot-up jumpers and he seems most comfortable in the corners. He's not really asked to do much in his minutes with the senior team, so he doesn't really run off screens. Therefore, it's a bit unclear if he can shoot on the move. In late shot clock situations, he'll try to take a quick pull-up jumper, but he has some trouble keeping his balance and getting his shot off quickly. Based on this information, he may be limited to being a stationary shooter. He's very effective off the ball because his high motor allows him to score on hustle plays. He'll cut hard to the rim if a defender overplays his shot and he'll run the floor to fill lanes in transition. With the ball in his hands, he's limited to making straight-line drives to the rim. He doesn't quite have the quickness to get all the way to the rim, but he will seek out contact to draw fouls and get to the free throw line. He's also an unselfish player that can make simple plays to keep the ball moving or avoid turnovers.

Defensively, he doesn't have the ideal physical tools, but he compensates for them by being a solid team defender. From an athletic standpoint, he is going to be limited at the NBA level because he has shorter than average arms to go along with below average lateral quickness and jumping ability. Therefore, he may have some struggles in keeping up with NBA level wing players in the future. He also isn't tested a whole lot because he was hidden in some favorable matchups due to his youth. However, in the limited number of times where he was tested, he plays hard enough and shows the awareness to be in the right place, so he's a decent defender with his team in Europe. He plays angles fairly well, which allows him to either stay in front of his man or funnel him into help. He also shows enough functional strength to decently hold position inside while defending bigger players on post-ups. As it was mentioned earlier, he was generally a solid team defender that would close out on shooters in spot-up situations. In addition to this, he was also effective at fighting through screens to either stay attached to shooters off the ball or contain pick-and-roll ball handlers. He also maintains sound rebounding position and he's consistent at blocking his man out, which allows him to be a fairly good defensive rebounding wing player. He's more of a stay-at-home, position defender at this stage, so he rarely looks to roam on the weak side. On the other hand, he has shown solid awareness to jump passing lanes or dive on loose balls to get steals at a decent rate.

Deividas Sirvydis is an intriguing prospect that could eventually develop into a three-and-D wing player in the future. He still needs to spend another couple of years in Lithuania to physically mature and prove himself against an increasing level of competition. Also, his chances of making the NBA would increase if he added another high-end offensive skill. If he continues to make positive progress, he could resurface in the future as a rotational, three-and-D wing similar to a player like Allen Crabbe. Otherwise, if his growth is stunted in any way, he will likely stay overseas to continue his solid career.

Abdoulaye N'Doye   35/40/45

College/Country	Height	Weight	Age on July 1
France	6'7"	183	21.312

Wingspan	Standing Reach	No Step Vert	Max Vert
N/A	N/A	N/A	N/A

Basic Stats		Advanced Stats	
GP	30	TS%	0.575
MIN/G	25.4	3PTA/FGA	0.480
PTS/G	6.4	FTA/FGA	0.224
REB/G	3.3	OREB%	3.0
AST/G	2.2	DREB%	13.6
STL/G	1.4	TRB%	8.0
BLK/G	0.2	AST%	14.4
FG%	0.474	STL%	3.0
3PT%	0.411	BLK%	0.9
FT%	0.529	TOV%	22.3
		USG%	13.5

Projected Draft Range: 2nd Round to Undrafted

Top 10 Comps (Second Rounders Only)

	SIMsc			Year
1	861.5	J.P.	Tokoto	2015
2	851.5	DeAndre	Liggins	2011
3	842.3	Alvin	Williams	1997
4	839.7	John	Celestand	1999
5	831.4	Steve	Bardo	1990
6	831.4	Royal	Ivey	2004
7	831.0	Brian	Davis	1992
8	831.0	Orien	Greene	2005
9	830.8	Michael	Gbinije	2016
10	825.9	Patrick	McCaw	2016

Abdoulaye N'Doye has been playing for Cholet Basket in the French Elite for the last three seasons. After being a reserve in the previous two years, he worked way his up to become a starter this season. With more playing time, his production level has increased to the point where he could be considered for selection in this year's draft. He still has the option of withdrawing his name in June, but if he stays in the draft, there's a possibility that he could be taken at some point in the second round.

Right now, N'Doye is a little more advanced on defense than he is on offense. He has very good raw athleticism that could allow him to hold up against NBA wing players. He has an extremely long wingspan to go along with very good lateral mobility and fairly explosive leaping ability. These tools allow him to be a fairly good on-ball defender because he has the quickness to stay with his man and he'll aggressively pressure ball handlers to force turnovers. He also will actively contest shots. On the downside, he tends to be a bit too aggressive, so he's prone to committing fouls at a very high rate. As a team defender, he's fairly solid. He'll close out on shooters in spot-up situations and he'll fight through screens off the ball. He has potential as a pick-and-roll defender because he can use his quickness and willingness to fight over the screen to contain ball handler and he's strong and long enough to switch onto the roll man. He's more of a stay-at-home defender because he doesn't really look to roam on the weak side. He doesn't really get blocks, but he can use his length to play passing lanes to get steals. He also is good at boxing his man out, so he's a solid defensive rebounder.

Offensively, he has improved his production level from his previous seasons, but he's still unpolished at this stage. With Cholet Basket, N'Doye plays a very low volume role. Often times, he'll be stationed off the ball in a spot-up position. He was much better at knocking down open shots, as he made 39.5% of his threes this past season. However, his stroke is still rather inconsistent because he continues to be a poor free throw shooter, as he's never had a Free Throw Percentage above 60% in any of the last three seasons. Therefore, he still needs to work on his ability to make standstill shots to prove that he can consistently space the floor at the next level. In general, he's an unselfish player that can make a few plays to find open teammates inside or on the perimeter. On the other hand, he tends to be a little bit careless with the ball, so he'll commit turnovers at a fairly high rate. Right now, he has a limited ability to create his own shot because he may only be about an average ball handler at best. He can occasionally beat his man off the dribble with a straight-line drive, but he doesn't really change directions well and he'll tend to mishandle the ball when he's pressured. Off the ball, he moves fairly well because his athleticism allows him to be very good in transition, as he'll finish plays above the rim, and he'll run the floor to fill lanes. He also is a fairly good cutter in a half-court set.

Abdoulaye N'Doye has the athleticism and defensive skills to compete in the NBA, but he needs to work on his offensive skills to avoid being a spacing liability at the next level. His profile is somewhat similar to Mickael Gelabale. If he rushes to come over to the NBA, his career could follow a similar path, as he would have a short stint in the league as a fringe roster player before he spends the rest of his career overseas. However, if he improves his shooting to at least a passable level, he could develop into a situational defensive specialist along the lines of a poor man's Thabo Sefolosha.

Yovel Zoosman 35/40/45

College/Country	Height	Weight	Age on July 1
Israel	6'6"	200	21.137

Wingspan	Standing Reach	No Step Vert	Max Vert
N/A	N/A	N/A	N/A

Basic Stats		Advanced Stats	
GP	62	TS%	0.576
MIN/G	19.8	3PTA/FGA	0.469
PTS/G	5.4	FTA/FGA	0.275
REB/G	2.8	OREB%	4.0
AST/G	1.7	DREB%	13.5
STL/G	1.0	TRB%	8.7
BLK/G	0.2	AST%	12.8
FG%	0.461	STL%	2.9
3PT%	0.355	BLK%	1.2
FT%	0.732	TOV%	18.6
		USG%	13.5

Projected Draft Range: 2nd Round to Undrafted

Top 10 Comps (Second Rounders Only)

	SIMsc			Year
1	890.9	Michael	Gbinije	2016
2	888.6	Josh	Richardson	2015
3	888.3	Danny	Green	2009
4	886.1	DeAndre	Liggins	2011
5	882.5	Sterling	Brown	2017
6	880.7	Kevin	Lynch	1991
7	879.7	Malcolm	Lee	2011
8	879.6	Brian	Davis	1992
9	874.6	Darrun	Hilliard	2015
10	874.1	James	White	2006

Yovel Zoosman has been a regular rotational player for Maccabi Tel Aviv for the last two seasons. He plays as a starter when the team plays in the Israeli Premier League due to foreign player restrictions, but then he comes off the bench during EuroLeague play. Even so, he's built up a solid international pedigree. He was named MVP of the FIBA Europe Under-20 Championship and he was also an Israeli Premier League All-Star this season. Based on these accomplishments, there's a chance that a team could take a flyer on him at some point in the second round if he stays in the draft.

Offensively, Zoosman plays in a very low usage role for Maccabi, so they don't really run many plays for him. He mainly gets his points off open spot-up jumpers and hustle plays. At this stage, he only makes threes at a rate that's slightly above break-even. His motion is fairly smooth and he stays balanced, but he has something of a slow, long windup. Therefore, he's most effective when he's wide open. When he has to get a shot off quickly, his release point becomes a little more inconsistent, which results in more misses. If he can work on releasing the ball quicker, he could eventually be a more dynamic shooter because he's occasionally been able to come off screens. Off the ball, he plays with a pretty high motor. He'll cut hard to the rim and he's quick to run the floor to fill a lane in transition. He has a good sense of when to pick his spots to crash the offensive glass to score on put-backs. He has some skill with the ball in his hands, but he's much better suited for a complementary role. He can make straight-line drives to the basket, but he's not especially quick and he's about average as a ball handler. This means that he can't really change directions well and he doesn't always get all the way to the rim on his drives. He will seek out contact, so he draws fouls at a decent rate. He's a very unselfish player that will find open teammates on the perimeter or on cuts inside. However, he can be a bit careless with his passes, so he is somewhat prone to committing turnovers.

As a defender, he lacks the ideal tools. He does have a fairly long wingspan relative to his height, but his lateral movements can be a bit stiff. He has some trouble staying with quicker players in isolation situations. He somewhat compensates for his lack of quickness by competing hard to stay in decent position and he'll contest shots. This allows him to be an adequate defender at the EuroLeague level, but he might not be able to hold up quite as well at the NBA level. He's a solid team defender that will usually make proper rotations. He'll fight through screens to keep himself attached to shooters off the ball and contain ball handlers in pick-and-roll situations. He also will consistently close out to contest perimeter shots. Additionally, he stays in good rebounding position and he usually blocks out his man, so he's a fairly good defensive rebounding wing player as a result. He's also solid as a help defender because he'll use his length to play passing lanes to get steals and he can rotate from the weak side to block a shot. He also will dive on the floor for loose balls and he's adept at drawing charges.

Yovel Zoosman is a prospect with some translatable skills, but he needs some more seasoning to improve his overall game to compete at the NBA level. Ideally, it would be best for him to stay with Maccabi for another couple of years to progress into a larger role and produce against a high-level of competition. If he shows that he can defend NBA level athletes and consistently knock down shots, he could resurface in a few years as a situational, three-and-D role player along the lines of somebody like Darius Miller. Otherwise, he's likely to remain overseas to continue his relatively accomplished international career.

THANK YOU

Thank you to everybody that made this book possible. I am very thankful of all the support from all of my readers and I hope you enjoyed this new edition. If you have any comments or questions, please feel free to send me an email and look out for new book releases from my Amazon author page. I'm also developing some new ways to produce content to enrich your overall experience. If you liked this book and you want to more content to expand on everything that you have read, you can make a small donation to help turn my new ideas into reality. Thanks once again and all of the necessary information can be found in the credits section.

Made in the
USA
Middletown, DE

77273305R00256